Resilience, Enviro and the City

Urban centres are bastions of inequalities, where poverty, marginalization, segregation and health insecurity are magnified. Minorities and the poor – often residing in neighbourhoods characterized by degraded infrastructure, food and job insecurity, limited access to transport and health care, and other inadequate public services – are inherently vulnerable, especially at risk in times of shock or change as they lack the option to avoid, mitigate and adapt to threats.

Offering both theoretical and practical approaches, this book proposes critical perspectives and an interdisciplinary lens on urban inequalities in light of individual, group, community and system vulnerabilities and resilience. Touching upon current research trends in food justice, environmental injustice through socio-spatial tactics and solution-based approaches towards urban community resilience, *Resilience, Environmental Justice and the City* promotes perspectives which transition away from the traditional discussions surrounding environmental justice and pinpoints the need to address urban social inequalities beyond the built environment, championing approaches that help embed social vulnerabilities and resilience in urban planning.

With its methodological and dynamic approach to the intertwined nature of resilience and environmental justice in urban cities, this book will be of great interest to students, scholars and practitioners within urban studies, environmental management, environmental sociology and public administration.

Beth Schaefer Caniglia is the Director of the Sustainable Economic & Enterprise Development (SEED) Institute and Faculty Research Director in the College of Business and Economics at Regis University, USA.

Manuel Vallée is a Lecturer in the Department of Sociology at the University of Auckland, New Zealand.

Beatrice Frank is the Social Science Specialist of Regional Parks, Capital Regional District of Victoria, Canada.

Routledge Equity, Justice and the Sustainable City series
Series editors: Julian Agyeman, Zarina Patel, AbdouMaliq Simone and Stephen Zavestoski

This series positions equity and justice as central elements of the transition towards sustainable cities. The series introduces critical perspectives and new approaches to the practice and theory of urban planning and policy that ask how the world's cities can become 'greener' while becoming more fair, equitable and just.

The Routledge Equity, Justice and the Sustainable City series addresses sustainable city trends in the global North and South and investigates them for their potential to ensure a transition to urban sustainability that is equitable and just for all. These trends include municipal climate action plans; resource scarcity as tipping points into a vortex of urban dysfunction; inclusive urbanization; 'complete streets' as a tool for realizing more 'liveable cities'; and the use of information and analytics towards the creation of 'smart cities'.

The series welcomes submissions for high-level cutting-edge research books that push thinking about sustainability, cities, justice and equity in new directions by challenging current conceptualizations and developing new ones. The series offers theoretical, methodological and empirical advances that can be used by professionals and as supplementary reading in courses in urban geography, urban sociology, urban policy, environment and sustainability, development studies, planning, and a wide range of academic disciplines.

Incomplete Streets
Processes, practices and possibilities
Edited by Stephen Zavestoski and Julian Agyeman

Planning Sustainable Cities and Regions
Towards more equitable development
Karen Chapple

The Urban Struggle for Economic, Environmental and Social Justice
Deepening their roots
Malo Hutson

Bicycle Justice and Urban Transformation
Biking for all?
Edited by Aaron Golub, Melody L. Hoffmann, Adonia E. Lugo and Gerardo Sandoval

Green Gentrification
Urban sustainability and the struggle for environmental justice
Kenneth Gould and Tammy Lewis

Resilience, Environmental Justice and the City
Edited by Beth Schaefer Caniglia, Manuel Vallée and Beatrice Frank

Resilience, Environmental Justice and the City

Edited by Beth Schaefer Caniglia,
Manuel Vallée and Beatrice Frank

First published 2017 by Routledge

2 Park Square, Milton Park, Abingdon, Oxfordshire OX14 4RN
711 Third Avenue, New York, NY 10017

Routledge is an imprint of the Taylor & Francis Group, an informa business

First issued in paperback 2018

© 2017 selection and editorial matter, Beth Schaefer Caniglia, Beatrice Frank and Manuel Vallée; individual chapters, the contributors

The right of the editors to be identified as the author of the editorial material, and of the authors for their individual chapters, has been asserted in accordance with sections 77 and 78 of the Copyright, Designs and Patents Act 1988.

All rights reserved. No part of this book may be reprinted or reproduced or utilised in any form or by any electronic, mechanical, or other means, now known or hereafter invented, including photocopying and recording, or in any information storage or retrieval system, without permission in writing from the publishers.

Trademark notice: Product or corporate names may be trademarks or registered trademarks, and are used only for identification and explanation without intent to infringe.

British Library Cataloguing-in-Publication Data
A catalogue record for this book is available from the British Library

Library of Congress Cataloging-in-Publication Data
A catalog record for this title has been requested

ISBN: 978-1-138-11989-5 (hbk)
ISBN: 978-1-138-31587-7 (pbk)

Typeset in Goudy
by Swales & Willis, Exeter, Devon, UK

Contents

List of illustrations	vii
List of contributors	viii
1 Resilience, environmental justice and the city: an introduction BETH SCHAEFER CANIGLIA, BEATRICE FRANK AND MANUEL VALLÉE	1

PART I
Theoretical frameworks   15

2 Critical environmental justice studies DAVID N. PELLOW	17
3 A framework for improving resilience: adaptation in urban contexts BRIAN MAYER	37
4 Revealing the resilience infrastructure of cities: preventing environmental injustices-in-waiting BETH SCHAEFER CANIGLIA AND BEATRICE FRANK	57

PART II
Practices   77

5 "There is just a stigma here": historical legacies, food justice, and solutions-based approaches toward urban community resilience TAMARA L. MIX, ANDREW RARIDON AND JULIE M. CROFF	79

6 Nurturing an acquiescence to toxicity: the state's naturework in urban aerial pesticide spraying campaigns 97
MANUEL VALLÉE

7 Water connections: output-based aid for the urban poor and the pursuit of water justice in Jakarta, Indonesia 118
RITA PADAWANGI AND MANUEL VALLÉE

8 Ecological resilience and New York City's water supply system: the role of adaptive governance in combating vulnerabilities 138
SARAH E. BLAKE

PART III
Governance and policy 155

9 Rethinking the politics of water: risk, resilience, and the rights of future generations 157
JOANNA L. ROBINSON

10 The pitfalls and promises of climate action plans: transformative adaptation as resilience strategy in US cities 177
CHANDRA RUSSO AND ANDREW PATTISON

11 Resisting environmental injustice through socio-spatial tactics: experiences of community reconstruction in Boston, Havana, and Barcelona 195
ISABELLE ANGUELOVSKI

12 Environmental justice initiatives for community resilience: ecovillages, just transitions, and human rights cities 216
JACQUELINE PATTERSON AND JACKIE SMITH

13 Conclusion 234
BEATRICE FRANK, BETH SCHAEFER CANIGLIA
AND MANUEL VALLÉE

Index 243

Illustrations

Figures

3.1	The Resilience Activation Framework (RAF)	47
4.1	Socio-ecological systems resilience formation	60
7.1	Number of customers by category, PALYJA (1998–2009)	126
7.2	Number of customers by category, AETRA (2011)	126

Tables

4.1	Summary of resilience-specific systems theory assumptions	62
4.2	Summary of systems theory assumptions applied toward socio-cultural systems	62
4.3	Summary of the criticisms of structural-functionalism	63
4.4	Summary of the key assumptions of critical theory	67
7.1	Comparison of service levels of PALYJA and AETRA in 2009	125
7.2	Jakarta water tariff structure, selected categories	125
7.3	Goals of the GPOBA Water Supply Project in Western Jakarta	129
10.1	Examples of policies that address mitigation vs. adaptation and inequality concerns	181
11.1	A summary of neighborhood changes in Dudley, Casc Antic, and Cayo Hueso	200
11.2	Strategic and tactical development in Dudley, Casc Antic, and Cayo Hueso	202

Map

5.1	Location of Greenwood Historic District within Tulsa's contemporary food desert	84

Contributors

Isabelle Anguelovski, Institute for Environmental Science and Technology (ICTA), Universitat Autònoma de Barcelona (UAB)

Sarah E. Blake, Department of Sociology, Washington State University

Beth Schaefer Caniglia, Director of the Sustainable Economic and Enterprise Development (SEED) Institute and Faculty Research Director in the College of Business and Economics at Regis University

Julie M. Croff, School of Applied Health and Educational Psychology, Oklahoma State University

Beatrice Frank, Regional Parks, Capital Regional District of Victoria

Brian Mayer, School of Sociology, University of Arizona

Tamara L. Mix, Department of Sociology, Oklahoma State University

Rita Padawangi, Asia Research Institute, National University of Singapore

Jacqueline Patterson, Climate Program, National Association for the Advancement of Colored People

Andrew Pattison, Department of Sociology and Anthropology, Colgate University

David N. Pellow, Environmental Studies Program, University of California

Andrew Raridon, Department of Sociology, Purdue University

Joanna L. Robinson, Department of Sociology, Glendon College, York University

Chandra Russo, Department of Sociology and Anthropology, Colgate University

Jackie Smith, Department of Sociology, University of Pittsburgh

Manuel Vallée, Department of Sociology, University of Auckland

1 Resilience, environmental justice and the city

An introduction

Beth Schaefer Caniglia,[1] Beatrice Frank[2] and Manuel Vallée[3]

Introduction

The certainty of human-induced climate change is unequivocal (IPCC 2014; Melililo, Richmond and Yohe 2014). Even more concerning is that the impacts of climate change are no longer coming; they are here. We continue to break records for global temperatures. Melting ice caps, rising seawaters, bleaching coral reefs, increasing droughts, wildfires, intensity and number of storms, and the spread of diseases are empirically documented. Even more urgent than the consequences of climate change today are the projections for the future. Global temperature increases are expected between 3°F and 10°F by the end of the twenty-first century, which will further intensify the social and environmental stressors.

Certain sectors of the economy will be especially hard hit by the impacts of climate change. The U.S. National Climate Assessment (Melililo et al. 2014, 11) lists agriculture, water, health, energy, transportation, forests and ecosystems as especially vulnerable. So, too, certain human sectors of society are significantly more vulnerable than others. Most sources highlight that people of color, indigenous communities, children, the elderly, the disabled and ill, and the poor are front-line communities seriously threatened by current and impending climate impacts (Pellow and Brehm 2013; Melililo et al. 2014; Harlan et al. 2015). Additionally, these populations are the most disadvantaged when it comes to income, wealth, health, personal security, political power, educational and occupational achievement (Harlan et al. 2015), and climate and environmental change portends widespread environmental injustices (Caniglia et al. 2014).

Cities are growing rapidly as the twenty-first century progresses (UNEP 2012; Wu 2014). In this book, cities are defined as human-built environments with high human populations and extensive impervious surface area (Wu 2014). Urban areas are the human-built regions including and surrounding such city centers. Half of the world's population already lives in cities, and it is expected that by 2050, 80% of humanity will reside in "vast urban conurbation[s] sometimes called mega-urban-regions" (Davis 2011, 21). Urban areas, including megacities with over 10 million inhabitants (e.g., Tokyo, New York, Delhi), are widespread across the globe, and their number is expected to rise in the coming decades (Davis 2011; Elmqvist et al. 2013; Grove 2009; Schewenius, McPhearson and Elmqvist 2014; UNEP 2012). With their flow of commodities, capital, energy and people, cities play a key role in shaping economic, social and environmental change (Grove 2009; UNEP 2012).

Urban centers are also bastions of inequalities, where poverty, marginalization, segregation and health insecurity are magnified (Jorgenson and Rice 2012; UN Habitat 2010; UNICEF Bangladesh 2010). Minorities and the poor – often residing in neighborhoods characterized by degraded infrastructures, food and job insecurity, limited access to transport and health care, and other inadequate public services – are inherently vulnerable (Anguelovski 2014; Barnett, Matthew and O'Brien 2010). Socially disadvantaged groups are especially at risk in times of shock or change as they lack: the *option* to avoid, mitigate and adapt to threats posed to the system's social, environmental and cultural integrity; the *capacity and freedom* to exercise the options that are available to them; and the ability to *actively participate* in obtaining these options (Brklacich, Chazan and Bohle 2010; Caniglia et al. 2014). Social capital, or the ability to cooperate within or among groups with shared values and understandings, might be missing or weakened in sections of society excluded by the wider community or perceived as outsiders (Liu and Foster 2011). Access to social support and networks can activate social resiliency, helping withstand the deleterious effects of post-disaster stress (Abramson et al. 2015). However, the absence of such capital hinders individuals and groups from accessing resources and networks, making disadvantaged populations inherently vulnerable and less able to recover after disasters (Aldrich 2012).

This convergence of vulnerabilities and opportunities has inspired this volume. While the literatures on climate justice, urbanization and resilience are each increasingly robust, they tend to incorporate each other's insights in only cursory ways. Given the urgent nexus of vulnerabilities that collide in cities facing climate change, our desire is to: (1) elaborate these more specifically; (2) theorize resilience in these contexts; and (3) explore leverage points for significantly reducing risks to the most vulnerable urban dwellers *before* the worst consequences of environmental and climate change arrive. In the coming sections, we elaborate briefly on the state of the literature in climate justice, urban socio-ecological systems and resilience before providing a roadmap for the rest of the book.

Climate injustice

There have been many in-depth reviews of the ways climate change unequally endangers the poor, people of color, the elderly and other vulnerable groups (Bullard and Wright 2009; Harlan et al. 2015; Roberts and Parks 2007). Here we provide a simplified overview of their findings, because the following chapters cover them in some depth. Ciplet, Roberts and Khan (2015) highlight that climate injustice is generally evaluated within three categories: climate change-related causes, impacts and responses.

It is commonly accepted knowledge that the burning of fossil fuels in processes such as production, transportation and mining is the primary contributor to climate change (Pacala and Sococlow 2004). These processes are largely driven by industrialized nations and those that are rapidly industrializing, such as India, China and Brazil (Burns and Caniglia 2016; Ciplet et al. 2015). Frequently, the consequences of consumption in industrialized nations are externalized to poor nations, and those consequences are often most acutely felt by the poor and people of color (Smith, Sonnenfeld and Pellow 2006). Therefore the economic development that fuels climate change around the world benefits a small number of corporations, nations and social classes, compared with the many who suffer from its consequences (Downey 2015).

The consequences of these activities intersect with existing inequalities in ways that make the poor, people of color, single women and other traditionally repressed groups at much higher risk of suffering from climate change (Harlan et al. 2015; Kasperson and Kasperson 2001). To begin with, the poor are exposed to the impacts of climate change in ways the rich can avoid. Poor housing and lack of land tenure, lack of modern plumbing and electricity, and legacies of being moved to the most marginal and degraded lands leave the poor directly exposed to rising temperatures and seawaters, and increases in infectious diseases. These vulnerable groups frequently lack access to early warning systems, transportation and financial capital to move away from rising tides or to escape approaching storms (Bullard and Wright 2009; Roberts and Parks 2007).

When climate justice scholars review responses to climate change, they generally refer to laws and policies. In their comprehensive review of this dimension of climate injustice, Harlan et al. (2015) find that governments consistently act too slowly, not assertively enough, and in ways that continue to favor and advance the rich over the poor and most vulnerable. These trends are illustrated using data from the international policy arena, where governments come together to build consensus policies to address climate change. This arena has come to be known for its failure to act on climate change (Ciplet et al. 2015). Decades of delays have resulted in haphazard and uncoordinated approaches to mitigation. While NGOs and other members of civil society are allowed to observe the activities of the IPCC negotiations, the number of observers and the extent that they can intervene are severely limited during the high-level segment of the meetings, and even representatives of poorer, developing nations have been consistently marginalized from the final documents adopted at the meetings.

In short, the literature provides ample evidence that climate injustice is a reality at multiple levels – a fact that will prove out extensively in the following chapters. Legacies of inequalities accumulate to create vulnerabilities that will only increase with advancing climate change. One weakness in this literature that we hope to address is the ways in which climate injustice specifically manifests itself in urban environments. The literature on urban socio-ecological systems rarely engages the climate justice literature, leaving the specific interfaces that characterize the vulnerabilities of the urban poor in need of elaboration. We turn now to an overview of vulnerabilities in urban socio-ecological systems as a means of further contextualizing the resilience, environmental justice and urbanization nexus.

Urban socio-ecological systems

Urbanization characterizes contemporary societies, influences well-being and, in many ways, increases both ecological and human vulnerabilities to environmental and climate change. From an ecological perspective, urban sprawl reduces ecological resiliency by converting ecosystems and agricultural land, reducing biodiversity, altering micro-climate patterns, eroding topsoil, diverting and interrupting water flows, and impacting the provisioning of many ecosystem services (Elmqvist et al. 2013; Grove 2009; Pickett et al. 2011; Schewenius et al. 2014). Urban expansion's environmental effects are not limited to their nearby surroundings (Elmqvist et al. 2013; Grimm et al. 2008). Production, transportation and consumption processes generate vulnerabilities in distant ecosystems by altering land, water and biodiversity across the world, and by altering global biogeochemical cycles and climate patterns (Grimm et al. 2008; Smith et al. 2006). Such local and global changes alter urban environmental functions, the ability to withstand natural disasters or disrupting weather events, and affects the ability of human communities to withstand environmental crises (Aldrich 2012). This is particularly evident in urban areas, where social and environmental injustices intersect.

With drastic increases in urbanization and the growing concern for how cities affect human livelihoods, a variety of social issues have been explored in urban areas. These include issues related to the economy, the impact on well-being of those living in urban areas, and political systems and institutions (Buyantuyev and Wu 2009; Grimm et al. 2008; Nassauer and Raskin 2014; Wolch, Byrne and Newell 2014). Within the economic dimension, scholars have explored the evolution of cities from preindustrial to contemporary settings (i.e., capitalism, industrial restructuring, globalization) (Aguilar 2009; Knox and Pinch 2010; Hall and Barrett 2012). Provisioning and access to businesses, goods and services have become key themes in this area of study. Difficulties encountered by citizens in accessing job markets and the competition between urban areas in offering employment, for example, are some of the economic dimensions that have been explored (Aguilar 2009; Da Cunha et al. 2012; Romero, Solís and De Ureña 2014). Access to housing and household indebtedness, neighborhood gentrification, international trade and the geographies of consumption are additional key topics within this research cluster (Da Cunha et al. 2012; Knox and Pinch 2010; Short and Yeong-Hyun 1999; Stenning et al. 2010; Walks 2013). Studies on global firms, markets and digital communication have drawn attention to the role played by networks of cities in shaping economies (Sassen 2008; Spencer 2015). Globalization, indeed, has favored the spatial dispersal of economic activities outside cities, enhanced urban areas' centralization effects and emphasized the linkages binding these areas. Accordingly, a new economic configuration of urban areas has been described in urban studies, one that is more complex, transboundary and service-intense (Sassen 2008; Spencer 2015).

Social injustices frequently overlap and are amplified by environmental inequalities. Environmental justice – or the right of all people "regardless from their race, color, origin, or income [. . .] to enjoy the same degree of protection from environmental and health hazards and equal access to the decision-making process to have a healthy environment in which to live, learn, and work"[4] – is indeed not equally distributed among urban residents. Disadvantaged populations often reside in degraded neighborhoods where hazardous pollutants, toxins and noxious environmental facilities are concentrated (Anguelovski 2014; Bullard and Wright 2012; Pellow and Brehm 2013; Schlosberg 2013). Goods and hazards are unevenly distributed – while minorities and the poor lack access to the benefits and services offered to the rest of the city, they bear the deleterious side effects caused by the multiple and cumulative sources of environmental "bads", generated in the process of providing benefits to their powerful and often white counterparts (Caniglia et al. 2014; Mohai, Pellow and Roberts 2009; Pellow 2007). Environmental injustices are perpetuated in distressed neighborhoods as minorities and the poor frequently lack the ability, opportunity and resources to fight against long-term environmental bads. The inability of such populations to organize themselves, gain power and influence decision-making feeds the treadmill of production, perpetuating the vicious cycle of dumping environmental bads in already socially vulnerable neighborhoods (Mohai et al. 2009).

Exposure to risk differs in cities based on race, color, origin and/or income, and is magnified in neighborhoods where environmental bads are concentrated. Thus, risk exposure becomes extreme when inherently vulnerable populations live in inherently unjust environments. Often, disasters or other extreme events illuminate the full extent of such social and environmental risks, or vulnerabilities. Tornados, hurricanes, earthquakes, droughts or floods, just to mention some, frequently uncover the *injustices-in-waiting* engrained in cities. Injustices-in-waiting are the inequalities existing below the surface and perpetuated over time through environmental disruption, social inequalities, poor urban planning, as well as governance and power imbalances. Because of existing injustices-in-waiting, inherently vulnerable socio-ecological systems lack resources and have little to no capacity to absorb disturbances and reorganize when exposed to an environmental shock. Thus, insecure communities residing in impoverished environments are the ones hit hardest by extreme environmental and climatological events, often bearing disproportionate environmental harms, economic losses and human fatalities (Caniglia et al. 2014). This book's *leitmotiv*, injustices-in-waiting, draws our attention to the fact that social and environmental injustices are present and deep-rooted, even when they are not fully documented or visible. It also underscores the need to reflect on how we can build resiliency in cities when disadvantaged individuals, groups and communities are chronically vulnerable and enclosed in degraded socio-ecological systems.

Hurricane Katrina clearly exemplifies the injustices-in-waiting and the unequal distribution of environmental bads. New Orleans, situated below sea level, was built by deeply modifying the Mississippi River and delta. Changes in this area's spatial ecological patterns created vulnerabilities to floods and extreme weather events. An aging population and the city's racial and residential segregation further enhanced the vulnerability of specific individuals and groups (e.g., blacks, the elderly, single women) to environmental bads. These vulnerabilities were fully exposed when Hurricane Katrina hit the city. New Orleans' flooding can be attributed to its lack of natural barriers and the ineffectiveness of human-built structures to buffer the hurricane. Vulnerable populations (i.e., poor, black and elderly) had insufficient means to evacuate, thereby staying behind and suffering health and safety risks, as well as the highest economic and human losses (Aldrich 2012; Bullard and Wright 2009). The combination of an ecologically impoverished environment, deep-rooted social inequalities and inadequate institutional preparedness resulted in reduced human security and unjustly distributed environmental bads. To build a more resilient and equitable New Orleans, post-disaster efforts have focused on reducing local vulnerabilities through better education, health care, governance and land use planning (Liu and Foster 2011). Yet, the ability to recover from a crisis does not rely solely on the magnitude of the environmental or climatological event, the resources available or the provisioning of grassroots, charitable and government aid; it also stems from the environmental health and the social capital imbued in the community struck by the disaster (Aldrich 2012). While many argue that New Orleans' tourist economy and housing market recovered over time, the African-American community suffered significant population losses, and lost significant property holdings in an increasingly white city. The lack of strong community ties and networks within and across New Orleans' neighborhoods resulted in the migration of people and resources from the city, further undermining the urban center's social capital. Even more disturbing is that many communities that experienced the largest loss of life and property remain inadequately connected, exposed to environmental bads and poorly protected against future flooding – continuing to be vulnerable and exposed to injustices-in-waiting. These are the confluences of vulnerabilities our case studies highlight in an array of urban centers.

Resilience

Resilience and sustainability have been suggested as the panacea for social and environmental injustices. While resilience stresses the need to anticipate, cope with and adapt to change, sustainability is the process of balancing natural resources use, economic development and conservation for current and future generations. The scholarship on resilience emerged in the 1970s, when ecologists conducted careful observations regarding the ways stochastic events (e.g., wildfires) influence the primary functions and thresholds of ecosystems (Folke 2006; Folke et al. 2010; Lake 2013). The resilience term was introduced by C.S. Holling (1973) and describes the capacity of a system to absorb external shocks without drastically altering the key relationships between species and other ecosystem variables. In general, resilience was characterized in two ways: how long the system took to recover from the external shock, or how much external stimuli the system could withstand before significant thresholds were reached (Barr and Devine-Wright 2012; Brand and Jax 2007; Folke et al. 2010).

Sociocultural scholars have taken the resilience metaphor and applied it to social systems (Walker and Salt 2006; Adger 2000; Fiksel 2006). The same definitions apply in this burgeoning field, except we find much less conceptual consensus and more uncoordinated research efforts than exist in the natural sciences. Insights can be gleaned from the fields of human security, vulnerabilities, coupled human and natural systems, and environmental/climate justice. As detailed by the authors in our theoretical section, social resilience studies also draw from psychology, critical theory, critical race theory and ethnic studies, among others. However, these contributions tend to be overlooked by scholars outside of the social sciences. Key indicators drawn from these disparate literatures suggest that social resilience pertains to multiple levels of resilience. The earlier description of hurricane Katrina's impact on New Orleans highlights that calculating the resilience of an entire system can turn a blind eye to the consequences of climate change and other disasters on sub-populations *within* the system (Caniglia et al. 2014).

From these literatures Caniglia et al. (2014) drew numerous variables, including a wide range of structural or contextual variables. From the human security literature (Barnett et al. 2010), they list governance, food security, economic security, access to healthcare, personal security and safety, and general environmental security as the types of background variables that condition vulnerability when a shock hits the system. The human security literature also highlights: (1) adaptation/recovery options must be available; (2) citizens must know of their existence; and (3) they must possess the capacity to avail themselves of these resources. If knowledge of and ability to access recovery/adaptation resources are not equally available, injustices are in waiting. Finally, from the vulnerabilities literature, exposure and sensitivity condition both the extent to which individuals and communities are impacted by climate change, as well as the need for proactive adaptation in the face of future disasters (Adger 2006; Birkmann 2006; Gallopín 2006; Kasperson et al. 2005). These factors combine to produce overall resilience within the system.

Urban areas are increasingly viewed as a central nexus where complex and dynamic socio-ecological systems and processes interact at multiple levels and scales. Such places are described simultaneously as centers of environmental bads and social inequalities, and as novel ecosystems, able to create challenges and offer opportunities for humankind's current and future resiliency and sustainability (Anderson and Elmqvist 2012; Elmqvist et al. 2013; Grimm et al. 2008; Grove 2009). Understanding the connection between vulnerabilities and injustices in cities is critical to identifying injustices-in-waiting and building mechanisms that enhance individual, group and community ability to cope with and adapt to environmental and climate change. However, studies of cities have yet to capture the intertwined and complex ties between environmental justice and resilience. Environmental justice scholars have largely documented the unjust exposure of specific social groups (i.e., gender, ethnicity) to environmental bads, but have struggled to propose alternative frameworks with which to identify injustices-in-waiting and build mechanisms for mitigating crises before they strike. A much stronger emphasis is needed on fostering resilience, one that is socially and environmentally just (Pellow 2016; Mayer 2016). Such resilience should be nurtured before environmental harms occur, in order to build community proactivity and enhance preparedness to change, uncertainty, unpredictability and surprise (Barr and Devine-Wright 2012; Berkes and Ross 2012; Magis 2010). "Only humans, indeed, are able to anticipate, react to and prevent risk by building up buffers to environmental shocks and other threats to the system" (Caniglia et al. 2014, 419). Resilience can influence and enhance entire communities' ability to mobilize physical, sociopolitical, sociocultural and psychological resources (Berkes and Ross 2012; Davidson 2010; Magis 2010). To propel the shift from cities as bastions of inequalities to resilient, thriving and sustainable environments, this volume offers critical perspectives and a social science lens on equity, justice and the transition towards sustainable cities. It proposes a toolkit of frameworks, practices, governance and policy approaches that shed light on resilience and environmental justice in urban environments. As well, it advances discussions, and propels discourses about the intertwined nature of urban vulnerability and injustice-in-waiting as issues to be identified and addressed in the quest to moving towards resilient, sustainable cities.

Outline of the book

The volume's introductory section offers three framework chapters that push the boundaries of existing perspectives on resilience and environmental justice in urban contexts. Because resilience is a systems framework, scholars tend to emphasize the functional capacity of cities to bounce back after external shocks. Yet, vulnerable individuals, groups and communities might not be able to cope, adapt or even withstand an environmental crisis, especially if injustices-in-waiting are engrained in the impacted urban socio-ecological systems. Furthermore, power's influence on resilience and adaptation, uneven distribution of environmental bads in cities, and disparities across groups of marginalized populations can intensify social injustices. To better understand these challenges, Chapter 2 presents a critical environmental justices framework that discusses the relation between social and environmental injustice, the interrelated nature of such inequalities and their awaiting to be exposed, and the role played by humans and other species as key elements of sustainable, just and resilient urban spaces. Such a framework offers a new perspective on "the way to resist the current social order and bring new imaginings, visions, practices, relationships, and communities into being that are anti-authoritarian and sustainable, and that embody *just resilience*—a resilience marked by social and environmental justice" (Pellow 2016, 25). The chapter is followed by a critical review of the resilience concept and its relation to building resiliency in communities. This contribution goes further by linking positive adaption strategies among individuals, groups and communities through social networks, which can represent an adaptive mechanism to mobilize resources in case of environmental crisis. These frameworks offer us theoretical bridges between cities, individuals, groups and community vulnerabilities, as a means to think about urban socio-ecological systems and their resilience to changing environments and climate.

The book's central section focuses on practices. Case studies varying in geographical areas, emphasis and scale are used to elucidate the relationship between power and differential access to environmental goods, resiliency and environmental justice in cities. A food justice project in northern Tulsa explores the issue of food justice projects "placed" into communities, rather than "based" in existing communities, and what such efforts mean for community engagement, resilience and sustainability. Another case study elucidates how government-backed urban pesticide spraying campaigns undermined natural and community resilience in Auckland, New Zealand, while two others illuminate the social forces mediating water justice and resilience in Jakarta, Indonesia, and New York City. The case studies point to context-specific situations and timeframes in which individuals, communities and nation-states must respond to shocks and disturbances to build more resilient and sustainable urban communities. A real-world perspective based on practice is essential for moving from simply documenting unjust exposures to environmental bads, to actually proposing alternative social arrangements that both help prevent injustices-in-waiting and build social and infrastructural mechanisms that mitigate crises before they strike. The aforementioned case studies aim to empower readers to transition from looking at the causes of environmental injustice to thinking about pathways that can be used to prevent injustices-in-waiting and enhance socio-ecological resiliency before harms occur.

The final section of the book examines how governance and policies create challenges and offer opportunities to enhance equity and justice in cities. Contributions on the imperatives of water politics, alliance-building in climate justice organizations, pitfalls and promises of climate action plans, community activism and empowerment, and environmental justice movements illuminate the many institutional barriers encountered while dealing with injustice, poverty and a lack of sociopolitical access to decision-making. These contributions offer an alternative model for distributive justice, for both current and future generations, thereby providing a pathway to enhance urban resilience amidst environmental and climate change. By bringing frameworks, practices, governance and policy approaches together, we create common ground for new theories and praxis that better address the key elements cities need to enhance their resilience and equity. This cross-fertilization encourages "the transitions from a rather defensive position that is constantly compelled to prove that environmental injustices plague communities of color and the poor more than their richer, White counterparts" (Caniglia et al. 2014, 423) to a more active and applied environmental justice scholarship – one that enhances resiliency by helping to develop mechanisms that help us anticipate, prevent and cope with environmental bads.

Conclusion

Though methodologically challenging to study, urban environments are ideal laboratories to explore the linkages between environmental justice, resiliency and the transition towards sustainable cities. Such an understanding is instrumental to identifying what is needed to enhance both local and global adaptability to change, and transforming cities into a central nexus for the long-term functioning and sustainability of economies, societies and ecosystems. With an increasingly urbanizing society, there is a more urgent need for cities to become stewards of sustainability and resource efficiency, from both an infrastructural and social perspective. Scholars need, therefore, to transition from documenting environmental injustice made visible through disasters towards proposing pathways that make urban socio-ecological systems adaptable to a range of environmental and climate changes. This book draws attention to the contexts that enable or constrain urban resilience, such as governance structures, power relations, capacity-building and meeting basic needs, such as health and food security. Unless these are available to citizens, urban areas will remain vulnerable and will have limited adaptive capacity to respond to disasters and climate changes. How environmental justice and resilience shape the long-term sustainability of cities is and will remain one of the driving challenges of our century.

Notes

1 Director of the Sustainable Economic & Enterprise Development (SEED) Institute and Faculty Research Director in the College of Business and Economics at Regis University, beth.caniglia@oksatate.edu
2 Regional Parks, Capital Regional District of Victoria, bfrank@crd.bc.ca
3 Department of Sociology, University of Auckland, m.vallee@auckland.ac.nz
4 Source https://www.epa.gov/environmentaljustice

References

Abramson, D.M., Grattan, L.M., Mayer, B., Colten, C.E., Arosemena, F.A., Bedimo-Rung, A. and Lichtveld, M. (2015). The resilience activation framework: A conceptual model of how access to social resources promotes adaptation and rapid recovery in post-disaster settings. *Journal of Behavioral Health Services & Research*, 42, 42–57.

Adger, N.W. (2000). Social and ecological resilience: Are they related? *Progress in Human Geography*, 24(3), 347–364.

Aguilar, A.G. (2009). Urban geography. In M. Sala (Ed.), *Encyclopedia of life support systems (EOLSS), UNESCO: Geography – volume II* (pp. 127–140). Oxford: Eolss Publishers.

Aldrich, D.P. (Ed.) (2012). *Building resilience: Social capital in post-disaster recovery*. Chicago: University of Chicago Press.

Anderson, P. and Elmqvist, T. (2012). Urban ecological and social-ecological research in the city of Cape Town: Insights emerging from an urban ecology CityLab. *Ecology and Society*, 17(4), 23.

Anguelovski, I. (2014). *Neighborhood as refuge: Community reconstruction, place remaking, and environmental justice in the city.* Cambridge, MA: The MIT Press.

Barnett, J., Matthew, R.A. and O'Brien, K.L. (2010). Global environmental change and human security: an introduction. In A.M. Richard, J. Barnett, B. McDonald and K.L. O'Brien (Eds.) *Global environmental change and human security* (pp. 5–32). Cambridge, MA: The MIT Press.

Barr, S. and Devine-Wright, P. (2012). Resilient communities: Sustainabilities in transition. *Local Environment: The International Journal of Justice and Sustainability, 17(5)*, 525–532.

Berkes, F. and Ross, H. (2012). Community resilience: Toward an integrated approach. *Society and Natural Resource, 26(1)*, 5–20.

Birkmann, J. (2006). *Measuring vulnerability to natural hazards: towards disaster resilient societies.* New Delhi: TERI Press.

Brand, F.S. and Jax, K. (2007). Focusing the meaning(s) of resilience: Resilience as a descriptive concept and a boundary object. *Ecology and Society, 12(1)*, 23.

Brklacich, M., Chazan, M. and Bohle, H.G. (2010). Human security, vulnerability, and global environmental change. In A.M. Richard, J. Barnett, B. McDonald and K.L. O'Brien (Eds.) *Global environmental change and human security* (pp. 35–51) Cambridge, MA: The MIT Press.

Bullard, R.D. and Wright, B. (2009). *Race, place, and environmental justice after Hurricane Katrina: Struggles to reclaim, rebuild, and revitalize New Orleans and the Gulf Coast.* Philadelphia: Westview Press.

Bullard, R.D. and Wright, B. (2012). *The wrong complexion for protection: How the government response to disaster endangers African American communities.* New York: New York University.

Burns, T.J. and Caniglia, B.S. (2016). *Environmental sociology: The ecology of late modernity.* Norman, OK: Mercury Academic.

Buyantuyev, A. and Wu, J. (2009). Urbanization alters spatiotemporal patterns of ecosystem primary production: A case study of the Phoenix metropolitan region, USA. *Journal of Arid Environments, 73*, 512–520.

Caniglia, B.S., Frank, B., Delano, D. and Kerner, B. (2014). Enhancing environmental justice research and praxis: The inclusion of human security, resilience and vulnerabilities literature. *International Journal of Innovation and Sustainable Development, 4*, 409–426.

Ciplet, D., Roberts, J.T. and Khan, M.R. (2015). *Power in a warming world: The new global politics of climate change and the remaking of environmental inequality.* Cambridge, MA: MIT Press.

Da Cunha, A., Mager, C., Matthey, L., Pini, G., Rozenblat, C. and Véron, R. (2012). Urban geography in the era of globalization: The cities of the future emerging knowledge and urban regulations. *Geographica Helvetica, 67*, 67–76.

Davidson, D.J. (2010) The applicability of the concept of resilience to social systems: some sources of optimism and nagging doubts. *Society and Natural Resources, 23(12)*, 1135–1149.

Davis, K. (2011). The urbanization of the human population. In R.T. LeGates and F. Stout (Eds.) *The city reader* (5th ed.) (pp. 20–31). Abingdon: Routledge.

Downey, L. (2015). *Inequality, democracy and the environment.* New York: New York University Press.

Elmqvist, T., Fragkias, M., Goodness, J., Güneralp, B., Marcotullio, P.J., McDonald, R.I., et al. (2013). Stewardship of the biosphere in the urban era. In T. Elmqvist T.,

Fragkias M., Goodness J., Güneralp B., Marcotullio P.J., McDonald R.I., et al. (Eds.) *Urbanization, biodiversity and ecosystem services, challenges and opportunities* (pp. 719–747). New York: Spring.

Fiksel, J. (2006). A framework for sustainable materials management. *Journal of Materials*, 58(8), 15–22.

Folke, C. (2006). Resilience: the emergence of a perspective for social-ecological system analyses. *Global Environmental Change*, 16(3), 253–267.

Folke, C., Carpenter, S.R., Walker, B., Scheffer, M., Chapin, T. and Rockström, J. (2010). Resilience thinking: Integrating resilience, adaptability and transformability. *Ecology and Society*, 15(4), 20.

Gallopín, C.G. (2006). Linkages between vulnerability, resilience, and adaptive capacity. *Global Environmental Change*, 16(3), 293–303.

Grimm, N.B., Faeth, S.H., Golubiewski, N.E., Redman, C.L., Wu, J., Bai, X. and Briggs, J.M. (2008). Global change and the ecology of cities. *Science*, 319, 756–760.

Grove, M.J. (2009). Cities: Managing densely settled social–ecological systems. In S.F. Chapin III, G.P. Kofinas and C. Folke (Eds.) *Principles of ecosystem stewardship* (pp. 381–394). New York: Springer.

Hall, T. and Barrett, H.L. (2012). *Urban geography* (4th ed.). Abingdon: Routledge.

Harlan, S.L., Pellow, D.N., Roberts, T., Bell, S.E., Holt, W.G. and Nagel, J. (2015). Climate justice and inequality In R. Dunlap and R.J. Brulle (Eds.) *Climate change and society* (pp. 127–163). Oxford: Oxford University Press.

Holling, C.S. (1973). Resilience and stability of ecological systems. *Annual Review of Ecology and Systematics*, 4, 1–23.

Intergovernmental Panel on Climate Change (IPCC) (2014). *Climate change 2014: Impacts, adaptation, and vulnerability*. Retrieved 9 December 2014 from: http://www.ipcc.ch/pdf/assessment-report/ ar5/wg2/WGIIAR5-FrontMatterA_FINAL.pdf

Jorgenson, A.K. and Rice, J. (2012). Urban slums and children's health in less developed countries. *American Sociological Association*, XVIII(1), 103–116.

Kasperson, R.E. and Kasperson, J.X. (2001). *Climate change, vulnerability, and social justice*. Stockholm: Stockholm Environment Institute.

Kasperson, R.E., Dow, K., Archer, E.R.M., Cáceres, D., Downing, T.E., Elmqvist, T., et al. (2005). Vulnerable people and places. In Millennium Ecosystem Assessment Board, *Ecosystems and human well-being: current state and trends assessment* (pp. 143–164). Washington: Island Press.

Knox, P. and Pinch, S. (2010). *Urban social geography: an introduction* (6th ed.). Harlow: Pearson Education.

Lake, P.S. (2013). Resistance, resilience and restoration. *Ecological Management & Restoration*, 14(1), 20–24.

Liu, A. and Foster, K. (Eds.) (2011). *Resilience and opportunity: Lessons from the US Gulf Coast after Katrina and Rita*. Chicago: Brookings Institution Press.

Liu, G.Y., Yang, Z.F., Chen, B. and Ulgiati, S. (2011). Monitoring trends of urban development and environmental impact of Beijing. *Science of the Total Environment*, 409, 3295–3308.

Magis, K. (2010). Community resilience: an indicator of social sustainability. *Society and Natural Resources*, 23(5), 401–416.

Mayer, B. (2016). A framework for improving resilience: Adaptation in urban contexts. In B.S. Caniglia, M. Vallee and B. Frank (Eds.) *Resilience, environmental justice and the city*. New York: Routledge.

Melililo, J.M., Richmond, T.C. and Yohe, G.W. (Eds.) (2014). *Highlights of climate change impacts in the United States: The third national climate assessment.* U.S. Global Change Research Program.

Mohai, P., Pellow, D. and Roberts, J.T. (2009). Environmental justice. *Annual Review of Environmental and Resources, 34,* 405–430.

Nassauer, J.I. and Raskin, J. (2014). Urban vacancy and land use legacies: A frontier for urban ecological research, design, and planning. *Landscape and Urban Planning, 125,* 245–253.

Pacala, S. and Socolow, R. (2004). Stabilization wedges: Solving the climate problem for the next 50 years with current technologies. *Science, 305*(5686), 968–972.

Pellow, D. (2007). *Resisting global toxics: Transnational movements for environmental justice.* Cambridge, MA: MIT Press.

Pellow, D. (2016). Critical environmental justice studies. In B.S. Caniglia, M. Vallee and B. Frank (Eds.) *Resilience, environmental justice and the city.* New York: Routledge.

Pellow, D.N. and Brehm, H.N. (2013). An environmental sociology for the twenty-first century. *Annual Review of Sociology, 39,* 229–250.

Pickett, S.T.A., Cadenasso, M.L., Grove, M.J., Boone, C.G., Groffman, P.M., Irwin, E., et al. (2011). Urban ecological systems: scientific foundations and a decade of progress. *Journal of Environmental Management, 92,* 331–362.

Roberts, T. and Parks, B. (2007). *A climate of injustice: Global inequality, north-south politics, and climate policy.* Cambridge: Cambridge University Press.

Romero, V., Solís, E. and De Ureña, J.M. (2014). Beyond the metropolis: new employment centers and historic administrative cities in the Madrid global city region. *Urban Geography, 35*(6), 889–915.

Sassen, S. (2008). Urban sociology in the 21st century. In C.D. Bryant and D.L. Peck (Eds.) *21st century sociology* (pp. 476–486). Thousand Oaks, CA: Sage Publications.

Schewenius, M., McPhearson, T. and Elmqvist, T. (2014). Opportunities for increasing resilience and sustainability of urban social–ecological systems: insights from the URBES and the cities and biodiversity outlook projects. *Ambio, 43,* 434–444.

Schlosberg, D. (2013). Theorising environmental justice: the expanding sphere of a discourse. *Environmental Politics, 22*(1), 37–55.

Short, J.R. and Yeong-Hyun, K. (1999). The global urban system. In J.R. Short and K. Yeong-Hyun (Eds.) *Globalization and the city* (pp. 24–57). Longman: The University of Michigan.

Smith, T., Sonnenfeld, D.A. and Pellow, D.N. (2006). *Challenging the chip: Labor rights and environmental justice in the global electronics industry.* Philadelphia: Temple University Press.

Spencer, J.H. (2015). *Globalization and urbanization.* London: Rowan & Littlefield.

Stenning, A., Smith, A., Rochovska, A. and Swiatek, D. (2010). Credit, debt, and everyday financial practices: Low-income households in two postsocialist cities. *Economic Geography, 86*(2), 119–145.

UNEP. (2012). *The Asia-Pacific issue brief series on urbanization and climate change.* Retrieved 5 May 2016 from http://www.urbangateway.org/system/files/documents/urbangateway/addressing_urban_poverty_inequality_and_vulnerability_in_a_warming_world.pdf

UN-HABITAT. (2010). *State of Asia Cities 2010/11.* Fukuoka: UN-HABITAT. Retrieved 13 May 2016 from www.rrojasdatabank.onfo/citiesasia1011.pdf

UNICEF Bangladesh. (2010). Understanding urban inequalities in Bangladesh: A prerequisite for achieving vision 2021. A study based on the results of the 2009 multiple indicator cluster survey. Retrieved 13 May 2016 from http://www.unicef.org/bangladesh/Urban_paper_lowres.pdf

Walker, B. and Salt, D. (2006). *Resilience thinking: Sustaining ecosystems and people in a changing world.* Washington: Island Press.

Walks, A. (2013). Mapping the urban debtscape: The geography of household debt in Canadian cities. *Urban Geography, 34(2),* 153–187.

Wolch, J.R., Byrne, J. and Newell, J.P. (2014). Urban green space, public health and environmental justice: The challenge of making cities 'just green enough'. *Landscape and Urban Planning, 125,* 234–244.

Wu, J. (2014). Urban ecology and sustainability: the state-of-the-science and future directions. *Landscape and Urban Planning, 125,* 209–221.

Part I
Theoretical frameworks

2 Critical environmental justice studies

David N. Pellow[1]

Introduction

In our book *Power, Justice, and the Environment*, Robert Brulle and I used the term "critical environmental justice studies" (Pellow and Brulle 2005), which has since been adopted by other scholars working to expand the academic field and politics of environmental justice (EJ) (Adamson 2011, Holifield, Porter and Walker 2010). This concept is meant to build on recent scholarship in EJ studies questioning assumptions and gaps in earlier work in the field, by embracing greater interdisciplinarity and moving toward methodologies and epistemologies including and beyond the social sciences. As this direction in scholarship is still in its formative stages, here I take the opportunity to offer some guidance for what critical EJ studies might look like, with particular attention to the ways that urban space shapes struggles for environmental justice and resilient communities.

Environmental justice studies: an overview of the field

Why critical environmental justice studies? In order to answer that question, I must first offer a brief overview of the field of environmental justice studies. EJ studies has moved us toward a clear understanding that, where we find social inequalities by race and class, we tend to also find environmental inequalities in the form of marginalized groups being exposed to greater levels of pollution, toxics, "natural" disasters and the effects of climate change/disruption, as well as their exclusion from policy-making bodies that influence those outcomes (Bullard 2000; Bullard and Wright 2012; Fothergill and Peek 2004; Fothergill, Maestas and Darlington 1999; Harlan et al. 2006; Hunter 2000; Klinenberg 2002). Thus environmental risks disproportionately affect poor communities, communities of color, immigrants, indigenous peoples, and other marginalized communities around the globe. Scholars have been studying this problem for many years, and while many important cases have emerged from rural communities, it is a problem and struggle largely based in urban spaces. Researchers have also refined and improved our ability to measure the details and granularity of spatial environmental inequalities by race, class, and space (Bullard et al. 2007; Crowder and Downey 2010; Downey 2006; Mennis and Jordan 2005; Mohai and Saha 2007).

A small but growing group of researchers—including and especially environmental humanities scholars—have focused on the ways that gender, sexuality, citizenship, indigeneity, and nation shape the terrain of ecological inequalities, but those areas of scholarship remain in need of further development (Adamson 2011; Bell 2013; Brown and Ferguson 1995; Buckingham and Kulcur 2010; Holifield et al. 2010; Krakoff 2002; Krauss 1993; Park and Pellow 2011; Smith 2005; Stein 2004; Taylor 1997).

Recent scholarship divides EJ studies into two phases: (1) the "first generation," which was focused primarily on documenting the existence of environmental inequality through the lens of race and class; and (2) "second generation" studies that extend beyond questions of distribution to incorporate a deeper consideration of theory and the ways that gender, sexuality, and other categories of difference shape EJ struggles (Buckingham and Kulcur 2010; Holifield et al. 2010; Walker 2010). The aim of this framing is to push the field into a greater embrace of methodologically creative and interdisciplinary approaches to EJ studies. I agree with much of that principle, but I find this framing somewhat lacking. That is, while it describes the majority of social scientific articles published during the early years—which were based on quantitative, positivist models that sought to measure environmental inequality—this perspective overlooks a wealth of highly visible and impactful books, edited collections, and qualitative studies published in academic and non-academic presses and journals that offer a very different perspective on EJ studies. For example, during the so-called first generation of EJ studies, some scholars were actually engaged in exploring the gendered dimensions of EJ conflicts (Brown and Ferguson 1995; Krauss 1993), extending beyond the question of whether race versus class were the primary drivers of unequal risk distribution and asking what the health and psychological impacts of environmental inequalities might be in residential communities and workplaces (Cable and Cable 1995; Bullard 2000; Pellow and Park 2000). Significant "first generation" scholarship involved excavating the historical, social, and political forces that produce environmental injustices in the first place (Gottlieb 1994; Hurley 1995; Park and Pellow 2002; Pellow 2000; Pulido 1996; Szasz 1994; Szasz and Meuser 1997). During that "first generation" period, scholars were also exploring: (1) the complexities and contradictions of claims-making around environmental racism/injustice in cases where communities of color and indigenous communities declared the right to welcome hazardous and toxic industries and wastes in the name of environmental justice and sorely needed economic development (Krakoff 2002; Pellow 2000); (2) the historical process of social identity construction and the intersections of race, class, and gender as they relate to environmental injustice (Taylor 1997); and (3) EJ struggles across a variety of social spaces, including the workplace (Hossfeld 1990; Pellow and Park 2002; Wright and Bullard 1993).

In my view, what actually distinguishes the second from the first generation of EJ studies is that the second generation emphasizes greater methodological creativity and interdisciplinarity, the extension of scholarship into areas of greater theoretical breadth, and the expansion of social categories under consideration, particularly a stronger attention to gender, sexuality, and increasingly, nonhuman natures. There is also an increased depth with which scholars are envisioning and grappling with questions of justice and sustainability (Agyeman 2005; Agyeman, Bullard and Evans 2003; Schlosberg 2004).

Recent scholarship has grappled with the various ways to theorize the meaning of *justice*, and how this can include justice defined as distribution, inclusion, participation, recognition, fairness/procedure, capabilities, and so on (Banerjee 2014; Harrison 2011; Schlosberg 2004, 2007; Walker 2010), thus raising complex questions about how the scholarship and the movement have imagined both the problem and solution. Schlosberg (2004, 529) rightly points to the importance of "recognition" of marginalized groups in EJ conflicts, but there remains one major fallback of this approach. It often (though not always) relies on maintaining and reinforcing the state and state power, which is problematic because the state is one of the primary forces contributing to environmental injustice and related institutionalized violence. Recognition of various marginalized and aggrieved populations facing environmental injustice is important in a liberal-reformist paradigm that seeks to maintain state hegemony, but I suggest that scholars and activists might consider going beyond a state-centric orientation because state hegemony will likely not be productive to achieving environmental justice. The recent scholarship that calls for thinking about more expansive forms of justice might then consider doing so in a way that takes more seriously the depths and problem of distribution and the troubling limits of a state-centric approach.

Finally, as Caniglia, Frank, Delano, and Kerner (2014) point out, with few exceptions, EJ studies has done a poor job of articulating a vision and path toward environmental justice (for one exception see Anguelovski 2014). Critical EJ studies offers one such approach.

Toward critical environmental justice studies

Critical EJ studies is a perspective intended to address a number of important limitations and tensions within "first generation" EJ studies. These include, for example: (1) questions concerning the degree to which scholars should place emphasis on one or more social categories of difference (e.g., race, class, gender, sexuality, species, etc.) versus a focus on multiple forms of inequality; (2) the extent to which scholars studying EJ issues should focus on single-scale versus multiscalar analyses of the causes, consequences, and possible resolutions of EJ struggles; (3) the degree to which various forms of social inequality and power—including state power—are viewed as entrenched and embedded in society; and (4) the largely unexamined question of the expendability of human and nonhuman populations facing socioecological threats from states, industries, and other political economic forces.

On the first point above, EJ scholars have a tendency to focus on only one or two forms of social inequality in studies of environmental injustice. For example, some scholars continue to debate the relative importance of race versus class in terms of which category is most important with respect to the unequal and/or discriminatory distribution of environmental hazards (Mohai, Pellow and Roberts 2009), while only a small group of scholars have explored the role of gender and sexuality in EJ studies (Adamson, Evans and Stein 2004; Buckingham and Kulcur 2010; Stein 2004). Moreover, the key social category *species* remains, at best, at the margins of the field of EJ studies, despite the fact that, generally, when and where humans suffer from environmental inequalities, so does the more-than-human world (and vice versa) and often as a result of ideological frameworks that link marginalized humans to "nature." A small number of researchers are grappling with these ideas, primarily in the fields of ecological feminism and critical animal studies (Best, Nocella, Kahn, Gigliotti and Kemmerer 2007; Gaard 2004). My point is that since *multiple* forms of inequality drive and characterize the experience of environmental injustice, the field would do well to expand in that direction.

With respect to the second point above concerning *scale*, the EJ studies literature tends to be characterized by research at one scale or another, rather than a multiscalar approach. In other words, most researchers focus on the local, regional, national, or sometimes transnational or global scale, but few studies attempt to grasp how EJ struggles function at multiple scales, from the cellular and bodily level to the global and back (Herod 2011; Sze 2016). Some scholars have addressed this important question by exploring cases in which pollutants produced in one part of the world travel across national borders and impact human and ecological health in another hemisphere (Sze 2006). Scale is of critical importance because it allows us to understand how environmental injustices are facilitated by decision-makers who behave as if sites where hazards are produced "out of sight and out of mind" are somehow irrelevant to the health of people and ecosystems at the original sites of decision-making power and consumption. Attention to scale also assists us in observing how social movement *responses* to environmental injustices draw on spatial frameworks, networks, and knowledge to make the connections between hazards in one place and harm in another. CEJ studies thus advocates multiscalar methodological and theoretical approaches to studying EJ issues in order to better comprehend the complex spatial and temporal causes, consequences, and possible resolutions of EJ struggles.

Regarding the third point above—the degree to which various forms of inequality and power are viewed as entrenched in society—this concern stems from my conclusion that the vision of change articulated by many EJ studies scholars and many leading EJ activists generally looks to the state and capital to accommodate demands via legislation, institutional reforms, and other policy concessions. The concern here is that such an approach leaves intact the very power structures that produced environmental injustice in the first place. Yes, it names those institutions and structures as sources of the problems and seeks to reform them, but by working in collaboration with those entities, such efforts ultimately risk reinforcing their legitimacy and ensuring their future status. A critical EJ studies approach might, at the very least, raise the question as to whether scholars and activists aiming for transformational analyses and social change should look to the primary actors responsible for producing environmental injustices to offer remedies for those harms. From a simple criminal justice perspective, that approach might seem logical (i.e., the perpetrator should offer recompense for a crime); but from a systemic justice perspective, it is entirely *il*logical (i.e., if the system is designed to produce the harms of environmental injustice, what is needed is a redesign or a new system altogether).

Regarding the fourth point above, EJ studies suggests that various marginalized human populations are treated—if not viewed—as inferior and less valuable to society than others. This point is largely under-theorized in the literature (Pulido 1996). Critical EJ studies makes this point more explicit by arguing that these populations are marked for erasure and death, and links that ideological and institutional othering to the more-than-human world as well. Moreover, critical EJ contends that these threatened populations and spaces are critical to building socially and environmentally just and resilient futures for us all.

Thus, what critical EJ studies offers "first generation" EJ studies is the following, which I call the four pillars of critical EJ: (1) greater attention to how multiple social categories of difference are entangled in the production of environmental injustice, from race, gender, sexuality, ability, and class to species, which would attend to the ways that both the human and the more-than-human world are impacted by and respond to environmental injustice and related forms of state-corporate violence; (2) an embrace of multiscalar methodological and theoretical approaches to studying EJ issues in order to better comprehend the complex spatial and temporal causes, consequences, and possible resolutions of EJ struggles; (3) a deeper grasp on the entrenched and embedded character of social inequality—including speciesism and state power—in society and therefore a reckoning with the need for transformative (rather than exclusively reformist) approaches to realize environmental justice. In other words, critical EJ studies seeks to push our analyses and actions beyond the state and capital via a broad anti-authoritarian perspective; and (4) greater attention to and articulation of the ways that humans and more-than-human actors are *indispensable* to the present and for building sustainable, just, and resilient urban spaces. As EJ studies has had difficulty promoting a productive and transformative vision of change (Caniglia et al. 2014), indispensability is a key ingredient in that effort.

In the following sections I elaborate on the four pillars noted above, with the aim of articulating a more robust framework for future scholarship and action around environmental justice that is not usually contained in "first generation" EJ studies scholarship.

What does critical environmental justice studies look like?

Building on the work of scholars across numerous fields that only periodically intersect (i.e., environmental justice studies, critical race theory, critical race feminism, ethnic studies, gender and sexuality studies, political ecology, anti-authoritarian/anarchist theory, and ecological feminism), I propose *critical environmental justice studies* as a framework built on the following four pillars:

First pillar

The first pillar of critical EJ studies involves the recognition that social inequality and oppression in all forms intersect and that actors in the more-than-human world are subjects of oppression and are frequently agents of social change. I will first consider the issue of intersecting oppressions. The fields of critical race theory, critical race feminism, gender and sexuality studies, queer theory, eco-feminism, disability studies, and critical animal studies all speak to the ways in which various social categories of difference work to place particular bodies at risk of exclusion, marginalization, erasure, discrimination, violence, and othering. These insights are important for building an understanding of the ways that intra-human inequality and oppressions function and how they intersect with human-nonhuman oppression. As David Nibert and Michael Fox put it, "[T]he oppression of various devalued groups in human societies is not independent and unrelated; rather, the arrangements that lead to various forms of oppression are integrated in such a way that the exploitation of one group frequently augments and compounds the mistreatment of others" (Nibert and Fox 2002, 13). Some of those "[v]arious devalued groups in human societies" include women, immigrants, lesbian/gay/bisexual/transgender/queer (LGBTQ) persons, people of color, indigenous peoples, disabled persons, the elderly, children, low-income people, and nonhuman species. And while the *experiences* of these various groups are qualitatively distinct (i.e., not equivalent), the *logic* of domination and othering as practiced by more powerful groups against them provides the thread of intersectionality through each of their oppressions.

Thus critical EJ views racism, heteropatriarchy, classism, nativism, ableism, ageism, speciesism, and other forms of inequality as intersecting axes of domination and control. That is, these inequalities are mutually reinforcing in that they tend to act together to produce and maintain systems of individual and collective power, privilege, and subordination. With respect to speciesism, critical EJ extends beyond the category of the human to include the more-than-human world (from nonhuman animals to the built environment) as subjects of oppression and as agents of social change. The built environment, and in particular, the urban environment, is a vast assemblage of what urban political ecologists call "socionatures" or nature/culture hybrids (Heynen, Kaika and Swyngedouw 2006) that reflect the entangled and inseparable character of buildings, roads, communication technologies, residential, commercial, and public spaces, and to some extent, the entire biosphere. The urban built environment is a "socionature" because it is impossible to delineate where its human imprint ends and its nonhuman imprint begins, or vice versa. They are linked in what Freudenburg, Frickel, and Gramling (1995) called "conjoint constitution." And since most of the human beings on this planet are living in cities and other urban spaces, the future of environmental justice studies, and efforts to create resilience and sustainability, will have to focus more energy on cities.

Second pillar

The second pillar of critical EJ studies is a focus on the role of *scale* in the production and possible resolution of environmental injustices. As Julie Sze writes, "thinking globally and acting locally also demands that people more fully comprehend the relationship between the local and the global or, in other words, to consider scale" (2016, 178). And by scale, environmental studies scholars mean both spatial and temporal dimensions of how objects, ideas, bodies, beings, things, and environmental harms and resilient practices are linked, how they are connected ecologically. While much of the EJ literature pays attention to only one scale of analysis (e.g., a neighborhood, census tracts, etc.), some scholars have grappled with this problem using multiple scales, pointing to the ways that, for example, persistent organic pollutants produced thousands of miles away from the Artic nevertheless end up in high concentrations in the breast milk of indigenous Nunavik women (Sze 2016) and how EJ activists in Louisiana collaborate with and stand in solidarity with activists in Nigeria, the Philippines, and other parts of the world because they are fighting the same global oil corporation—Shell (Kurtz 2003). A critical EJ studies framework suggests that multiscalar spatial and temporal analyses are a productive direction for this body of scholarship. This approach allows us to examine how, for example, pollution generated by a coal-fired power plant in the Bronx can emit carbon and other substances that contribute to respiratory disorders like asthma in children who live in New York City, but also how that pollution exacerbates the broader challenge of global climate change/disruption.

But scale is about much more than size and space. Attention to the *temporal* dimensions of scale allows us to explore, for example, how the emergence and use of coal-fired power plants and petroleum-based economies developed and changed over historical periods, thus unveiling some of the social causes of our ecological crises and perhaps revealing clues as to how things might have unfolded differently and therefore inviting interventions for the future. The production of a molecule of carbon dioxide or nitrous oxide can occur in an instant, but it remains in the atmosphere for more than a century, so the decisions we make at one point in time can have dramatic ramifications for generations to come (Sayre 2005). The decisions by European colonizers to enslave peoples of African descent and conquer the indigenous peoples and lands of what became the United States of America have dramatic consequences for human and environmental health that are evident today. For example, Native American and African American communities today face some of the most intense impacts of climate change. Native peoples often live on lands that are targeted for fossil fuel drilling (which pollutes their water tables and endangers the lives of flora and fauna they depend on) and African Americans are more likely than other communities to live near health-impairing coal-fired power plants. Both of these examples of environmental racism reveal the ongoing violence associated with the reservation system, the violation of treaties with indigenous peoples, and residential segregation. In the case of the community of Diamond in the city of Norco, Louisiana, the close proximity of this African American community to a hazardous oil production facility is a legacy of that land being a former slave plantation and the people living nearby being the descendants of enslaved peoples (Lerner 2006). Norco is named after the New Orleans Refinery Company, an affiliate of the Royal Dutch Shell Corporation, which bought up the land where the refinery stands from the owners of two former slave plantation sites. The

Diamond community is a subdivision created by African American sharecroppers who moved across the street when Shell announced that it was building a chemical plant on the site where they lived. Today the descendants of slaves and sharecroppers bear the full force of living next to the refinery and chemical plant. There have been a number of major spills, leaks, explosions, and other industrial accidents at the site that residents claim have contributed to a number of deaths and illnesses (Lerner 2006). One cannot begin to understand why environmental racism affects the Diamond community without also understanding the history of racism, segregation, sharecropping, slavery, and the development of the petroleum industry in the U.S. South and globally. Efforts at enabling or producing *resilience* will have to take scale (both spatial and temporal) into account.

Third pillar

The third pillar of critical EJ studies is the view that social inequalities—from racism to speciesism—are deeply embedded in society (rather than aberrations) and reinforced by state power and market systems, and that therefore the current social order stands as a fundamental obstacle to social and environmental justice. The logical conclusion of that observation is that social change movements may be better off thinking and acting beyond the state and capital as targets of reform and reliable partners.

As far as a vision of change is concerned, the general thrust of "first generation" EJ studies and the EJ movement is that scholars and activists are *not* asking how we might build environmentally just resilient communities *beyond* the state, but rather how we might do so with a *different* kind of state intervention. While perhaps generative and seemingly firmly on the political cutting edge, this view is also limited and contradictory, if we consider the work of scholars who conclude that states are both inherently racially exclusionary and ecologically unsustainable (Goldberg 2002; Smith 2011). EJ scholars and activists tend to argue for the dedication and expansion of state resources away from anti-ecological and anti-humanist purposes to the cause of ecological protection, environmental justice, civil and human rights—in some ways part of a classic progressive-Left platform. The problem with this approach is that it assumes that states can and do perform such functions separately, when in fact they tend to be integrally linked in a fashion that serves to reinforce state power and various forms of inequality (including institutional racism and speciesism). For example, policies aimed at environmental protection often result in unequal enforcement along race and class lines (Lavelle and Coyle 1992; Lombardi, Buford and Greene 2015) and/or the shifting of environmental harms from privileged communities onto other, less politically powerful communities (Bullard 2000; Pellow 2007; Szasz 1994). Public welfare policies associated with food stamps tend to be linked directly to and support agricultural practices that involve the exploitation of low-wage farm labor, massive industrial herbicide and pesticide usage, and the consumption of nonhuman animals (livestock) raised in often cruel conditions that also negatively harm human workers and pollute local water tables and surrounding landscapes. Public welfare policies associated with job training and workforce development rarely if ever are linked to enterprises that are characterized by low ecological footprints and a unionized employee population. These are not anomalies. In the view of many scholars, this is because the *purpose* of a state is to exert control over populations, ecosystems, and territory, among other things (Amster, DeLeon, Fernandez, Nocella and Shannon 2009; Goldberg 2002; Scott 1999, 2010; Weber, Owen, Strong and Livingstone 2004). Thus the EJ studies and EJ movement's goal of pushing the state to shift resources from harmful to progressive aims will likely meet with the usual challenges from conservatives who find these ideas too radical. More importantly, since "progressive" state practices—like conservative state practices—tend to support state dominance and reflect the state's inherently exclusionary and anti-ecological practices, even a "successful" end result will be limited at best since it will likely strengthen the very state responsible for the environmental inequalities that scholars and activists decry.

The EJ movement and EJ scholarship generally share a consensus that they are looking to the state and its legal systems to deliver justice, to self-regulate or police itself, and to regulate industry (Benford 2005). Thus far, as studies have demonstrated conclusively, the track record of state-based regulation and enforcement of environmental and civil rights legislation in communities of color has not been promising (Cole and Foster 2000; Lavelle and Coyle 1992; Lombardi et al. 2015). Yet, as Robert Benford (2005) argues, the EJ movement continues to seek justice through a system that was never intended to provide justice for marginalized peoples and nonhuman natures.

To restate the third pillar, critical EJ views social inequality—including speciesism—as deeply entrenched and embedded in human society (rather than as aberrations), and reinforced by state power and market systems. Thus critical EJ views socioecological violence (i.e., violence directed against both humans and the more-than-human world) as *foundational* to the current social order. Hence a critical EJ perspective sees that social order as a fundamental obstacle to social and environmental justice and therefore refuses reformist approaches to social change. Accordingly, critical EJ urges scholars and activists to go beyond the boundaries of the state and capital to explore the ways that humans and more-than-humans can and do resist the current social order to bring new imaginings, visions, practices, relationships, and communities into being that are anti-authoritarian and sustainable, and that embody what I call *just resilience*—a resilience marked by social and environmental justice. *Just resilience* is an important concept for environmental studies scholars because, among many reasons, there are forms of resilience that are *unjust* and we should distinguish between them. For example, as scholars of political economy have noted for decades, one of the defining features of states, capital markets, and dominant social institutions is that these systems and structures are often forced to display resilience, as they frequently deflect, displace, absorb, incorporate, and assimilate myriad challenges from various corners of society, whether it be the entry of new ethnic groups, the emergence of revolutionary social movements, or the growth of political ideologies that might challenge their hegemony (Ahmed 2012; Ferguson 2012; Piven and Cloward 1978; Scott 2010;

Selznick 1949). States, corporations, markets, and their constituent institutions seek to maintain their dominance through various forms of *unjust resilience* on a routine basis. When workers' rights movements demand the right to form unions, corporations often repress those movements or incorporate some of the least disruptive demands, gaining acceptance and minimizing the possibility of ongoing future protests. When environmentalists demand that universities divest from fossil fuel markets, as the 350.org movement has done, academic institutions that have agreed to this demand tend to do so only when it has little impact on their actual stock portfolio's returns. These are examples of how dominant institutions retain their hegemony through *unjust resilience*. That resilience is unjust because it maintains socially and ecologically unequal, discriminatory, and unsustainable practices and relationships. *Just resilience* would be a set of practices and relationships characterized by deeper commitments to equity, social, and environmental justice. Just resilience builds on Agyeman, Bullard, and Evans's (2003) concept of just sustainability, which is defined as "the need to ensure a better quality of life for all, now and into the future, in a just and equitable manner, whilst living within the limits of supporting ecosystems." Just sustainability is an integration of environmental justice and sustainability, but does not directly address the need for a community's capacity to rebound and rebuild (i.e., resilience) in the wake of myriad threats and harms and to do so with a focus on justice. Just resilience does just that. An example of what just resilience might look like could be the work that community-based organizations did when they came together in the wake of Hurricane Katrina to rebuild and strengthen existing grassroots groups and social networks and to create new ones (like the Common Ground Collective) that would facilitate the capacity of the Gulf Coast region's most marginalized populations to recover after that disaster, and chart a future characterized by greater democratic practices and relationships among humans and between humans and the more-than-human world (Crow 2014).

The charge from the critical EJ perspective that scholars must be aware of how deeply entrenched social inequalities are in society reflects the concept of "injustices-in-waiting" (Caniglia et al. 2014) in that power imbalances produced by states, corporations, and existing social hierarchies enable greater vulnerabilities and risks for human and more-than-human populations and communities across the globe. That is, while ecological threats to various bodies and spaces are dangerous in and of themselves, once we take into account the unequal political and social terrain that gives rise to and supports those threats, we become more fully aware of how multiple layers of power function to create and sustain various risks for some populations while protecting others. These social hierarchies and power imbalances constitute injustices in and of themselves as well as "injustices-in-waiting" because, while constructing unequal relationships, they also heighten certain vulnerabilities and risks for certain bodies and spaces.

Fourth pillar

The fourth pillar of the critical EJ studies framework centers on the concept of *indispensability*. In the book *Black and Brown Solidarity*, critical race and ethnic studies scholar John Márquez (2014) introduces the concept "racial expendability" to argue that black and brown bodies are, in the eyes of the state and its constituent legal system, generally viewed as criminal, deficient, threatening, and deserving of violent discipline and even obliteration. Márquez and other ethnic studies scholars (Cacho 2012; Da Silva 2007; Mills 2001; Vargas 2010) contend that, in a society centered on whiteness, people of color are constructed as and rendered expendable. Philosopher and critical race theorist Charles Mills (2001) argues that people of African descent, for example, are considered "black trash" by policy-makers and institutions that foment environmental racism because these populations are associated with filth, waste, and uncleanliness, so locating pollution in their communities actually makes cultural common sense.

A critical EJ studies perspective builds on this work by countering the ideology of white supremacy (Goldberg 2004; Márquez 2014) and human dominionism (Mason 2004), and articulating the perspective that excluded, marginalized, and othered populations, beings, and things—both human and more-than-human— must be viewed not as expendable but rather as *indispensable* to our collective futures. This is what I term *racial indispensability* (when speaking particularly about people of color) and *socioecological indispensability* (when speaking about broader communities within and across the human/more-than-human divide and their relationships to one another). Racial indispensability is intended to challenge the logic of racial expendability and is the idea that institutions, policies, and practices that support and perpetuate racism suffer from the illogical assumption that the future of people of color is de-linked from the future of white communities. In fact, white communities have always been dependent upon communities of color, for labor, for consumers, for political support, and for the existence of the idea of whiteness itself, which provides what W.E.B. DuBois called a "psychological wage" (1935) even for the poorest white Americans who could feel the pride of knowing that at least they were, for example, "not black." In other words, whiteness has no meaning without people of color. Those are troubling reasons why people of color are indispensable to this society. More positively, people of color are members of our society, are core participants in our social systems, and more broadly, are members of our socioecological systems and are therefore key to ensuring the continued functioning, sustainability, and just resilience of our society and planet. Hence, people of color are indispensable to our collective futures. Only when we understand that all of our communities are indispensable to a healthy and sustainable present and future can we envision and practice (critical) environmental justice.

The idea of indispensability is distinct from an assimilationist perspective, which seeks to (often involuntarily and violently) incorporate "others" into one's own vision of a society (Smith 2005). Rather, indispensability honors key EJ and ecological principles by seeing all communities (more-than-human and human) as interconnected, interdependent, but also sovereign and requiring the solidarity of others. Indispensability should also not be confused with a functionalist view of society and socioecological relations as it is meant to serve as a call for solidarity of all members of our socioecological communities, even in the face of great conflict, inequality, and tension. Indispensability recognizes that roles, positions, and behaviors among various populations can and do conflict and change over time, and that the character of inequality and state and market power in most societies is highly unjust and must be confronted. Functionalism, on the other hand, posits that whatever the character of inequality, roles, and behaviors may be, it must be positive for that society and therefore is in no need of change (Davis and Moore 1945; Parsons 1954). Indispensability argues against that logic because critical EJ is fundamentally focused on securing justice and sustainability in a highly unjust and unsustainable system. Thus indispensability demands dramatic change but does so from the perspective that all members of society and socioecological systems have something to contribute to that process and to our collective futures.

Socially, politically, philosophically, and ecologically, what this means is that we are all linked in webs of social interdependence, so that what happens to one group affects, in some way, all others. As Dr. Martin Luther King, Jr. famously wrote in his landmark "Letter from a Birmingham Jail" with regard to racism and the future of the U.S.:

> Injustice anywhere is injustice everywhere [. . .] In a real sense all life is interrelated. All men are caught in an inescapable network of mutuality, tied in a single garment of destiny. Whatever affects one directly, affects all indirectly. Never again can we afford to live with the narrow, provincial "outside agitator" idea. Anyone who lives inside the United States can never be considered an outsider.
>
> (King 1963)

King demonstrated a profound understanding of indispensability. The point of racial and socioecological indispensability is that since we are all linked in socioecological relationships, the harm that one group experiences has consequences for all others. But the idea of indispensability takes that basic ecological observation even further to argue that since what affects one affects all, then all are indispensable to our collective future, particularly those groups disproportionately and negatively impacted by systems of inequality and/or state-corporate violence.

The impacts of climate change offer a telling example of environmental racism in the face of indispensability. While the findings and conclusions of climate scientists are remarkably clear that anthropogenic climate change is occurring at a dramatic pace and with increasing intensity, this is also happening unevenly, with people of color, the poor, indigenous peoples, people in the global south, and women suffering the most (Harlan et al. 2015). This is a clear case of environmental racism and inequality, but the fossil fuel industries, national governments, and religious conservatives have invested enormous sums of energy, time, and money into denying these facts. Even Pope Francis has spoken clearly on this matter and sees it as an example of climate injustice that is placing the planet and its people in peril (Francis 2015). Yet the climate change deniers see it in their interests to ignore and/or actively work against the recognition of the problem (Dunlap and McCright 2010; Dunlap and McCright 2015; Norgaard 2011;

Oreskes and Conway 2010). A critical EJ studies framework allows us to see that, regardless of perceptions and politics, this approach is not only harmful to marginalized communities around the globe, it is also self-defeating for those who appear to be operating in their own short-term self-interests. Thus, the problem of climate change/disruption reveals in stark terms the fact of racial indispensability and socioecological indispensability—the fourth pillar of critical EJ studies.

Critical EJ extends the work of scholars and activists who argue that, in this society, people of color are constructed as and rendered expendable (Cacho 2012; Da Silva 2007; Márquez 2014; Mills 2001; Vargas 2010). Building on those ideas and challenging the ideology of white supremacy and human dominionism, critical EJ articulates the perspective that excluded, marginalized, and othered populations, beings, and things—both human and more-than-human—must be viewed as *indispensable* to our collective futures. Indispensability can be linked to debates focused on resilience through the concept of just resilience, which poses the key question, "resilience for whom?" and answers that question with a resounding "everyone!"

Discussion and conclusion

The term "critical environmental justice studies" (Pellow and Brulle 2006) is used by scholars working to expand EJ studies beyond its first-generation focus on the basic questions concerning the racial and class dimensions of environmental inequality using either quantitative or small case study methods (Adamson 2011; Holifield et al. 2010). This concept is meant to build on that earlier scholarship in EJ studies and move beyond its conceptual, theoretical, disciplinary, and methodological limitations. Since that path is still very much in formation, this chapter is an effort to chart one course in that direction with greater specificity.

Thus critical EJ studies is a framework whose goal is to address important limitations and tensions within EJ studies. There are four key issues from "first generation" EJ studies that critical EJ studies can speak to that I focus on in this chapter. First is the tendency for EJ scholars to focus on only one or two social categories of difference (for example, race and/or class), when in fact, environmental injustices are driven by and impact actors across multiple forms of inequality (e.g., race, class, gender, sexuality, age, ability, species, etc.). While a small but growing number of scholars are exploring the ways that, for example, gender and sexuality shape EJ struggles (Adamson et al. 2004; Buckingham and Kulcur 2010; Stein 2004), that work is still in its early stages. Further, the category of species remains almost entirely at the margins of the field despite the very clear and documented ways that EJ conflicts reflect tensions and intersections between humans and the more-than-human world (Best et al. 2007; Gaard 2004; Jacoby 2001). The evidence and perspectives from fields such as ecological feminism, political ecology, critical race theory, ethnic studies, critical race feminism, the environmental humanities, and critical animal studies suggests that multiple forms of inequality fuel environmental injustice and shape the experiences of the actors involved, so EJ studies would be strengthened with greater attention to these dynamics.

Second, the EJ studies literature tends to be characterized by research at one scale or another, rather than a multiscalar approach. In other words, most researchers focus on the local, regional, national, and sometimes transnational or global scale, but few studies attempt to grasp how EJ struggles function at multiple scales, from the cellular and bodily level to the global, and back. Scale is of critical importance because it allows us to understand how environmental injustices are facilitated by decision-makers who, for example, behave as if sites where hazards are produced "out of sight and out of mind" are somehow irrelevant to the health of people and ecosystems at the original sites of decision-making power and consumption. Attention to scale also assists us in observing how social movement *responses* to environmental injustices draw on spatial frameworks, networks, and knowledge to make the connections between hazards in one place and harm in another. Scholars have demonstrated that the environmental justice and climate justice movements are examples of networks of activists from local communities who collaborate with partners at the transnational and global scales, launching campaigns directed at multinational corporations and/or participating in United Nations-sponsored gatherings to implement a stronger global climate treaty (Ciplet, Roberts and Khan 2015). This is important for understanding and addressing environmental injustice because it functions at all scales in both its driving forces and its consequences. That is, environmental threats "jump" scale by crossing vast expanses of geographic space and time by refusing to be contained by artificial boundaries such as national borders and election cycles. A critical EJ studies approach embraces multiscalar analyses for producing more robust understandings of the reasons why environmental inequalities exist and for developing more effective responses to them.

Third is the tendency within EJ studies to name and critique the problems of social inequality and power imbalances among various populations versus states and corporations, paired with an unwillingness to see those social relations as deeply entrenched and as fundamental obstacles to achieving environmental justice. In other words, despite a strong condemnation of the scourges of racism, class domination, and the abuse of state and corporate power in the literature, EJ studies generally offers prescriptions for change that rely on dominant institutions serving as partners and collaborators in forging a just and sustainable future. The evidence and analysis from fields such as anarchist studies, critical race theory, critical race feminism, ethnic studies, and critical animal studies suggests that these inequalities are foundational to the formation and maintenance of states and capital and that it would likely be counterproductive for environmental justice scholars and advocates to seek remedies from dominant institutions. A critical EJ studies approach asks whether scholars and activists aiming for transformational analyses and social change should expect the very institutions that are largely driving socioecological inequalities to offer remedies for these harms (and what the implications of doing so might be).

Fourth, EJ studies suggests that certain human populations are devalued via environmental racism, yet stops short of theorizing this point beyond that largely implicit claim. Critical EJ studies takes this claim more seriously by linking it to scholarship that concludes that these bodies are expendable (a much stronger claim than the contention that they are viewed as inferior), and links that ideological and institutional othering to the more-than-human world as well. Furthermore, critical EJ confronts that hegemonic view with the perspective that these bodies, populations, and spaces at risk are indispensable to our collective futures. Rather, all are understood to be linked to one another in complex webs of social and ecological interdependence that are in constant fluctuation, change, conflict, and negotiation, but that require one another's presence and participation for our future collective well-being.

Critical EJ studies draws from numerous fields of scholarship in order to produce more robust and richer accounts for why environmental injustices occur and persist, for how human and nonhuman forces shape and are shaped by them, and for what environmental justice could look like. That is, the promise of critical EJ studies lies in its capacity to more fully explain the sources and consequences of our socioecological crises and develop more generative analyses of how social change efforts within and across species may meet those challenges.

Finally, critical EJ studies can aid scholars and advocates in thinking through a *redefinition of the concept of environmental justice itself* to reflect and encompass the above four pillars. Following White (2008) and Brisman (2008), perhaps any discussion regarding the future of environmental justice studies and the environmental justice movements might begin by connecting a "first generation" framing of environmental justice, which centers primarily around the intersection of social inequality and environmental harm, with the concept of *ecological justice*, which centers on the relationship of human beings to the broader nonhuman world. These two concepts are infinitely productive for each other. In my view, critical EJ studies would offer a redefinition or expansive view of environmental justice that reached out to and merged with ecological justice. By the term ecological justice, I mean to suggest a more respectful and egalitarian relationship of human beings to one another and to the broader nonhuman world. This model of analysis and politics begins with humans taking responsibility for practicing transformative socioecological political work and extends to understanding inequalities within and across species and space to imagine and struggle for a more democratic multispecies world. Nonhuman species and ecosystems may not engage in politics the way humans tend to, but they can and do exert influence in many ways (Bennett 2009; Braun and Whatmore 2010; Robbins 2007). Ecological justice destabilizes the notion of the human as a biological category at the apex of a human/nature hierarchy and, instead, embraces it as a political category that engages with the broader ecological community. This model of politics also rejects the state as an arbiter of justice and inclusion. Generally speaking, states have managed, included, excluded, homogenized, and controlled humans and nonhuman natures for the benefit of a small elite. That should be reason enough to embrace an anarchist or broadly anti-authoritarian approach to socioecological change. Curiously, this concept of ecological justice closely mirrors and parallels the principles of environmental justice—a sort of founding document of the U.S. EJ movement, suggesting that, in many ways, the EJ movement and EJ studies have yet to catch up to the vision of the movement's founding principles, which are largely aligned with a critical EJ perspective. Moreover, the concept and practice of *just resilience* would play an important role in future research and action concerning environmental justice because it reflects the need to incorporate and support practices that produce the capacity of people, nonhumans, and ecosystems to rebuild and regain strength and vitality in the face of myriad threats.

Note

1 Environmental Studies Program, University of California, pellow@es.ucsb.edu

References

Adamson J. (2011). Medicine food: Critical environmental justice studies, native North American literature, and the movement for food sovereignty. *Environmental Justice*, 4, 213–219.

Adamson J., Evans M.M. and Stein R. (Eds.) (2004). *The environmental justice reader: Politics, poetics, and pedagogy*. Tucson: University of Arizona.

Agyeman J. (Ed.) (2005). *Sustainable communities and the challenge of environmental justice*. New York: New York University Press.

Agyeman J., Bullard R. and Evans B. (Ed.) (2003). *Just sustainabilities: Development in an unequal world*. Cambridge, MA: The MIT Press.

Ahmed S. (2012). *On being included: Racism and diversity in institutional life*. Raleigh, NC: Duke University.

Amster R., DeLeon A., Fernandez A.L., Nocella II A.J. and Shannon D. (Eds.) (2009). *Contemporary anarchist studies*. New York: Routledge.

Anguelovski I. (2014). *Neighborhood as refuge: Community reconstruction, place remaking, and environmental justice in the city*. Cambridge, MA: The MIT Press.

Banerjee D. (2014). Toward an integrative framework for environmental justice research: A synthesis and extension of the literature. *Society and Natural Resources*, 27, 805–819.

Bell S.E. (2013). *Our roots run deep as ironweed: Appalachian women and the fight for environmental justice*. Champaign: University of Illinois Press.

Benford R. (2005). The half-life of the environmental justice frame: Innovation, diffusion, and stagnation. In D.N. Pellow and R.J. Brulle (Eds.) *Power, justice, and the environment: A critical appraisal of the environmental justice movement* (pp. 37–55). Cambridge, MA: MIT Press.

Bennett J. (2009). *Vibrant matter: A political ecology of things*. Durham, NC: Duke University.

Best S., Nocella A., Kahn R., Gigliotti C. and Kemmerer L. (2007). Introducing critical animal studies. *Journal for Critical Animal Studies*, 5(1), 3–4.

Braun B. and Whatmore S.J. (Eds.) (2010). *Political matter: Technoscience, democracy, and public life*. Minneapolis: University of Minnesota.

Brisman A. (2008). Crime-environment relationships and environmental justice. *Seattle Journal for Social Justice*, 6, 727–817.

Brown P. and Ferguson F (1995). "Making a big stink": Women's work, women's relationships, and toxic waste activism. *Gender & Society*, 9, 145–172.

Buckingham S. and Kulcur R. (2010). Gendered geographies of environmental justice. In R. Holifield, M. Porter and G. Walker (Eds.) *Spaces of environmental justice*. New York: Wiley-Blackwell.

Bullard R.D. (2000). *Dumping in Dixie: Race, class, and environmental quality* (3rd ed.). Boulder, CO: Westview.

Bullard R.D. and Wright B. (2012). *The wrong complexion for protection: How the government response to disaster endangers African American communities*. New York: New York University.

Bullard R.D., Mohai P., Saha R. and Wright B. (2007). *Toxic wastes and race at twenty, 1987–2007*. New York: United Church of Christ.

Cable S. and Cable C. (1995). *Environmental problems, grassroots solutions*. New York: St. Martin's Press.

Cacho L. (2012). *Social death: Racialized rightlessness and the criminalization of the unprotected*. New York: New York University.

Caniglia B.S., Frank B., Delano D. and Kerner B. (2014). Enhancing environmental justice research and praxis: The inclusion of human security, resilience and vulnerabilities literature. *International Journal of Innovation and Sustainable Development*, 8, 409–426.

Ciplet D., Roberts J.T. and Khan M.R. (2015). *Power in a warming world: The new global politics of climate change and the remaking of environmental inequality*. Cambridge, MA: The MIT Press.

Cole L. and Foster S. (2000). *From the ground up: Environmental racism and the rise of the environmental justice movement*. New York: New York University.

Crow S. (2014). *Black flags and windmills: Hope, anarchy, and the common ground collective*. Oakland, CA: PM Press.

Crowder K. and Downey L. (2010). Inter-neighborhood migration, race, and environmental hazards. *American Journal of Sociology*, 115, 1110–1149.

Da Silva D.F. (2007). *The global idea of race*. Minneapolis: University of Minnesota.

Davis K. and Moore W.E. (1945). Some principles of stratification. *American Sociological Review*, 10, 242–249.

Downey L. (2006). Environmental racial inequality in Detroit. *Social Forces*, 85(2), 771–796.

DuBois W.E.B. (1977 [1935]). *Black reconstruction*. New York: Atheneum.

Dunlap R. and McCright A. (2010). Climate change denial: Sources, actors and strategies. In C. Lever-Tracy (Ed.) *Routledge handbook of climate change and society* (pp. 240–259). New York: Routledge.

Dunlap R. and McCright A. (2015). Challenging climate change: The denial countermovement. In R. Dunlap and R.J. Brulle (Eds.) *Climate change and society: Sociological perspectives* (pp. 300–332). Oxford: Oxford University Press.

Ferguson R. (2012). *The reorder of things: The university and its pedagogies of minority difference*. Minneapolis: University of Minnesota.

Fothergill A. and Peek L. (2004). Poverty and disasters in the United States: A review of recent sociological findings. *Natural Hazards*, 32, 89–110.

Fothergill A., Maestas E. and Darlington J. (1999). Race, ethnicity, and disasters in the United States: A review of the literature. *Disasters*, 23, 156–173.

Francis P. (2015). *Laudato si': on care for our common home*. Second Encyclical. Vatican City: The Vatican.

Freudenburg W., Frickel S. and Gramling R. (1995). Beyond the society/nature divide: Learning to think about a mountain. *Sociological Forum*, 10, 361–392.

Gaard G. (2004). Toward a queer ecofeminism. In R. Stein (Ed.) *New perspectives on environmental justice: Gender, sexuality, and activism* (pp. 21–44). New Brunswick: Rutgers University Press.

Goldberg D.T. (2002). *The racial state*. New York: Blackwell Publishers
Gottlieb R. (1994). *Forcing the spring: The transformation of the American environmental movement*. San Francisco: Island Press.
Harlan S.L., Brazel A.J., Prashad L., Stefanov W.L. and Larsen L. (2006). Neighborhood microclimates and vulnerability to heat stress. *Social Science & Medicine*, 63, 2847–2863.
Harlan S., Pellow D.N., Roberts J.T., Bell S.E., Holt W.G. and Nagel J. (2015). Climate justice and inequality. In R. Dunlap and R.J. Brulle (Eds.) *Climate change and society: Sociological perspectives* (pp. 127–163). Oxford: Oxford University Press.
Harrison J.L. (2011). *Pesticide drift and the pursuit of environmental justice*. Cambridge, MA: The MIT Press.
Herod A. (2011). *Scale*. London: Routledge.
Heynen N., Kaika M. and Swyngedouw E. (Eds.) (2006). *In the nature of cities*. New York: Routledge.
Holifield R., Porter M. and Walker G. (2010). Introduction—Spaces of environmental justice—Frameworks for critical engagement. In R. Holifield, M. Porter and G. Walker (Eds.) *Spaces of environmental justice*. New York: Wiley-Blackwell.
Hossfeld K. (1990). 'Their logic against them': Contradictions in sex, race, and class in Silicon Valley. In K. Ward (Ed.) *Women workers and global restructuring*. Ithaca, NY: Institute for Labor Relations Press.
Hunter L. (2000). The spatial association between U.S. immigrant residential concentration and environmental hazards. *International Migration Review*, 34, 460–488.
Hurley A. (1995). *Environmental inequalities: Class, race, and industrial pollution in Gary, Indiana, 1945–1980*. Raleigh, NC: University of North Carolina.
Jacoby K. (2001). *Crimes against nature: Squatters, poachers, thieves, and the hidden history of American conservation*. Berkeley, CA: University of California Press.
King M.L., Jr. (1994). [1963] *Letter from Birmingham Jail*. New York: HarperCollins.
Klinenberg E. (2002). *Heat wave*. Chicago: University of Chicago Press.
Krakoff S. (2002). Tribal sovereignty and environmental justice. In K. Mutz, G. Bryner and D. Kenney (Eds.) *Justice and natural resources*. San Francisco: Island Press.
Krauss C. (1993). Blue collar women and toxic waste protests. In R. Hofrichter (Eds.) *Toxic struggles*. Philadelphia: New Society Publishers.
Kurtz H. (2003). Scales, frames, and counter-scale frames: Constructing the problem of environmental injustice. *Political Geography*, 22, 887–916.
Lavelle M. and Coyle M. (1992). Unequal protection: The racial divide in environmental law. *National Law Journal*, 15, SI–SI2.
Lerner S. (2006). *Diamond: A struggle for environmental justice in Louisiana's chemical corridor*. Cambridge, MA: The MIT Press.
Lombardi K., Buford T. and Greene R. (2015). Environmental justice, denied. *Center for Public Integrity*, August 3.
Márquez J. (2014). *Black-brown solidarity: Racial politics in the new Gulf south*. Austin: University of Texas Press.
Mason J. (2004). *An unnatural order: Roots of our destruction of nature*. Brooklyn: Lantern Books.
Mennis J. and Jordan L. (2005). The distribution of environmental equity: Exploring spatial nonstationarity in multivariate models of air toxic releases. *Annual Association of American Geographers*, 95, 249–268.
Mills C. (1999). *The racial contract*. Ithaca, NY: Cornell University Press.
Mills C. (2001). Black trash. In L. Westra and B.E. Lawson (Eds.) *Faces of environmental racism* (pp. 73–93). New York: Rowman & Littlefield.

Mohai P., Pellow D. and Roberts J.T. (2009). Environmental justice. *Annual Review of Environmental and Resources*, 34, 405–430.

Mohai P. and Saha R. (2007). Racial inequality in the distribution of hazardous waste: A national-level reassessment. *Social Problems*, 54, 343–370.

Nibert D. and Fox M.W. (2002). *Animal rights/human rights: Entanglements of oppression and liberation*. New York: Rowman & Littlefield Publishers.

Norgaard K.M. (2011). *Living in denial: Climate change, emotions, and everyday life*. Cambridge, MA: The MIT Press.

Oreskes N. and Conway E.M. (2010). *Merchants of doubt: How a handful of scientists obscured the truth on issues from tobacco smoke to global warming*. New York: Bloomsbury Press.

Park L.S. and Pellow D.N. (2011). *The slums of Aspen: Immigrants vs. the environment in America's Eden*. New York: New York University.

Parsons T. (1954). *Essays in sociological theory*. New York: The Free Press.

Pellow D.N. (2000). Environmental inequality formation: Toward a theory of environmental injustice. *American Behavioral Scientist*, 43, 581–601.

Pellow D.N. (2007). *Resisting global toxics: transnational movements for environmental justice*. Cambridge, MA: MIT Press.

Pellow D.N. and Brulle R.J. (Eds.) (2005). *Power, justice, and the environment: A critical appraisal of the environmental justice movement*. Cambridge, MA: The MIT Press.

Pellow D.N. and Park L.S. (2002). *The Silicon Valley of dreams: Environmental injustice, immigrant workers, and the high-tech global economy*. New York: New York University.

Piven F.F. and Cloward R. (1978). *Poor people's movements*. New York: Vintage.

Pulido L. (1996). A critical review of the methodology of environmental racism research. *Antipode*, 28, 142–159.

Robbins P. (2007). *Lawn people: How grasses, weeds, and chemicals make us who we are*. Philadelphia: Temple University Press.

Sayre N. (2005). Ecological and geographical scale: Parallels and potential for integration. *Progress in Human Geography*, 29(3), 276–290.

Schlosberg D. (2004). Reconceiving environmental justice: Global movements and political theories. *Environmental Politics*, 13, 517–540.

Schlosberg D. (2007). *Defining environmental justice: Theories, movements, and nature*. Oxford: Oxford University Press.

Schlosberg D. and Carruthers D. (2010). Indigenous struggles, environmental justice, and community capabilities. *Global Environmental Politics*, 10, 12–35.

Scott J. (1999). *Seeing like a state*. New Haven, CT: Yale University Press.

Scott J. (2010). *The art of not being governed: An anarchist history of upland southeast Asia*. New Haven, CT: Yale University Press.

Selznick P. (1949). *TVA and the grass roots: A study in the sociology of formal organization*. Berkeley, CA: University of California Press. Smith A. (2005). *Conquest: Sexual violence and American Indian genocide*. Cambridge: South End Press.

Smith M. (2011). *Against ecological sovereignty*. Minneapolis: University of Minnesota Press.Stein R. (Ed.) (2004). *New perspectives on environmental justice: Gender, sexuality, and activism*. New Brunswick: Rutgers University Press.

Szasz A. (1994). *Ecopopulism: Toxic waste and the movement for environmental justice*. Minneapolis: University of Minnesota Press.

Szasz A. and Meuser M. (1997). Environmental inequalities. Literature review and proposals for new directions in research and theory. *Current Sociology*, 45, 99–120.

Sze J. (2006). Boundaries and border wars: DES, technology, and environmental justice. *American Quarterly*, 58(3), 791–814.

Sze J. (2016). Scale. In J. Adamson, W. Gleason and D.N. Pellow (Eds.) *Keywords for environmental studies* (pp. 178–180). New York: New York University Press.

Taylor D. (1997). Women of color, environmental justice, and ecofeminism. *Sturgeon*, 38–81.

Vargas J.H.C. (2010). *Never meant to survive: Genocide and utopias in black diaspora communities*. New York: Rowman & Littlefield.

Walker G. (2010). Beyond distribution and proximity: Exploring the multiple spatialities of environmental justice. In R. Holifield, M. Porter and G. Walker (Eds.) *Spaces of environmental justice*. New York: Wiley-Blackwell.

Weber M., Owen D.S., Strong T.B. and Livingstone R. (2004). *The vocation lectures*. Cambridge: Hackett.

White R. (2008). *Crimes against nature: Environmental criminology and ecological justice*. Cullompton, UK: Willan Publishing.

Wright B. and Bullard R.D. (1993). The effects of occupational injury, illness, and disease on the health status of Black Americans: A review. In R. Hofrichter (Ed.) *Toxic struggles*. Philadelphia: New Society Publishers.

3 A framework for improving resilience
Adaptation in urban contexts

Brian Mayer[1]

Introduction

There are many roads towards resilience, yet not all are equally socially or environmentally just. As we enter into a new era of climate change and disaster planning and preparation, now often guided by resilience thinking, it is vitally import to consider the implications of past, current, and future social and environmental injustices, and identify strategies for addressing them while working towards a resilient future. Resilience can be a particularly compelling paradigm, as it is often perceived as apolitical and grounded in sound ecological sciences. But as many of resilience thinking's critics note, extending an ecological metaphor to studying a range of individual-level phenomena (Bonanno 2004), community structure (Hatt 2013), and larger cultural systems (Adger, Barnett, Brown, Marshall and O'Brien 2013; Lyon and Parkins 2013) has potentially stretched the idea beyond practical application. Despite these critiques, resilience thinking continues to grow in prominence in both theoretical and applied fields related to environmental change, thereby necessitating further attention and refinement.

The resilience concept's transformation from a 1970s ecological metaphor to today's international paradigm for managing environmental change has led to an important opportunity to shape the field into an effective tool for understanding the dynamics of changing social-ecological systems. Despite resilience thinking's rapid growth across many academic and professional disciplines, attention to the sociocultural contexts in which adaptive change occurs has largely been minimal (Cote and Nightingale 2012). Social science insights borrowed by the natural sciences are often outdated and counterproductive to the goal of building resilient and just societies. This chapter's purpose is to explore resilience thinking's epistemological history and to identify key advances and potential opportunities to better integrate social sciences' insights into social and environmental stratification systems, which should be addressed as a core part of resilience thinking.

That social and ecological systems are interlinked in their vulnerability to environmental change is not a new phenomenon or realization. The rationality of addressing "social-ecological systems" is an academic construct driven by advances in our analytical toolkits and growing realizations that current and future generations face an unprecedented level of environmental instability and change. The resilience of these social-ecological systems has been defined in a broad variety of ways, but most definitions emphasize "a capacity for successful adaptation in the face of disturbance, stress, or adversity" (Norris, Stevens, Pfefferbaum, Wyche and Pfefferbaum 2008, 129). Whereas the concept of sustainability, which is perhaps being supplanted by resilience in many policy arenas, emphasized the need to find equilibrium between growth and conservation without jeopardizing future generations, resilience thinking focuses on the necessity for adaptability to anticipated social and environmental changes. Thus, in an era of rapid and visible climatic change, resilience thinking, with its emphasis on uncertainty and adaption, continues to grow in academic and professional prominence.

With the realization that change is imminent, short-term resilience thinking is an important component of identifying social-ecological systems' strengths and weaknesses. However, an emphasis on interim planning and evaluation of incremental improvement can fail to address the long-term goals outlined in sustainability of linking social, environmental and economic justice. Overemphasizing temporary resilience can lead to greater crises down the road. Our social systems can and have effectively postponed the catastrophic effects of ecological system disruption, through the imposition of technological solutions that often lead to greater disruption to people elsewhere in place and in time (Catton 1982; Davidson 2010). These delays and offsets disproportionately affect the disadvantaged and obfuscate ongoing social and environmental inequalities. Examining the static social-ecological resilience of such settings may lead us to falsely conclude them to be resilient. However, it is only because of limited operationalization of the resilience concept. Resilience thinking's tendency to emphasize narrow timeframes can create problems of "injustices-in-waiting," whereby social and environmental inequalities existing just below the surface and, contained by present-day planning and policy, can easily be brought to the surface and exacerbated by a crisis. Despite any level of adaptive capacity, when great enough – as illustrated by the disastrous aftermath of Hurricane Katrina in New Orleans – these injustices-in-waiting can devastatingly be made present and collapse communities previously seen as resilient.

There are alternative visions for resilience thinking, stemming largely from the work on community resilience, which do see the potential for radical transformation of unjust social systems – especially following the disruption caused by a major disaster (Cretney 2014; Cretney and Bond 2014). While not all visions of resilience incorporate transformation, community resilience – with its attention to specific community capacities for social and ecological change – offers the most promise for incorporating environmental and social justice into the logic and praxis of contemporary resilience thinking. Reviewing the development of the resilience concept and its relation to the potential for building community resilience, as well as the theoretical criticisms that have developed in response, is an important first step towards outlining a socially just road to resilience. This chapter explores the genealogy of resilience thinking, finding promise for addressing environmental inequalities through emerging approaches to building community resilience. In focusing on a model for a "resilience activation framework," I attempt to offer a model for linking individual and community attributes that allows us to build adaptive capacity across scales. Finally, I conclude by proposing that resilience offers much potential for addressing environmental qualities if considered holistically, but if applied without a critical approach could also be a tool for maintaining the status quo.

A genealogy of resilience

In 2013, *Time* magazine declared "resilience" the buzzword of the year (Walsh 2013). Indeed, the resilience concept had been growing in popularity over several decades, reaching particular prominence in discussions ranging from the United Nation's Rio +20 Conference on Sustainable Development to the U.S. Center for Disease Control's state-level guidance on disaster preparation. How did a concept grow from a radical departure from equilibrium-based theories of ecological stability to global environmental governance paradigm? The following section explores three evolutions within resilience thinking, tracing its growth from an individual-level phenomenon to a systems-level metaphor with some refinement down to the level of the community.

Psycho-social resilience

Although Holling's (1973) seminal work on ecological resilience is often viewed as the beginning of this paradigm shift, multiple natural and social science discourses describe some type of ability to withstand an external stressor and return to a desirable condition (Welsh 2014). For example, "psycho-social resilience" originates from the child development literature of the 1970s (Garmezy 1971; Murphy 1974; Werner 1993; Werner, Bierman and French 1971). As Masten (2001) argues, these early studies sought to explain why certain at-risk children rose above their surroundings and, unlike their peers, avoided common psychopathological outcomes and were thus seen as "invulnerable" or "invincible" (Buggie 1995; Pines 1975). Decades later, this unique property of select individuals became understood as a much more common phenomenon, leading Masten and others to label this individual resilience instead as an "ordinary magic" (Bonanno 2004; Masten 2001; Sheldon and King 2001).

In the fields of psychology and social epidemiology, individual resilience is seen as the ability in all of us to recover from personal trauma and the capacity to cope with either acute or chronic adversity. The factors most associated with an individual's ability to cope with these adverse circumstances include personality factors (e.g., hardiness, self-efficacy, self-esteem), attitudinal factors (e.g., positive worldview, faith, altruism), attachment factors (e.g., communal solidarity, social support, connections to competent adults or peers), cognitive factors (e.g., intellectual and reasoning abilities), and specific adaptation and coping skills (e.g., including stress-reduction competencies) (Abramson et al. 2015;

Bonanno and Diminich 2013; Masten and Narayan 2012). Common to these more recent studies is the assumption that all individuals are inherently resilient, but the ability to maintain that resilience can be limited by personal and community deficits in personal experiences and trauma, inequalities in access to key resources, and environmental exposures (Abramson et al. 2015).

This approach to identifying which individual and social factors activate or inhibit resilience is only what Wright and colleagues (2013) refer to as the first wave of psycho-social resilience studies, with subsequent research programs investigating more complex interactions between resilience factors, interventions, and the neurobiological and epigenetic influences on resilience. Following the growth of studies and interventions in individual resilience, a literature of self-help books and guides has also developed to encourage individuals to build their coping skills and self-esteem, and is taught in a wide range of fields from the military to childhood development (Meredith et al. 2011; Richardson 2002).

Social-ecological resilience

Returning back to the 1970s, the ecological sciences experienced a transition from an equilibrium-based paradigm of understanding how to manage fragile systems through a "balance of nature" approach to a nonequilibrium approach emphasizing the "capacity of a system to absorb disturbances and reorganize while undergoing change so as to still retain the same function, structure, identity and feedbacks" (Walker, Holling, Carpenter and Kinzig 2004). Holling (1973) first articulated this concept as "ecological resilience," where the more resilient an ecological system is, the greater the shock it can absorb without shifting into an alternative regime or collapse (Weichselgartner and Kelman 2014). Resilient ecological systems are also seen as possessing the ability to regenerate to their "original" forms after a significant disturbance (Resilience Alliance 2009).

In the 1990s, this approach to seeing ecological systems in dynamic flux was extended to include the social systems interacting with and dependent on those ecologies. Observations that natural-resource-dependent communities are fundamentally linked to ecological and social systems helped drive the growth in attention, within the natural sciences, to the synergistic and coevolutionary relationships between human society and the environment (Noorgard 1994). However, as Adger (2000) argues, simply applying Holling's ecological resilience concept to social systems "assumes that there are no essential differences in behaviour and structure between socialized institutions and ecological systems" (1973, 350). Several attempts to address this fundamental problem of matching scales in social and natural systems have been proposed, such as Warren's (2005) model of linking ecological hierarchy theory and the structuration theories of Giddens (1981) and Sewell (1992). However, few of these complex models appear to have been picked in further elaborations or practical applications. Despite these past challenges, "social-ecological" literature has grown within certain academic disciplines and practitioner fields into a robust field of understanding and managing interdependent communities and ecosystems, although with limited input from the social sciences.

The rapid growth of social-ecological applications led to the formation of the Resilience Alliance in 1999, which lists its research mission to "fortif[y] a paradigm shift in natural resource management from top-down, command-and-control optimization, to the promotion of resilience and self-organization" (Resilience Alliance 2009). Gunderson and Holling's (2002) "panarchy" meta-concept captures all permutations of interactions and feedback loops of the multiple scales of social-ecological systems interacting across space, time, and governance regimes. However, social systems in these social-ecological systems are essentially boiled down to environmental governance institutions (O'Riordan et al. 1998) and tend to overlook the influence of individual agency and cultural context (Adger 2000). This lack of agency perpetuates a trend found in most analyses that integrate the natural and social sciences, and continues the trend towards a decidedly functionalist approach. A more conflict-oriented approach that views resilience as a process as opposed to an outcome would emphasize adaption towards a desired outcome instead of the maintenance of the existing status quo. Likewise, observations of social resilience tend to conflate economic equity with economic stability, where the indicator of system resiliency is most often resistance to change, not equitable (re)distribution.

Community resilience

Both the psycho-social and social-ecological resilience paradigms have been converging towards what Berkes and Ross (2013) refer to as an appreciation of community-level effects on resilience. Building on these individual- and systems-level approaches, researchers in the natural hazards and disaster management fields have argued that the resilience concept is scalable from the individual to the community to social and ecological systems (Abramson et al. 2015; Welsh 2014). Whereas the psycho-social tradition emphasizes individual agency and the social-ecological tradition that of management institutions, community resilience research has sought to integrate individual agency with structural conditions that either enable or inhibit resilient outcomes (Abramson et al. 2015; Norris et al. 2008). Recognizing resilience as a broad metaphor referring to some type of adaptive capacity, community resilience research has adopted the dynamic and complex systems thinking of the other two traditions, while maintaining an interventionist approach to identifying means of enhancing those capacities (Welsh 2014).

"Community resilience" can be defined as the enduring capacity of geographically, politically, or affinity-bound communities to define and account for their vulnerabilities to disaster and develop capabilities to prevent, withstand, or mitigate for a traumatic event (Abramson et al. 2015). Importantly, resilience is perceived as an ability or process as opposed to a static outcome or quality of a system – resilience may be activated, or it may not (Brown and Kulig 1996; Pfefferbaum, Pfefferbaum, Van Horn, Klomp, Norris and Reissman 2013). With this adaptation-centric approach, a stable system that fails to change or adapt – even if it returns to an equilibrium state – may in fact suggest a lack of resilience (Norris et al. 2008). This is an important departure from the previous two resilience traditions, where equilibrium states are the guiding assumption for modeling individual- or social-ecological resilience. The community resilience literature is instead guided by an emphasis on adaptive capacity, leading Norris and colleagues (2008) to define it as "a process linking a set of capacities to a positive trajectory of functioning and adaptation after a disturbance" (130).

This emphasis on adaptation is largely due to the influence of the social vulnerabilities literature and on the disaster scholars researching and promoting community resilience. There are many fundamental linkages between the concepts of vulnerability and resilience, but they are kept artificially separated because of distinct epistemological traditions between the natural (social-ecological resilience) and social (psycho-individual resilience) sciences. Nonetheless, the vulnerability literature's influence, particularly from hazard studies and political ecology, on community resilience makes this tradition the most suitable for addressing environmental inequalities while enhancing resilience (Miller et al. 2010).

Norris et al. (2008) conceptualize resilience as a set of networked capacities that relies both on the availability of resources and their distribution within a system, and this conceptualization offers the greatest opportunity for integrating it to the environmental inequalities literature. These networked capacities are processes through which vital resources for disaster preparedness and response can be mobilized, emphasizing vital forms of capital: economic, social, human, and political. Significantly, their model recognizes the potential for an unequal distribution of these resources, based on well-documented sources of inequities, such as race, class, location, and gender. In fact, efforts to develop indicators of community resilience are largely modeled on social vulnerability (Cutter, Boruff and Shirley 2003) and find fairly robust inverse relationships between social vulnerability and community resilience (Bergstrand, Mayer, Brumback and Zhang 2014; Sherrieb, Norris and Galea 2010). This approach to community resilience offers important advantages to the vulnerability model – whereas the resource-deficit approach of the vulnerabilities literature can identify significant individual risk factors, resilience, and in particular community resilience, envisions the vulnerability and adaptive capacities of individuals located not in isolation, but within the systematic distribution of resources and their community's adaptive capacity.

Resilience thinking and planning is increasingly used in governance circles across all geographic scales – from local emergency planning at the community level, national policy-making and federal research funding, to international aid and development (Brown 2014; Cote and Nightingale 2012; Cretney 2014; Reid 2012; Walker and Cooper 2011; Welsh 2014). This range raises an additional set of complications, as the meaning of "community" itself is often debated (Norris et al. 2008). For whom resilience is being built, whether through individual mental strengthening, management of complex social and natural systems, or enhancing community adaptive capacity, remains a challenging question to answer. Although the practical answer would be "everyone," not all resilience interventions start from a position of full participation and equal outcomes. The next section addresses two major critiques of resilience thinking that are premised on the question: "resilience for whom?"

Resilience for whom?

Resilience thinking's rise as a new paradigm for managing social-environmental systems has attracted numerous critiques, particularly from political ecology. These critiques center on the argument that while resilience thinking can be effective in modeling complex social-ecological systems, it generally fails to address normative questions about social justice and equity, and fails to recognize that resilience as an outcome or state may be socially and temporally contingent (Brown 2014). The resilience literature has a different set of core questions than the hazards and vulnerability literature. The hazards and vulnerabilities literature focuses on structural inequalities and agency-based approaches to addressing them. By contrast, resilience thinking emphasizes outlining a complex system's functions and its various tipping points for change. Implicit in this framework is a different set of normative questions, where there is less attention on alleviating social inequalities and more attention directed towards stability and adaptation.

The stability metaphor is particularly attractive in a complex world, but its widespread usage also invites problems. Despite the many refrains that resilience is only a metaphor for understanding complex systems, feedback loops, or nonequilibrium states in ecology and natural resource management, it is being increasingly used by academics and practitioners, who are applying it in governance regimes without much consideration for its practical elements. Additionally, as Cote and Nightingale (2012) argue, the conceptual "slippage" that occurs when a metaphor for complex processes transitions from a descriptive to a prescriptive tool can result in problematic and risky social interventions. For example, the desired outcome of a resilience intervention may be a priority for some while being opposed by others – in other words, agreement around ideal states is likely to be much more complex in the real world than can be hypothetically modeled. The geography literature, in particular, has passionately debated the ontological challenges of applying a systems-modeling concept from the positivist ecological sciences to the constructivist social sciences (Davoudi and Porter 2012; Weichselgartner and Kelman 2014). Emphasizing the functionalist overtones of resilience thinking's systems-level approach, these critiques focus on the lack of agency ascribed to individuals and the role of stability in resilient systems. Both lines of critique stress the need to ask normative questions alongside the empirical analyses of resilient individuals, communities, and systems.

Creating resilient subjects

The first major criticism of resilience thinking views the concept as ontologically facilitating a world of resilient subjects no longer dependent on a formal state for welfare assistance, but rather fully adaptable through their own capacities to the various conditions of their lives. In the postcolonial neoliberal world, resilience can be critiqued for being an externally defined imperative of self-reliance and resourcefulness – encouraging coping with harsh and unequal social conditions as opposed to transforming them. Furthermore, the shift towards resilience-style interventions, particularly in the developing world, is criticized for only being a temporary response to neoliberalism's failure to create stable economies and societies in the first place (Pugh 2014). In this vein, resilience thinking is interpreted as generating a false consciousness that encourages us to embrace the idea of living dangerously in an ever more uncertain world – one created by the same neoliberal institutions now developing resilience interventions and governance models.

As the psycho-social tradition in resilience has taken hold in psychological practice and related self-help literatures (O'Malley 2010), it is increasingly being applied to populations living in areas seen as socially vulnerable, due to high rates of poverty, low educational attainment, high unemployment, gang violence, or other highly visible social problems (Cretney 2014). At risk here is the potential creation of an interventionist approach that blames the existing culture of the socially vulnerable for their unequal status while promoting a "new" culture of self-sufficiency and resourcefulness that fits well with a dependence on neoliberal markets. Although this is by no means a new approach for justifying the welfare state's retraction, the overemphasis on personal resilience without reflexivity about social conditions jeopardizes resilience thinking's usefulness for increasing sustainability and adaptability. Furthermore, the psycho-social tradition on its own potentially legitimates the state's abdication of responsibility for caring for the socially vulnerable. As Reid (2012) argues, "'resilient' peoples do not look to states to secure their wellbeing because they have been disciplined into believing in the necessity to secure it for themselves" (69).

There is an inherent contradiction in asking those in our society with the least to become more adaptable to living with scarce resources in a system that simultaneously fosters those vulnerabilities. Lacking insights from contemporary stratification or cultural theory, a systems-thinking approach to resilience does not adequately address the unequal distribution of resources and risk within a social-ecological system. This resilient human subject is conceived by resilience's critics "as resilient in so far as it adapts to rather than resists the conditions of its suffering in the world. To be resilient is to forego the very power of resistance" (Reid 2012, 76). While improving individual adaptability and flexibility can lead to increased community and political engagement, by working to identify vulnerabilities and opportunities to enhance adaptive capacities, the psycho-social approach's functionalist undercurrents have the potential to create what Peck and Tickell (2002, 386) call "responsibility without power." The question of "resilience for whom" looms large when we consider the implications of encouraging equilibrium-based personal adaptability. Will resilient individuals be trapped by their own resourcefulness and independence, unable to fundamentally alter socially unjust systems that are by their nature "resilient"? Or is there an emancipatory potential in resilience thinking that has yet to be fully articulated?

Adaptation or revolution?

"Resilience and not revolution is the rallying cry of the early twenty-first century" (Hornborg 2009, 252). In trying to create socially just and resilient systems, a second critique argues that contemporary conceptualizations of systems resilience lack attention to agency and power. Instead, there is a disproportionate focus on adaptation to exogenous system stressors as opposed to questioning or challenging the endogenous social dynamics of the system (Brown 2014; Hornborg 2009). This trend likely stems from the epistemological misapplication of ecological systems thinking to a social context that sees social actors and institutions as homogenous functionaries supporting homeostasis. For example, the classic text on resilience in social-ecological systems, *Panarchy* from Gunderson and Holling (2002), includes a chapter from Westley (2002, 107) that cites Parsons in likening the functions of social systems to the natural world: "[l]ike natural systems, social systems must fulfill key functions. They must be oriented toward certain goals or objectives, they must create mechanisms for integration and adaptation, and they must create mechanisms for self-reproduction." Without delving too deeply into the refutation of Parsonian functionalism within sociology (c.f., Mills 1963), the tendency of contemporary resilience thinking towards equilibrium, whether due to a metaphor mismatch or implicit political agenda, presents an important opportunity for dialogue with social scientists.

Much contemporary resilience thinking in development studies proposes an alternative to the top-down resource management. By focusing on the need for better integration of local context and cultural differences across social-ecological systems, the application of resilience thinking through adaptive management strongly emphasizes consensus-building. For example, Holling (2001) considers shifting resource control a part of the adaptive cycle, consensually moving between parties or institutions when the necessity arises for a change in management. Within this hypothetical system of power exchanges, however, human agency is almost never reflected upon (Davidson 2010). Instead, the resilience literature tends to emphasize consensus in the management of social-ecological systems, leading to cooperative governance dominating over any references to individual or collective concerns (Hatt 2013). Systematic failures in adaptive management then are seen as stemming from the inflexibility of social regimes and the limitations of financial and social resources as opposed to human errors or uneven participation in such management programs (Adger et al. 2009). According to Hatt (2013, 34), "[i]n transposing the social into a system, the impact of individual agency, the role of power, and structural arrangements have been conflated by an attachment to consensus that has consistently been criticized as a weakness in functionalism." These limits to resilience fail to recognize what Cote and Nightingale refer to as the "inherent contextual aspects of social systems" (2012, 480), but may be better understood as social inequalities in access to the information, economic resources, and political power within that social system, which leads to unrest and a lack of the cooperation that many social-ecological resilience paradigms presume.

Managing social-ecological systems and thus influencing resilience has historically been the privilege of the elite. Neoliberal political power is closely associated with control over essential resources, such as energy, food, and bodies (Davidson 2010; Pugh 2014; Reid 2012). Yet, the broader discourse in resilience thinking is viewed by some as blind toward the role of power, which Hornborg, among others, views as a major weakness: "[resilience is] oblivious not only of power, conflict, and contradiction, but also of culture" (2009, 255). Welsh (2014) concludes that political power's omission is not unintentional, but rather an intended move designed to instill resilience thinking with a political neutrality more in line with a technocratic solution than a revolutionary paradigm. Even adaptive capacity is limited in its ability to address fundamental inequalities when it is conceived as small, incremental changes along a preconceived development pathway that follows a neoliberal paradigm (Cretney 2014; Pike, Dawley and Tomaney 2010).

Furthermore, as Cote and Nightingale (2012, 480) argue, introducing new participatory and inclusive management systems can potentially exacerbate existing inequalities-in-waiting, or potentially create new social vulnerabilities and inequalities. Scale here is important. Although advocating for the enhancement of local resilience does build on regional strengths and cultural norms, the complete absence of attention to national or international politics has also produced several failed resilience-building initiatives (MacKinnon and Derickson 2013). Without addressing the normative questions around "resilience for whom," interventions meant to create stability around social and environmental change have the potential for being unjust. Hence, resilience approaches emphasizing adaptation over resistance offer guidance on how to build resilience, such as community resilience, that has the greatest potential for addressing environmental inequalities.

Linking agency and structure in resilience

While certainly the debate around what a resilient individual, community, or system truly looks like is an important endeavor, other scholars argue that resilience thinking's objective benefits lie in the process of building adaptive capacities that may lead to resilience (Norris et al. 2008). One such approach stems from the study of the impact and recovery from the 2010 *Deepwater Horizon* oil spill (DWHOS). Considered to be the largest maritime oil spill in history, the DWHOS impacted the five coastal states in the Gulf of Mexico region by damaging commercial fisheries, contaminating beaches and marshes, and disrupting the seafood and tourism industries (Freudenburg and Gramling 2011). Whereas past oil spills received only limited research attention from federal agencies, the National Institute of Environmental Health Sciences sought to quickly establish a multi-state research consortium to examine the spill's physical, mental, and community health effects.

Across four separate research projects consisting of multiple partner universities and community partners, the NIEHS Deepwater Horizon Consortia emphasize personal and community resilience to the oil spill's detrimental effects. Through the Resilience Working Group, academic partners from each of the four projects integrated their analytical approaches studying post-spill resilience and inductively assembled the proposed model to account for the interaction between individual and structural community factors that might lead to resilient outcomes.

The Resilience Activation Framework (RAF) draws on Hobfoll's (1989; 2002) conservation of resources model of stress and adaption, a core theory from the psycho-social resilience tradition. In this model, individuals are assumed to be driven to acquire, preserve, and protect essential resources for their well-being, including "objects (car, house), conditions (marriage, seniority), personal characteristics (self-esteem, optimism), and energies (time, knowledge, money), which facilitate the ability to acquire other important entities" (Abramson et al. 2015). When these resources are lost, threatened, and/or fail to be acquired, individuals experience a stressful situation that leads to a loss of well-being and potential mental health problems. Resilient individuals are then those who are capable of either better acquiring these resources or coping with their short-term loss. Like Holling's (1973) resilient ecological system, an external stressor tests individuals' ability to adapt to a shift in available energies and other resources. However, the psycho-social tradition's use of this concept largely assumes that these energies and resources are regularly available even in the face of an immediate crisis or as part of broader social inequalities in access to resources. The RAF model seeks to address the limits of these assumptions by including structural elements that potentially limit the availability and access to those essential resources.

The model for the RAF (Figure 3.1) incorporates both the resource deficit model outlined by Norris et al. (2008), as well as the assumption that resilience is a metaphor for a set of adaptive processes that function both at the individual

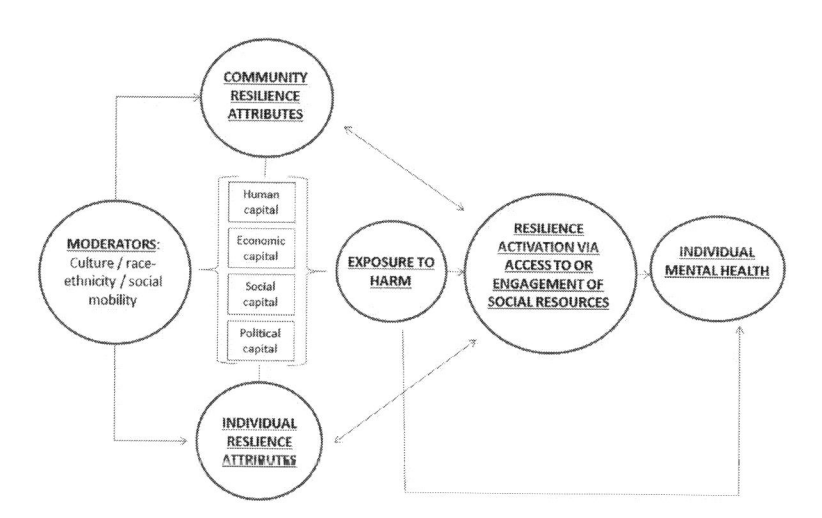

Figure 3.1 The Resilience Activation Framework (RAF)

(psycho-social resilience) and at the community (community resilience) levels. The framework suggests two pathways by which access to social resources can activate resilience processes: (1) the deficits are addressed by increasing individual or community assets or facilitating access to them; and (2) the provision of formal or informal social resources enhances or activates positive adaptive traits (Abramson et al. 2015).

In the RAF model, the activation of latent resiliency processes operates through the ability to create linkages between individual and community resources. Most stress and disaster recovery models argue that people who have access to better social resources or social support are better able to resist the deleterious effect of post-disaster stress (Hobfoll 2002; Kaniasty and Norris 1993; Norris et al. 2008; Palinkas, Petterson, Russell and Downs 1993). In the RAF model, resilience activation hinges on the ability of better social resources to activate resilience attributes toward maintaining psychological vitality, stability, and mental health, as well as adequate physical health and well-being (Abramson et al. 2015). Social support could potentially activate resilience processes by providing knowledge and assistance for practical needs, helping with problem-solving, promoting positive emotions and attitudes associated with resilience, and facilitating adaptive coping behaviors.

A major lacuna across all the resilience traditions is the absence of culture. Although resilience studies and interventions take place across the globe in a variety of sociocultural milieus, few consider cultural-specific definitions of resilience, resilience attributes, or vital resources. The few besides aboriginal or indigenous studies – where resilience takes on a distinct definition outside of a nature-society interaction model – typically treat culture as an additional system of beliefs operationalized at the same level as ecosystems and governance institutions (Crane 2010). In addressing this gap, Adger (2000) notes that several key elements separate biophysical and human resilience, including human institutions. These institutions provide a means for individuals and communities to sustain resilient capacities and to pass that wisdom on to subsequent generations through social memory (Abramson et al. 2015). As human constructs, these institutions reflect cultural influences and are largely local in scale. Thus, they mediate how a community prepares for and responds to a disruption and activates its resilient capacities. From the community level, culture, ethnicity, gender and race are prime mechanisms for enabling or inhibiting resilience. Important lessons learned in the aftermath of both domestic and global disasters have confirmed culture's pivotal role in resource supply as well as redevelopment practices (DeVries 1995; Oliver-Smith 1996; Rich, Edelstein, Hallman and Wandersman 1995). The RAF attempts to include these important sociocultural differences as moderating factors that influence access and valuation of individual and community attributes/resources. Although treating culture as a moderating factor may fail to account for all of its influence and variability across cases, the RAF model leaves open both endogenous cultural variation and the broader national and international heterogeneity as significant resilience factors.

Resilience and environmental justice

Environmental justice studies grew out of a powerful social force for change, which grew out of the resistance from communities of color and working-class communities to growing ecological degradation and unequal distributions of environmental hazards in the late 1970s and early 1980s (Roberts and Toffolon-Weiss 2001). At the heart of this new social movement was a challenge to existing social, economic, and political systems that disproportionately placed poor and minority communities at risk of exposure to toxic and hazardous pollution, and increased environmental deterioration. To address these inequalities, environmental justice advocates for "the concept that every individual, regardless of race, ethnicity, or class, has the right to be free from ecological destruction and deserves equal protection of his or her environment, health, employment, housing, and transportation" (Roberts and Toffolon-Weiss 2001, 10). The study of environmental inequalities similarly emerges from this political and cultural space, emphasizing the study of racial and economic stratification in producing unequal patterns of environmental risks and vulnerabilities (Pellow 2000). Despite the national and global integration of environmental justice language into several political arenas and institutions such as the Intergovernmental Panel on Climate Change and the Basel Convention on the transboundary movement of hazardous waste, there have been relatively few attempts to integrate environmental justice into resilience thinking.

Like its complementary fit with sustainable development, environmental justice studies offers a ground-up approach to examining social-ecological problems, which can help inform the often top-down institutional approach prominent in contemporary resilience thinking (Agyeman 2005). The challenge of environmental justice scholars and activists to sustainable development was one of equal participation and benefit in the promotion of environmentally-conscious growth. One can imagine the environmental justice movement will make similar critiques of the resilience paradigm – resilient for whom and when? And furthermore, who gets to determine what resilience looks like? Are there, in fact, practices, behaviors, and institutions that normatively need modification and thus become increasingly problematic if they are resilient to change?

One advantage of integrating environmental justice principles into resilience thinking is that it increases attention to the social sphere's role in the social-ecological system. A critical component of environmental justice is the inclusion of "where we live, work, and play" into the definition of a just environment. The implementation of resilience thinking and policy can often focus on immediate ecological threats, such as rising sea levels, hurricanes, or flooding – leading to the most visible areas or populations receiving the bulk of attention and intervention. By including not only the highly visible ecological risks but also the less witnessed private spaces in which interactions with the environment occur, we can ensure that all groups are included in resilience-building. For example, in response to the 2010 *Deepwater Horizon* oil spill, much attention was directed towards the toxicological safety of commercial fisheries, with the U.S.

Environmental Protection Agency, Food and Drug Administration, and National Oceanic and Atmospheric Administration developing and implementing rapid seafood testing programs and outreach activities for seafood harvesters. Yet, comparatively little effort was granted to the potential risks to subsistence fishers, most often represented in poor and minority populations along the Gulf Coast. Although the government agencies used the language of building resilience and analytic capacity among the commercial seafood industry, the interventions emphasized the economic value of the threatened ecology over the basic livelihood necessities the Gulf provided to its most vulnerable populations.

As many of resilience thinking's critics argue, incremental changes are the most common advancement along the metaphorical road towards resilience. For those groups, marginalized by social and economic inequalities, these small changes in adaptive capacity or institutional development do not suffice. Although this emphasis on adaptation and stability can be a strength of resilience thinking, environmental justice is much more visionary in its approach to addressing inequality. Much of the strength of the environmental justice paradigm is its theoretical attention towards both the equitable distribution of environmental goods and hazards, as well as the procedural components of equal recognition and democratic participation of all stakeholders. While aspects of these core elements of an environmentally just society can be accounted for in resilience thinking, such as the assessment of material distributions and democratic institutions, they are typically accounted for as potential components of a resilient social-ecological system. Environmental justice studies would see them instead as goals of a resilient society. An even broader goal for a just *and* resilient social-ecological system could be radical transformation of existing status quos, fundamentally addressing inequitable social and economic conditions such as segregation, unemployment, and uneven educational opportunities.

What might a just resilience approach look like? Although resilience thinking is informed by studies of social vulnerability, just resilience should exhibit greater attention to the current and historical political factors and socioeconomic conditions that shape resilience attributes and adaptive capacities, which range from the local to the global. Following Pellow's (2000) environmental inequality formation model, resilience thinking would also benefit from analyzing stakeholder participation and access to proposed resilience institutions. Resilience thinking would also benefit from analyzing individual agency and power in a nondiscriminatory fashion, as well as improving the modeling to cultural variation. As with the critique outlined above, a neoliberal approach to depending on global markets for personal resilience is unlikely to produce the truly resilient communities envisioned by many of resilience's proponents. Whether it is assigning some type of bounded agency within structure, as envisioned by Sewell (1992), or related approaches, such as the RAF. Understanding the interaction of individuals and their communities in determining resilient outcomes can also be a step toward integrating environmental justice's emphasis on stratification with resilience's emphasis on structures.

Resilience and the city

Cities and their diverse citizenry can highlight social vulnerabilities and thus the need for a resilience thinking informed by critical environmental justice. In urban centers we see the widest gaps between the rich and the poor and the extremes of environmental inequalities. Cities also offer many opportunities for resilience-building, as they are often more dynamic when it comes to policy and institutional change than rural areas. For example, Pelling (2012, 9) identifies four characteristics of urban systems that could be addressed by resilience thinking: (1) communication systems, (2) economic diversity, (3) local participation in decision-making, and (4) social services. Each of these characteristics highlights critical infrastructures that are key components of urban "social systems" and which are often ignored by sustainable design or resilient city principles (Pelling 2012). These local social and economic institutions are critical, as large-scale governmental institutions such as nation-states tend to play lesser roles in resilience planning (Reid 2012). Localities such as cities and counties take on much greater responsibility for disaster preparedness and adaption planning (Pugh 2014). Thus, cities and their complex social structures may offer the greatest opportunities to better understand what social factors enable resilient outcomes.

At the same time, cities are also more prone to catastrophic disasters, due to the density of highly socially vulnerable populations and the engineered divides between their social and ecological systems. Urbanization necessitates fundamental alterations to land-use patterns, which can strain patterns of social-ecological resilience, whether they be water source contamination, deforestation, or encroachment on endangered habitats. There is a logical justification for the majority of resilience planning case studies examining rural natural-resource management scenarios – there we can see the interactions between the natural and social spheres in greater detail than we may be able to in urban contexts. Yet, it is the urban contexts where adaptation is most needed and it is there that we should focus our efforts to develop a socially and environmentally just approach to resilience thinking.

Conclusion

Resilience thinking challenges us to create scholarly knowledge and practical applications of change in an uncertain and vulnerable environment. There are increasing calls for a political and social justice turn in resilience thinking. What began as a scholarly debate over the epistemological implications of applying natural science's systems-thinking approaches to the social world has helped refine the resilience concept in several ways. The resistance orientation is being replaced by an emphasis on adaptation and change. Community resilience, in particular, provides many analytical and practical tools for understanding what characteristics of social systems may produce more resilient outcomes. The RAF model builds on the community resilience literature by including the psycho-social model of resilience and examining its interface with structural patterns of resilience. This approach can help us understand the interaction of agency and structure in the development of interventions to enhance adaptive capacity and build resilience. Integrating environmental justice studies focuses attention on existing inequalities and the need for fundamental change. A just resilience thinking should emphasize the need for social reorganization and diversity, democratic participation, and a ground-up approach to understanding the resilience of poor and minority communities.

Could there ever be a scenario where resilience is not a desired outcome? With the ambiguity surrounding resilience's definition and applicability to social-ecological systems, there is certainly the possibility of a system being environmentally resilient but also socially unjust – and vice versa (Walker, Anderies, Kinzig and Ryan 2006; Walker and Cooper 2011). For example, is New Orleans more or less resilient following the diaspora that followed Hurricane Katrina? Most residents who left and never returned were among New Orleans' most socially vulnerable, leading to a hypothetical improvement in its overall social resilience. However, this would be a very biased analysis of resilience and one influenced by the limiting orientation towards resistance to change, as opposed to the resilience thinking influenced by adaptation to change. Resilience, informed by critical environmental justice studies, should be oriented toward reorganization and renewal. An environmental justice framework brings greater attention to agency, inequality, and historical accounting, which resilience thinking needs to bring about a more socially just world.

Acknowledgements

I'd like to acknowledge a grant from the National Institute of Environmental Health Sciences (U19ES020683) as part of the Deepwater Horizon Research Consortium.

Note

1 University of Arizona, School of Sociology, branmayer@email.arizona.edu

References

Abramson D.M., Grattan L.M., Mayer B., Colten C.E., Arosemena F.A., Bedimo-Rung A. and Lichtveld M. (2015). The Resilience Activation Framework: A conceptual model of how access to social resources promotes adaptation and rapid recovery in post-disaster settings. *Journal of Behavioral Health Services & Research*, 42, 42–57.

Adger W.N. (2000). Social and ecological resilience: are they related? *Progress in Human Geography*, 24, 347–364.

Adger W.N., Barnett J., Brown K., Marshall N. and O'Brien K. (2013). Cultural dimensions of climate change impacts and adaptation. *Nature Climate Change*, 3, 112–117.

Adger W.N., Dessai S., Goulden M., Hulme M., Lorenzoni I., Nelson D.R., et al. (2009). Are there social limits to adaptation to climate change? *Climatic Change*, 93, 335–354.

Agyeman J. (2005). *Sustainable communities and the challenge of environmental justice*. New York: New York University Press.

Bergstrand K., Mayer B., Brumback B. and Zhang Y. (2014). Assessing the relationship between social vulnerability and community resilience to hazards. *Social Indicators Research*, 122, 391–409.

Berkes F. and Ross H. (2013). Community resilience: toward an integrated approach. *Society & Natural Resources*, 26(1), 5–20.

Bonanno G.A. (2004). Loss, trauma, and human resilience: Have we underestimated the human capacity to thrive after extremely aversive events? *American Psychologist*, 59, 20.

Bonanno G.A. and Diminich E.D. (2013). Annual research review: Positive adjustment to adversity–trajectories of minimal–impact resilience and emergent resilience. *Journal of Child Psychology and Psychiatry*, 54, 378–401.

Brown D.D. and Kulig J.C. (1996). The concepts of resiliency: Theoretical lessons from community research. Retrieved 14 April 2016 from https://www.uleth.ca/dspace/bitstream/handle/10133/1275/JK%20-%20The%20Concept%20of%20Resiliency%20-%20Theoretical%20Lessons%20from%20Community%20Research.pdf?sequence=1

Brown K. (2014). Global environmental change IA social turn for resilience? *Progress in Human Geography*, 38, 107–117.

Buggie S.E. (1995). Superkids of the ghetto. *Contemporary Psychology: APA Review of Books*, 40(12), 1164–1165.

Catton W.R. (1982). *Overshoot: The ecological basis of revolutionary change*. Chicago: University of Illinois Press.

Cote M. and Nightingale A.J. (2012). Resilience thinking meets social theory: Situating social change in socio-ecological systems (SES) research. *Progress in Human Geography*, 36, 475–489.

Crane T.A. (2010). Of models and meanings: Cultural resilience in social-ecological systems. *Ecology and Society*, 15, 19.

Cretney R. (2014). Resilience for whom? Emerging critical geographies of socio-ecological resilience. *Geography Compass*, 8, 627–640.

Cretney R. and Bond S. (2014). 'Bouncing back' to capitalism? Grass-roots autonomous activism in shaping discourses of resilience and transformation following disaster. *Resilience*, 2, 18–31.

Cutter S.L., Boruff B.J. and Shirley W.L. (2003). Social vulnerability to environmental hazards. *Social Science Quarterly*, 84, 242–261.

Davidson D.J. (2010). The applicability of the concept of resilience to social systems: Some sources of optimism and nagging doubts. *Society and Natural Resources*, 23, 1135–1149.

Davoudi S. and Porter L. (2012). Resilience: A bridging concept or a dead end? Reframing resilience: Challenges for planning theory and practice interacting traps: Resilience assessment of a pasture management system in northern Afghanistan urban resilience: What does it mean in planning practice? Resilience as a useful concept for climate change adaptation? The politics of resilience for planning: A cautionary note. *Planning Theory & Practice*, 13, 299–333.

DeVries M.W. (1995). Culture, community and catastrophe: Issues in understanding communities under difficult conditions. *NATO ASI Series D Behavioural and Social Science*, 80, 375–393.

Freudenburg W.R. and Gramling R. (2011). *Blowout in the Gulf: the BP oil spill disaster and the future of energy in America*. Boston: MIT Press.

Garmezy N. (1971). Vulnerability research and the issue of primary prevention. *American Journal of Orthopsychiatry*, 41, 101.

Giddens A. (1981). Agency, institution, and time-space analysis. In K. Knorr Cetina and A.V. Cicourel (Eds.) *Advances in social theory and methodology: toward an integration of micro- and macro-sociologies* (pp. 161–174). London: Routledge.

Gunderson L.H. and Holling C.S. (Eds.) (2002). *Panarchy: understanding transformations in human and natural systems.* Washington, DC: Island Press.

Hatt K. (2013). Social attractors: A proposal to enhance resilience thinking about the social. *Society & Natural Resources*, 26, 30–43.

Hobfoll S.E. (1989). Conservation of resources: a new attempt at conceptualizing stress. *American Psychologist*, 44(3), 513.

Hobfoll S.E. (2002). Social and psychological resources and adaptation. *Review of General Psychology*, 6, 307.

Holling C.S. (1973). Resilience and stability of ecological systems. *Annual Review of Ecology and Systematics*, 1–23.

Holling C.S. (2001). Understanding the complexity of economic, ecological, and social systems. *Ecosystems*, 4(5), 390–405.

Hornborg A. (2009). Zero-sum world challenges in conceptualizing environmental load displacement and ecologically unequal exchange in the world-system. *International Journal of Comparative Sociology*, 50, 237–262.

Kaniasty K. and Norris, F.H. (1993). A test of the social support deterioration model in the context of natural disaster. *Journal of Personality and Social Psychology*, 64, 395.

Lyon C. and Parkins J.R. (2013). Toward a social theory of resilience: Social systems, cultural systems, and collective action in transitioning forest-based communities. *Rural Sociology*, 78, 528–549.

MacKinnon D. and Derickson K.D. (2013). From resilience to resourcefulness: a critique of resilience policy and activism. *Progress in Human Geography*, 37(2), 253–270.

Masten A.S. (2001). Ordinary magic: Resilience processes in development. *American Psychologist*, 56, 227.

Masten A.S. and Narayan A.J. (2012). Child development in the context of disaster, war, and terrorism: Pathways of risk and resilience. *Psychology*, 63.

Meredith L.S., Sherbourne C.D., Gaillot S., Hansel L., Ritschard H., Parker A. and Wrenn G. (2011). Promoting psychological resilience in the U.S. Military. *RAND Center for Military Health Policy Research*.

Miller F., Osbahr H., Boyd E., Thomalla F., Bharawani S., Ziervogel G., et al. (2010). Resilience and vulnerability: complementary or conflicting concepts? *Ecology and Society*, 15.

Mills C.W. (1963). *Power, politics, and people: the collected essays of C. Wright Mills.* New York: Oxford University Press.

Murphy L.B. (1974). Coping, vulnerability, and resilience in childhood. *Coping and Adaptation*, 69–100.

Noorgard R. (1994). *Development betrayed: The end of progress and coevolutionary revisioning of the future.* London: Routledge.

Norris F.H., Stevens S.P., Pfefferbaum B., Wyche K.F. and Pfefferbaum R.L. (2008). Community resilience as a metaphor, theory, set of capacities, and strategy for disaster readiness. *American Journal of Community Psychology*, 41, 127–150.

O'Malley P. (2010). Resilient subjects: Uncertainty, warfare and liberalism. *Economy and Society*, 39, 488–509.

O'Riordan T., Cooper C.L., Jordan A., Rayner S., Richards K.R., Runci P. and Yoffe S. (1998). Institutional frameworks for political action. *Human Choice and Climate Change*, 1, 345–439.

Oliver-Smith A. (1996). Anthropological research on hazards and disasters. *Annual Review of Anthropology*, 303–328.

Palinkas L.A., Petterson J.S., Russell J. and Downs M.A. (1993). Community patterns of psychiatric disorders after the Exxon Valdez oil spill. *American Journal of Psychiatry*, 150, 1517–1523.

Peck J. and Tickell A. (2002). Neoliberalizing space. *Antipode*, 34(3), 380–404.

Pelling M. (2012). *The vulnerability of cities: Natural disasters and social resilience*. New York: Earthscan.

Pellow D.N. (2000). Environmental inequality formation toward a theory of environmental injustice. *American Behavioral Scientist*, 43, 581–601.

Pfefferbaum R.L., Pfefferbaum B., Van Horn R.L., Klomp R.W., Norris F.H. and Reissman D.B. (2013). The communities advancing resilience toolkit (CART): An intervention to build community resilience to disasters. *Journal of Public Health Management and Practice*, 19, 250–258.

Pike A., Dawley S. and Tomaney J. (2010). Resilience, adaptation and adaptability. *Cambridge Journal of Regions, Economy and Society*, 3(1), 59–70.

Pines M. (1975). In praise of invulnerables. *APA Monitor*, 7.

Pugh J. (2014). Resilience, complexity and post-liberalism. *Area*, 46, 313–319.

Reid J. (2012). The disastrous and politically debased subject of resilience. *Development Dialogue*, 58, 67–79.

Resilience Alliance (2009). Adaptive capacity. Retrieved 14 April 2016 from http://www.resalliance.org/565.php

Rich R.C., Edelstein M., Hallman W.K. and Wandersman A.H. (1995). Citizen participation and emprowerment: The case of local environmental hazards. *American Journal of Community Psychology*, 23, 657–676.

Richardson G.E. (2002). The metatheory of resilience and resiliency. *Journal of Clinical Psychology*, 58, 307–321.

Roberts J.T. and Toffolon-Weiss M.M. (2001). *Chronicles from the environmental justice frontline*. Cambridge: Cambridge University Press.

Sewell W.H. (1992). *A theory of structure: duality, agency, and transformation*. Chicago, IL: University of Chicago Press.

Sheldon K.M. and King L. (2001). Why positive psychology is necessary. *American Psychologist*, 56, 216.

Sherrieb K., Norris F.H. and Galea S. (2010). Measuring capacities for community resilience. *Social Indicators Research*, 99, 227–247.

Walker B., Holling C.S., Carpenter S.R. and Kinzig A. (2004). Resilience, adaptability and transformability in social-ecological systems. *Ecology and Society*, 9, 5.

Walker B.H., Anderies J.M., Kinzig A. and Ryan P. (2006). *Exploring resilience in social-ecological systems: Comparative studies and theory development*. Sydney: CSIRO Publishing.

Walker J. and Cooper M. (2011). Genealogies of resilience from systems ecology to the political economy of crisis adaptation. *Security Dialogue*, 42, 143–160.

Walsh B. (2013). Adapt or die: Why the environmental buzzword of 2013 will be resilience. *Time: Science and Space*, 8.

Warren W.A. (2005). Hierarchy theory in sociology, ecology, and resource management: a conceptual model for natural resource or environmental sociology and socioecological systems. *Society and Natural Resources*, 18(5), 447–466.

Weichselgartner J. and Kelman I. (2014). Geographies of resilience: Challenges and opportunities of a descriptive concept. Retrieved 14 April 2016 from http://phg.sagepub.com/content/early/2014/04/02/0309132513518834.full.pdf

Welsh M. (2014). Resilience and responsibility: Governing uncertainty in a complex world. *Geographical Journal*, 180, 15–26.

Werner E.E. (1993). Risk, resilience, and recovery: Perspectives from the Kauai longitudinal study. *Development and Psychopathology*, 5, 503–515.

Werner E.E., Bierman J.M. and French F.E. (1971). *The children of Kauai: A longitudinal study from the prenatal period to age ten.* Honolulu: University of Hawaii Press.

Westley F. (2002). The devil in the dynamics: adaptive management on the front lines. In L.H. Gunderson and C.S. Holling (Eds.) *Panarchy: understanding transformations in human and natural systems.* Washington, DC: Island Press.

Wright M.O., Masten A.S. and Narayan A.J. (2013). Resilience processes in development: four waves of research on positive adaptation in the context of adversity. In S. Goldstein and R.B. Brooks (Eds.) *Handbook of Resilience in Children* (pp. 15–37). New York: Springer.

4 Revealing the resilience infrastructure of cities

Preventing environmental injustices-in-waiting

Beth Schaefer Caniglia[1] and Beatrice Frank[2]

Introduction

People of color and the poor bear an inordinate amount of negative consequences related to environmental degradation, pollution, natural and technological disasters (Harlan et al. 2015; Pellow and Brehm 2013; Roberts and Parks 2007). This fact is problematic for the concept of resilience, which is based upon the desire to maintain socio-ecological systems in balance after having faced external shocks. An important underpinning assumption of ecological resilience theory states that systems are adaptable and can return to an environmental state of balance, making them resilient. We argue in this chapter that the application of such an assumption to social resilience requires us to ask: resilient for whom? A social resilience theory has to acknowledge and address the inherent inequalities that are structured into current socio-ecological systems. Urbanization is particularly problematic for resilience, because it is taking place so quickly in many places, exerting pressure on cities to accommodate the growth without fully comprehending its consequences. As a result, cities – places well-known to be bastions of inequality (UN-HABITAT 2010; UNICEF Bangladesh 2010) – often adapt to external shocks in ways that actually reinforce inequality and structure vulnerability in ways that are difficult to reverse. Our goal in this chapter is to unpack resilience theory to highlight its key weaknesses in the face of environmental injustice. We argue that an infusion of critical theory is necessary to adapt what was originally an ecological theory to the human resilience context, which often results in severe exploitation of the many for the benefit of increasingly fewer elites.

The advent of the concepts of resilience and vulnerability has enabled social scientists to view environmental injustice through new lenses. However, to date, very few scholars of resilience have engaged the environmental justice literature (Caniglia, Frank, Delano and Kerner 2014). We suspect this oversight stems from the fact that the concept of resilience evolved from the ecological sciences and draws from a set of assumptions that emphasize stability, equilibrium and environmental fit, while the environmental justice tradition focuses on inequality, conflict and critical theory. These approaches to seeing the world around us are not incompatible, but to merge them productively requires us to carefully examine particular underpinning assumptions that overlook the powerful structuring influence of human selfishness. In this chapter, we argue that social resilience cannot be achieved without addressing inequality and conflict. Our contemporary world is mired in conflict, and increasingly large portions of people on Earth are excluded from access to the basic resources needed to thrive in the new climate era.

To facilitate the development of a resilience theory that explains and predicts resilience for the most vulnerable groups, we trace the theoretical roots and approaches used by resilience scholars. We particularly evaluate the underpinning assumptions that mark systems theory, highlight a series of warrants that are embedded in systems theory that lead to inaccurate conclusions and approaches, and, ultimately, we argue that an infusion of critical theory can advance resilience studies in ways that promote the common good.

Background: a basic understanding of resilience

Early studies on ecological structures and functions focused on the effects of internal and external disturbances and stochastic events on the integrity of environmental systems (Folke 2006; Folke et al. 2010; Lake 2013). The ability of ecological structures to withstand stressors is defined as the resistance and resilience of the system. Resistance theorists advocate that ecological systems are able to remain stable in the face of disturbances (Lake 2013; Lopez et al. 2013). Resistance is therefore measured as the degree of stress needed to bring the system to a new state (Walker, Holling, Carpenter and Kinzig 2004). Resilience, instead, consists in the system being able to absorb disturbances while returning to its original state (i.e., engineering resilience) or to move across different stability domains while maintaining the system functions (i.e., ecological resilience) (Barr and Devine-Wright 2012; Brand and Jax 2007; Fiksel 2006; Folke 2006; Gunderson 2000; Holling 1973; Lake 2013; Lopez et al. 2013; Webb 2007). Resilience is measured as the time needed by a system to rejoin stability after disturbance (i.e., engineering resilience) or as the quantity of disturbance a system can bear before shifting to a new stability domain (e.g., ecological resilience) (Barr and Devine-Wright 2012; Brand and Jax 2007; Folke et al. 2010).

While over time the concept of engineering resilience has been discarded, the idea of ecological resilience and its dynamic nature has become a key concept in ecology. Increasingly research has demonstrated that dynamic and complex systems can cross thresholds and move into new states without losing structure, processes, and identity (Barr and Devine-Wright 2012; Brand and Jax 2007; Gunderson 2000; Holling 1996; Schwartz et al. 2011; Webb 2007). As clarified through Walker and Salt's (2006) metaphor of a ball in a basin, systems are adaptive and can exist in multiple stable domains, retaining their overall features. Indeed, the ball can move across different domains within its basin while seemingly remaining in an equilibrium status. Yet, when extreme events or external forces push the ball beyond the basin boundary, the ball lands in a new basin with different feedbacks and structure (Walker and Salt 2006, 55). After crossing such a threshold, the ball is no longer able to return to its previous status.

Social groups and their dynamics comply as well with the ball in the basin metaphor (Caniglia et al. 2014). The concept of resilience has been widely used to describe communities' abilities to withstand and respond to change. In the case of society, resilience is a human-driven response that enables social groups to survive, function and recover from change, uncertainty, unpredictability and surprise (Adger 2000; Barr and Devine-Wright 2012; Berkes and Ross 2012; Magis 2010). Resilience is built across society levels, from the single individual (i.e., ability to face life adversity) to entire groups and communities (i.e., social cohesion, human agency). Such resilience enables society to prepare for change, create buffers and prevent risk, and develop and mobilize resources in case of need (Barr and Wright 2012; Berkes and Ross 2012; Davidson 2010; Folke et al. 2010). Social resilience can be measured through social exclusion, marginalization and social capital, as well as by the governance structure of social systems (Adger 2000; Caniglia et al. 2014). Resilient social systems depend on social diversity, efficiency, adaptability and cohesion, as much as from the context in which they are placed when dealing with stressors, might they be society, policy and/or environmentally driven (Adger 2000; Barr and Devine-Wright 2012; Fiksel 2006; Davidson 2010; Walker and Salt 2006). Yet, while the majority of society may be resilient and bounce back to their previous livelihood after a regime shift, sensitive populations might not. Vulnerable individuals and groups often depend upon a determined status or structure for their well-being, having little to no coping capacity to change. Such lack of resilience makes those groups especially exposed, which are often hit the most and the hardest by regime shifts and changes. As underlined by Caniglia and colleagues (2014, 418), "the effects of regime shifts on groups and places are therefore particularly important for environmental justice scholarship, especially when focusing on which vulnerable social groups and individuals will suffer the most from such system transitions."

A general model of social resilience: community and individual resilience

In 2014, Caniglia et al. published a review of several literatures that provide insights into the links between resilience and inequality, including the literatures related to resilience, vulnerability, human security, coupled human and natural systems (CHANS) and environmental justice. The review combed these literatures for overlapping and contradicting concept definitions as a means for creating a model of social resilience to tie these lines of inquiry together. The literature pointed toward an understanding of resilience at two levels – the community/systems level and the individual level.

The most novel finding from this review of the literature is that social resilience can exist at the systems/society level, while particular subgroups of individuals/communities are distinctly more vulnerable. It is a critical responsibility in contemporary cities for leaders to create resilience for all of their occupants, particularly the most vulnerable (Caniglia et al. 2014). The human security literature highlights several structural/institutional dimensions of societies that determine a large portion of a society's ability to react to external shocks in ways

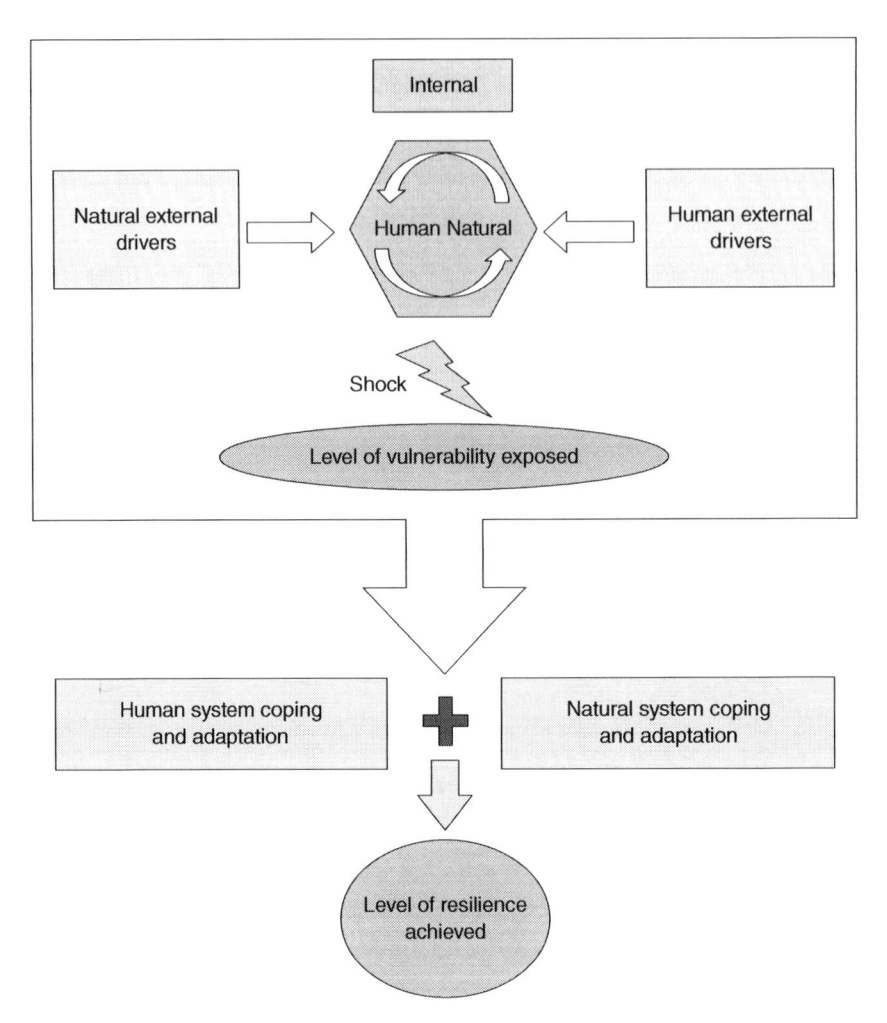

Figure 4.1 Socio-ecological systems resilience formation
Source: Caniglia et al. (2014)

that preserve the overall social system. Political, economic and social control institutions, for example, can be organized in ways that facilitate recovery from disasters or in ways that are too rigid to adapt (Commission of Human Security 2003, 4). Human security scholars also highlight the importance of food security, access to healthcare, environmental quality and social capital as characteristics of resilient systems/societies (Barnett, Matthew and O'Brien 2010). In other words, societies that offer access to these services to their residents are most resilient to external shocks at both the individual and system levels.

Preparedness for external shocks is also critically important in determining the resilience of a society (Morss, Wilhelmi, Meehl and Dilling 2011; Paton et al.

2008; Roberts and Parks 2007). A society that has relegated resources to disaster recovery is more resilient than a society that has not set aside recovery resources. It is equally important, however, for all members of society to know how to access those resources and be physically, and psychologically able to take advantage of those resources. From the literature on vulnerabilities, we also know that particular groups are more sensitive and/or exposed to external shocks (Zahran, Peek, Snodgrass, Weiler and Hempel 2011). Farmers, for example, are more exposed to climate-related disasters, such as drought and increased temperatures. The elderly are more sensitive to heat waves, as illustrated by the large loss of life among the elderly in heat waves in Paris and Chicago. Children are more sensitive to lead in drinking water and are more vulnerable in disasters (Peek and Stough 2010), as highlighted by recent events in Flint, Michigan. The poor and people of color are more vulnerable to shocks in the economy than their white, wealthier counterparts (Bullard and Wright 2009).

Overall, the literature suggests that the preparedness of a society, the exposure and sensitivity of that society's citizens, and the pre-existing characteristics of the society in terms of environmental governance, economics and social services work together to predict how broadly and how quickly societies and their citizens can recover from a variety of external shocks. It is critical for cities to acknowledge and plan for the risks they face in terms of environmental, technical and financial shocks (among others). However, preparedness and recovery planning alone will not eliminate the vulnerabilities that exist because of exposure, sensitivity and other barriers that limit knowledge of or access to a society's preparedness and recovery resources. If resilience for everyone is our goal, we must examine and address the factors that predict vulnerability, sensitivity and access to financial and social capital before, during and after disasters strike. Our current treatment of these dimensions of resilience-preparedness often turns a largely blind eye to the ways that inequality in society is structured, and exposes and impacts sensitive groups during both long- and short-term disasters. Therefore, in the next section of this chapter, we carefully unpack the assumptions of systems theory as it applies to ecological and human communities and highlight areas where an infusion of critical theory can improve our scholarly efforts to describe and predict resilience and increase the common good in the face of contemporary environmental and climate change.

Resilience and systems theory

According to Laszlo and Krippner (1998, 2), "a 'system' may be described as a complex of interacting components together with the relationships among them that permit the identification of a boundary-maintaining entity or process." As social scientists have adopted the resilience language into their examination of disaster recovery and the vulnerability of social systems, we have done so without adequate consideration of the underpinning structural-functionalist orientation of systems theories. Therefore, in the following sections we review the underpinning assumptions of systems theories in general. We further

Table 4.1 Summary of resilience-specific systems theory assumptions

- System dynamic equilibrium is good, because the self-organizing properties of systems have emerged as appropriate for the surrounding environment (Holling 1973).
- The key components and relationships within the system should be maintained in order to ensure survival of the system (Davis and Moore 1945).

review the ways systems theories have been applied historically in the social sciences, along with the critiques that led them to be largely discarded and replaced by critical theories.

The concept of resilience refers to the capacity of a system to absorb changes and withstand disturbances *while maintaining its central functions* (Holling 1973). There are important assumptions embedded in this definition that need to be unpacked. The key assumptions of systems theory envision socio-ecological systems to comprise interdependent elements that co-vary in complex, adaptive ways that can be apprehended by observing key patterns, properties and behaviors within the system (von Bertalanffy 1968). Systems theory also evokes the assumptions of structural-functionalism and holds that properties and behaviors within the system tend toward a steady state of relationships and interactions that self-replicate to maintain the critical functions of the system (Parsons 1954, 1966). A system is considered resilient when the primary functions in the system can be maintained or quickly resumed after an external shock to the system (Walker and Salt 2006). In a vulnerable system, an external shock can push elements of the system beyond their ability to recover, which can cause widespread system transformation.

Table 4.2 Summary of systems theory assumptions applied toward socio-cultural systems

- Socio-cultural systems consist of interdependent parts that improve the function of societies by promoting stability and solidarity (Durkheim 2014).
- The structures within society, such as norms and social institutions, provide system regulation, rather than the acts of individuals (Durkheim 2014; Parsons 1966).
- The more elaborate/complex a society, the more interdependence emerges, since the maintenance of important functions cannot be accomplished by one entity alone (Durkheim 2014); based on the metaphor of an organism (where many parts are necessary to maintain the survival of the whole), Emile Durkheim called this *organic solidarity* (Parsons 1960).
- The social roles people play in a social system are more important and constitute more enduring effects on society than the individuals who occupy those roles (Weber 2009).
- Stability and social cohesion are required for social systems to survive over time (Durkheim 2014; Parsons 1960).
- Existing social and cultural features are seen as functional in producing a cohesive and stable society (Davis and Moore 1945); therefore, these social and cultural features are analyzed in terms of their functions (Parsons 1966).
- Changes in the external environment, however, can require adaptive actions.
- A society will recognize the need to adapt in time to adjust to changing environmental demands (Davis and Moore 1954; Parsons 1966; Holland 2006).

Table 4.3 Summary of the criticisms of structural-functionalism

- It cannot account for social change, structural contradictions or conflict (Holmwood 2010).
- It does not address grievances in society (Buechler 2004).
- Feminist critiques illustrate that the functionalist interpretivist frame can be biased, rather than evidence based (Holmwood 2010).
- The existence of a particular element in society implies that its existence is coherent with the surrounding environment, but not that it was caused by those environmental features (Tumin 1953).

Another fundamental assumption contained in systems theory is that the maintenance and replication of core system functions is good – an assumption that largely stems from the tenet that the properties and behaviors of systems have evolved in ways that are best adapted to the external environment (Davis and Moore 1945; Holling 1973). In social systems, the market is an example of a central organizing institution that Parsons and other structural-functionalists highlight, where markets are described as self-regulating and self-adjusting to external shocks and changing circumstances (Parsons 1966). Laissez-faire approaches like these ask us to believe that the market takes into account all of the relevant functions of production, consumption and distribution, not only of products but of capital more broadly, through a network of interactions, relationships and feedback loops that have evolved over time to be ideally adapted to contemporary conditions. This same set of underpinning assumptions can be applied to other functions of systems, such as socialization and education, lawmaking, governance, healthcare provision and food security.

Laissez-faire approaches to disaster recovery rest on the assumption that the system will find its way back to equilibrium without excessive external interference. In fact, we should allow the system to right itself, rather than to intercede (Parsons 1966). The assumption is that the core organizing institutions within the social system will get back to work and restore their core functions. *The major problem we find with this approach is that it assumes that the core organizing institutions, patterns and feedback loops are adapted to the environment in ways that promote widespread survivability across the system* – an assumption that is clearly untenable given widespread and growing inequality in contemporary social systems and the uneven death rates experienced by the poor and people of color from environmental and climate-related disasters.

These assumptions take on an unjust orientation when they are applied to socio-cultural systems. In sociology, systems theory forms the basis for structural-functionalism (Holmwood 2010). Unlike scientists before them, functionalists explain the utility of particular components of society in reference to their existence, rather than in reference to their effects. In other words, structural functionalists explain the positive function of particular processes or institutions with the starting assumption that existing processes and institutions in fact serve a positive function for that society; they, then, work back from the institution or process of relevance in search of the particular function being served. *However,* when so many of our existing institutions – national and global – fail to provide widespread benefits for the majority of citizens, we are severely remiss to believe that those institutions are functional.

The market serves as an excellent example of the blind spots contained within complex-adaptive systems. While the data, in fact, show that the networks and feedback loops of the market resume after external shocks hit the system, the data also show that after external shocks particular people are able to recover while others are not. In other words, the laissez-faire approach is proven, but not with the positive outcomes we are asked to expect. Rather, the data consistently show that the central functions of society favor those in power when they experience external shocks; they systematically fail the poor, the elderly, youth, women, indigenous peoples and nearly all people of color (Harlan et al. 2015; Pellow and Brehm 2013). During recovery the data show that the systematic vulnerability of these groups *prior to external shocks* compared with their white, wealthy and male counterparts often serves to super-exclude the vulnerable and significantly advances the advantage of those in power *in the aftermath of external shocks*. So, while the self-replicating dimensions of systems such as the market appear to play out, they do not play out in ways that foster broad-based resilience, rather they structure inequalities that are deeper than they were at pre-disaster times.

For example, Benjamin Landy (2013) examined recovery from the 2008 economic crisis with a special eye toward the rich compared with the middle and lower classes in the United States. He found that two years after the recession, inequality between the rich and poor had grown larger than it was prior to the recession. And, because of the way the housing market was implicated in this particular recession, Landy (2013) cites that "low- and middle-income homeowners were hit particularly hard, with households in the bottom four-fifths of the wealth distribution experiencing a 39.1 percent decline in net worth between 2007 and 2010. The top 20 percent, by contrast, lost just 14 percent of their net worth." The data becomes particularly alarming as Landy (2013) digs deeper:

> According to a Pew Research Center analysis, every dollar and more of aggregate gains in household wealth between 2009 and 2011 went to the richest 7 percent of households. Aggregate net worth among this top group rose 28 percent during the first two years of the recovery, from $19.8 trillion to $25.4 trillion. The bottom 93 percent, meanwhile, saw their aggregate net worth fall 4 percent, from $15.4 trillion to $14.8 trillion. As a result, wealth inequality increased substantially over the 2009–2011 period, with the wealthiest 7 percent of U.S. households increasing their aggregate share of the nation's overall wealth from 56 percent to 63 percent.

Fry and Taylor (2013) cite similar data:

> On an individual household basis, the mean wealth of households in this more affluent group (the top 7%) was almost 24 times that of those in the less affluent group in 2011. At the start of the recovery in 2009, that ratio had been less than 18-to-1.

When we look at recovery from these events based on race, we find that disasters such as the economic crisis of 2007 set back people of color at much higher rates than whites (Cooper, Gable and Austin 2012) and their recovery has been considerably slower.

Stewart Lansley of the *Observer* casts dispersion on the laissez-faire approach to markets in the aftermath of crises (2012). He explains that many macro-economists argue that inequality is supposed to foster economic growth, yet both the most recent recession and the great depression of the 1930s were preceded by increased inequality. He states:

> Then there have been two periods when wages have seriously lagged behind productivity – in the 1920s and the post-1980s. Both of them culminating in prolonged slumps. Between 1990 and 2007, real wages in the UK rose more slowly than productivity, and at a worsening rate. In the US, the decoupling started earlier and has led to an even larger gap. [. . .]. The significance of a growing "wage-productivity gap" is that it upsets the natural mechanisms necessary to achieve economic balance. Purchasing power shrinks and consumer societies suddenly lack the capacity to consume.

He further argues that these wage–productivity gaps increase when regulation in an economy goes down, further highlighting the correlation between laissez-faire approaches to systems and instability. It seems clear that carefully planned prevention and recovery plans are a much better way to insure broad-based resilience than laissez-faire approaches, but we also need targeted pre-disaster efforts to lessen the unequal vulnerabilities of the groups predicted to suffer the most.

The social sciences have had this type of debate before. We need only briefly examine Davis and Moore's (1945) famous discussion of the positive functions of inequality in America to remind ourselves of our structural-functionalist past. In this article, Davis and Moore take inequality as the institution of interest. They argue that inequality plays several positive functions in America, most saliently to induce the most talented people into the most important occupational positions. The argument holds that unequal inducements in the forms of salary and benefits serve as incentives for the most talented people to endure the costs and delayed gratification required to acquire more complex occupational-specific skills. Without such differences in incentive structures, why would talented people delay income-earning capacity by attending school or acquiring credentials when they could simply work at a less important position for equal pay?

Of course, Melvin Tumin (1953) posed a cogent point-by-point critique of Davis and Moore's thesis based on a more critical theoretical orientation. First, he argued that inequality is perpetuated: the benefits acquired by one generation's work result in advantages for future generations. Tumin argues that talent cannot be developed if one does not have access to the funding needed to pursue an education, which means that the talent of the poor is repressed by their poverty; likewise, the rich can pursue education and delay gratification whether they are talented or not, because their education and their livelihood during education is generally paid for by their parents. Turning Davis and Moore's argument on its head, Tumin asks: What is the incentive to go to work when one can pursue education on his/her parents' dime? Tumin's arguments ring true today. To begin with, children with lower IQs from upper-class families attain a college education at a considerably higher rate than high-IQ children from the lowest quartile income bracket (Gilbert 2015).

The fundamental argument at stake here is whether more inequality produces a greater common good than less when societies are faced with external shocks; and the data we have cited so far indicate that inequality spikes appear to cause economic instability. Furthermore, economic inequality prior to disasters seems to predict who will recover afterwards. And, most important to our current argument, it appears that *contemporary rates of inequality portend increased inequality in the future and widespread suffering in the face of future economic and natural disasters*. Climate change points to serious increases in disasters, such as floods, heat waves, wildfires and hurricanes, suggesting we really have a lot of work to do to prevent the environmental injustices that are coming down the pike (Caniglia et al. 2014; Ciplet, Roberts and Khan 2015; Roberts and Parks 2007). If we begin with the structural-functionalist assumptions that existing social relationships and institutions are serving the common good, we will accept the laissez-faire approach that relies on existing "functions" to return to normal after external shocks. However, if we acknowledge the fact that contemporary institutions have failed the majority of citizens (Caniglia et al. 2014), we are required to make changes to those institutions *before future disasters strike*. If we do not, we are simply accepting a world that condemns all but the upper echelons of society to the suffering predicted by climate change.

Challenges to structural-functionalism

The social sciences have almost entirely replaced outdated structural-functionalist explanations for social phenomena with critical explanations. Many failures of the theory to account for empirical reality led to its demise. For example, the argument that stability within social systems arises from solidarity and consensus was not born out in the empirical world (Holmwood 2010). The social movements of the twentieth century highlighted conflict based on racial inequality, women's rights, exclusion of the poor from satisfactory housing, and severe cleavages regarding the war in Vietnam. These conflicts made any theory untenable that tried to explain the functions of social systems with solidarity and consensus at its center. Inequality and persistent poverty brought about serious questions regarding whether the existing social institutions were, in fact, designed to serve the broader common good; and contemporary evidence continues to support the argument that social institutions such as the economy and educational systems are decidedly tweaked toward service of the rich and white elites, rather than the broader common good.

One central dimension of structural-functionalism is that it is predicated upon maintaining the central organizing features of a system and relying on their networks of relationships, roles and feedback loops to self-replicate. When we view

Table 4.4 Summary of the key assumptions of critical theory

- Human ideology is the key to liberation from oppression (Mayo 1999).
- Social institutions often serve as sites of oppression (Habermas 1987; Brulle 2000).
- Reflexive analysis pinpoints the ways people in general and particular social groups are oppressed by social institutions (Beck, Giddens and Nash 1994).
- Social change stems from conflict/critical perspectives (Coser 1957).
- The concepts and ideologies used in society to justify/explain characteristics in society must be evaluated according to their underpinning assumptions and the interests those concepts and ideologies propagate (Adorno and Horkheimer 1997; Thompson 2013).

this proposition through the lens of environmental justice, it is very problematic, because the central organizing characteristics of contemporary socio-ecological systems are consistently associated with outcomes that privilege the rich, while disadvantaging the poor, women, the elderly, youth and people of color. That's a lot of disadvantage that resilience theory overlooks. Let's examine the factual evidence that illustrates this privilege.

In the United States, the accumulation of wealth, income, educational and occupational attainment, upward mobility and political power have become increasingly concentrated among the top 10% of the population. The richest 20% of the U.S. population earns 50% of the income. The concentration is even more spectacular when we look at wealth, where the top 10% of wealth-holders possess 90% of stocks, 98% of bonds, and 93% of business equity. Neighborhood segregation has simultaneously increased in the United States, with the top and bottom 10% of households increasingly separate from those in the middle. In resilience terms, such segregation has significant implications, because higher-income neighborhoods have safer streets, better schools, and stronger civic associations – all indicators of higher resilience in the face of external shocks. Upward mobility in the United States has declined, while downward mobility has increased; and statistics show that upward mobility is considerably more dependent upon educational attainment than it was in the decades immediately following World War II. Since educational attainment is decidedly predicted by social class status, the solid implication is that the rich are getting consistently richer and advantage is passed down through the generations, while the poor are falling seriously behind (Gilbert 2015).

Many of these trends are more serious when we control for race, ethnicity, age and gender. After the 2009 recession, blacks, Hispanics and youth exhibited the slowest rate of recovery in the labor market (Cooper et al. 2012). Children in the United States are at a higher risk of poverty than the American population as a whole (Gornick and Jantti 2016). This fact has very serious implications for resilience, because "low-income children in the U.S. tend to have less stable and lower-income families, less secure families, and parents who have less time to devote to their children" (Corak 2016, 51). Blacks and Hispanics in the United States experience twice the risk of poverty as whites. Black and Hispanic female heads of households have the highest risk of poverty. Black children experience a 37% risk of poverty, compared with white children, who experience 18% risk. Although poverty tends to be a transitory situation for most Americans, those who are born poor have a 25% risk of remaining poor, compared with only 4% risk of becoming poor if you were *not* born poor. This likelihood increases by race. Blacks who were born poor have a 33% chance of being poor in adulthood (Gilbert 2015).

When we look at inequality and resilience at the international level, three critical dimensions are highlighted in the sociological literature: the exposure and impacts of natural disasters; the ability of elites to exclude the poor from decision-making and available resources; and the power of industrialized nations to dominate the international institutions that create policies, treaties and other cooperative agreements.

Roberts and Parks (2007) provide the most extensive review of vulnerability to natural disasters to date. According to their examination, industrialized nations are less vulnerable to natural disasters because they are better able to prepare for their consequences. They can install early warning systems, prepare for large-scale evacuations, and set aside resources for recovery efforts after disasters strike. Developing countries also have centralized health services that are there to serve victims, stronger police forces to protect citizens until systems return to normal, and economic institutions that get back on line more quickly. When measuring the effects of disasters that took place in the 1980s and 1990s, Roberts and Parks examine the importance of several factors: institutional democracy, national wealth, civil society pressure, inequality, urbanization, environmental vulnerability and coastal population. When predicting homelessness and death from disasters, their model found that coastal populations, rurality, and domestic income inequality were consistently associated with higher vulnerability. A legacy of colonialism within a country was also a strong predictor of death and homelessness from droughts, floods, windstorms and heat waves.

Perhaps the most recent treatment of the impacts of environmental degradation on the poor is Liam Downey's book (2015) *Inequality, Democracy, and the Environment*. Downey highlights the ways that the power of elites structures the unequal impacts of environmental problems. Specifically, elites are able to manipulate the best of environmental outcomes for themselves through several mechanisms. First, they are able to monopolize decision-making power in the major international institutions, such as the World Trade Organization and the International Monetary Fund. Because of this power, they influence policies in ways that shift environmental costs and burdens onto less powerful states. However, more subtly, because of their advantageous positions, they can control information in ways that frame the truth to their own advantage, distract from the dangers of their political and economic activities, and spread doubt among less knowledgeable groups regarding the real consequences of our contemporary relationship with natural resources. Downey places the vast majority of blame for our contemporary environmental crisis on these elites and their ability to manipulate the rest of the world.

Ciplet, Roberts and Khan (2015, 5) define climate injustice as "heightened and disproportionate vulnerability to climate-related harm by disadvantaged social groups." They argue that extractive industries, such as the fossil fuel and mining industries, disproportionately expose the poor to waste chemicals and other toxic conditions. In addition, vulnerability to drought, floods, disease and displacement are highly correlated with being poor, elderly and otherwise marginalized. Rising temperatures put global food supplies at risk, and rising prices for the basic necessities, such as food and shelter, inordinately impact the poor and people of color around the world. They highlight that people in the 48 least developed countries (LDCs) are more likely to die in disasters that stem from climate change than those in the rest of the world.

Facts such as these highlight that existing social institutions, relationships and feedback loops must be changed in ways that shift the burdens of climate change and other external shocks back into balance. An infusion of critical theory into resilience perspectives is absolutely required. Therefore, let us examine the central assumptions of critical theory.

Critical theory is often considered a broad umbrella under which one can find a variety of schools of thought, such as critical race theory, queer theory and feminist theory (Guba and Lincoln 1994). These schools encourage voice and representation of empirical data from within the communities being studied, rather than from the perspective of scholars whose own identities are not shared with those they are studying. This school of thought arose from the teachings of Karl Marx – especially the concepts of inequality in the means of production, exploitation of labor, and the use of ideology to distract the proletariat from class consciousness. The engines of the Industrial Revolution produced a concentration of wealth that crystalized itself in a variety of institutions, relationships and feedback loops that resulted in the creation of a power elite (Wright 1969) that consisted of political, military and economic leaders. The Frankfurt School in Germany, which operated between World War I and World War II, brought together social scientists whose primary orientation was to elaborate and reinterpret Marx's critique of capitalism, champion education aimed at liberating oppression with knowledge, and foster critical thinking and empowerment (Calhoun 1995).

As a theory of knowledge, critical theory argues that the underpinning assumptions of our understanding of the empirical world must be interrogated. While there are certain ways of seeing the world that are widely accepted, many of those ideas have come from systems of knowledge and institutions that are not objective. Rather, much of human knowledge has been created by those in power as a means of repressing conflict by convincing the oppressed that those institutions and practices are natural expressions of reality that hold opportunity for everyone (Foucault 1980). Drawing upon Marx's concept of ideology, the Frankfurt School scholars, such as Adorno, Horkheimer and Habermas, argue that many cultural tropes related to opportunity and the fulfillment of human nature through the means of production merely serve to perpetuate capitalism as the most natural economic system. Max Weber (2002) elaborates this argument in his book *The Protestant Ethic and the Spirit of Capitalism*.

While the original critical theorists studied and critiqued capitalism and the rise of the fascist Nazi Party in Germany, contemporary critical theory has expanded its examinations to include a variety of forms of oppression, including slavery, colonialism, patriarchy, homophobia and environmental justice, among others (Calhoun 1995). The ideology of capitalism remains a common theme; however, broader critiques of social institutions, such as voting, education, marriage, national and international policies, multinational corporations and tax systems have become targets for critical analyses. The fundamental approach entails an examination of social institutions in terms of how inclusively/exclusively they operate, the transparency and consistency of their rules of engagement, the fairness and equality of the outcomes they produced, and how they are structured – both formally and informally – to handle grievances. Institutions are also examined in their historical context by asking who they were originally designed to serve and how they have evolved as their constituency grew larger and more diverse.

Critical examinations have shown consistently that particular social facts are especially difficult to change – especially those that protect the powerful. Institutions such as the market and marriage are typically protected by a complex mesh of overlapping protections, such as free trade agreements, national and international institutions, religious, state and federal frameworks (Zucker 1992). Many of these institutions are reinforced by informal socialization processes and cultural practices in homes, schools and churches. The underpinning ideologies are used to justify the laws, and the system of laws and punishments feeds back to teach citizens about good behavior. The best critical theorists argue that these tight feedback loops create a society that fails to incorporate inputs from the external environment, even when that environment is heading for extinction (Beck 1992; Habermas 1987). In essence, the feedback loops are so tight and self-referential that they gain an authoritarianism that encourages turning a blind eye to empirical reality.

To correct this type of blindness in our studies of climate-related disasters, critical theory offers an insightful lens. We can introduce five simple steps into our analysis of existing social systems. Specifically, when approaching a social system, begin with a contextual analysis of existing inequality by posing the following questions:

- Which social institutions are the most favorable targets for reducing systematic vulnerability of sensitive and exposed groups? Where are the largest roadblocks to reducing those vulnerabilities?
- Are there any cultural ideologies that serve to perpetuate the vulnerability of marginalized groups? How might the ideologies be combatted or transformed?
- Are disaster preparedness and recovery system resources available to everyone? Do all groups know about those resources and have the ability to access them?
- Are the most vulnerable groups at the table during disaster preparedness and recovery planning? How can we insure that we design preparedness and recovery systems that serve these exposed and sensitive populations?
- Are there ways we can increase resilience for everyone before embedded injustices are experienced? Can we decrease vulnerability before disasters strike?

These types of reflexive approaches can open the doors for inclusion in decision-making (Beck 1992; Habermas 1987) and help us to move toward just resilience (see Chapter 2 of this volume). Critical theory can help identify injustices-in-waiting before a crisis or disaster strikes by systematically examining existing inequality and the institutions and ideologies that perpetuate unjust exposure and sensitivity of marginalized groups in society. Reflexive approaches are fundamental to uncovering such social vulnerabilities, even when inequalities are not fully documented or apparently visible to our eyes. Furthermore, exploring how populations with different coping capacity may be impacted by, react to and respond to disasters and changes can help develop preparedness plans and risk assessments that are inclusive of the most vulnerable sectors of society. Critical theory and the idea of just resilience can thus advance resilience studies in ways that promote the common goods and allow us to answer the question: social resilience for whom? For everybody.

Conclusion: state change now for disaster equality

Our goal in this chapter is to advocate a critical revolution in the way scholars theorize preparedness and recovery for climate-related disasters. Existing inequality within socio-economic systems will result in environmental injustices as environmental and climate-related disasters occur. Certain populations are systematically more exposed and more vulnerable to heat waves, floods, intense storms and infectious diseases. The poor, youth, women, the elderly and people of color around the world stand to carry the largest burden of the climate crisis. However, our scholarly approaches to socio-ecological system studies largely fail to address these realities. By omission we become perpetrators of environmental injustices.

We have highlighted above the ways that systems theory and structural-functionalism tend to turn a blind eye to inequality and injustice. We drew upon extensive statistics to highlight contemporary inequality and the ways disasters and external economic shocks actually accrue advantage to those who are most well-off before those shocks. In this light, we argue that scholars of resilience and vulnerability must systematically examine existing inequality, and the institutions and ideologies that perpetuate unjust exposure and sensitivity of marginalized groups in society. By incorporating a handful of steps into our research process, we can better describe the existing contexts of the societies we hope to make resilient. We can better serve decision-makers by highlighting the institutional features of their communities that serve as roadblocks to improved resilience and offer the best potential to reduce vulnerabilities. Rather than beginning our analyses with the assumption that existing institutions need to be protected against disasters and restored after they occur, we should *ask* whether existing institutions can be strengthened before disasters strike. Can they be made more transparent, more democratic, more successful in serving the common good? Can we draw on the insights of the human security framework to significantly reduce vulnerability among the most marginalized communities? Can we insure that everyone – including the elderly, disabled and youth, among others – has knowledge of and access to disaster preparedness and recovery resources? Can we incorporate the voices of those on the margins in the creation of disaster preparedness and recovery plans?

Although our examination confirms many of the assumptions of systems theory, it highlights that a laissez-faire approach to disaster recovery and preparedness will result in continued super-exclusion of the groups most vulnerable to the consequences of environmental and climate change. However, we can start addressing vulnerability by acknowledging existing inequality and targeting the perpetrating institutions for the necessary reforms. These reforms must be based on an emphasis on the need to serve the common good as we respond to messages from the environment. We have to understand why we find ourselves in this place of systematic inequality in order to address it. Systems reproduce themselves; however, for a system to reproduce something that we want – such as justice, equality or resilience – its infrastructure has to be geared toward those goals. Over a century of policies have systematically favored whites and the rich over people of color, the elderly, youth and the poor. If we want to change this, we have to begin with the assumption that the status quo is not what we want. In fact, we have to begin with the factual realization that our current systems will continue to replicate inequality (and, in fact, make it worse over time) if left to laissez-faire approaches.

Notes

1 Director of the Sustainable Economic & Enterprise Development (SEED), Institute and Faculty Research Director in the College of Business and Economics at Regis University, beth.caniglia@oksatate.edu
2 Regional Parks, Capital Regional District of Victoria, bfrank@crd.bc.ca

References

Adger N.W. (2000). Social and ecological resilience: are they related? *Progress in Human Geography*, 24(3), 347–364.
Adorno T.W. and Horkheimer M. (1997). *Dialectic of enlightenment*. New York: Verso Books.
Barnett J., Matthew R.A. and O'Brien K.L. (2010). Global environmental change and human security: an introduction. In A.M. Richard, J. Barnett, B. McDonald and K.L. O'Brien (Eds.) *Global environmental change and human security* (pp. 5–32). Cambridge, MA: The MIT Press.
Barr S. and Devine-Wright P. (2012). Resilient communities: sustainabilities in transition. *Local Environment: The International Journal of Justice and Sustainability*, 17(5), 525–532.
Beck U. (1992). *The risk society: towards a new modernity*. Thousand Oaks, CA: Sage Publications.
Beck U., Giddens A. and Nash S. (1994). *Reflexive modernization: politics, tradition and aesthetics in the modern social order*. Palo Alto, CA: Stanford University Press.
Berkes F. and Ross H. (2012). Community resilience: toward an integrated approach. *Society and Natural Resource*, 26(1), 5–20.

Brand F.S. and Jax K. (2007). Focusing the meaning(s) of resilience: resilience as a descriptive concept and a boundary object. *Ecology and Society*, *12(1)*, 23.

Brulle R.J. (2000). *Agency, democracy, and nature: the US environmental movement from a critical theory perspective*. Cambridge, MA: MIT Press.

Buechler S.M. (2004). Strain and breakdown theories. In *The Wiley Blackwell encyclopedia of social and political movements*. Hoboken, NJ: Wiley Blackwell.

Bullard R.D. and Wright B. (2009). *Race, place, and environmental justice after Hurricane Katrina: struggles to reclaim, rebuild, and revitalize New Orleans and the Gulf Coast*. Philadelphia, PA: Westview Press.

Calhoun C. (1995). *Critical social theory: culture, history, and the challenge of difference*. Cambridge, MA: Wiley-Blackwell.

Caniglia B.S., Frank B., Delano D. and Kerner B. (2014). Enhancing environmental justice research and praxis: the inclusion of human security, resilience and vulnerabilities literature. *International Journal of Innovation and Sustainable Development*, *4*, 409–426.

Ciplet D., Roberts J.T. and Khan M.R. (2015). *Power in a warming world: the new global politics of climate change and the remaking of environmental inequality*. Cambridge, MA: MIT Press.

Commission of Human Security (2003). Human security now. Retrieved 5 May 2014 from http://reliefweb.int/sites/reliefweb.int/files/resources/91BAEEDBA50C6907C1256D19006A9353-chs-security-may03.pdf

Cooper D., Gable M. and Austin A. (2012). The public-sector jobs crisis: Women and African Americans hit hardest by job losses in state and local governments. Retrieved 11 March 2016 from http://www.epi.org/publication/bp339-public-sector-jobs-crisis

Corak M. (2016). Economic mobility. Retrieved 5 May 2014 from http://inequality.stanford.edu/sites/default/files/Pathways-SOTU-2016.pdf

Coser L.A. (1957). Social conflict and the theory of social change. *British Journal of Sociology*, *8(3)*, 197–207.

Davidson D.J. (2010). The applicability of the concept of resilience to social systems: some sources of optimism and nagging doubts. *Society and Natural Resources*, *23(12)*, 1135–1149.

Davis K. and Moore W. (1945). Some principles of stratification. *American Sociological Review*, *10(2)*, 242–249.

Dent E.B. and Umpleby S.A. (1998). Underlying assumptions of several traditions in systems theory and cybernetics. In R. Trappl (Ed.) *Cybernetics and systems* (pp. 513–518). Vienna: Austrian Society for Cybernetic Studies.

Downey L. (2015). *Inequality, democracy and the environment*. New York: New York University Press.

Durkheim E. (2014). *The division of labor in society*. New York: Free Press.

Fiksel J. (2006). A framework for sustainable materials management. *Journal of Materials*, *58(8)*, 15–22.

Folke C. (2006). Resilience: the emergence of a perspective for social-ecological system analyses. *Global Environmental Change*, *16(3)*, 253–267.

Folke C., Carpenter S.R., Walker B., Scheffer M., Chapin T. and Rockström J. (2010). Resilience thinking: integrating resilience, adaptability and transformability. *Ecology and Society*, *15(4)*, 20.

Foucault M. (Ed.) (1980). *Power/knowledge: Selected interviews & other writings, 1972–1977*. New York: Pantheon Books.

Fry R. and Taylor P. (2013). A rise in wealth for the wealthy; Declines for the lower 93%: An uneven recovery, 2009–2011. Retrieved 11 March 2016 from http://www.pewsocialtrends.org/2013/04/23/a-rise-in-wealth-for-the-wealthydeclines-for-the-lower-93

Gilbert D. (2015). *The American class structure in an age of growing inequality*. Thousand Oaks, CA: Sage Publishers.

Gornik J.C. and Jantti M. (2016). Poverty. Retrieved 5 May 2014 from http://inequality.stanford.edu/sites/default/files/Pathways-SOTU-2016.pdf

Guba E.G. and Lincoln Y.S. (1994). Competing paradigms in qualitative research. *Handbook of Qualitative Research*, 2(163–194), 105.

Gunderson L.H. (2000). Ecological resilience – in theory and application. *Annual Review of Ecology and Systematics*, 31, 425–439.

Habermas J. (1987). *The theory of communicative action: lifeworld and system – a critique of functionalist reason*. Boston: Beacon Press.

Harlan S.L., Pellow D.N., Roberts T., Bell S.E., Holt W.E. and Nagel J. (2015). Climate justice and inequality. In R. Dunlap and R.J. Brulle (Eds.) *Climate change and society* (pp. 127–163). Oxford: Oxford University Press.

Holland J.H. (2006). Studying complex adaptive systems. *Journal of Systems Science and Complexity*, 19(1), 1–8.

Holling C.S. (1996). Engineering resilience versus ecological resilience. In P.C. Schulze (Ed.) *Engineering within ecological constraints* (pp. 31–44). Washington: National Academy Press.

Holling S.C. (1973). Resilience and stability of ecological systems. *Annual Review of Ecology and Systematics*, 4, 1–23.

Holmwood J. (2010). Functionalism and its critics. In C. Crothers (Ed.) *Historical developments and theoretical approaches in sociology, volume II* (pp. 110–132). New York: EOLSS Publications/UNESCO.

Lake P.S. (2013). Resistance, resilience and restoration. *Ecological Management & Restoration*, 14(1), 20–24.

Landy B. (2013). A tale of two recoveries: wealth inequality after the great recession. Retrieved 24 March 2016 from https://tcf.org/content/commentary/a-tale-of-two-recoveries-wealth-inequality-after-the-great-recession

Lansley S. (2012). Why economic inequality leads to collapse. Retrieved 15 May 2016 from https://www.theguardian.com/business/2012/feb/05/inequality-leads-to-economic-collapse

Laszlo A. and Krippner S. (1998). Systems theories: their origins, foundations, and development. In J.S. Jordan (ed.) *System theories and a priori aspects of perception* (pp. 47–74). Amsterdam: Elsevier.

López D.R., Brizuela M.A., Willems P., Aguiar M.R., Siffredi G. and Bran D. (2013). Linking ecosystem resistance, resilience, and stability in steppes of North Patagonia. *Ecological Indicators*, 24(3), 1–11.

Magis K. (2010). Community resilience: an indicator of social sustainability. *Society & Natural Resources*, 23(5), 401–416.

Mayo P. (1999). *Gramsci, Freire and adult education: possibilities for transformative action*. Basingstoke: Palgrave Macmillan.

Morss R.E., Wilhelmi O.V., Meehl G. and Dilling L. (2011). Improving societal outcomes of extreme weather in a changing climate: an integrated perspective. *Annual Review of Environmental Resources*, 36(1–25).

Parsons T. (1954). *Essays in sociological theory*. New York: The Free Press.

Parsons T. (1960). *Durkheim's contribution to the theory of integration of social systems*. New York: The Free Press.

Parsons T. (1966). *Societies: evolutionary and comparative perspectives*. Upper Saddle River, NJ: Prentice-Hall.

Paton D., Houghton B.F., Gregg C.E., Gill D.A., Ritchie L.A, McIvor D., Larin P., Meinhold S., Horan J. and Johnston D.M. (2008). Managing tsunami risk in coastal communities: identifying predictors of preparedness. *Australian Journal of Emergency Management, 23(1)*.

Peek L. and Stough L.M. (2010). Children with disabilities in the context of disaster: a social vulnerability perspective. *Child Development, 81*, 1260–1270.

Pellow D.N. and Brehm H.N. (2013). An environmental sociology for the twenty-first century. *Annual Review of Sociology, 39*, 229–250.

Perkins O. (2014). Slowest economic recovery in decades, according to several indicators. Retrieved 3 November 2015 from http://www.cleveland.com/business/index.ssf/2014/11/slowest_economic_recovery_in_d.html

Roberts J.T. and Parks B. (2007). *A climate of injustice: global inequality, north-south politics, and climate policy*. Cambridge: Cambridge University Press.

Schwartz A., Béné C., Bennett G., Boso D., Hilly Z., Paul C., Posala R., Sibiti S. and Andrew N. (2011). Vulnerability and resilience of remote rural communities to shocks and global change: empirical analysis from Solomon Islands. *Global Environmental Change, 21(11)*, 1128–1140.

Thompson J.B. (2013). *Ideology and modern culture: critical social theory in the era of mass communication*. London: John Wiley & Sons.

Tumin M.M. (1953). Some principles of stratification: a critical analysis. *American Sociological Review, 18(4)*, 387–394.

UN-HABITAT (2010). *State of Asia cities 2010/11*. Fukuoka: UN-HABITAT. Retrieved 5 May 2016 from www.rrojasdatabank.onfo/citiesasia1011.pdf

UNICEF Bangladesh (2010). *Understanding urban inequalities in Bangladesh: a prerequisite for achieving vision 2021. A study based on the results of the 2009 multiple indicator cluster survey*. Dhaka: UNICEF Bangladesh.

U.S. Department of Labor (2012). African-American labor force in the recovery. Retrieved 3 November 2015 from http://www.dol.gov/_sec/media/reports/blacklaborforce/

von Bertalanffy L. (1968). *General system theory: foundations, development, applications*. New York: George Braziller.

Walker B., Holling C.S., Carpenter S.R. and Kinzig A. (2004). Resilience, adaptability and transformability in social-ecological systems. *Ecology and Society, 9(2)*, 5.

Walker B. and Salt D. (2006). *Resilience thinking: sustaining ecosystems and people in a changing world*. Washington: Island Press.

Webb C.T. (2007). What is the role of ecology in understanding ecosystem resilience? *BioScience, 57(6)*, 470–471.

Weber M. (2002). *The protestant ethic and the spirit of capitalism*. Los Angeles: Roxbury Publishing Company.

Weber M. (2009). *The theory of social and economic organization*. New York: The Free Press.

Wright M.C. (1969). *The power elite*. Oxford: Oxford University Press.

Zahran S., Peek L., Snodgrass J.G., Weiler S. and Hempel L. (2011). Economics of disaster risk, social vulnerability, and mental health resilience. *Risk Analysis, 31(7)*.

Zucker L. (1992). The role of institutionalization in cultural persistence. In W. Powell and P. DiMaggio (Eds.) *The new institutionalism in organizational analysis* (pp. 83–107). Chicago: University of Chicago Press.

Part II
Practices

5 "There is just a stigma here"

Historical legacies, food justice, and solutions-based approaches toward urban community resilience

Tamara L. Mix,[1] Andrew Raridon[2] and Julie M. Croff[3]

Introduction

After the Civil War, thousands of former slaves sought cheap land and opportunity by moving to the Oklahoma territory. The following land grab and oil boom brought prosperity for both whites and African Americans settling in the growing city of Tulsa. However, *de jure* segregation created two Tulsas—one white, one African American. African Americans were restricted to North Tulsa, settling and developing what became known as the Greenwood District into a prosperous community. In the midst of the Jim Crow era, segregation worked to strengthen community cohesion. Barred from patronizing white establishments and forced to provide for themselves, by 1921, 35 city blocks of North Tulsa had been established as a self-sufficient African American community complete with a bus system, schools, hospitals, newspapers, banks, and over 600 businesses (Ellsworth 1982). Greenwood Avenue, the main thoroughfare through the community, was dubbed "Negro Wall Street" by Booker T. Washington because of its many bustling businesses and the multiple African American millionaires that worked and lived on the street. Tulsa's white residents, while begrudgingly acknowledging the community's success, continued to refer to North Tulsa as "Little Africa," and intermittent lynchings and other displays of white supremacy served to remind African American residents of their place in Oklahoma's racial hierarchy (Johnson 2007).

In late spring 1921, racial animosity simmered throughout Tulsa, as it had in other US cities over the past three years—animosity fueled by whites' anxieties that African Americans were an economic threat and African Americans' frustration that despite their service in World War I they were still denied basic human rights at home. On May 30, false allegations that a young African American male assaulted a white female elevator operator escalated racial tensions in Tulsa to a breaking point (Halliburton 1972; Messer 2011; Messer and Bell 2010; Oklahoma Commission to Study the Tulsa Race Riot of 1921, 2001). Fueled by sensationalist newspaper editorials and deputized civilians, white mobs shot, lynched, beat, and dragged through the streets North Tulsa's African American residents, eventually killing more than 300 people. Over the next three days, the white rioters continued to loot and burn the Greenwood District, destroying 35 city blocks of residences and leaving thousands of African Americans homeless. Known now as the Tulsa Race Riot of 1921, the multi-day show of force and white supremacy has been described as "one of the most devastating single episodes of racial conflict in the post-slavery United States," yet the riot's occurrence was not formally acknowledged by Oklahoma authorities until 1997 (Ellsworth 1982; Messer and Bell 2010, 252).

After the National Guard cleared the area and African American residents were released from temporary detention centers, many residents had no homes to return to. The Tulsa City Commission quickly passed a fire ordinance preventing immediate rebuilding of the community, causing some of the populace to leave. Residents who chose to remain in Tulsa spent the winter following the riot in tents. Community rebuilding was able to take place upon an Oklahoma Supreme Court ruling that the fire ordinance was unconstitutional. In the decades that followed the riot, African Americans experienced continued racial intimidation by white Tulsans and the Ku Klux Klan, while parts of the Greenwood neighborhood were targeted by a series of urban renewal projects that demolished several city blocks to make way for the growing interstate system (Johnson 2007). Ultimately, the once self-sufficient community never fully recovered economically or socially. Today, North Tulsa remains racially segregated, housing more than two-fifths of the African American population of Tulsa County (43%) and nearly one-fifth of the county's Latinos (19%), while simultaneously losing over 40% of its population since 1960 (CSC 2011). North Tulsa also boasts the county's largest food desert, part of which includes a six-mile area with no grocery store of any kind, as well as a sprawling city layout that makes accessibility difficult for those who do not own vehicles.

North Tulsa has a complex social and economic history characterized by racial violence and discrimination—processes that, over time, have severely hindered efforts in the local political arena to engage in plans to facilitate community sustainability and resilience. Contemporary environmental inequalities are rooted in complex historical and cultural milieus (Downey, Dubois, Hawkins and Walker 2008; Pellow 2000). Historical legacies related to structured inequalities of race and class are linked to increased community vulnerability and likelihood for exposure to environmental risks (Mohai, Pellow and Roberts 2009). One dimension of community vulnerability is interconnected with limited physical and financial access to resources, including basic necessities such as food. Amid growing concern over racial inequality and low access to healthy food, a network of activists and scholars has coalesced in the pursuit and understanding of "food justice." Broadly situated in environmental justice narratives (Bryant 1995; Mohai et al. 2009; Pellow 2000), food justice scholarship places "access to healthy, affordable, and culturally appropriate food in the contexts of institutional racism, racial formation, and racialized geographies," thus taking into account the racial disparities in food access across the United States (Alkon and Norgaard 2009, 289). Food justice scholarship also borrows from environmental justice work by attending to the ways that food insecurity is rooted in a community's context, and the primacy of local factors in considering how inequality manifests and, ultimately, can be ameliorated.

That existing inequalities are related to historical injustices and may act as barriers to sustainable development and community resilience begs the question of what types of solutions-based actions may be taken to actively reduce the impact of potential environmental harms in areas prone to vulnerability (Brklacich, Chazan and Bohle 2010; Caniglia, Frank, Delano and Kerner 2014). In this chapter, we use the North Tulsa community as a case study to examine how historical conditions influence contemporary food inequalities, and thus contribute to potential food injustices-in-waiting. Drawing on interviews with 26 stakeholders and community leaders involved with developing a mobile grocer to service the North Tulsa area, we address how resilience is mediated by local context and historical legacies of institutional racism, reflecting on the impact that contemporary solutions-based food justice approaches may have in assisting with community response to unanticipated environmental harms. After considering how processes of racial segregation and discrimination have not only caused food insecurity, but limited sustainability, resilience, and opened opportunities for food injustices-in-waiting, we suggest steps that can be taken to prepare for and prevent future risks, and consider how any potential food justice projects must account for North Tulsa's unique historical context. In so doing, we contribute to sociological scholarship on environmental inequality, food justice, and solutions-based approaches useful in facilitating community resilience and proactive responses to environmental harms.

Environmental inequality, food justice, and community implications

Pellow and Nyseth Brehm clearly articulate that environmental inequality "is first and foremost a social problem, driven and legitimated by social structures and discourses" (2013, 235). Empirical evidence consistently finds that environmental hazards are situated in and disproportionately impact poor and racial minority communities (Bullard 1993; Mohai et al. 2009). Rooted in structured inequalities perpetuated by racial residential segregation and racial income inequality, environmental inequality is "highly contingent on local conditions that, in turn, are likely to be the product of historical forces that vary from one metropolitan area to another" (Downey et al. 2008, 273).

The food justice movement has emerged as one of many responses to environmental inequality. Food justice highlights the connections between inequality and various segments of the food system, including racial disparities in access to healthy food (Alkon and Agyeman 2011; Gottlieb and Joshi 2010). Examinations of food access demonstrate, for example, how minority communities have been negatively impacted by processes of deindustrialization and urban renewal that have suburbanized retail grocery markets, making impacted communities into areas of low food access (Morland, Wing, Roux and Poole 2002). Dynamics related to inequality have created food deserts, or low-income areas where residents have limited or no access to a supermarket offering affordable, fresh food, particularly produce (Coleman-Jensen, Gregory and Singh 2014; Guy and David 2004; Schafft, Jenses and Hinrichs 2009; USDA 2009). Residents of food deserts frequently suffer from food insecurity, whereby individuals experience "limited or uncertain availability of nutritionally adequate and safe foods or limited or uncertain ability to acquire acceptable foods in socially acceptable ways" (Anderson 1990, 120).

The racial disparities in food insecurity rates within food deserts are stark and well-documented. African American neighborhoods have on average between two and four times fewer supermarkets than white neighborhoods and up to six times as many fast food restaurants (Donley and Alwitt 1997; Powell, Slater, Mirtcheva, Bao and Chaloupka 2007). Moreover, supermarkets in white neighborhoods serve on average 3,800 residents per store, whereas in predominantly African American neighborhoods a supermarket can serve up to 23,000 residents (Morland et al. 2002). Even within food deserts, African Americans are at a greater disadvantage than whites, residing on average 1.1 miles farther from the nearest grocery store and having access to stores with less-desirable produce offerings than in stores closer to predominantly white neighborhoods (Zenk et al. 2005). Having a local supermarket is not just a matter of convenience, but has real effects on dietary patterns. Studies find that a supermarket's presence in a neighborhood led to a 32% increase in fresh fruit and vegetable consumption among African Americans and an 11% increase among whites (Morland et al. 2002).

Unless the existing food system is examined as a series of "racial projects," food insecurity will continue to disproportionately affect people of color (Alkon and Agyeman 2011; Omi and Winant 1994). Many programs, such as the Federal Supplemental Nutrition Assistance Program (SNAP), Women, Infants, and Children (WIC) programs, and private charity food services, aim to reduce food insecurity by providing residents with food or the means to procure food. Yet food justice initiatives move beyond addressing food insecurity by attending to the underlying racial causes of low food access and malnutrition. In this way food justice activists, similar to environmental and social justice activists, seek to create initiatives that increase the capacity of neighborhoods and communities to ameliorate (racial) inequality and then, by extension, food inequality.

Communities that experience food insecurity are left in a unique position of vulnerability, whereby structured inequalities lead to an inability to meet basic needs (Alkon et al. 2013; Emery and Flora 2006). Sustainable community development (SCD) projects, employing democratic processes to reorganize social, economic, and environmental relationships, have made inroads into addressing food inequity, but are limited in their ability to challenge existing power structures and plan for uncertainty (Agyeman and Evans 2004; Connelly, Markey and Roseland 2011; Pearsall and Pierce 2010; Roseland and Connelly 2005). Projects to promote resilience, or the ability of a community to recover and adapt to social and environmental harms, including human-induced risks or natural hazards, have transitioned from primarily ecological perspectives to include social dimensions of analysis (Adger 2000; Caniglia et al. 2014; Davidson 2010; Kasperson, Kasperson and Berberian 2005). Community resilience approaches offer an additional perspective from which to consider how projects can work to reduce community vulnerability by addressing food insecurity and planning for injustices-in-waiting. Community engagement, advanced planning, and organizational connections are preliminary steps toward reducing vulnerability. Additionally, investing in diverse community resources and enhancing social capital are central to understanding community-level vulnerabilities and limiting the impact of potential future risk events (Cutter, Boruff and Shirley 2003; Green, Gill and Kleiner 2006; Norris, Stevens, Pfefferbaum, Wyche and Pfefferbaum 2008; Ritchie and Gill 2007).

Contemporary North Tulsa: contextualizing racial inequality and food insecurity

State and local contexts are central to understanding the landscape and magnitude of food inequality. In Oklahoma, African Americans are more likely to live at or below poverty level (29%), while Latinos are somewhat less likely (21%), and whites match national rates (10%). One in four Oklahoman children suffers daily food insecurity and over 15% (600,000) of state residents receive food benefits in the form of either the SNAP or WIC programs (Elsheikh and Barsouth 2013). Of those who benefit from these programs, almost 60% are children and another 23% earn an income that places them far below the poverty level (Carter 2015; Sherman and Trisi 2015). Within Tulsa County, the heart of the Tulsa metropolitan area, 17% of residents are food insecure, 23% of which are children, and an additional 30% of residents are obese (Willingham and Jaworski 2013). Furthermore, food security is not distributed evenly across the city, but instead clusters in poorer areas of the city, and particularly in the North Tulsa area. North Tulsa is home to the city's largest food desert and some of the highest rates of poverty and low access to personal transportation (see Map 5.1). North Tulsa is predominantly populated by African Americans, housing more than two-fifths of the African American population of Tulsa County (43%) and nearly one-fifth of the county's Latinos (19%).

In this chapter, we make clear connections between historical dynamics of racial inequality and contemporary manifestations of vulnerability and resilience related to food insecurity using the case of North Tulsa. Designed as a simplified grocery store housed in a towable trailer, the mobile grocer was created to provide a variety of products, including staple items such as milk, bread, and eggs as well as affordable fresh fruits and vegetables, and accept both SNAP and WIC benefits. The emergence of the mobile grocer as a food access and distribution system offers an opportunity through which to examine how alternative food projects can work towards greater community sustainability, resilience, and justice and an occasion to consider solutions-based approaches to food injustices-in-waiting.

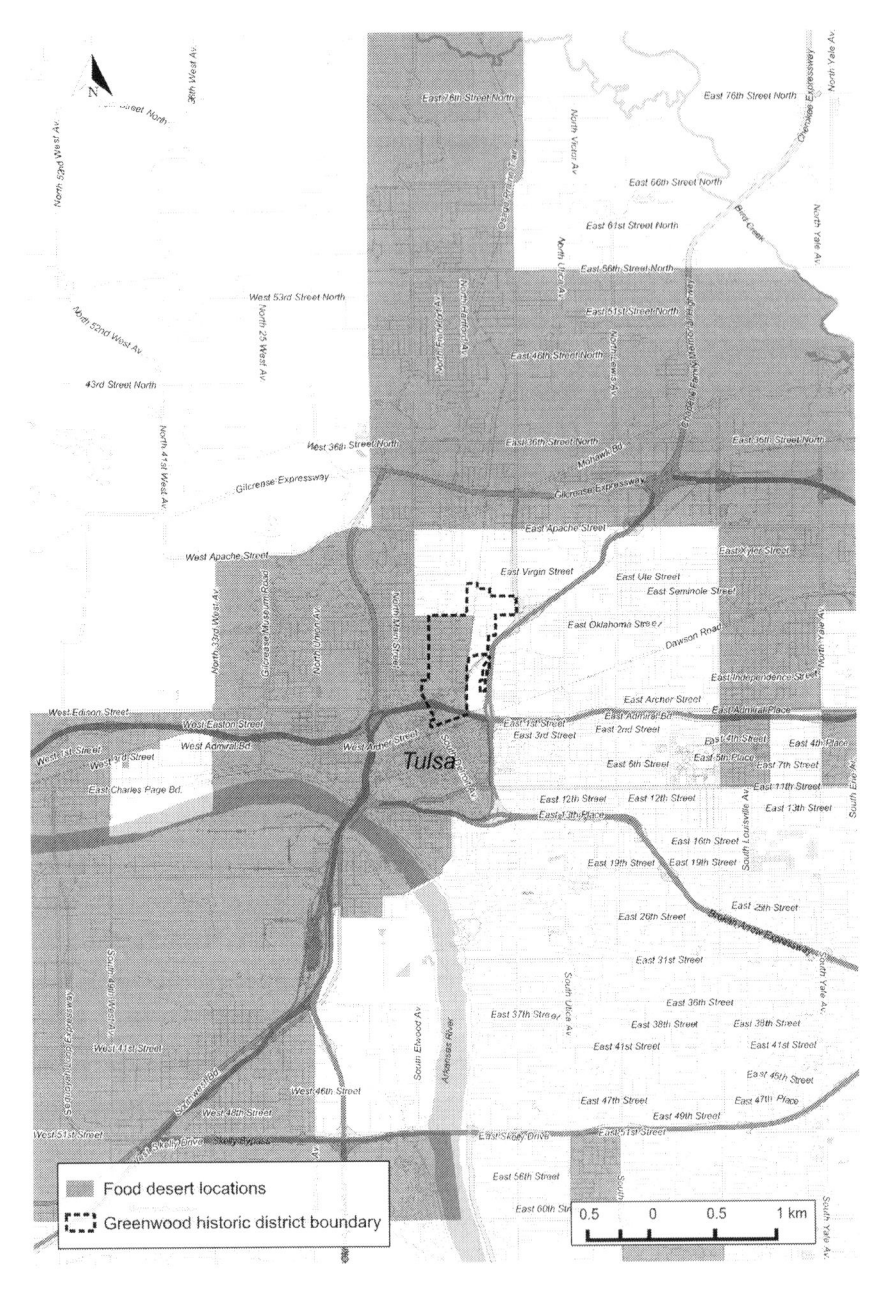

Map 5.1 Location of Greenwood Historic District within Tulsa's contemporary food desert

Cartographic work by Matthew Haffner

Research design

Using a constructivist grounded theory approach (Charmaz 2006), we employed qualitative semi-structured telephone and face-to-face interviews for data collection. A combination of purposive and snowball sampling (Hesse-Biber and Leavy 2011) was used to select participants from a list of key community leaders and stakeholders involved with food security efforts in the region and initial planning for the mobile grocer.

Qualitative interviews were conducted over a one-month period and were thirty minutes to an hour and a half in duration. Discussions with respondents allowed for the assessment of procedural preferences for the grocer including routes and ideal stock. We also considered the broader food environment of the North Tulsa community, especially taking into account deeper issues of racial discrimination. As such, interviewers addressed topics ranging from existing efforts toward food security in Tulsa, to the ways in which a mobile grocer might operate, and who might be best served. Notes and interview transcripts make up the data for this piece, representing our conversations with 26 interview respondents.

The leaders and stakeholders we interviewed were affiliated with organizations as varied as community gardens, churches, food banks, farms, Tribal Nations, and health services. Of our 26 interviewees, 16 (62%) indicated that their organizations served the North Tulsa community specifically; the remaining 38% of respondents operated organizations citywide, or in areas adjacent to North Tulsa. Of the 26 interviewees, 16 were women (62%). Racially, 17 identified as white (65%), 2 as African American (7%), 3 as American Indian (11%), 2 as African American and American Indian (7%) and 2 as some "other" race (7%). A majority of the respondents (61%) were between the ages of 55 and 64.

All data were organized and analyzed according to procedures broadly outlined by Charmaz (2006). Initial thematic coding was implemented to identify preliminary themes, including: barriers to food security in North Tulsa, community demographics, challenges for a mobile grocer, potential routes and service areas for the mobile grocer, and concerns for cultural sensitivity. After initial thematic coding, notes and interview transcripts were coded line-by-line and central themes and corresponding thematic categories were developed. Individual code sheets were created and corresponding text and quotations from the coded interview transcripts were compiled and aggregated for final analysis.

In the following sections, we illustrate how this varied group of respondents describe the components of food insecurity and present their interpretations of the role racial discrimination plays in creating and furthering food insecurity in the North Tulsa area. We conclude by considering how the legacies of past racial discrimination contribute to food injustices-in-waiting, and how we might begin to address these inequities in order to move towards a more food secure North Tulsa.

The surface-level components of community food insecurity: poor access to fresh and healthy food, knowledge gaps, and limited transportation

Anderson's (1990) definition provided earlier in this chapter illustrates how food insecurity can manifest in multiple ways depending on local context. What specific types of food are unavailable, what methods of procurement are socially unacceptable, and what physical and social barriers prevent accessibility for different demographic groups can all vary across time, space, and population. Our interviewees consistently identify three surface-level components of food insecurity: lack of access to healthy and affordable fresh food, food-related knowledge gaps, and insufficient transportation. While individually not unique to the North Tulsa community, together the surface-level components reflect the distinctive dynamics of food insecurity in the area.

Lack of access to healthy and affordable fresh food

The first component of food insecurity our interviewees identify is overall low access to healthy and affordable fresh food throughout North Tulsa. Respondents specify that there is a general "lack of grocery stores that carry fresh, healthy food in the area." Produce is a main concern of stakeholders. One stakeholder explains that "fruits and veggies are most needed [in North Tulsa] and hardest for low-income people to have access to," while another agrees that "selection is very limited and what is available costs far more than [other stores outside the community]." Lastly, interviewees contend that the overall higher prices of food in North Tulsa doubly impacts lower-income residents, not only by stretching their already limited budgets further, but because "many places do not accept SNAP." This means that the poorest residents must choose between either paying out of pocket for food with their already limited financial means or traveling longer distances to stores that will accept food assistance.

Food-related knowledge gaps: nutrition, cooking, and shopping

The second component of food insecurity within the North Tulsa community consists of three significant food-related knowledge gaps regarding: healthy eating habits and nutrition; how to properly cook healthy food; and how to shop for healthy food on a budget. While each represents a different dimension of food-related knowledge gaps, interviewees' responses demonstrate how these knowledge gaps frequently overlap and coincide.

Respondents suggest that many community residents are unfamiliar with nutritional guidelines and what foods are healthy to eat. One interviewee claims that any educational programs directed at the community would need to start with "general things like what is good and bad for [residents to eat] and serving sizes." This is particularly crucial in order to address some of the high rates of diet-related illness in North Tulsa. Respondents generally acknowledge that "diabetes is an issue in the community" and that "we have a lot of people with obesity and diabetes" throughout the area.

Limits to nutritional knowledge in the community are compounded by other food-related knowledge gaps relating to cooking abilities. One respondent bluntly asserts that throughout North Tulsa there is "a lack of knowledge about what is 'good food' and how to cook it," and that "most everyone understands how to fry food. We can cook soul food. We understand fat and grease." Another suggests that poverty further confounds food preparation, saying that "a lot of families get utilities cut off and can't cook . . . and lots don't know how to cook or they don't have pots, pans, tables, chairs." Even when residents have regular access to household utilities and cooking utensils, respondents suggest a lack of cooking knowledge remains an issue for many. One explains how at a local charity site "fresh produce . . . would go to waste because people would not buy it . . . because people don't know how to prepare produce." A local community garden proponent echoes these sentiments, stating that despite having improved access to community garden plots where residents could grow some of their own fresh produce, there seems to be a sustained disconnect between accessing and actually consuming healthy produce, saying "growing produce is great, but you can't just hand zucchini to people and have them eat it. You have to teach preparation; otherwise people will keep it on the counter and just look at it until it becomes flat."

Third, interviewees suggest that in addition to food-related knowledge gaps in nutrition and cooking, some residents also do not know how to effectively shop for healthy food on limited budgets, and that this gap further aggravates food insecurity in North Tulsa. One respondent draws connections between the three central food-related knowledge gaps, explaining:

> People don't buy healthy food because they don't know how to fix healthy food. You need to address how to grocery shop. How do you buy a week's worth of groceries with $20? How do you cook nutritionally? How do you avoid salt and oils? Exactly how do you grocery shop? People don't know how to cook. People don't know how to make food last on a small amount of money.

Another interviewee attributes residents' difficulties in shopping to a combination of low access, poverty, and loss of basic household skills, stating that "even though people were receiving [SNAP and WIC] benefits to buy food, they didn't use the benefits effectively. Those who received the benefits were young women, but these girls didn't know how to buy food and prepare it effectively." They suggest that challenges to budgeting are related to the structure of food benefit programs. As one respondent explains, "it's hard to budget food stamps for a month. I get paid once a month and it's hard for me. Being able to plan and save back to replenish is difficult. They tend to buy cheaper food so they can buy more."

Lastly, respondents suggest that the above-mentioned knowledge gaps are not recent phenomena, but rather have been slowly building over time as economic and social conditions in the community have worsened. One respondent claims that "in the last three generations, low-income people have lost the chance to know how to cook, manage a food budget, how to make healthy choices. All of this is now a 'lost art'," and now that there is a gap in the transfer of knowledge and skills from older to younger generations, the task of addressing food-related knowledge gaps becomes a larger issue for outside agencies to address.

Limited transportation and urban sprawl

Third and finally, interviewees identify limited access to transportation as a significant component of food insecurity in North Tulsa. Interviewees share that "this is a walking community," in part because "families don't own a car or only have one car that is shared so they may not be able to go to the store." Respondents suggest that residents who lack access to personal transportation rely on walking because the public transportation infrastructure is inadequate. They believe that in general the local "bus system is poor" and that "the city has no drive to serve our area" by improving public transportation schedules or routes to service the community.

Transportation access issues are compounded by the unique local context of the Tulsa built environment, which is characterized by urban and suburban sprawl. Interviewees assert that the "lack of [public] transportation is due to poor public infrastructure [and because] the population is spread out over a larger geographic area." Others explain that when people can access the bus system, they may not be able to use it very well to obtain groceries because groceries are bulky items to carry onto and off the bus, especially when residents are faced with multiple transfers or long rides with children in tow. One interviewee explains her realization of this potential difficulty for residents by recounting an instance when she was watching a mother struggling to juggle three small children while carrying grocery bags and gallons of milk onto the bus, and then suddenly understanding why a family might choose instead to pay two or three times as much for milk at the corner gas station within walking distance in order to avoid the hassle and the embarrassment of grocery shopping via public transit.

Stakeholders consistently identify poor access to affordable fresh and healthy food, food-related knowledge gaps, and limited transportation as surface-level components of food insecurity in North Tulsa. However, interviewees frequently cite racial tensions and discrimination as underlying drivers of these surface-level components. In particular, interviewees connect contemporary racial inequalities in the Tulsa-area food system to racially-motivated events in Oklahoma's past. In the following section, we present several interpretations by interviewees of how past racial injustices contribute to the North Tulsa area's contemporary food insecurity. We then conclude by considering how these past injustices contribute to food injustices-in-waiting, and what steps might help ameliorate potential food injustices and lead to greater community resilience.

Past, present, and future: racial legacies, vulnerability, and barriers to resilience

Our interviewees assert that food insecurity and race are intricately intertwined throughout North Tulsa. Some of these connections are more visible than others. One respondent demonstrates the racial disparities in the impacts of food insecurity that she witnesses regularly by recounting an experience she had in a nearby hospital:

> So in the dialysis unit, I noted that there were nothing but people of color in there. And that was shocking to me. And I remember asking the doctors and the nurses, "Why are there no white people in here? What's going on?" They said, "Well a lot of the people that are here, it's mostly the food that— you know, it's diet related." And it was Native American, Latino or African American people there [. . .] and it just didn't sit well with me.

Some respondents identify deeper connections between overt racial disparities in food insecurity in North Tulsa and the area's less addressed legacy of racial injustice stemming from the 1921 race riots. The economic decimation of the North Tulsa community following the events of 1921 resulted in decades of continued racial segregation and discriminatory lending practices, making North Tulsa into an area of concentrated racial segregation and poverty. Aspects of Tulsa's racial residential segregation were not formally addressed until the late 1960s, when Tulsa endured school desegregation lawsuits to close legal loopholes that allowed white families to skirt desegregation mandates (Fleming, Horn, Freeman, Ruiz and Saltzman 1977). During this period, the area was further blighted by a series of urban renewal projects that sited the growing interstate system through several North Tulsa neighborhoods. Today, charges of steering, blockbusting, and "reverse redlining" remain, as reports reveal that North Tulsa neighborhoods were primarily targeted by banks for subprime loans over the past decade, and that African Americans throughout Tulsa are experiencing higher foreclosure and loan denial rates than their white counterparts (Gobar 2011). In these ways, past and present racial issues are contributing factors making the area economically unappealing to grocery stores, creating a retail vacuum filled by fast food restaurants and corner convenience and liquor stores, and thus worsening the area's food insecurity.

Accordingly, our interviewees charge that even 90 years after the riots, 40 years after the desegregation lawsuits, and 8 years after the housing bubble burst, racial discrimination related to racial segregation still contributes to food insecurity in the area. Respondents suggest that part of the riot's lasting legacy of racial injustice is a continued stigma surrounding the community. Interviewees assert that today "North Tulsa has many negative perceptions as a forgotten part of Tulsa with unsafe neighborhoods." Others lament that "the community is forgotten" and that "there is a stigma associated with the areas where the . . . mobile grocer should go." When probed further, interviewees explain that the general "stigma" is a perception of the community as a high-crime area plagued by drugs and gang violence. One community member notes "discrimination is a factor [in North Tulsa's food insecurity] because some grocery store owners are unwilling to locate a grocery store in areas where they perceive higher crime; there's just a stigma here [in North Tulsa]." Another respondent suggests that grocery stores are hesitant to locate in the North Tulsa community because of the racial associations with public housing, stating that "yes, there is discrimination. The stores fear not making money and concerns over greater security needs, because there are two government housing communities within a four-mile radius." Respondents' general charges that negative perceptions of the community are rooted in racialized conceptions of African Americans and racial violence are partially validated by Tulsa's crime rates. Tulsa metro crime reports indicate that North Tulsa has had some of the lowest violent and nonviolent crime rates in the city since 2008— lower than the whiter and wealthier areas in East and Southwest Tulsa (Fullbright 2015). Interviewees suggest that the racial connotations of the community as crime-ridden stem in part from the area's association with the 1921 race riots and the poverty that has followed. Accordingly, they assert that "the residual effects [of the riots] need to be acknowledged" and that "the history of institutional discrimination in the area needs to be addressed first" before any true progress can be made toward alleviating the community's food insecurity.

Stakeholders also feel that in order to address North Tulsa's food security needs, the broader systems that control the community's infrastructure and food environment need to be challenged and reformed. Once again, interviewees argue that this hinges on dealing with the community's tumultuous racial history and present-day systems of institutional racism and discrimination. One local community organizer describes what she identifies as institutional racism and how it hampers her efforts to obtain support for local community initiatives. She portrays several local funding organizations and governmental institutions as heavily enmeshed in an "old boys' club," one that generally derides individuals or groups promoting issues related to race. She gives an example of how she must cope with this barrier when seeking resources for her organization's food security work, saying:

> Most everything in Oklahoma is really white run and it's from a white perspective. And then they say "you can do it, anybody can do it [obtain program funding]." Well, it's not the same [for people of color]. Some of the things I've had to do [as a community organizer], I've always had to have a white counterpart when I needed something done . . . to let them speak, you know. Some places I don't think I would have even had people talking to me if I hadn't of had him [my white counterpart] there to speak. So I'm thankful for him, but I know too that that was only one of the ways that I even got through a door. So, I guess that's just part of the stuff that's on the shelf that we just got to deal with.

Charges of institutional discrimination are difficult to prove. Nevertheless, that our interviewees interpret certain events through a racial lens highlights the salience of Tulsa's past racial injustices to those from and involved with the North

Tulsa community. It also indicates that community members are making direct connections to past racial events and current racial disparities in food security, and that addressing the community's legacy of racial injustices is an important step toward empowering community residents, whether or not acts of discrimination are actually informed by the legacies of the riots or ensuing poverty.

Discussion and conclusion: racial legacies, food insecurity, and food injustices-in-waiting

Our interviewees articulate several distinct components of food insecurity in North Tulsa and how they think durable racial legacies tied to the 1921 riots have caused and exacerbated food insecurity in the community. Racial segregation, institutional discrimination, and prejudicial associations with the community and its residents have made North Tulsa into an area of concentrated poverty, vulnerable not only to food insecurity, but other potential future hazards as well. If North Tulsa already struggles with food insecurity, what can we expect if the area is impacted by other socio-environmental stressors, such as a natural or man-made environmental disaster? That is, how have processes of racial segregation and discrimination not only caused food insecurity, but created food injustices-in-waiting? How can the mobile grocer be designed to service the North Tulsa community and help residents prepare for or prevent such injustices?

Respondents assert the necessity for the mobile grocer to incorporate elements of food justice activism and work beyond distributing food, to focus on efforts to strengthen the broader community. One respondent explains that "getting people food doesn't solve hunger issues. Providing food does not translate immediately into healthier lives." Another invokes food justice by name, stating that the mobile grocer must be "about more than just food security but about community and food justice . . . It needs to be more than just about food and access, especially for a community that lacks a lot of resources . . . [it needs to be about] empowerment to achieve goals, for people to be healthy."

North Tulsa is not the only community facing vulnerability, food insecurity, and food injustice-in-waiting. For instance, several historically African American New Orleans neighborhoods experience similar issues with concentrated poverty, food insecurity, and negative perceptions informed by race. During and immediately after Hurricane Katrina, these areas were not serviced as quickly as less-disadvantaged parts of the city—what some attribute to racial discrimination (Bullard and Wright 2009). In the years following Katrina, impacted neighborhoods saw sluggish rebuilding rates and much slower return rates of African American residents than less-disadvantaged areas of the city (Fussell, Sastry and VanLandingham 2010). Part of the issue is that homes in historically disadvantaged and segregated areas are appraised at low rates—a result of negative impacts of segregation and poverty. As a result, residents are given less for their homes than others because of the consequences of racial segregation beyond their control (Bates and Green 2009). Non-homeowners are also disadvantaged because of rising rental rates, in part because housing units are fewer and demand makes them more expensive. Relatedly, businesses are slow to return, meaning that there are even fewer grocery stores servicing lower-income neighborhoods than before, and larger chains are less inclined to rebuild in these areas (Bullard and Wright 2009). Residents in racially segregated areas perceive risk less seriously, and when they are impacted by events such as Katrina, are more likely to rely on faith and hope than services and social networks, in part because the areas in which they live and have lived are characterized by lower levels of social capital (Lachlan, Burke, Spence and Griffin 2009). Finally, the breadth of food-based projects, many argue, boosts local food security—home and community gardens, local farms, farmers' markets selling local seasonal produce—yet all are at risk because of natural disasters. For instance, in New Orleans much of the soil is contaminated, making it difficult and dangerous for residents to garden.

North Tulsa's experiences have created the potential for similar food injustices-in-waiting. The North Tulsa area is already negatively perceived by Tulsa residents and retailers alike, which may explain why grocery stores and other retail outlets are hesitant to locate there. Proponents of local food, and some interviewees represented in our sample, highly value local food production, and suggest that food security projects such as the mobile grocer should not only strive to sell local ingredients, but should offer plants and seeds to further encourage residents to take charge of their own food security by growing home and community gardens. While local and home-based strategies are a path to food independence, in the face of natural and technological disasters, including severe weather leading to droughts, fires, floods, and tornados, as well as earthquakes and water contamination, local food initiatives could be devastated even in the most resilient of communities. Because North Tulsa is perceived negatively, it is reasonable to assume that response and rebuilding efforts may be similar to those witnessed following Katrina—that is, North Tulsa may be given less attention by emergency response efforts and receive less remuneration following a disaster because the area has been artificially depressed because of decades of racial segregation and the cultivation of poverty. In short, legacies of racial injustice have not only contributed to contemporary food insecurity, but may also contribute to future food injustices that would be exacerbated by potential disasters.

We note that the creation of a mobile grocer is a good first step in moving toward a more resilient North Tulsa. We suggest two potential solutions to prepare for food injustices-in-waiting. First, the mobile grocer is designed for the North Tulsa community. Its specific context and components to reduce food insecurity are a strength of the project, serving to further enhance the community's resilience in case of a disaster. For instance, where other agencies and projects may overlook North Tulsa because of negative perceptions as a dangerous or economically risky locale, the mobile grocer may be poised to provide swift and steady services to the area. Second, while planners' suggestions that the mobile grocer both rely on and encourage the development of local and hyperlocal food systems and projects are laudable, in relation to potential disasters, a local sourcing focus may further exacerbate existing injustices in the area by setting the community up for a reversal of resilience by losing self-sufficiency when hyper-local projects are impacted by disasters. If the mobile grocer encourages the creation of regional foodsheds drawing upon diverse resources, not only would North Tulsa be better protected from disaster-induced food insecurity, but other areas could potentially benefit by sourcing food from them and strengthening regional economies.

Tulsa's history of racial violence and institutional discrimination has left areas of the urban region without appropriate resources to be self-sufficient and food secure. Long-term community sustainability and resilience rests on community participation and deeper economic revitalization. Balancing a community's short-term needs with long-term goals is challenging, especially when the community in question carries with it a history of marginalization and racialized discrimination. Based on stakeholder narratives, we argue that without addressing historical legacies of racial discrimination, North Tulsa and communities like it will remain vulnerable. As a result, the ability to foster community sustainability and resilience, and to effectively address injustices-in-waiting, will remain elusive.

Acknowledgements

Special thanks to our respondents for their candor and commitment to food justice work in Tulsa, Oklahoma, and to Nancy Betts, Regents Professor and Head of OSU Nutritional Sciences for her research support.

Notes

1 Oklahoma State University, Department of Sociology, tamara.mix@okstate.edu
2 Purdue University, Department of Sociology.
3 Oklahoma State University, School of Applied Health and Educational Psychology.

References

Adger W.N. (2000) Social and ecological resilience: Are they related? *Progress in Human Geography*, 24, 347–364.
Agyeman J. and Evans B. (2004) "Just sustainability": The emerging discourse of environmental justice in Britain? *Geographical Journal*, 170, 155–164.
Alkon A.H. and Agyeman, J. (2011) *Cultivating food justice: race, class, and sustainability*. Cambridge, MA: MIT Press.
Alkon A.H., Block D., Moore K., Gillis C., DiNuccio N. and Chavez N. (2013) Foodways of the urban poor. *Geoforum*, 48, 126–135.
Alkon A.H. and Norgaard K.M. (2009) Breaking the food chains: an investigation of food justice activism. *Sociological Inquiry*, 79, 289–305.
Anderson S.A. (1990). Core indicators of nutritional state for difficult-to-sample populations. *Journal of Nutrition*, 120.
Bates L.K. and Green R.A. (2009). Housing recovery in the Ninth Ward: disparities in policy, process, and prospects. In R.D. Bullard and B. Wright (Eds.) *Race, place, and environmental justice after Hurricane Katrina: struggles to reclaim, rebuild, and revitalize New Orleans and the Gulf Coast*. Boulder, CO: Westview Press.

Brklacich M., Chazan M. and Bohle H.G. (2010). Human security, vulnerability, and global environmental change. In A.M. Richard, J. Barnett, B. McDonald and K.L. O'Brien (Eds.) *Global environmental change and human security* (pp. 35–51). Cambridge, MA: MIT Press.

Bryant B. (1995). *Environmental justice: issues, policies and solutions.* Washington, DC: Island Press.

Bullard R.D. (1993). *Confronting environmental racism: voices from the grassroots.* New York: South End Press.

Bullard R.D. and Wright B. (2009). *Race, place, and the environment in post-Katrina New Orleans: struggles to reclaim, rebuild, and revitalize New Orleans and the Gulf Coast.* Boulder, CO: Westview Press.

Caniglia B.S., Frank B., Delano D. and Kerner B. (2014). Enhancing environmental justice research and praxis: the inclusion of human security, resilience and vulnerabilities literature. *International Journal of Innovation and Sustainable Development,* 8, 409–426.

Carter S. (2015). Food stamps and the working poor. Retrieved 20 July 2015 from http://www.tulsaworld.com/opinion/readersforum/scott-carter-food-stamps-and-the-working-poor/article_824485de-797f-5094-a3cf-c4eeae3aedde.html

Charmaz K. (2006). *Constructing grounded theory.* Thousand Oaks, CA: Sage Publications.

Coleman-Jensen A., Gregory C. and Singh A. (2014). *Household food security in the United States in 2013.* Washington, DC: U.S. Department of Agriculture Economic Research Service.

Community Service Council (2011). Population trends: Tulsa County, Tulsa and North Tulsa, 2000 to 2010. Retrieved 15 May 2014 from http://www.csctulsa.org/files/file/pop%20trends%202000%20to%202010%20tulsa%20co%20and%20north%20tulsa%20rev%207-13-11.pptx

Connelly S., Markey S. and Roseland M. (2011). Bridging sustainability and the social economy: achieving community transformation through local food initiatives. *Critical Social Policy,* 31, 308–324.

Cutter S., Boruff B. and Shirley W.L. (2003). Social vulnerability to environmental hazards. *Social Science Quarterly,* 84, 242–261.

Davidson D.J. (2010). The applicability of the concept of resilience to social systems: some sources of optimism and nagging doubts. *Society & Natural Resources,* 23, 1135–1149.

Donley T. and Alwitt L. (1997). Retail stores in poor urban neighborhoods. Retrieved 13 October 2013 from http://via.library.depaul.edu/econ_pubs/1

Downey L., Dubois S., Hawkins B. and Walker M. (2008). Environmental inequality in metropolitan America. *Organization and Environment,* 21, 270–294.

Ellsworth S. (1982). *Death in a promised land: the Tulsa race riot of 1921.* Baton Rouge: Louisiana State University Press.

Elsheikh E. and Barsouth N. (2013). *Structural racialization and food insecurity in the United States.* Berkeley, CA: Haas Institute for a Fair and Inclusive Society, University of California. Retrieved 9 September 2015 from http://diversity.berkeley.edu/sites/default/files/Structural%20Racialization%20%20%26%20Food%20Insecurity%20in%20the%20US-(Final).pdf

Emery M. and Flora C. (2006). Spiraling-up: mapping community transformation with community capitals framework. *Community Development,* 37, 19–35.

Fleming A.S., Horn S., Freeman F.M., Ruiz M. Jr. and Saltzman F.M. (1977). *School desegregation in Tulsa OK.* Oklahoma Advisory Committee to the United States Commission on Civil Rights. Retrieved 11 January 2016 from https://www.law.umaryland.edu/marshall/usccr/documents/cr12d4522.pdf

Fullbright L. (2015). Numbers show North Tulsa crime is lowest in the city. Retrieved 5 January 2016 from http://www.newson6.com/story/29601041/numbers-show-north-tulsa-crime-is-lowest-in-the-city

Fussell E., Sastry N. and VanLandingham M. (2010). Race, socioeconomic status, and return migration to New Orleans after Hurricane Katrina. *Population and Environment*, 31, 20–42.

Gobar A.M. (2011). *Oklahoma mortgage lending patterns: an analysis of patterns of subprime lending and homeownership and foreclosures among people of color in Tulsa and Oklahoma City MSAs*. Oklahoma Asset Building Partnership and Practice (OABPP) Initiative. Retrieved 5 January 2016 from http://okpolicy.org/wp-content/uploads/2012/08/CRW-Oklahoma-Study-2011-Angela-Gobar.pdf

Gottlieb R. and Joshi A. (2010). *Food justice*. Cambridge, MA: MIT Press.

Green J.J., Gill D.A. and Kleiner A.M. (2006). From vulnerability to resiliency: assessing impacts and responses to disaster. *Southern Rural Sociology*, 21, 89–99.

Guy C.M. and David G. (2004). Measuring physical access to 'healthy foods' in areas of social deprivation: a case study in Cardiff. *International Journal of Consumer Studies*, 28, 222–234.

Halliburton R. Jr. (1972). The Tulsa race war of 1921. *Journal of Black Studies*, 2, 333–357.

Hesse-Biber S.N. and Leavy P. (2011). *The practice of qualitative research*. Los Angeles: Sage Publications.

Johnson H. (2007). *Black Wall Street: from riot to renaissance in Tulsa's historic Greenwood District*. Woodway, TX: Eakin Press.

Kasperson J.X., Kasperson R.E. and Berberian M. (2005). *The social contours of risk* (Vol. 1). London: Earthscan.

Lachlan K.A., Burke J., Spence P.R. and Griffin D. (2009). Risk perceptions, race, and Hurricane Katrina. *Howard Journal of Communications*, 20, 295–309.

Messer C.M. (2011). The Tulsa race riot of 1921: toward an integrative theory of collective violence. *Journal of Social History*, 44, 1217–1232.

Messer C.M. and Bell P.A. (2010). Mass media and governmental framing of riots: the case of Tulsa, 1921. *Journal of Black Studies*, 40, 851–870.

Mohai P., Pellow D. and Roberts J.T. (2009). Environmental justice. *Annual Review of Environmental and Resources*, 34, 405–430.

Morland K., Wing S., Roux A.D. and Poole C. (2002). Neighborhood characteristics associated with the location of food stores and food service places. *American Journal of Preventive Medicine*, 22, 23–29.

Norris F.H., Stevens S.P., Pfefferbaum B., Wyche K.F. and Pfefferbaum R.L. (2008). Community resilience as a metaphor, theory, set of capacities, and strategy for disaster readiness. *American Journal of Community Psychology*, 41, 127–150.

Oklahoma Commission to Study the Tulsa Race Riot of 1921. (2001). Tulsa race riot. Retrieved 5 January 2016 from http://www.okhistory.org/research/forms/freport.pdf

Omi M. and Winant H. (1994). *Racial formation in the United States: from the 1960s to the 1990s*. New York: Routledge.

Pearsall H. and Pierce J. (2010). Urban sustainability and environmental justice: evaluating the linkages in public planning/policy discourse. *Local Environment*, 15, 569–580.

Pellow D.N. (2000). Environmental inequality formation: toward a theory of environmental injustice. *American Behavioral Scientist*, 43, 581–601.

Pellow D.N. and Nyseth Brehm H. (2013). An environmental sociology for the twenty-first century. *Annual Review of Sociology*, 39, 229–250.

Powell L.M., Slater S., Mirtcheva D., Bao Y. and Chaloupka F.J. (2007). Food store availability and neighborhood characteristics in the United States. *Preventive Medicine*, 44, 189–195.

Ritchie L.A. and Gill D.A. (2007). Social capital theory as an integrating theoretical framework in technological disaster research. *Sociological Spectrum*, 27, 103–129.

Roseland M. and Connelly S. (2005). *Toward sustainable communities: resources for citizens and their governments*. Gabriola Island, BC: New Society Publishers.

Schafft K., Jenses E. and Hinrichs C. (2009). Food deserts and overweight schoolchildren: evidence from Pennsylvania. *Rural Sociology*, 74, 153–177.

Sherman A. and Trisi D. (2015). *Safety net more effective against poverty than previously thought: correcting for underreporting of benefits reveals stronger reductions in poverty and deep poverty in all states*. Center on Budget and Policy Priorities. Retrieved 6 September 2015 from http://www.cbpp.org/research/poverty-and-inequality/safety-net-more-effective-against-poverty-than-previously-thought

USDA (2009). Access to affordable and nutritious food. Administrative Publication No. AP-036. June. Retrieved 15 September 2013 from http://www.ers.usda.gov/publications/ap-administrative-publication/ap-036.aspx#.Un6RgPmkrp4

Willingham F. and Jaworski D. (2013). A measure of hunger. Retrieved 9 September 2015 from http://oklahomawatch.org/2013/06/30/data-driven-a-measure-of-hunger/

Zenk S.N., Schulz A.J., Israel B.A., James S.A., Bao S. and Wilson M.L. (2005). Neighborhood racial composition, neighborhood poverty, and the spatial accessibility of supergrocers in metropolitan Detroit. *American Journal of Public Health*, 95, 660–667.

6 Nurturing an acquiescence to toxicity
The state's naturework in urban aerial pesticide spraying campaigns

Manuel Vallée[1]

Introduction

Since World War II industry has dramatically increased synthetic chemical production and dissemination. This growing toxification has contaminated spaces we inhabit, food we eat, water we drink, and air we breathe. Consequently, this contamination has led to chemical "injustices-in-waiting" (Caniglia, Frank, Delano and Kerner 2014), where chemical trespass has led humans to bio-accumulate chemicals, thereby predisposing them for disease (Steingraber 2009). While Rachel Carson's landmark book *Silent Spring* (1965) was a catalyst for bringing attention to the proliferation of man-made chemicals and their environmental destructiveness, Woodhouse and Howard (2009) point out:

> despite the environmental movement's success in reducing some specific hazards, such as those from persistent pesticides, chemical toxicity generally reaches more deeply and more broadly into the fabric of daily life in our era than it ever did in Carson's.
>
> (35)

This toxification's cumulative impact has led Foster (1999) to write, "today few can doubt that the system has crossed critical thresholds of ecological sustainability, raising questions about the vulnerability of the entire planet" (108).

Chemical pesticides are particularly salient to societal toxification as they contaminate the air humans breathe and the food we eat, the contamination of which have both been linked to numerous medical conditions, including: (1) neurological problems, such as depression; (2) Parkinson's disease; (3) male fertility problems, such as lowered sperm counts; (4) female infertility; (5) birth defects; (6) endocrine disruption; (7) respiratory problems, such asthma; and (8) and cancers, including breast, prostate, and lung cancers (Bell 2004; CHE 2016a). As others have emphasized (Bell 2004; Harrison 2011), such pesticide-induced health risks are most often borne by the poor and people of color, who are the ones most often placed in harm's way. As well, pesticides contribute to biodiversity loss, soil erosion, and the pollution of freshwater sources, all of which further undermine the sustainability and resilience of human communities (Hallberg 1987; Reganold, Elliott and Unger 1987).

The growing toxification of the planet represents a significant threat to the long-term sustainability and resilience of human communities, which underscores the need to better understand the processes leading to it. Much research has focused on the roles of industry, capitalism (Faber 2008; Foster 1999), and the state, with a focus on lax regulatory frameworks and policies that subsidize polluting processes (Bührs 1993; Faber 2008; Harrison 2011). However, less has been said about the state's ideological work to perpetuate an acceptance of toxifying processes. To shed light on this issue I examine urban aerial pesticide spraying campaigns.

These campaigns consist of government-sponsored operations that aim to eradicate invasive species through the aerial spraying of pesticides over densely-populated urban areas. Examples include campaigns conducted in: Spokane, WA (1993); Auckland, New Zealand (1996–97); Victoria, British Columbia (1998); Auckland, New Zealand (2002–03); Hamilton, New Zealand (2004); and Toronto, Ontario (2013). These campaigns are disturbing because they repeatedly expose large numbers of humans to synthetic chemicals, thereby increasing the individual's chances of developing or exacerbating respiratory and/or other chronic health problems – what can be defined as chemical injustices-in-waiting. This is particularly true of children and the elderly, who are society's most vulnerable members (Solomon 2000). These issues are further mediated by class, as lower-income groups are less likely to know about such campaigns or know how to adequately protect themselves and their families. An additional concern is that such campaigns could occur more frequently in the future, because of temperature shifts associated with climate change, which could enable species to migrate and settle in new habitats.

From an analytical perspective, these campaigns provide a unique opportunity to understand the social construction of pesticide cultures. While most pesticide use occurs in sparsely-populated rural areas – where people typically lack the political, economic, and cultural capital to effectively resist (Harrison 2011) – urban aerial spraying campaigns are occurring in densely-populated ones. Given the numbers of people affected, one would expect a high level of resistance to these campaigns, particularly when we consider urban populations tend to be more educated and are more likely to have the necessary social and financial resources to effectively resist. However, apart from the resistance against California's Light Brown Apple Moth campaign (Spiegelman 2010), opposition to the campaigns have been minimalist and noneffective, which begs us to ask "why?"

To shed light on this question I analyze New Zealand's 2002–03 campaign to eradicate the Painted Apple Moth (*Teia anartoides*) (PAM) from the Auckland region. This campaign consisted of 48 sprayings undertaken over a 17-month period, covering, at its peak, 12,000 hectares of densely populated areas in Auckland, New Zealand's largest city (Smith 2007). This urban spraying campaign was unprecedented in scale, whether we consider the area covered, the number of sprayings undertaken, or the number of people exposed (193,000 residents) (Smith 2007). One would imagine that the sheer number of people exposed would have produced a substantial backlash, but it did not. This chapter focuses on showing how that potential was defused by government ideological work that framed PAM as a three-pronged biosecurity threat that needed to be eradicated.

Capitalism, toxicants, the state, and an acquiescence to toxicity

In *The Vulnerable Planet* (1999), John Bellamy Foster discusses how the rise of monopoly capitalism led to the "scientific-technical revolution," where industry co-opted science and deployed it towards the scientific management of humans and nature, as well as the production of synthetic chemicals, which increasingly displaced the products of nature. This "technological displacement of nature" (Foster 1999) can be seen in the displacement of organic fertilizers in favor of chemical ones, and in the increasing use of pesticides instead of natural forms of insect control. Importantly, pesticide use increased as industry became increasingly beholden to an industrial view of nature, which emphasized monocultures to maximize profitability, but whose corollaries were diminished species diversity, genetic diversity and ecosystem resilience, as well as a continuously growing reliance on pesticides.

The state has played an important role in these matters, as there has been a long history of governments enacting environmental violence on behalf of industry, even in "Clean and Green New Zealand" (Bührs 1993). This violence often manifests itself in the unequal distribution of "environmental bads" (Bell 2004), where toxicants and pollution are steered disproportionately to poor communities and communities of color (Bell 2004; Pellow 2009). Additionally, the violence is often enabled by weak to nonexistent regulatory enforcement, or policies that subsidize destructive practices (Bührs 1993; Faber 2008; Harrison 2011). Pellow (2009) argues that such violence can be attributed to the fact that far from being democratic and pluralist entities, governments largely exist to advance the interests of the rich over those of the poor. Moreover, Harvey (1996) suggests such inequities are advanced through utilitarianism's dominance in the state's environmental management practices. While utilitarianism is supposed to maximize welfare for the most people, Harvey (1996) emphasizes that such perspectives can be distorted to serve the interests of capital, arguing that under such perspectives the "only serious question is how best to manage the environment for capital accumulation, economic efficiency and growth" (Harvey 1996, 375). Relatedly, in her analysis of pesticide drift, Harrison (2011) concluded that a prioritization of economic interests handcuffs the state's ability to protect people, thereby encouraging the toxification of society:

> in a context that privileges economic growth, the state is generally only able to intervene where there is quantified, certain scientific evidence documenting links between an environmental hazard and sufficiently egregious harm.
>
> (16)

While others have stressed the role played by industry and governments (Faber 2008; Foster 1999; Harrison 2011), Woodhouse and Howard (2009) focus on the role of citizen complicity. They attribute growing toxification to citizens' acquiescence to toxicants, which they ascribe to three key governing mentalities: (1) the assumption that business executives should enjoy broad authority to decide what products will be made and marketed, how they will be made, and how chemicals will be formulated and manufactured; (2) the assumption that academic scientists and engineers should have nearly complete freedom to pursue research trajectories of their own choosing; and (3) the assumption that extensive toxicity is the price to pay for participating in an affluent consumer society. Moreover, they trace this acquiescence to the hegemony the ruling class established through a diffusion of their values, beliefs, attitudes, and social norms.

The focus on citizen complicity fills an important void in a literature that tends to focus on industry and government. Moreover, it seems to provide some explanatory power for the PAM aerial spraying campaign as the Auckland population displayed a surprising level of passivity vis-à-vis the proposed spraying campaign. In one survey, 67% of participants agreed with the statement "the eradication programme is inconvenient, but ultimately worth it to stop the environmental damage and health effects the moth could cause," with only 13% disagreeing with the statement (Smith 2007, 50). More telling is that when protests were held, they were sparsely attended. For example, a January 2002 protest outside the Ministry of Agriculture and Forestry (MAF) only yielded 50 protestors, while only 80 people showed up for an October protest outside the Prime Minister's Auckland home (TVNZ 2007). A week later a few hundred participated in a protest march in Auckland, but that was just a fraction of the 193,000 residents ultimately affected by the spraying campaign (ibid).

This analysis addresses two limitations with Woodhouse and Howard's work. First, while their use of the hegemony concept outlines how ruling-class ideological work perpetuates the acquiescence to toxicity, their analysis focuses on industry and fails to discuss the government's role in the process. Second, while they explain how power is achieved through the diffusion of values, beliefs, attitudes, and norms, theirs is a general explanation that is short on details. For a more fine-grained understanding of how diffusion occurs, I turn to Stella Capek's (2009) work on naturework, which uses a symbolic interactionist approach to explain that our perceptions of the environment are socially constructed through "naturework," the ideological work that constructs the lens through which we perceive "nature." Using this concept I demonstrate how the New Zealand government's "naturework" framed PAM as a three-pronged biosecurity threat: to human health, to New Zealand's native ecology, and to the country's economy. Beyond the PAM case, this analysis can help us better understand the way government ideological work can nurture an acquiescence to urban aerial pesticide spraying campaigns, and pesticide use more generally.

New Zealand's Painted Apple Moth eradication program

PAM is native to Southern Australia, where it is considered a common, but minor urban garden pest (Elliott, Ohmart and Wylie 1998; Suckling et al. 2014). While the males can fly, the females can not, which reduces their mobility to 200–300 meter hops and considerably slows the population's spread (New Zealand Audit Office 2003). Because the moth is polyphagous (able to eat different foods), it has a wide host range, including acacia, eucalyptus and radiata pine trees (Ministry for Primary Industries 2003). PAM can cause low-level defoliation of pine trees, which would make it a concern for the plantation forestry sector. However, such defoliation tends to be concentrated on individual trees (McEntee 2005). For example, in its native Australia it "typically affects less than 1 per cent of individual trees in an infested radiata pine compartment" (Ministry of Agriculture and Forestry 2000, 3).

In May 1999 authorities discovered a population of this alien species on 22 properties in West Auckland (Auckland District Health Board 2002). This prompted the Ministry of Agriculture and Forestry (MAF) to start eradication efforts, which included ground spraying with Chlorpyrifos (an organophosphate pesticide) and removing host trees (ibid). In October a second population was found 15 kilometers away in Mt. Wellington, and MAF began spraying with Decis Fort (a synthetic pyrethroid insecticide containing the active ingredient Deltamethrin) (Auckland District Health Board 2002; Pesticide Action Network 2010).

In 2000 MAF conducted an economic impact assessment of a possible PAM incursion based on data relating to another alien species, the White-Spotted Tussock Moth (orgyia thyellina). While this species belongs to the same family, they differ in feeding and breeding habits, and PAM is less impactful on its environment (Smith 2007). Despite these differences, MAF reported that a lack of government response to PAM could cost the plantation forestry industry, municipal governments, and the horticultural sector $16.5–$115 million over the subsequent twenty years (MAF 2000). In turn, this report was to lay the underlying rationale for pursuing an aerial spraying program.

In August 2000 the government Cabinet approved $1.75 million to continue tree host removal and ground spraying with insecticides, which it re-authorized in May 2001 (Smith 2007). By October 2001 the moth had been found in surrounding suburbs, including Avondale, Titirangi, Kelston, Glen Eden and Mt. Wellington (ibid), which led the Cabinet to give the Committee for Infrastructure and Environment power to handle the situation as they saw fit. This led to the development of an aerial spraying campaign, which began in January 2002 and was to include six to eight sprayings over an area covering 600 hectares in West Auckland (Goven, Kerns, Quijano and Wihongi 2007). The insecticide chosen for this campaign was Foray 48B, a commercial insecticide containing Bacillus thuringiensis subspecies kurstaki (Btk) (a live bacterium that kills the larvae of moths and butterflies) (Swadener 1994), as well as a host of man-made chemicals with toxic effects. The decision to use this pesticide was based on the belief it was less toxic than other pesticide options.

After the Labour government's re-election in August 2002, the Cabinet approved $88 million for a five-year eradication campaign, which allowed MAF to extend the spray zone to 900 ha in September, to 8,000 ha in October, and

10,000 ha in December (Smith 2007). The spraying campaign concluded in May 2003, after 40 aerial sprayings had sprayed 97,000 liters of pesticide over the West Auckland region (ibid). At its peak the spray area exposed 193,000 residents to numerous sprayings, with many experiencing multiple sprayings on the same day (ibid). Importantly, the 193,000 figure does not account for the transient population, who had to enter the spray zone for work or other reasons (ibid). The campaign's official cost was $65 million (Smith 2007; Suckling et al. 2014), but that amount fails to capture uncalculated damage to the environment, long-term health (both physical and psychological) effects and the lowered productivity associated with those health problems.

Ecological concerns with the spraying program

While the spraying campaign eradicated PAM, it is thought to have exacted a high toll on ecological biodiversity. First, it is likely to have decimated populations of indigenous moths and butterflies, due to Btk's indiscriminate effects on all caterpillars (Upton and Caspar 2008). A 1994 study in Oregon found that a Btk treatment reduced the total weight of local caterpillars by 90–95%, the number of caterpillars by 80%, and the number of caterpillar species by 60% (Savonen 1994). In turn, such population losses reduce ecosystem services provided by these species, such as pollination, weed control, and serving as a food source for birds, bats, and other species (Swadener 1994).

Another concern is the spray's likely impact on other species. For example, in other contexts the use of Bt-based sprays have decreased numerous beneficial insects, such as parasitic wasps, spider mites, and aphid-eating flies (Swadener 1994). Such sprays have also been shown to be toxic to some birds (Jones 1986), water insects (Kreutzweiser, Holmes, Capell and Eichenberg 1992), and rainbow trout (Swadener 1994). Land mammals have also been affected, with lab rats experiencing respiratory depression when exposed to air containing Btk spores (ibid). In another study rabbits exposed to Bt experienced irritation to the skin and eyes (Seigel, Shadduck and Szabo 1987). As well, sheep exposed to Btk through diet had loose stools, with some displaying microscopic damage to their colons (Goven et al. 2007). Part of the reason for these effects is that while Bt is naturally found in the environment, the strains being used are applied at rates far exceeding naturally occurring levels (No Spray Zone website).

Besides the effects of Bt bacteria, lab studies have shown that the inert chemicals in Foray 48B can, by themselves, impact land mammals. For example, propylene glycol causes renal and hepatic damage, as well as fetal toxicity and embryo death (Goven et al. 2007). As well, in an inhalation exposure study, rats exposed to benzoates displayed lung and trachea irritation, decreased kidney weight, decreased liver weight, and significant death rates (1 out of 6) at the highest exposure rates (Goven et al. 2007).

Another ecological concern is pesticide persistence. While MAF originally assured residents the spray would break down after two hours, MAF scientists subsequently found that it can persist up to eleven days (West Aucklanders

Against Aerial Spraying 2002). The latter is in line with some previous research, which found the insecticide's half-life to be nine days (West and Burges 1985). However, some studies suggest the insecticide would have survived longer than that. In one case viable Btk spores were recovered from tree foliage a full year after application (Feitelson, Payne and Kim 1992), and in another Bt persisted in a citrus orchard for two years and retained its toxicity vis-à-vis caterpillars (Huang, Huang and Kunhua 1990). Moreover, in Denmark Btk was found in a cabbage field seven years after application (Van Cuyk et al. 2011). A related problem is persistence in water. In some cases Btk has been detected in the rivers and public water systems after aerial spraying, and it has been found that Btk spores are not adequately destroyed by standard water treatment processes (Menon and Mestral 1985). In another experiment, researchers detected viable Bt cells in the water for up to 200 days after application, and up to 270 days in the sediment (Hoti and Balaraman 1991).

Another ecological concern is contamination with genetically modified organisms (GMO) as the spray's bacterial ingredient was grown on a nutrient broth consisting largely of soy and corn from the United States, where virtually all supplies are GMO-contaminated (Pesticide Action Network Aotearoa 2002). While MAF confirmed the spray contained soy and corn, they did not test it for GMO contamination, which suggests Western Auckland was thoroughly polluted with GMO ingredients, thereby undermining attempts at organic agriculture in the area. This should have been particularly concerning for a country that bills itself as being "100% pure and natural" and free of genetically engineered organisms.

Human health concerns with the spraying

The spray campaign introduced numerous concerns for human health. For instance, the pesticides used for ground spraying contain Chlorpyrifos, an organophosphate pesticide that can lead to developmental problems, particularly in children whose mothers were exposed during pregnancy (Rauh et al. 2011). As well, the chemical is associated with: (1) severe neurological effects; (2) reproductive harms; (3) metabolic effects (such as obesity and diabetes); (4) respiratory problems, including asthma; and (5) childhood cancers (Californians for Pesticide Reform 2007; CHE 2016b; Rauh et al. 2011).

Regarding the aerial spray chemicals, while the government assured the public that Foray 48B was completely safe (Smith 2007), health problems have been linked to the spray's ingredients, including the inert ingredients as well as the Btk microorganism. For instance, studies have shown that Btk spores can enter the vegetative state in humans with healthy immune systems (Jensen et al. 2002; Valadares, Whittome, Shore and Levin 2001). As well, researchers have found that 25% of exposed humans manifest immune responses that can last up to three years, which suggests the bodies are fighting off a reproducing population (Ginsburg 2006). The aforementioned effects on mammals should raise further concerns for human safety.

As for the inert ingredients, while the government concealed their identity from the public, scientists managed to identify three: hydrochloric acid, propylene glycol, and benzoic acid (Kedgley 2003). The inhalation of hydrochloric acid fumes is known to cause choking and inflammation of the respiratory tract (ibid), with medical research also linking it to asthma (Vizcaya et al. 2011), lung cancer (CHE 2016c), and bronchitis (Brunekeef and Holgate 2002; CHE 2016c). Regarding propylene glycol, it has been linked to hearing loss, skin irritation, intestinal damage, depression, and has been found to affect children's central nervous systems (CHE 2016d; Kedgley 2003). While benzoic acid is a food preservative, it causes asthma, and irritates the skin and eyes (Kedgley 2003). Beyond those three chemicals, community scientists have uncovered two chemicals from previous 48B formulations, two of which are associated with serious health effects: (1) sulfuric acid, which causes laryngeal cancer (CHE 2016e); and (2) phosphine, which is related to hepatitis, pulmonary edema, and seizures (CHE 2016f). As well, there is preliminary evidence linking phosphine to cataracts, chronic renal disease, heart attacks, and peripheral neuropathy (ibid).

Besides what is known about Foray 48B's individual components, data exists on the spray's impact on exposed populations. During the 1996–97 spraying campaign against the White-Spotted Tussock Moth, also in Auckland, the government's use of Foray 48B led 375 residents to complain about a variety of symptoms, including: respiratory symptoms (including asthma), headaches, skin irritation, eye irritation, diarrhea, and lethargy (Smith 2007). During the 2002–03 PAM eradication campaign, MAF's Health Service fielded 22,643 calls about health problems related to the spraying and provided clinical assessments to 840 people, with 100 of those being referred on for specialist consultation (ibid).[2] Furthermore, during the 2002–04 period there was a doubling in the asthma discharge rate for boys aged 0–4 who were in the spray zone, and a 50% increase for girls of the same age (Gallagher, Pirie and Hales 2005). In 2006, three years after completing the PAM spraying campaign, the government acknowledged Foray 48B was associated with neuropsychiatric problems (i.e., anxiety, dizziness, sleep problems, concentration difficulties) and with physical symptoms (i.e., flu-like symptoms, stomach discomfort, diarrhea, chest tightness, irritation of the throat, nose, eyes and skin) (Hales et al. 2004; Smith 2007).

Framing PAM as a biosecurity threat

The use of any pesticide should raise serious concerns about public health, ecosystem health, and community resilience. One would imagine the public would be particularly sensitized to these issues for urban aerial spraying campaigns, where residents can literally see, smell, and feel the pesticides. Thus, if the New Zealand government was to succeed with its spraying campaign, it was essential to build public support for it. Toward that end, the New Zealand government conducted "naturework" (Capek 2009) aimed at framing PAM as a threefold biosecurity threat: a threat to human health, New Zealand's indigenous flora, and the country's economy.

Framing PAM as a threat to human health

During the PAM campaign the New Zealand government repeatedly portrayed the species as a threat to human health. This began in March 2002, when the Auckland District Health Board (ADHB) released a report alleging "the painted apple moth is known to cause adverse health effects, including skin lesions, eye irritation, and respiratory reactions" (ADHB 2002, 50). Then, on December 10, during a parliamentary debate, Marian Hobbs (Member of Parliament) argued PAM's eradication was important for public health reasons: "scientific evidence is that about 95 percent of people are allergic to the painted apple moth" (NZ Parliamentary Debate 2002). A week later Jim Sutton (director of the Biosecurity government agency) put out a press release stating the PAM eradication campaign was partially driven by the public health risk associated with the moth, arguing that overseas experience had demonstrated that 95% of humans are allergic to PAM hairs (Sutton 2002a). In February 2003 a MAF media release announced that scientists working with PAM had serious reactions to PAM hairs, with one experiencing a severe reaction when a hair contacted her eye (MAF 2003). The media release also declared that "just about everyone who has had a reasonable level of exposure to the moths have developed some degree of reaction to the hairs" and that "the impact this moth is having on the PAM project workers will be the same the public would suffer if the moth was allowed to establish here" (ibid, 1). MAF authorities also emphasized that PAM's establishment would have a devastating impact on the New Zealand lifestyle, arguing "an infestation of Painted Apple Moth in our native forests could cause authorities to close areas to the public during the height of the moth breeding season because of the impact it could have on public health" (ibid). As well, the release stated "we [MAF] strongly advise anyone who thinks they have come in contact with a Painted Apple Moth to seek medical attention" (ibid). This ideological work was further strengthened by MAF's use of 30-second radio advertisements that portrayed the moth as scary and dangerous (Derraik 2008). In 2007, three years after the spraying campaign had ended, Jim Anderton (new Biosecurity Minister) reiterated the frame, stating that PAM's "caterpillar has a very toxic effect on human beings" and that skin contact provokes serious toxic reactions (Radio New Zealand 2007). He reiterated that the spraying campaign was partially driven by concerns for public health, including the "extreme allergic reactions most people tend to have to the caterpillars of the moth" (Anderton 2007, 1).

These communications signaled to the public that PAM was a significant health threat, which bolstered support for the government's eradication efforts. However, there were several problems with framing the moth as a human health menace. First, the frame lacked any empirical support, starting with the 2002 ADHB report, which failed to provide any empirical evidence for its claim that PAM causes adverse health effects. This is surprising given that the moth is a common pest in suburban orchards and urban gardens throughout South Australia, including most of Tasmania (ADHB 2002; Derraik 2008). As Derraik (2008) points out, "if the claims of widespread human susceptibility and consequent adverse reactions were indeed accurate, one would expect case reports of human exposure in Australia" (37).

Instead of relying on actual data, the ADHB's assertions were based on the reported health effects associated with two other members of the moth family: the tussock moth (Lymantrilnae) and the gypsy moth (Lymantria dispar dispar). While they belong to the same moth family, there seems to be no other rationale for using them as a basis for evaluating the potential health impact of the PAM (Derraik 2008). In particular, Derraik (2008) emphasizes there is no evidence that their biochemical profiles are similar enough to cause equivalent reactions in humans, and what evidence does exist suggests the opposite. Moreover, while the scientific literature provides extensive evidence about the health effects of other moths, very little is reported about PAM, and what is reported suggests any health effects would be minor (ibid).

Besides the ADHB report, the government officials' assertions also fare poorly under closer scrutiny, as they too failed to provide empirical support for their claims. While Marian Hobbs and Jim Sutton asserted 95% of humans are allergic to PAM, neither provided any support for their claims. Similarly, MAF failed to substantiate their claim that a lab technician suffered an extreme allergic reaction to handling the moths. Moreover, one case is hardly sufficient to generalize the problem to 95% of the human population, particularly when we consider the majority of the population would have less exposure than lab technicians did. Such discrepancies between evidence and claims elucidate a mechanism through which governments shape public perceptions about nature in order to advance their aims.

Furthermore, the government's concern for protecting public health seems disingenuous when we consider its long track record of placing citizens at risk. First, during the 1960s, 1970s, and 1980s, the government allowed the aerial spraying of 2,4,5-T throughout New Zealand, a chemical that was laced with carcinogenic dioxins and associated with severe skin rashes, malaise, peripheral nervous system disturbances, liver toxicity, cancer, birth defects, and miscarriages (Bunting 2013; Dew 1999; Wildblood-Crawford 2008). Beyond allowing the spraying, between 1981 and 1985 the government actually subsidized farmers to use herbicide, resulting in 53,795,834 liters being sprayed in 1985 alone (Takoko and Gibbs 2004). Second, for forty years the government allowed the logging industry to use pentachlorophenol (PCPs) as a wood preservative for their radiata pine exports (Dew 1999). Besides being associated with a host of health effects (including fever, fatigue, weight loss, nausea, and mood swings), the PCP grades used in New Zealand contained toxic impurities, including dioxins and furans, which were associated with their own set of health problems. This went on for forty years before an inquiry into the situation was finally called in 1991 (ibid). A third example is the 1996–97 urban aerial spraying campaign to eliminate the White-Spotted Tussock Moth from the Auckland region, which also relied on the Foray 48B pesticide, and which led 375 residents to complain about health effects (Smith 2007). Fourth, as of 2004 the New Zealand government was aware of 7,000 locations that were potentially contaminated by hazardous substances, but were withholding the information from the public (Gardiner and Gamble 2004). What, in fact, emerges is a pattern where New Zealand governments have repeatedly placed industry interests above public health, thereby placing citizens in harm's way and encouraging both chemical trespass and chemical "injustices-in-waiting."

Framing PAM as a threat to New Zealand's ecology

The government's second justification for the spray campaign was PAM's threat to New Zealand's native flora. In a January 2002 newspaper op-ed, Ruth Frampton (the PAM spray campaign's original director) mentioned that while the moths prefer wattles (a weed) and acacia trees (non-native to New Zealand), they can also feed on three native species (kowhai, karaka, and mountain ribbonwood) (Frampton 2002a). In a press release she further asserts that while aerial spraying was not an ideal solution, it was necessary "to protect New Zealand's forestry and environmental interests" (Frampton 2002b, 1). In September of that year Jim Sutton (the Biosecurity Minister) made a similar point. In the face of public pressure for having dramatically expanded the program from 550 hectares to 8,521 hectares, Sutton argued the spray campaign was necessary for protecting New Zealand's natural environment against the moth (Aeraqua Medical Services 2005; Sutton 2002a). He reiterated this point three months later, when facing renewed criticism for yet another expansion in the campaign, stating "the Cabinet decided to proceed with an eradication attempt because of the incalculable risk the painted apple moth poses to our indigenous forests" (Sutton 2002b, 1). Similarly, in March 2003 Judith Tizard (the Member of Parliament representing Central Auckland) argued New Zealand's indigenous forests are threatened by the moth's damage (Tizard 2003, 1). The line of reasoning was replicated four years later, when, following the release of the Ombudsman's report, Jim Anderton (the new Biosecurity Minister) maintained, "These moths could have done real damage to our native plants. As a former Aucklander, I know just how important the Waitakere Ranges are to Aucklanders, and Cabinet was well aware of that when we made the decision to try to eradicate the painted apple moth" (Anderton 2007, 1).

These statements encouraged the public to view the moth as a significant ecosystem menace, which would have bolstered support for calls to eradicate it. This frame is likely to have been particularly effective with New Zealanders, who pride themselves on having a close relationship to the land (Dew 1999). The problem with the frame, however, is that there is much to suggest the representation of the threat was overstated. While it is true that PAM is able to eat different foods and its spread would have been unhindered by the natural predators it *might* have in Australia, the Island Resource Allocation Hypothesis (Suckling et al. 2014) suggests such invaders have a hard time settling in isolated island floras, such as New Zealand. The reason is that plant species in these settings are less reliant on top–down regulation offered by natural predators, and are more protected by "bottom–up" defenses (e.g. phytochemicals or plant architecture) that constrain herbivore reproduction (ibid). Moreover, Suckling et al. (2014) argue this hypothesis was supported by PAM's incursion in New Zealand: while the moth was found on three native species, lab studies show that two of those (the karaka and ribbonwood) did not support the development of female insects (Suckling et al. 2014).

In the field PAM was most often found on wattles, a very common weed in Auckland, whose numbers were very high in the heavy infestation areas (Suckling et al. 2014). Numerous moths were also found in naturalized acacia and, to a lesser extent, radiata pine, but neither species is indigenous to New Zealand. While neither is indigenous, both are important to New Zealand's plantation forestry industry, with radiata pine representing 90% of the sector. Interestingly, it is representatives from this sector that spoke most forcefully against the moth, and in 2002 they made their displeasure known when MAF manifested an inability to eradicate the moth (Beston 2002).

Framing PAM as an economic threat

In 2000 MAF produced an economic assessment that predicted that, in the absence of government intervention, the PAM incursion would entail negative impacts on: private amenity, public amenity, plantation forestry, horticulture, the conservation estate, watershed conservation, human health, and trade prospects. Basing themselves on estimates produced for the 1996–97 White-Spotted Tussock Moth incursion, MAF predicted the PAM incursion would cost the country $16–$116 million over the subsequent 20 years, with a likely total cost of $48 million (MAF 2000). In the 2002 reassessment MAF analysts increased the estimate to $58–$356 million. The higher estimates were later echoed by government officials. For instance, in March 2003 Judith Tizard (Auckland Central MP) declared "the painted apple moth represents a projected cost to the economy of up to $358 million over the next 20 years" (Tizard 2003, 1). Similarly, in May 2004 Jim Sutton (Biosecurity Minister) maintained "this moth is a serious threat to our urban, native and commercial trees with an estimated economic impact of about $258 million" (Sutton 2004, 1)

Framing the moth as an economic threat was another way to stoke fears about the moth's incursion and support for eradication action. However, like the other two, this frame also falters under closer scrutiny. First, while it was presented as an economic threat to all of New Zealand, in reality it was the plantation forestry sector that was most likely to be impacted. Specifically, in a low-impact scenario (i.e., $58 million), MAF estimated the plantation forestry sector would shoulder 78% of the economic impacts, which would increase to 87% in a high-impact scenario (i.e., $356 million) (MAF 2002).

Second, most of the estimated economic impacts were not increased costs brought on by the incursion, but rather estimated profits the plantation sector *might* lose *if* the PAM incursion led to defoliation and *if* the defoliation was sufficient to stunt tree growth. Whereas production losses were estimated to represent 55% of the economic impacts in a high-impact scenario (i.e., $356 million), they represented 100% of the economic impacts in a low-impact scenario (i.e., $58 million). If we exclude profit loss estimates from the calculation, the 20-year estimate would be reduced from $58–$358 million to $12.76–$160 million, with the lower figure being five times lower than the eradication campaign's final official cost of $65 million (Suckling et al. 2014).

Third, the economic estimates were based on numerous questionable assumptions. For example, the assessment was based on moth incidence rates that were substantially higher than is found in the moth's natural habitat. When radiata pine forests experience a PAM infestation in Australia, less than 1% of the trees are affected (Suckling et al. 2014). By contrast, the MAF assessment was based on incidence rates that ranged from double to twenty-five times the Australian rate. The analysts' justification for the elevated rates is that PAM's natural predators would be absent in New Zealand. However, they failed to provide any empirical support for choosing incidence rates that were so much higher than in PAM's native habitat. A related problem is that the analysts' justification was based on the following unsupported assumptions: (A) the moth has natural predators in Australia; (B) it is these predators that restrict the moth's spread in that country; and (C) New Zealand flora would have no resistance to the moth, an assumption that is at odds with the Island Resource Allocation Hypothesis stated above (Suckling et al. 2014). Lastly, the economic assessment assumed defoliation resulting from the infestation would lead to an average 60% reduction in tree growth. This was based on losses following Cyclaneusma needle cast (a pine tree fungal infection), but no justification was given for using this case to estimate defoliation rates from a PAM infestation (MAF 2002). At a minimum, they should have used the 1% defoliation rates radiata pines suffered in the moth's homeland of Australia (Suckling et al. 2014).

A fourth problem is that MAF analysts failed to articulate the economic costs that would be associated with an eradication campaign. This is particularly troublesome when we consider the official final cost of the eradication campaign came in at $65 million (Suckling et al. 2014), which exceeds the government's lower-end estimates of what the PAM incursion would cost if they took no action ($58 million), and far exceeds the estimate ($12.76 million) that excludes the industry's potential lost profits. The problem is accentuated when we consider that the $65 million final cost does not consider the eradication campaign's damage to the local ecology, the long-term health costs associated with the residents' exposure to the spray, nor the economic impact of their lost productivity and well-being.

In the final analysis, MAF's one-sided economic assessment served to stoke fears about what might be lost from the PAM incursion, rather than providing an honest assessment of the costs and benefits associated with each potential line of action. In turn, this contributed to chemical trespass, illness for some, predispositions to illness for others, and the development of ecological "injustices-in-waiting."

Conclusion

This chapter's overarching aim has been to elucidate how governments nurture the public's acquiescence to toxicity. As illustrated with the PAM spraying campaign, urban aerial spraying campaigns are associated with numerous ecological and public health concerns that undermine ecological and community resilience, and create "injustices-in-waiting." Yet, the public continues to allow such campaigns to occur. The "acquiescence to toxicity" concept (Woodhouse and Howard 2009) suggests that citizens acquiesce to harmful chemicals because these are viewed as a necessary evil for participating in a "modern" society. Building on that concept, this chapter shows how such acquiescence is manufactured and perpetuated by state "naturework," which encourages us to view certain aspects of nature as a threat to be eradicated, thereby heightening support for pesticide spraying. In PAM's case the New Zealand government portrayed the species as a multi-pronged biosecurity threat, a framing that bolstered support for the government's call to eradicate the species with a pesticide spraying campaign.

Given the environmental concerns and injustices associated with the PAM campaign and that climate change is likely to create more species migration and biosecurity concerns, there is a need to critically assess the state's deployment of the biosecurity frame, which includes asking "a biosecurity threat for whom?" In the final analysis, it was the plantation forestry industry that was most threatened by the moth, due to the moths' slight affinity for radiata pine trees. It was also this industry who benefitted most from the eradication campaign, as it prevented lost profits associated with diminished tree growth and having to pay for pesticide applications over their plantations. Other beneficiaries of the spraying campaign included Abbot Laboratories (which manufactures Foray 48B), and Asurequality Limited (the state-owned enterprise responsible for carrying out the spraying campaign).

Conversely, losers in this story were the West Auckland residents, for whom the biosecurity intervention turned into 17 months of chemical terrorism, and whose health was sacrificed on the altar of industry profitability. Adding salt to the wounds was the fact the sacrifices were made for an industry that was mostly outside the Auckland Region (Ministry of Agriculture and Forestry 2002) and which profited from growing radiata pine, a non-native species that the government itself views as an invasive species (Department of Conservation website). As well, it can be argued the plantation sector's vulnerability was a result of their "counter-ecological" production practices. Foster (1999) argues that the scientific management of forests has reduced genetic and species diversity, which makes forestry plantations more vulnerable to insect infestations, and thus more reliant on pesticides. Besides Auckland residents, other losers were the New Zealand taxpayers, who had to pick up the $65 million operation cost, as well as bear the costs of residents' long-term health problems and lowered productivity. In essence, New Zealand citizens ended up subsidizing (through taxpayer dollars, sacrificed human health, and injustices-in-waiting) the plantation industry's counter-ecological production processes.

Such situations call for a human-rights approach to pesticides (Steingraber 2009), where human rights and well-being are placed ahead of industry profits, and where society adopts a greater adherence to the precautionary principle, so that public and private interests act to prevent human harm *before* it happens, and to the principle of reverse onus, where the onus is on government and corporations to prove that a pesticide is safe, rather than on citizens to prove it is harmful (ibid). Beyond minimizing exposures to toxicants, a human-rights approach to pesticides includes informing people of the chemicals they might be exposed to, the health effects associated with those pesticides, as well as providing them with resources to adequately protect themselves against exposure.

Better understanding the PAM case can help us move closer to that goal. First, there were many instances where the public was either inadequately informed or entirely misled about key facts or decision-making processes. This underscores the need for greater transparency around government processes related to pesticides, which includes passing laws that require government agencies to open up official meetings and records to the public (i.e., sunshine laws), passing legislation that obligates political officials to reveal their interactions with industry, and adding significant community representation to all government bodies that handle pesticide-related issues. Greater public engagement can empower communities to more effectively resist and reduce harmful pesticide applications, thereby preventing chemical injustices-in-waiting.

Second, the public's failure to mobilize en masse against the spray campaign betrays an acquiescence to the government's scientific expertise, which itself suggests the public does not adequately understand pesticides' toxic effects, both on humans and ecosystems. This problem can be traced back to the education system, which is geared toward preparing students for jobs in an environmentally destructive economic system (Schnaiberg and Gould 1994), but which fails to adequately educate all students about the harms associated with pesticides and other toxicants (Woodhouse and Howard 2009). At the moment few universities offer courses on the toxic effects of pesticides and toxicants, and no universities require such coursework (Woodhouse and Howard 2009). Universities also fail to transmit a deep eco-literacy to their students. Even though many universities now offer individual courses on environmental subjects and even degrees in environmental science, these are, with few exceptions, elective components of a university education (Haigh 2005). The result is that most students opt out of such courses, leading most to graduate without a deep understanding of ecosystems, how they can be harmed, and how they can be preserved. Thus, what is needed is university curriculum reform that provides students with greater knowledge about these issues, as well as the skills needed to effectively change their world.

Third, the government's deployment of the "biosecurity" frame helped stoke fears about PAM, bolstered support for the eradication campaign, and stifled dissent. This is not the first time governments have used this frame to advance industry interests (Cockburn 2015), but its use here underscores the need to educate citizens about: (1) the assumptions behind the frame; (2) the circumstances under which the government tends to utilize the frame; (3) the interested parties who invariably benefit from its use; (4) the parties who are compromised by its use; and (5) how the concept can be used as a mechanism of social control to stifle dissent.

The biosecurity frame rests on the utilitarian idea that the state has a duty to manage the environment in a way that maximizes welfare for the most people, and that harm to some is justified for the benefit of the many (Bell 2004). However, in the PAM case the utilitarian concept was flipped on its head, with the government harming the majority in order to maximize the plantation owners' economic returns. This underscores David Harvey's (1996) point that utilitarian perspectives can be distorted to serve capital's interests. Given utilitarianism's limitations, we need to work to institutionalize environmental justice in government decision-making processes, so that human well-being ceases to be subordinated to industry profitability. This would facilitate the institutionalization of a human-rights approach to pesticides, as well as toxicants more generally (Steingraber 2009).

Finally, a key element of the PAM story is that the spraying was pursued to preserve plantation forestry's profitability, an industry whose production practices undermines its own resilience vis-à-vis insect infestations. This problem has to be addressed to prevent similar environmental injustices in the future. Toward that end we can draw insights from John McKinlay's article "A Case for Refocusing Upstream: The Political Economy of Illness" (2005), which makes a strong case for an upstream public health approach that targets the manufacturers of disease – such as cigarette manufacturers and other entities who injure people through the products they sell and/or their production processes – and requires them to pay a tax to offset the destructiveness of their business products. This approach can be applied to industries that undermine biodiversity and ecological resilience more generally, such as the plantation forestry sector. If such industries had to pay significant fines for ecology-damaging practices, it would force them to at least consider less destructive production practices. Far from just penalizing ecological malfeasance, we can also support policies that reward companies who enhance biodiversity, thereby incentivizing ecology-protecting behavior that will increase ecological resilience and enhance environmental justice for humans and non-human species alike.

Acknowledgements

Research for this chapter was supported by the Faculty of Arts at the University of Auckland, through a 2013–14 Summer Scholars grant. I also want to thank Brittany Whiley and Florence Reynolds for their research assistance on this project, as well as Beatrice Frank for comments on an earlier draft of the chapter.

Notes

1 Department of Sociology, University of Auckland, m.vallee@auckland.ac.nz
2 This, in all likelihood, represents an underreporting as health workers typically overlook the chronic effects of pesticide exposure (Solomon 2000).

References

Aeraqua Medical Services (2005). *A study of presentations of householder concerns to the Painted Apple Moth (PAM) Health Service & Auckland Summer Symptom Survey.* New Zealand Biosecurity [online]. Retrieved 15 September 2015 from http://www.biosecurity.govt.nz/files/pests/painted-apple-moth/pam-health-report.pdf

Anderton J. (2007). *Painted Apple Moth spray campaign was vital.* 12 November. beehive.govt.nz [online]. Retrieved 15 December 2015 from http://www.beehive.govt.nz/node/31259

Auckland District Health Board, Public Health Service (2002). *Health risk assessment of the 2002 aerial spray eradication programme for the Painted Apple Moth in some Western suburbs of Auckland.* Auckland District Health Board.

Bell M. (2004). *An invitation to environmental sociology.* Thousand Oaks, CA: Pine Forge Press.

Beston A. (2002). $11m moth blitz risking failure. *New Zealand Herald [online].* 15 February. Retrieved 2 December 2015 from http://www.nzherald.co.nz/nz/news/article.cfm?c_id=1&objectid=939414

Brunekeef B. and Holgate S. (2002). Air pollution and health. *Lancet*, 360(9341), 1233–1242.

Bührs T. (1993). The role of the state: from 'state vandalism' towards a 'market-led' environment. In T. Bührs and R. Bartlett (Eds.) *Environmental policy in New Zealand: the politics of clean & green?* (pp. 90–112). Auckland: Ton Oxford University Press.

Bunting Z. (2013). *Subsidising agricultural expansion at the expense of public health: the case of 2,4,5-T and the role of the New Zealand government.* Unpublished MA thesis. Department of Sociology, University of Auckland.

Californians for Pesticide Reform (2007). *Airborne poisons: pesticides in our air and in our bodies [online].* Retrieved 4 March 2016 from http://pesticidereform.org/downloads/Biodrift-Summary-Eng.pdf

Caniglia B., Frank B., Delano D. and Kerner B. (2014). Enhancing environmental justice research and praxis: the inclusion of human security, resilience and vulnerabilities literature. *International Journal of Innovation and Sustainable Development*, 8, 409–426.

Capek S. (2009). The social construction of nature: of computers, butterflies, dogs, and trucks. In K. Gould and T. Lewis (Eds.) *Twenty lessons in environmental sociology* (pp. 11–24). New York: Oxford University Press.

Carson R. (1965). *Silent spring.* Hammondsworth: Penguin Books.

CHE (2016a). CHE toxicant and disease database entry for 'pesticides' [online]. Retrieved 3 April 2016 from http://www.healthandenvironment.org/tddb/contam/?itemid=2380

CHE (2016b). CHE toxicant and disease database entry for 'chlorpyrifos' [online]. Retrieved 3 April 2016 from http://www.healthandenvironment.org/tddb/contam/?itemid=2696

CHE (2016c). CHE toxicant and disease database entry for 'hydrochloric acid' [online]. Retrieved 3 April 2016 from http://www.healthandenvironment.org/tddb/contam/?itemid=2651

CHE (2016d). CHE toxicant and disease database entry for 'propylene glycol' [online]. Retrieved 3 April 2016 from http://www.healthandenvironment.org/tddb/contam/?itemid=2995

CHE (2016e). CHE toxicant and disease database entry for 'sulfuric acid' [online]. Retrieved 3 April 2016 from http://www.healthandenvironment.org/tddb/contam/?itemid=2798

CHE (2016f). CHE toxicant and disease database entry for 'phosphine' [online]. Retrieved 3 April 2016 from http://www.healthandenvironment.org/tddb/contam/?itemid=2364

Cockburn A. (2015). Weed whackers: Monsanto, glyphosate, and the war on invasive species. *Harper's Magazine*, September. Retrieved 2 December 2015 from https://harpers.org/archive/2015/09/weed-whackers/

Department of Conservation (no date). Wilding pines are invasive weeds [online]. Retrieved 15 February 2016 from http://www.doc.govt.nz/nature/pests-and-threats/common-weeds/wilding-pines/

Derraik J. (2008). The potential direct impacts on human health resulting from the establishment of the painted apple moth (Teia anartoides) in New Zealand. *New Zealand Medical Journal*, 121(1278), 35–40.

Dew K. (1999). National identity and controversy: New Zealand's clean green image and pentachlorophenol. *Health and Place*, 5, 45–57.

Elliott H., Ohmart C. and Wylie F. (1998). *Insect pests of Australian forests: ecology and management*. Chatswood, NSW: Reed International Books.

Faber D. (2008). *Capitalizing on environmental justice: the polluter-industrial complex in the age of globalization*. Lanham, MD: Rowman & Littlefield.

Feitalson J., Payne J. and Kim L. (1992). Bacillus thuringiensis insects and beyond. *Nature Biotechnology*, 10, 271–275.

Foster J.B. (1999). *The vulnerable planet: a short economic history of the environment*. New York: Monthly Review Press.

Frampton R. (2002a). Dialogue: well-considered approach to swatting indiscriminate pest [online]. *New Zealand Herald*. 14 January. Retrieved 30 September 2015 from http://www.nzherald.co.nz/nz/news/article.cfm?c_id=1&objectid=586604

Frampton R. (2002b). Response to Meriel Watts article MAF bungles the biosecurity in West Auckland [online]. *Ministry of Primary Industries*. Retrieved 22 January 2015 from http://www.mpi.govt.nz/news-resources/news/response-to-meriel-watts-article-maf-bungles-the

Gallagher L., Pirie R. and Hales S. (2005). *Descriptive study of hospital discharges for respiratory diseases in spray zone for Painted Apple Moth (Auckland), relative to local and national statistics 1999–2004* [online]. Retrieved 30 November 2015 from http://www.moh.govt.nz/notebook/nbbooks.nsf/0/BEBE29D3D3476AEDCC25712F006F8775?OpenDocument

Gardiner J. and Gamble W. (2004). Secrecy keeps lid on toxic cesspits [online]. *New Zealand Herald*. 9 September. Retrieved 15 October 2015 from http://www.nzherald.co.nz/nz/news/article.cfm?c_id=1&objectid=173615

Ginsburg C. (2006). The safety to humans of bacillus thuringiensis insecticidal sprays: a reassessment [online]. *No Spray Zone*. Retrieved 7 December 2015 from http://nosprayzone.number6.org/wp-content/uploads/2016/01/NSZPaper.pdf

Goven J., Kerns T., Quijano R. and Wihongi D. (2007). *Report of the March 2006 people's inquiry into the impacts and effects of aerial spraying pesticide over urban areas of Auckland* [online]. Action Plan & Print, Auckland. Retrieved 7 December 2015 from https://peoplesinquiry.wordpress.com/

Haigh M. (2005). Greening the university curriculum: appraising an international movement. *Journal of Geography in Higher Education*, 29(1), 31–48.

Hales S., Baker V., Dew K., Moata'ane L., Martin J., Rochford T., Slaney D. and Woodward A. (2004). *Assessment of the potential health impacts of the 'Painted Apple Moth' aerial spraying programme, Auckland, for the New Zealand Ministry of Health*.

Hallberg G. (1987). The impacts of agricultural chemicals on ground water quality. *GeoJournal*, 15(3), 283–295.

Harrison J. (2011). *Pesticide drift and the pursuit of environmental justice*. Cambridge, MA: MIT Press.

Harvey D. (1996). *Justice, nature, and the geography of difference*. Malden: Blackwell Books.

Hoti S. and Balaraman K. (1991). Changes in the populations of Bacillus thuringiensis H-14 and Bacillus spasacus applied to vector breeding sites. *The Environmentalist*, 11(1), 39–44.

Huang Y., Huang R. and Kunhua L. (1990). A field study of the persisting effects of Bacillus thuringiensis in citrus groves. *Chinese Journal of Biological Control*, 6(3), 131–133.

Jensen G., Larsen P., Jacobsen B., Madsen B., Smidt L. and Andrup L. (2002). Bacillus thuringiensis in fecal samples from greenhouse workers after exposure to B. thuringiensis-based pesticides. *Applied and Environmental Microbiology*, 68(10), 4900–4905.

Jones I. (1986). *Summary report: effect of Dipel and Plyac on hatchability of ringneck pheasant eggs*. Oregon Department of Fish and Wildlife.

Kedgley S. (2003). Toxic ingredients of Painted Apple Moth spray: tabled Parliament Speech [online]. Retrieved 15 November 2015 from http://www.greens.org.nz/speeches/toxic-ingredients-painted-apple-moth-spray-tabled

Kreutzweiser D., Holmes S., Capell S. and Eichenberg D. (1992). Lethal and sublethal effects of Bacillus thuringiensis var. kurstaki on aquatic insects in laboratory bioassays and outdoor stream channels. *Bulletin of Environmental Contamination and Toxicology*, 49, 252–258.

McEntee M. (2005). *Science communication in an age of risk: a case study of two biosecurity incursions*. Unpublished MA thesis. Department of Geography, University of Auckland.

McKinlay J. (2005). A case for refocusing upstream: the political economy of illness. In P. Conrad (Ed.) *The sociology of health & illness: critical perspectives* (pp. 551–564). New York: Worth Publishers.

Menon A. and De Mestral J. (1985). Survival of Bacillus thuringiensis var. kurstaki. *Water, Air Soil Pollution*, 25, 265–274.

Ministry of Agriculture and Forestry (2000). *Potential economic impact on New Zealand of the Painted Apple Moth*. July. MAF Policy.

Ministry of Agriculture and Forestry (2002). *Painted Apple Moth: reassessment of potential economic impacts [online]*. May. Retrieved 9 November 2015 from http://www.biosecurity.govt.nz/files/pests/painted-apple-moth/pam-reassessment-economic-impacts.pdf

Ministry of Agriculture and Forestry (2003). Technician removed from painted apple moth rearing project after reaction to moth hairs [online]. 3 February. Retrieved 5 December 2015 from http://www.mpi.govt.nz/news-resources/news/technician-removed-frompainted-applemoth-rearing.aspx

Ministry for Primary Industries (2003). Environmental assessment of aerial spraying in New Zealand for painted apple moth. Retrieved 9 September 2015 from http://www.biosecurity.govt.nz/pests-diseases/forests/painted-apple-moth/environmental-impact.htm

New Zealand Audit Office (2003). *Case study 3 – response to the incursion of the Painted Apple Moth*. Wellington, New Zealand.

New Zealand Parliamentary Debate (2002). Questions for oral answer questions to ministers: industry and regional development: Painted Apple Moth—vegetation control zone, West Auckland [online]. 10 December. Retrieved 2 September 2015 from http://www.vdig.net/hansard/archive.jsp?y=2002&m=12&d=10&o=9&p=9

No Spray Zone (no date). BT: organic pesticide or environmental disaster [online]. Retrieved 30 January 2016 from http://nosprayzone.number6.org/bt-info/bt-organic-pesticide-or-environmental-disaster/

Pellow D. (2009). The state and policy: imperialism, exclusion, and ecological violence in state policy. In K. Gould and T. Lewis (Eds.) *Twenty lessons in environmental sociology* (pp. 47–58). New York: Oxford Press.

Pesticide Action Network (2010). 'Deltamethrin' in PAN pesticide database [online]. Retrieved 2 December 2015 from http://www.pesticideinfo.org/Detail_Chemical.jsp?Rec_Id=PC33475

Pesticide Action Network Aotearoa (2002). MAF admit they don't know if aerial spray is OK [online]. *Scoop Independent News*. 7 October. Retrieved 14 November 2015 from http://www.scoop.co.nz/stories/AK0210/S00040.htm

Radio New Zealand (2007). Good Morning New Zealand, Jim Anderton interviewed by Sean Plunket. 13 November.

Rauh V., Arunajadai S., Horton M., Perera F., Hoepner L., Barr D. and Whyatt R. (2011). Seven-year neurodevelopmental scores and prenatal exposure to chlorpyrifos, a common agricultural pesticide. *Environmental Health Perspectives*, 119(8), 1196–1201.

Reganold J., Elliott L. and Unger Y. (1987). Long-term effects of organic and conventional farming on soil erosion. *Nature*, 330, 370–372.

Savonen C. (1994). Btk spraying for forest pest kills many other species. *OSU News*. Corvallis, OR: Oregon State University Agricultural Communications.

Schnaiberg A. and Gould K. (1994). *Environment and society: the enduring conflict*. Caldwell, NJ: Blackburn Press.

Seigel J., Shadduck J. and Szabo J. (1987). Safety of the entomopathogen Bacillus thuringiensis var. Israeliensis for mammals. *Journal of Economic Entomology*, 80, 717–723.

Smith M. (2007). *Report of the opinion of Ombudsman Mel Smith on complaints arising from aerial spraying of the biological insecticide Foray 48B on the population of parts of Auckland and Hamilton to destroy incursions of Painted Apple Moths, and Asian Gypsy Moths, respectively*. Wellington: Office of the Ombudsman.

Solomon G. (2000). *Pesticides and human health: a resource for health care professionals* [online]. Berkeley, CA: Physicians for Social Responsibility. Retrieved 10 December 2015 from http://www.psr-la.org/files/pesticides_and_human_health.pdf

Spiegelman A. (2010). The Light Brown Apple Moth (LBAM) doesn't deserve the starring role [online]. *Huffington Post*. 24 June. Retrieved 10 February 2016 from http://www.huffingtonpost.com/annie-spiegelman/the-light-brown-apple-mot_b_523306.html

Steingraber S. (2009). The social construction of cancer: a walk upstream. In L. King and D. McCarthy (Eds.) *Environmental sociology: from analysis to action* (pp. 287–299). Lanham, MD: Rowman & Littlefield.

Suckling D., Charles J., Kay M., Kean J., Burnip G., Chhagan A., et al. (2014). Host range testing for risk assessment of a sexually dimorphic polyphagous invader, painted apple moth. *Agricultural and Forest Entomology*, 16, 1–13.

Sutton J. (2002a). *Cabinet decides to expand eradication measure against painted apple moth* [online]. beehive.govt.nz. 9 September. Retrieved 11 October 2015 from http://www.beehive.govt.nz/release/cabinet-decides-expand-eradication-measure-against-painted-apple-moth

Sutton J. (2002b). *All New Zealanders need to work together for effective biosecurity* [online]. beehive.govt.nz. 17 December. Retrieved 11 October 2015 from http://www.beehive.govt.nz/release/all-new-zealanders-need-work-together-effective-biosecurity

Sutton J. (2004). *Painted Apple Moth spray programme ends* [online]. beehive.govt.nz. 13 May. Retrieved 17 October 2015 from http://www.beehive.govt.nz/release/painted-apple-moth-spray-programme-ends

Swadener C. (1994). Bacillus Thuringiensis (B.T.). *Journal of Pesticide Reform*, 14(3), 13–20.

Takoko M. and Gibbs A. (2004). *Nga Matitapu o te Hakino: people poisoned daily*. Auckland: Greenpeace NZ.

Tizard J. (2003). *Painted Apple Moth eradication campaign necessary* [online]. beehive.govt.nz. 28 March. Retrieved 17 October 2015 from http://www.beehive.govt.nz/release/painted-apple-moth-eradication-campaign-necessary

TVNZ (2007). Painted apple moth timeline [online]. *TVNZ*. 12 November. Retrieved 19 October 2015 from http://tvnz.co.nz/content/1443394/2591764/article.html

Upton R. and Caspar L. (2008). Bacillus thuringiensis – safety review [online]. Retrieved 23 January 2016 from http://www.lbamspray.com/Reports/BacillusthuringiensisSafetyReview031208.pdf

Van Cuyk S., Deshpande A., Hollander A., Duval N., Ticknor L., Layshock J., Gallegos-Graves L. and Omberg K. (2011). Persistence of *Bacillus thuringiensis* subsp. *kurstaki* in urban environments following spraying. *Applied and Environmental Microbiology*, 77(22), 7954–7961.

Valadares de Amorim G., Whittome B., Shore B. and Levin, D. (2001). Identification of Bacillus thuringiensis subjsp. kurstaki strain HD-1-like bacteria from environmental and human samples after aerial spraying of Victoria, British Columbia, Canada, with Foray 48B. *Applied and Environmental Microbiology*, 67(3), 1035–1043.

Vizcaya D., Mirabelli M., Antó J., Orriols R., Burgos F., Arjona L. and Zock J. (2011). A workforce-based study of occupational exposures and asthma symptoms in cleaning works. *Occupational and Environmental Medicine*, 68(12), 914–919.

West Aucklanders Against Aerial Spraying (2002). Painted Apple Moth Foray 48b aerial spraying [online]. *Scoop Independent News*. 26 August. Retrieved 12 November 2015 from http://www.scoop.co.nz/stories/PO0208/S00094.htm

West A. and Burges H. (1985). Persistence of Bacillus thuringiensis and Bacillus cereus in soil supplanted with grass or manure. *Plant and Soil*, 83, 389–398.

Wildblood-Crawford B. (2008). *Environmental (in)justice and 'expert knowledge': the discursive construction of dioxins, 2,4,5-T and human health in New Zealand, 1940 to 2007*. Unpublished PhD thesis. Department of Geography, University of Canterbury.

Woodhouse E. and Howard J. (2009). Stealthy killers and governing mentalities: chemicals in consumer products. In M. Singer and H. Baer (Eds.) *Killer commodities: public health and the corporate production of harm* (pp. 35–66). Plymouth: AltaMira Press.

7 Water connections
Output-based aid for the urban poor and the pursuit of water justice in Jakarta, Indonesia

Rita Padawangi[1] and Manuel Vallée[2]

Introduction

Even though water is necessary for survival, accessing it is often difficult for the urban poor in developing countries. In Jakarta, Indonesia, low-income households are much less likely to be connected to the water system, and poorer neighborhoods that are connected are more likely to experience unreliable or no water flow (Bakker and Kooy 2008; Bakker, Kooy, Shofiani and Martijn 2006).

Development financing institutions often blame such water inequities on the state's inability to function effectively, and they propose market-based mechanisms as the preferred solution. For instance, the World Bank and the Asian Development Bank promote private sector and market principles – such as business management, competition, and stakeholder representation – for managing infrastructures and basic services (Allouche and Finger 2002; Birkenholtz 2010). Additionally, over the last three decades the International Finance Corporation – the World Bank's private arm – has loaned more than US$75 million to countries worldwide to encourage private sector participation in water and sanitation projects, and water privatization has grown significantly. Relatedly, the World Bank claims that privatization projects have helped spread water access to an additional 24 million people in a range of countries since 1990 (Marin 2009).

However, water privatization hasn't been without its problems. While the World Bank lauds the fact privatization projects have increased the number of people connected to water networks, they fail to mention that most privatization projects fall well short of their stipulated targets. Additionally, social scientists have criticized water privatization projects for reducing water to an economic good, and for its tendency to obscure water's nonmarket values, including socio-ecological values, political values, as well as individual and collective values (Ioris 2011). As well, urban justice scholars have criticized market-based approaches for their tendency to reduce water services to a question of service distribution, which ignores the processes that establish, maintain, and mediate injustices (Dikeç 2001; Soja 2010; Young 1990). Solving uneven water access for the poor through privatization and its subsequent patches is problematic because they overlook the larger social inequalities that set the stage for unequal water access.

To shed more light on these issues, we analyze the privatization of Jakarta's water management, analyzing it through a social justice frame, and focusing particularly on the output-based aid (OBA) program that was implemented in 2007. OBA programs are a World Bank grant-funding scheme that encourages private sector operators to provide basic infrastructure to the poor. Jakarta, a city with a history of unequal water access, is a strategic case to analyze because it was one of the largest water privatization experiments in the world. Poor areas in the city that were not yet served by a piped water network were seen as "ungovernable" and "unserviceable" by the water utility companies (Bakker and Kooy 2008, 1900) until the OBA water supply program came along. OBA is a key program to analyze because it is now the World Bank's preferred means of addressing water inequalities and, as you will see, served as a Trojan horse for water privatization. While Jakarta's OBA program increased the number of poor households connected to the water network, it did little to address water service problems experienced by the poor or the underlying social justice issues that foster water injustices, which included land tenure barriers to obtaining a water connection, lower prioritization of water services, and enduring geographical difficulties in getting reliable services. In turn, the failure to address these issues helped perpetuate water injustices. Moreover, while it failed to address deep-seated water justice issues, it served as a mechanism to legitimize market-based approaches to water management, which helped further water's commodification and privatization.

Jakarta's OBA water supply program was introduced a decade into water privatization, as part of the effort to increase piped water network coverage and for private water companies to meet contract obligations. However, the OBA encountered community resistance in its implementation. We analyze the program's benefits, limitations, and contradictions to further understand the relationship between privatized water's pro-poor agenda and water justice. This analysis is informed by field observation, documents relating to Jakarta's OBA water supply[3] program, and in-depth interviews with officials and community.

In what follows we provide the chapter's conceptual framework, which includes a discussion of water privatization and the benefits of using a social justice frame to analyze Jakarta's OBA water program. We then discuss the output-based aid programs, Jakarta's water distribution history, the OBA program's implementation in Jakarta, as well as the program's benefits, limitations, and contradictions. Beyond shedding light on Jakarta's case, this analysis highlights why OBA water supply programs, more generally, fail to eliminate water injustices and actually perpetuate them.

Water privatization, the urban poor, and water justice

For the last three decades international institutions such as the World Bank, the Asian Development Bank, and the United Nations have hailed water privatization as the preferred answer to improving water delivery services. As of 2015 the International Finance Corporation (IFC) – the private arm of the World Bank – had loaned more than US$75 billion to countries worldwide to support private sector participation in water and sanitation projects (Vidal 2015). Between 1990 and 2015, 64 countries experienced private sector participation, with 49% in Latin America and the Caribbean (World Bank 2015). During the same time span more than US$31 billion was invested in East Asia and the Pacific for private sector participation in water and sewerage. However, 63 projects (26%) were "cancelled under distress," and most of these were in East Asia and the Pacific, representing a total investment of US$11.6 billion (World Bank 2015).

Water privatization proponents claim that applying market principles to water would ensure that water utility companies get enough revenue to cover system operation and maintenance and that this would improve service delivery to the poor (Goldman 2005). Additionally, the World Bank claims that improving access through privatization would lower water costs for poor households (Marin 2009). In practice, however, "the record of new connections by private companies for poor customers is disappointing" (Bakker 2010, 99), which is to be expected because privatized water services prioritize "good business climate" before social well-being (Harvey 2006, 25). It turns out that full cost recovery in water pricing and subsidies for reducing water tariffs, which are celebrated by water privatization proponents as best water management practices, are insufficient to ensure service delivery to the poor (Ingram, Whiteley and Perry 2008). Moreover, scholars have criticized the trend towards reducing water issues to delivery service, operation, and maintenance. For example, Ioris (2011) argued that water has numerous nonmarket values, including socio-ecological values, political values, individual and collective values, which are left out of the equation in water privatization. As well, others have charged that market-based water values: (1) disregard changes in water quality and people's incomes; (2) are too static and predetermined to frame water as a market value; (3) disregard social inequalities and environmental issues; and (4) overlook cultural identities related to water (Gibbs 2010; Ioris 2011; Laurie and Marvin 1999; Roberts 2008; Scruggs 1998; Sheehan 2005; Swyngedouw 2005). Furthermore, Robinson (2013) argued such problems increased the potential for exacerbating social inequalities, which have prompted many social movements against water privatization.

While the social science literature has highlighted water privatization's limitations, it has underanalyzed output-based aid water supply programs. This is an important gap because the policy world has celebrated the OBA program as the preferred solution for resolving tensions between water privatization and servicing the poor. A 2001 World Bank publication gives this rationale: "Output-based aid extends some of the core features of traditional government contracting and private infrastructure reforms ... [by increasing] the potential for mobilizing private funding for critical public services while ensuring a high level of accountability for the use of public funds" (Brook and Petrie 2001, 5). Since the first OBA grant approval in 2006, the program's reach has become worldwide, and yet the concept and practices are still inadequately addressed by the social sciences.

To address this gap we analyze Jakarta's OBA program through a social justice lens. Jakarta is an important case to analyze because it has a history of providing poor water access to the poor. Moreover, water companies introduced its OBA program despite significant agitation against privatization by non-government organizations (NGOs). Interestingly, not only was the program targeting areas with a history of poor water access, but the chosen areas were locations where NGO opposition was well organized. Furthermore, beyond the claim the program would benefit the poor, the program was advertised as a means for water utility companies to meet their contractual obligation to connect 100% of the population to the water network. Thus, Jakarta's OBA water supply program represented not only a benevolent service for the poor and a way of achieving citywide coverage, but perhaps more importantly a means of bolstering water privatization's legitimacy.

There are several benefits from pursuing the analysis through a social justice frame. First, social justice discussions have distinguished between three forms of justice: distributive justice, procedural justice, and interactive justice (Neal, Lukasiewicz and Syme 2014; Perreault 2014). A market-based emphasis on service delivery efficiency reduces water problems to an issue of distributional justice, which urban studies scholars have criticized because it obscures the processes that establish, maintain, and mediate injustices (Dikeç 2001; Soja 2010; Young 1990). For instance, procedural justice calls for attention to processes in making perceivably just decisions, while interactive justice looks at relationships among stakeholders and decision-makers (Neal et al. 2014; Skitka 2009). A focus on procedural and interactive justice is essential for evaluating pro-poor water services because these programs are targeted towards an economic class predisposed to facing urban service inequities.

A water justice lens also provides sensitivity to water's material and spatial dimensions, which can help us better see the incompatibility between privatized water and the pro-poor agenda. Water "captures and embodies processes that are simultaneously material, discursive, and symbolic" (Swyngedouw 2004, 28), but the discursive and symbolic processes are often discussed separately from the material. Water's materiality refers to the geo-hydrological and climatological dimensions that affect water availability and allocation patterns in the city (Zwarteveen and Boelens 2014). It also concerns water's role as a biological need that makes it inseparable from the pragmatism of everyday life. This pragmatism often depoliticizes water and emphasizes outcomes in water distribution, rather than process. While water justice scholars have critiqued inequities in water distribution processes, water's materiality demands more attention from social scientists because water and its infrastructures, as objects, are "capable of affecting and producing the world in distinct and sometimes forceful ways" (Meehan 2014, 216). Regarding the spatial dimension, it is also important to relate water programs to the broader spatial injustices in cities. Environmental injustices, including access to water, affect poorer members of society, who are marginalized in the capitalist production of urban space (Lefebvre 1991; Smith 2008). Water is a component of urban space, and the inseparability between water and urban geographies translates spatial inequalities into water injustices.

By exploring water's material and spatial dimensions in Jakarta's OBA water supply program, our specific contribution is to ground the understanding of these programs in the broader social justice context. While contradictions between privatized water and the well-being of the poor are bound to exist, as suggested by the literature, it is also important to recognize possible benefits experienced by residents because unequal water access was and continues to be a reality in Jakarta. Thus, the provision of water connections to the poor requires a nuanced view of water privatization impacts.

Output-based aid for urban water supply

Privatizing urban water supplies has not eliminated pro-poor water programs, despite the seeming contradictions between profit-making pursuits and the well-being of the poor. In fact, privatized water services can feature pro-poor programs, which are aimed at expanding services to the poor. The OBA program is one example. The OBA framework's key feature is providing a one-time grant to catalyze service delivery to the poor and it "is used in cases where poor people are being excluded from basic services because they cannot afford to pay the full cost of user fees such as connection fees" (GPOBA website 2011). As it pertains to water, financial institutions highlight the OBA program as the answer to water privatization's failure to serve the poor; it is touted as the "missing link" between the welfare of the poor and the private sector's financial needs (Mumssen, Johannes and Kumar 2010).

Also known as "performance-based aid" or "results-based financing," OBA applications must specifically define outputs prior to a particular project's implementation and funds are only reimbursed after the project delivers the promised output. These requirements have given the program key advantages over traditional funding approaches – which give funds at the beginning of development project – and they include: (1) increased transparency; (2) increased accountability; (3) increased engagement of private sector capital; (4) increased innovation and efficiency; (5) increased sustainability of public funding; and (6) enhanced results monitoring (Mumssen et al. 2010).

The OBA framework's reach is worldwide. For example, in 2010 there were 200 OBA projects in the World Bank Group, totaling more than US$3.5 billion. These funds were expected to increase "aid effectiveness" by acting as incentives to "mobilize private sector finance and expertise" (GPOBA 2009, 1). The OBA program's size indicates the private sector's growing importance in development. While only 5% of the amount is allocated to water and sanitation projects (Mumssen et al. 2010), water remains an important sector to analyze because of its centrality to people's livelihoods and its contradictions within privatization.

As a framework introduced by the World Bank Group's Private Sector Development Strategy, it is unsurprising to see that OBA prioritizes market-based mechanisms. First, the OBA program emphasizes the private sector's role in "improving service delivery for the poor" (GPOBA 2009, 2; Mumssen et al. 2010), which it does by providing subsidies for connection fees. Also, projects are developed in consultation with private sector entities. If the implementation is deemed too risky, the project's scale can be reduced, to lower the risks of substantial loss. If it is successful, the project can be showcased as a successful corporate pro-poor initiative, to burnish the program's pro-poor image. Importantly, privatized pro-poor programs do not question water's commodification. These programs actually encourage water's commodification by widening the water operator's consumer base to include groups that would not be able to otherwise afford the connection.

It is also important to discuss how private sector pro-poor initiatives, such as OBA projects, are implemented in unjust urban landscapes. Large cities in Southeast Asia have shown inequalities throughout their development, and these were exacerbated after recovering from the 1997 economic crisis, when consumption-driven development became more dominant (Douglass 2010; Rimmer and Dick 2009). Many urban poor settlements are close to rivers, but high pollution in many cities prevents using waterways as direct sources of drinking water (Padawangi 2012). Moreover, raw water for city piped water networks is usually channeled from the hinterlands, is often limited, and is unequally distributed. Piped water often perpetuates spatial injustices through water connection costs, which are quite high relative to urban poor incomes, and which leads them to buy water from vendors who often charge much higher prices (WHO 2015). However, city water injustices are conjoined with spatial injustice more generally, as marginalized populations are often situated in locations that are also deprived of other infrastructure services and land tenure security. Subsidizing connection fees may bring piped water into the community, but unresolved spatial injustices will continue to affect water accessibility, further perpetuating injustices-in-waiting.

The impact of Jakarta's output-based aid on water injustices

Water injustices in Jakarta

Jakarta is Indonesia's Special Capital Region and, as a result of decades of centralized development policies, has become the center of economic resources and political powers. The city has continuously drawn within-country migrants, as job opportunities are scarcer in the countryside (Jones and Douglass 2008). With a population of over 8.5 million in 2011 and at least twice as many in its metropolitan area, Jakarta is the largest city and mega-urban region in the country (DKI Jakarta Government 2016). By contrast, the population of the next largest city, Surabaya, is around 3 million (Widiantono and Soepriadi 2009).

Jakarta's urban poor have been historically disadvantaged in getting water provisions. For instance, during the Dutch colonial period piped water supply was limited to European neighborhoods (Bakker et al. 2006), and the poor's water needs were supplied through public hydrants and water vendors. In 1945, following independence, two water treatment plants – Pejompongan I and II – were built to represent modern Jakarta (Bakker et al. 2006). However, at the end of the 1960s only 15% of the residents had household connections. Monumental developments and mega projects grew in the city, but water service provision to the poor has tended to lag behind. For example, in the 1970s urban villages housed 80% of the population and covered 60% of Jakarta's land area, but only 10% of them could access piped water (Bakker et al. 2006). Moreover, while a subsidized network extension was built in 1968, it only served affluent neighborhoods. In 1990, with a population of approximately 8 million, the service coverage was somewhere between 38% and 42% (ADB 2007). Meanwhile, the nonrevenue water – which typically consists of leakage and illegal connections – hovered between 53% and 57% of produced water (ADB 2007).

Water challenges are closely related to spatial injustice in Jakarta, especially as it pertains to housing. Many urban poor settlements concentrate in environmentally-degraded riverbanks, seafronts, and old *kampung* (urban village) neighborhoods (Padawangi 2012; Swyngedouw 2004). The coverage of low-income public housing programs is limited and is marred by insufficient infrastructure services (Kompas 2011). One exception was the Kampung Improvement Program (KIP), which improved infrastructures in poor settlements during the 1970s and 1980s, and was internationally praised for doing so. However, many of those settlements have since been bought out for real estate speculation (McCarthy 2003; World Bank 1995).

Privatizing water services for Jakarta's urban poor

Jakarta's water privatization was part of the 1990s global expansion of multinational water companies' cross-border investments. In 1997 PAM Jaya – Jakarta's public water utility company – started 25-year concession contracts with private sector operators that divided Jakarta into two service areas (PAM Jaya website 2016). The West Zone was contracted to Suez Lyonnaise des Eaux, a France-based water utility operator and one of the world's largest private water companies. The East Zone was contracted to Thames Water, a UK-based company. The concession contracts required service improvements and achieving 100% coverage by 2023 (Argo and Laquian 2004). In the following years both concessionaires claimed they significantly improved the management of Jakarta's water system, including expanding the piped water network from 30% in 1997 to more than 60% in 2009, and reducing nonrevenue water from 60% to less than 50% (see Table 7.1).

One problem with the privatization project is that the expansion of piped water was uneven across income groups. According to Jakarta's water tariff structure, the urban poor are represented by Category K II 2A1 (house floor size less than 28 square meters), and while these residents had the highest percentage increase (584%) between 1998 and 2009 (see Table 7.2), the most new connections occurred for the K III A and above categories, with nearly 130,000 new connections since 1998.

Another problem is that PAM Jaya's progressive tariff structure is a strong disincentive for connecting the poor (Bakker et al. 2006). Specifically, those in Category K II 2A1 pay significantly lower per cubic meter tariff than the "key accounts" in Category K III A and above. The collected payments from all

Table 7.1 Comparison of service levels of PALYJA and AETRA in 2009

	West Zone	East Zone
	PT PAM Lyonnaise Jaya	PT AETRA Air Jakarta
Owner	Suez Environnement (51%) ASTRATEL (30%) CITI Group (19%)	Acuatico (95%) Alberta (5%)
Population	4,446,024	4,352,666*
Customers	412,456	382,693
Service Coverage	63.9%	66%*
Nonrevenue Water	43.9%	48.62%
Average Tariff	Rp 7,713 (approx. US$0.85)	Rp 6,100 (approx. US$0.70)
Volume	380,000 m3/day	354,500 m3/day
	Source: PALYJA	Source: AETRA Fact Sheet *Source: KRuHA

customers are put into a joint account between PAM Jaya and the operators, from which the private water companies receive their dues. Although poor customers pay less than a third of the rate paid by the middle class and above, all distributed water is billed on a flat per cubic meter water charge. In other words, the greater the number of poor households that are connected, the larger the shortfall between the collected tariff and the flat water charge paid to the operators – a shortfall PAM Jaya is responsible for covering.

Output-based aid (OBA) approach in Jakarta water supply

Despite extending piped water coverage, the two concessionaires' achievements were not enough to keep them on track to reach 100% coverage by 2023, which

Table 7.2 Jakarta water tariff structure, selected categories

Class	Description	Tariff since 15 January 2007		
		$0-10\ m^3$	$11-20\ m^3$	$>20\ m^3$
K I	Social Customers	1,050	1,050	1,050
K II	Low Income Domestic	1,050	1,050	1,575
K III A	Middle Class	3,550	4,700	5,500
K III B	Upper Class and Small Business	4,900	6,000	7,450
K IV A		6,825	8,150	9,800
K IV B	Non Domestic	12,550	12,550	12,550

US$1 = Rp 9,000 at the time of the GPOBA project completion
Source: PAM Jaya website 2016

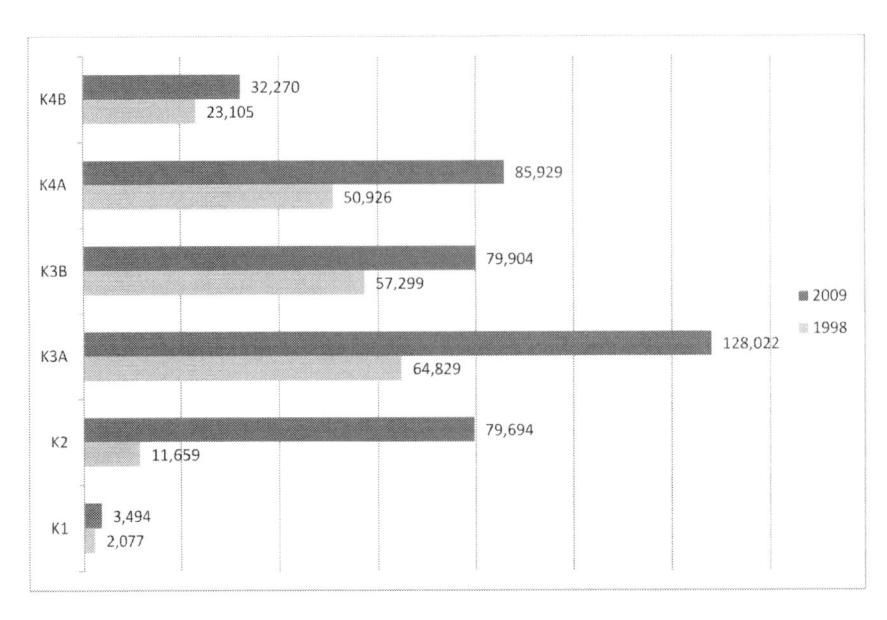

Figure 7.1 Number of customers by category, PALYJA (1998–2009)

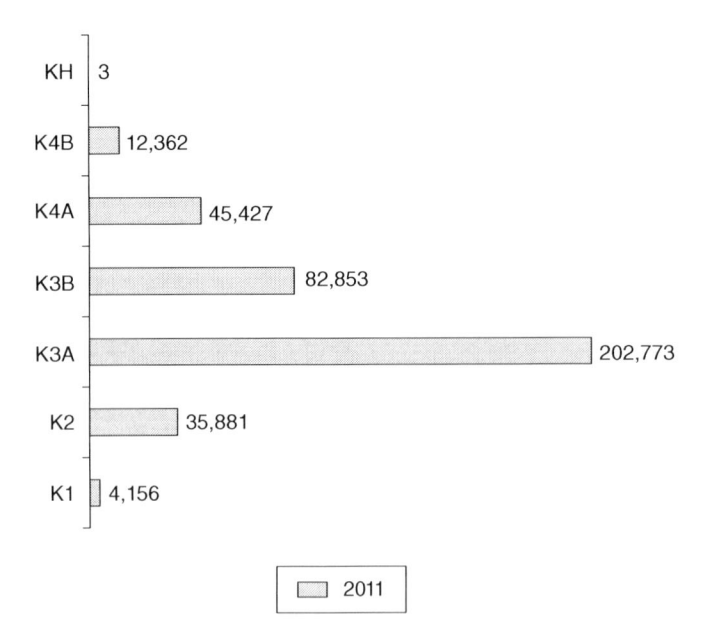

Category	2009	1998
K4B	32,270	23,105
K4A	85,929	50,926
K3B	79,904	57,299
K3A	128,022	64,829
K2	79,694	11,659
K1	3,494	2,077

Figure 7.2 Number of customers by category, AETRA (2011)

Category	2011
KH	3
K4B	12,362
K4A	45,427
K3B	82,853
K3A	202,773
K2	35,881
K1	4,156

was required by the privatization contracts. Under pressure to meet the 2023 coverage in an environment where connection fees were still prohibitive for the poor, the water companies viewed the OBA water supply program as an alternative funding source meeting their coverage goal. In 2005 PALYJA and AETRA approached Global Partnership for Output-Based Aid (GPOBA), a main funder of the OBA program, and requested support for expanding piped water access to low-income, "informal or slum communities" (Menzies and Setiono 2010, 1). In November 2007, GPOBA awarded PALYJA a US$2.57 million grant, with a timeline to complete the project in 2009.

Prior to the OBA program the urban poor (i.e., category KII) represented 17% of PALYJA's customer base. However, there were still many poor households in Jakarta who lived in places that lacked infrastructure services. Although the statistics bureau claimed that the poverty rate was only 4.09%, Jakarta's governor admitted that official poverty statistics were "deceiving" and that he would not be surprised if the actual poverty figure was at 40% (Detiknews 2014). Those who were not connected were likely to be those unable to afford homes with better infrastructure, and were unlikely to be able to afford the connection fee on their own. The OBA was expected to connect these communities as PALYJA's customers. With OBA-supported additional customers, PALYJA's K II customer category in 2009 reached almost 20%, compared with AETRA at nearly 10%.

The OBA project's objective, as stated in the Operating Manual, was to "connect poor communities containing some 11,600 households in western Jakarta to the piped water distribution network" (GPOBA 2008, 1). Similar to the GPOBA's pro-poor tagline, the project was to target low-income households, with the OBA subsidy targeted for covering the initial water connection fees. According to the OBA approach, PALYJA and AETRA had to fully shoulder the investment costs, and would be reimbursed *after* project completion *and* satisfactory delivery over the first three months.

Jakarta's OBA water supply program was implemented in two service arrangements, both of which are based on the legal status of the community's land: (1) Type I ("standard metered household connection"), with a Rp 120,000 connection fee for each household; and (2) Type II ("high density, very low income areas") for households with no legal land tenure, which were to use a "master meter" system, and charge each household a Rp 12,000 connection fee. The Type II connection is in response to Jakarta's legal requirements for piped water connections, which bars houses with no land titles from getting individual connections. Houses in the master meter arrangement have individual meters, but monthly bills are based on master meter readings. Also, recipients of type II connections are required to form a community-based organization (CBO) that takes responsibility for collecting payments from each household to cover the monthly bills. Out of the ten areas selected for GPOBA program's first phase, only one was planned for a Type II connection (i.e., Muara Baru in Penjaringan, which had 500 households) (GPOBA 2008).

Benefits of Jakarta's OBA water supply program

The first direct benefit of Jakarta's OBA program was the connection fee subsidy, which helped the urban poor connect to the water network. This benefit is widely viewed by water operators and financial institutions, such as the World Bank and the Asian Development Bank, as the answer to delivering piped water to the urban poor. PALYJA's President Director claimed that "socially and economically it is not good if the poor are not connected" (Interview, July 2010), and he strongly believed there should be a connection fee subsidy. In Jakarta's OBA program the connection fees for poor households were far below the standard connection fees of Rp 600,000 (approximately US$45) per household for mass connections or Rp 1.8 million (approximately US$135) for individual connections.

The second benefit is that the program lowered water expenses for those who get connected. Those lacking a connection had to buy water from local vendors, who charge much more. For example, the water cost from pushcart vendors was Rp 1,500 for 20 liters of water, equal to Rp 75,000 per cubic meter. In contrast, piped water for K II 2A1 customers was Rp 1,050 per cubic meter, plus a Rp 1,575 monthly subscription fee and taxes. A 2010 interview with Muara Baru residents revealed that each household usually spent Rp 90,000 to Rp 300,000 per month (about US$9–30, based on the exchange rate at the time) for water sold by pushcart vendors, depending on the household size and usage. With piped water, based on PAM Jaya's bill simulator, a K II 2AI household monthly bill is now less than Rp 10,000 for consuming up to 1 cubic meter, or less than Rp 20,000 for consuming up to 10 cubic meters.

The OBA program's third benefit was challenging land-tenure regulations that previously barred some Muara Baru residents from obtaining individual water connections. Such land-tenure regulations had long discriminated against the poor who could not afford to have legal homes, or could not afford to convert their land status to ownership, or were not informed of the necessity to obtain land certificates for areas they have lived on for generations. However, when the Muara Baru community members were offered Type II service (i.e., master meter) they refused it, insisting instead on obtaining individual connections. This posed a problem for PALYJA as the GPOBA program's agreed-upon targets stipulated that a minimum number of households had to be connected. Fearing that the OBA water supply program would not reach the minimum target, PALYJA advocated to the Jakarta government to permit individual connections in Muara Baru. Thus, the OBA program enabled Muara Baru to overcome discriminatory legal regulations, and allowed "squatters" to get piped water connections.

Limitations of Jakarta's OBA water supply program

Increasing the urban poor's connection to piped water has the potential to dramatically increase the equity of Jakarta's water system. However, while OBA's Phase I target was to connect 10,000 households, only 5,042 households were connected (GPOBA 2008; PALYJA 2011). One reason for this failure was that some had previous piped water connections that were terminated, which made them ineligible for the OBA program, as they were considered capable of paying the connection fee without the subsidy. A second reason was that many residents were unwilling to get connected (Interview with PALYJA representatives on the GPOBA program, July 2010).

Another limitation was that the OBA program's goals (see Table 7.3) failed to address issues specific to Jakarta. While the first goal was to provide affordable, reliable, and clean water, Jakarta's water supply was limited because it relied on sources outside the city that had to be shared with agricultural areas in West Java. Thus, the water service might not be reliable for 24 hours a day, especially for those in the far north of Jakarta, at the end of the pipe network, where pipe water pressure was the weakest. Relatedly, the national water provision agency rated Jakarta as having "unreliable" water service in 2006, 2007, and 2008 (BPP SPAM 2010), with water quality, service disruptions, and poor water pressure being common problems (AMRTA Institute 2015). The program's second goal emphasized the relationship between health and unsafe water, but many water-borne diseases in Jakarta were caused by floods, clogged drains, as well as unsanitary toilets and garbage disposal (Texier 2008). The third goal was to achieve economic benefits from satisfying the first two goals. However, if the first two goals could not be satisfied, achieving the third goal was unlikely. If water services remained unreliable because of unequal water pressure and limited supply, the urban poor with water connections still needed to rely on water vendors or wells to complement piped water. Furthermore, because many urban poor neighborhoods were prone to flooding, water-borne diseases would persist. Other than the fourth goal that referred specifically to Jakarta's spatial planning policy, the OBA water supply goals appeared as generic goals of water supply projects, which failed to address the specific water issues of Jakarta's urban poor, once again perpetuating injustices-in-waiting.

The Jakarta OBA program's three main benefits (i.e., connection subsidy, lowered water expenses, and eligibility) were also limited because they revolved around monetary measurements and land status, which were largely materialistic.

Table 7.3 Goals of the GPOBA Water Supply Project in Western Jakarta

1 Access to affordable and reliable clean water services;
2 Health benefits from reduced exposure to environmental risks posed by unsafe water (reduced morbidity and mortality rates – especially in infants);
3 Economic benefits from reduction in medical expenses to treat water borne diseases, increased productivity and capacity to work due to reduced morbidity and associated reduction in sickness related absence from work, reduced household expenditure of clean water (water tariff lower than cost of many alternative sources); and
4 Social benefits from equitable access to clean water for informal/illegal communities currently disbarred from access by DKI Jakarta spatial planning policy.

Source: GPOBA Water Supply Western Jakarta – Expansion of Water Services Project Operational Manual, 2007

The water supply program did not challenge injustices in the city, but rather used existing water systems, such as the water tariff. When combined with water privatization contracts, the water tariff became a source of injustice because the tariff structure and the escrow account system associated the poor with a shortfall in the escrow account. Regarding the OBA program's challenge to existing land status regulations, this challenge was only carried out for the Muara Baru community, thereby leaving unjust regulations in place to discriminate against other poor communities. These limitations indicate the OBA programs have deep contradictions between pro-poor and privatization perspectives, and elucidating these contradictions is what we now turn to.

Perpetuating water injustices

The inability of Jakarta's OBA program to achieve water justice can be traced to at least three contradictions within it. First, the program was tailored for the poor, but failed to involve the poor in designing the program and projects. While the program's second phase planned to establish 1,700 Type II connections (i.e., geared toward high-density, very low-income areas with no legal land tenure), the program faced difficulties because of its failure to engage with the local community. An example was the Muara Baru community, where the houses scheduled for Type II connections included those on stilts on the reservoir, with residents who were increasingly stigmatized in the popular realm as illegal and "out of control." The program's proposal for Type II connections was an effort to circumvent the legal issue that forbade individual connections for houses without land titles. The drafting of this plan did not include local voices and the Muara Baru community eventually resisted the Type II connections. The World Bank attributed the connection rejections to a "preference for standard, individual household metered connections" (Menzies and Setiono 2010, 2), but the reasons for the rejection were actually more complicated.

Bottom–up resistance to the OBA program represented the community's aspirations to be recognized, but it was also enmeshed with the local power hierarchy. Resistance could be attributed to the collective billing system, the necessity to form a community-based organization (CBO), and the existing water businesses operating in the area. Existing water businesses (often referred to as the "water mafia" by the private water operator) saw the program as a threat to their business, and encouraged the district head to withdraw support for the OBA water supply program and persuaded households to reject the master meter plan (Fournier, Folliasson, Martin and Arfiansyah 2010). PALYJA's problems were compounded by undeveloped networks with the community. While the company usually relied on NGOs to facilitate relationships and communication with communities, there was no NGO to communicate with in Muara Baru. After a year of negotiations with the local water vendors, PALYJA took them on as employees, thereby ending the resistance and allowing PALYJA to add 132 water connections. In turn, this allowed the OBA water supply program to meet its minimum target. This process showed that resistance to the OBA program was more complicated than just anti-privatization; the resistance reflected social and political dynamics within the community as well as personal interests.

The second contradiction was the reliance on exceptions for some beneficiaries, but not for others. For example, the program's challenge to land tenure requirements for individual connections was only specific to Muara Baru and did not become a precedent for the whole city. Moreover, it did not change Jakarta's limited raw water supply, nor did it challenge the unjust water tariff structure, both of which eventually affected beneficiaries. This showed that program implementation depended on special considerations rather than on changing an unjust system.

The third contradiction was that the OBA program's measurements of success were based on average output from all communities, which concealed spatial inequalities and failed to capture continuing water service injustices. There were at least two ways in which OBA water supply obscured injustices. First, although PALYJA's OBA water supply was deemed successful and led the company to get reimbursed for the connection fees, PALYJA admitted that not all communities in Muara Baru could get uninterrupted water service. Piped water service in Muara Baru continued to be problematic, due to their low-lying location at the northern coastal tip of Jakarta. While all OBA households were integrated as customers in the market – and were subjected to the basic monthly charges – not all of them got reliable services. In fact, unreliable water services is one of the reasons the Muara Baru community had a history of protesting against water privatization prior to the OBA water project. These were long-term customers who obtained individual piped water connections long before OBA, but whose homes ceased to get water after 1997 (Haryanto 2010). Instead of addressing the water supply problems of existing customers, the OBA program added more Muara Baru customers to the unreliable piped water network, generating the prerequisite for enhanced and more widespread injustices-in-waiting.

The GPOBA measured the Jakarta water supply program as a success, but water activists –including the ones from Muara Baru – continued to advocate for cancelling the privatization contracts. Suez intended to sell its 51% share of PALYJA to Manila Water, but was subsequently turned down by PAM Jaya in 2013, citing that Manila Water did not have the "reliable finances" to rebalance the contract (Global Water Intelligence 2012; Setiawati and Muhammadi 2013). A lawsuit by a coalition of residents, trade unions, and water justice activists, who had been advocating against water privatization for years, resulted in the Central Jakarta District Court ruling, in March 2015, to annul the contracts (TNI 2015). Despite the 2015 court ruling, the two concessionaires continued to run the water service, with Suez appealing against the ruling two weeks after the judgment (de Clercq 2015), and subsequently overturning the District Court ruling at the High Court appeal (Elyda 2016).

Conclusion: privatized water services and water injustices

This chapter's overarching objective has been to elucidate the fundamental incompatibilities between water privatization and pro-poor agendas. Towards that end we analyzed the privatization of Jakarta's water system, with a particular focus on the OBA water program introduced in 2007. This chapter's social justice focus has exposed water's material and spatial dimensions for the poor, which uncovered benefits, limitations, and contradictions in Jakarta's OBA water program. On the surface it looked like the Jakarta OBA program paved the way for delivering basic water services to the poor. However, the program also served to expand water privatization, enabling PALYJA to reach groups previously excluded because of financial and legal barriers, and to expand water delivery to communities that usually did not need the water companies.

While the OBA program provided the poor with tangible material benefits, it had significant limitations. Benefits included decreased water connection costs, an increase in the number of poor households connected to the water network, water connections for some who previously faced legal land-based obstacles, and lower water expenses for those who obtained connections. While these benefits are tangible and undeniable, the program also had significant limitations, such as failing to meet the stated goal of connecting 100% of the city's poor households, and that unjust land-based legal restrictions continue to deprive many from obtaining water connections.

The limitations can, to some degree, be attributed to the program's fundamental orientation toward market-based water management approaches, with two noticeable manifestations. First, the program's template-based goals preserved the inequalities in profit-based privatized water services by failing to recognize specific issues in Jakarta's unequal urban landscapes. For example, an expansion in the piped water network does not equate to reliable services, especially when Jakarta still faces a water supply shortage, and service reliability is unequally distributed across the city. The expansion is also insensitive toward geographic differences between poor communities. This is clearly indicated in the service expansion to poor areas in Muara Baru, where people who were connected before the OBA program were already experiencing intermittent and even nonexistent water services. This community, being at the far north end of the city, was spatially disadvantaged in water distribution but the OBA expanded the network without responding to those spatial disadvantages. Second, the program failed to challenge the root of water injustices in the city. The program appeared more as a "band aid" to a problematic profit-based system than an actual solution. The OBA program's limitations made it unable to address the root causes of water injustices, and it served more as a means of expanding water markets to the poor, validating water's commodification, and perpetuating water injustices.

Studying Jakarta's OBA program reveals that expanding services to the poor through market mechanisms serves to validate water's commodification and perpetuates water injustices, which will result, over time, in more injustices in waiting. Funders' and PALYJA's celebrations of OBA achievements, in delivering water for Jakarta's urban poor, are an example of how water's materiality still dominates the policy realm, leaving out the most essential questions of discriminatory practices and spatial inequalities, both of which perpetuate the poor's marginalization. Moreover, examining water's material and spatial aspects contributes to the water privatization literature because it underscores that water justice is tied to the larger context of social and spatial justice, and that efforts to achieve water justice will continue to fall short if we continue to treat water in isolation of the urban poor's social and spatial marginalization.

A limitation of this analysis is that it is based on one case. While Jakarta remains a strategic case to study water privatization's social impacts, the case's specificities might not generalize to other contexts. Thus, we need grounded observations in multiple sites to build more generalizable knowledge about the relationship between water privatization and pro-poor agendas. Towards that end, an interesting case might be Metro Manila, Philippines, where municipal water was also privatized to two concessionaires, but where one water company's service record has been celebrated by the Asian Development Bank. This distinction suggests that Manila may have enjoyed better water justice outcomes. If so, contrasting these cases could help illuminate factors that lead to better water justice in some locales, but not others. In turn, such knowledge could be used to better address water injustices, and improve the lives of millions in this region of the world.

Acknowledgements

The fieldwork for this chapter was supported by a research grant from the Institute of Water Policy, Lee Kuan Yew School of Public Policy, National University of Singapore.

Notes

1 Asia Research Institute, National University of Singapore.
2 Department of Sociology, University of Auckland, New Zealand.
3 Twenty interviews, conducted in 2010, involved representatives from each of the private water concessionaires, a representative of PAM Jaya (Perusahaan Air Minum Jakarta Raya) as the water utility company, several PALYJA representatives who managed the GPOBA water supply program in Jakarta, a representative of the program at the World Bank, a member of the Jakarta Water Regulatory Body at the time, leaders of a non-governmental organization (NGO) coalition on water, and residents in the OBA target area. These interviews are complemented by field observations of the OBA water supply areas in Jakarta.

References

ADB (Asian Development Bank) (2007). West Jakarta Water Supply Development Project. *Proposed Loan to the Republic of Indonesia*. Manila: Asian Development Bank.
Allouche J. and Finger M. (2002). *Water privatisation: trans-national corporations and the re-regulation of the water industry*. London and New York: Spon Press.
AMRTA Institute (2015). *Dry pipes: the problems of water services in Jakarta* (documentary film). Retrieved 26 August 2016 from https://www.youtube.com/watch?v=Rk75O5cVF1w

Argo T. and Laquian A.A. (2004). Privatization of water utilities and its effects on the urban poor in Jakarta Raya and Metro Manila. In Woodrow Wilson International Center for Scholars and the National Institute of Urban Affairs (Ed.) *Forum on urban infrastructure and public service delivery for the urban poor, regional focus: Asia.* New Delhi: India Habitat Centre.

Bakker K. (2010). *Privatizing water: Governance failure and the world's urban water crisis* (Singapore edition). Ithaca, NY: Cornell University Press.

Bakker K. (2007). The 'commons' versus the 'commodity': alter-globalization, anti-privatization, and the human right to water in the Global South. *Antipode*, 39(3), 430–455.

Bakker K. and Kooy M. (2008). Governance failure: rethinking the institutional dimensions of urban water supply to poor households. *World Development*, 36(10), 1891–1915.

Bakker K., Kooy M., Shofiani N.E. and Martijn E-J. (2006). *Disconnected: poverty, water supply and development in Jakarta, Indonesia.* Human Development Report 2006. Human Development Office Occasional Paper 2006/1.

Birkenholtz T. (2010). 'Full-cost recovery': producing differentiated water collection practices and responses to centralized water networks in Jaipur, India. *Environment and Planning, A(42)*, 2238–2253.

BPP SPAM (2010). *Kinerja PDAM tahun 2009 wilayah I, Pulau Jawa.* Badan Pendukung Pengembangan Sistem Penyediaan Air Minum (BPP SPAM), Kementrian Pekerjaan Umum.

Brook P.J. and Petrie M. (2001). Output-based aid: precedents, promises, and challenges. In P.J. Brook and S. Smith (Eds.) *Contracting for public services: output-based aid and its applications* (pp. 3–11). Washington: World Bank.

Carroll T. (2010). *Delusions of development: The World Bank and the post-Washington consensus in Southeast Asia.* London: Palgrave Macmillan.

de Clercq G. (2015). Suez will fight to keep its Jakarta water contract. *Reuters* (Technology). Retrieved 11 May 2016 from http://www.reuters.com/article/us-suez-jakarta-idUSKBN0N126W20150410

Conca K. (2005). *Governing water: contentious transnational politics and global institution building.* Cambridge, MA: MIT Press.

Detiknews (2014). Ahok Imbau BPS Ukur Angka Kemiskinan DKI Pakai KHL, Bukan Standar Kalori. *Detiknews*, 30 April. Retrieved 26 August 2016 from http://news.detik.com/berita/2569710/ahok-imbau-bps-ukur-angka-kemiskinan-dki-pakai-khl-bukan-standar-kalori

DKI Jakarta Government (2016). Dinas Kependudukan dan Catatan Sipil Provinsi DKI Jakarta. Retrieved 1 February 2016 from http://www.kependudukancapil.go.id/index.php?Itemid=63&id=4&option=com_content&view=article

Douglass M. (2010). Globalisation, mega-projects and the environment: Urban form and water in Jakarta. *Environment and Urbanisation Asia*, 1(1), 45–65.

Dumol M. (2000). *The Manila Water concession: a key government official's diary of the world's largest water privatization.* Washington: World Bank.

Dikeç M. (2001). Justice and the spatial imagination. *Environment and Planning, A(33)*, 1785–1805.

Elyda C. (2016). High court rules in favor of Jakarta water privatization. *Jakarta Post.* 2 March. Retrieved 11 May 2016 from http://www.thejakartapost.com/news/2016/03/02/high-court-rules-favor-jakarta-water-privatization.html

Fournier V., Folliasson P., Martin L. and Arfiansyah (2010). PALYJA Water For All programs in Western Jakarta. *Water Droplet.*

Furlong K. and Bakker K. (2010). The contradictions in 'alternative' service delivery: governance, business models, and sustainability in municipal water supply. *Environment and Planning C: Government and Policy*, 28, 349–368.

Gibbs L.M. (2010). 'A beautiful soaking rain': environmental value and water beyond Eurocentrism. *Environment and Planning D: Society and Space*, 28, 363–378.

Global Water Intelligence Magazine (2012). Tie-ups and buy-ups: Manila Water has agreed to buy Suez Environnement's 51% stake in PALYJA, the Jakarta west zone concessionaire, 14 years into a 25-year contract. *Global Water Intelligence Magazine*, November.

Goldman M. (2005). *Imperial nature: The World Bank and struggles for social justice in the age of globalization*. New Haven, CT: Yale University Press.

GPOBA website (http://www.gpoba.org/gpoba/what-is-oba) Accessed 19 October 2011.

GPOBA (2008). Global Partnership on Output Based Aid Western Jakarta: Expansion of Water Services Project, Operational Manual. Retrieved 26 August 2016 from https://www.gpoba.org/sites/gpoba/files/OperationsManual/GPOBA%20%20Indonesia%20Jakarta%20_%20PALYJA_Operational%20Manual.pdf

GPOBA (2009). Output-based aid – fact sheet. Retrieved 16 May 2016 from https://www.gpoba.org/sites/gpoba.org/files/GPOBA_fact_sheet_english_0.pdf

Harvey D. (2006). *Spaces of global capitalism: towards a theory of uneven geographical development*. London and New York: Verso.

Haryanto U. (2010). Indonesian water warriors flood streets of Jakarta. *Jakarta Globe*, 23 March, 2.

Heynen N., Kaika M. and Swyngedouw E. (Eds.) (2006). *In the nature of cities: urban political ecology and the politics of urban metabolism*. London and New York: Routledge.

Ingram H., Whiteley J.M. and Perry R.W. (2008). The importance of equity and the limits of efficiency in water resources. In J.M. Whiteley, H. Ingram and R.W. Perry (Eds.) *Water, place, and equity*. Cambridge, MA: MIT Press.

Ioris A.A.R. (2011). Values, meanings, and positionalities: the controversial valuation of water in Rio de Janeiro. *Environment and Planning C: Government and Policy*, 29, 872–888.

Ioris A.A.R. (2016). Water scarcity and the exclusionary city: the struggle for water justice in Lima, Peru. *Water International*, 41(1), 125–139.

Jones G. and Douglass M. (Eds.) (2008). *Mega-urban regions in Pacific Asia*. Singapore: NUS Press.

Kompas (2011). Ribuan Unit Rumah Susun Terlantar. *Kompas*, 28 February.

Laurie N. and Marvin S. (1999). Globalisation, neoliberalism, and negotiated development in the Andes: water projects and regional identity in Cochabamba, Bolivia. *Environment and Planning, A(31)*, 1401–1415.

Lefebvre H. (1991). *The production of space* (reprint edition). Oxford: Blackwell Publishers.

Loftus A. (2006). Reification and the dictatorship of the water meter. *Antipode*, 38(5), 1023–1045.

Marin P. (2009). *Public-private partnerships for urban water utilities: a review of experiences in developing countries*. Washington: World Bank and PPIAF.

McCarthy P. (2003). Understanding slums: case studies for the global report 2003: Jakarta, Indonesia UN-HABITAT. Retrieved 25 April 2016 from http://www.ucl.ac.uk/dpu-projects/Global_Report/cities/jakarta.htm

Meehan K. (2014). Tool-power: water infrastructure as wellsprings of state power. *Geoforum*, 57, 215–224.

Menzies I. and Setiono I. (2010). Output-based aid in Indonesia: improved access to better services for poor households in Western Jakarta. *GPOBA Approaches Note*. Washington, DC: The World Bank.

Morgan B. (2012). *Water on tap: rights and regulation in the transnational governance of urban water services*. Cambridge: Cambridge University Press.

Mumssen Y., Johannes L. and Kumar G. (2010). *Output-based aid: lessons learned and best practices*. Washington: World Bank.

Neal (Patrick) M.J., Lukasiewicz A. and Syme G.J. (2014). Why justice matters in water governance: some ideas for a 'water justice framework'. *Water Policy*, 16, 1–18.

Padawangi R. (2012). Climate change and the north coast of Jakarta: environmental justice and the social construction of space in urban poor communities. In W.G. Holt III (Ed.) *Research in urban sociology, vol. 12 (Urban areas and climate change)* (pp. 321–339). Bingley: Emerald.

Padawangi R. and Douglass M. (2015). Water, water everywhere: toward participatory solutions to chronic urban flooding in Jakarta. *Pacific Affairs*, 88(3), 517–550.

PALYJA (2011). *Annual report 2011*. Jakarta: PT PAM Lyonnaise Jaya.

PAM Jaya website (http://www.pamjaya.co.id) Accessed 11 May 2016.

Patrick M.J. (2014). The cycles and spirals of justice in water-allocation decision making. *Water International*, 39(1), 63–80.

Perreault T. (2014). What kind of governance for what kind of equity? Towards a theorization of justice in water governance. *Water International*, 39(2), 233–245.

Prasad N. (2007). Privatisation of water: a historical perspective. *Law, Environment and Development Journal*, 3(2), 217–235.

Rimmer P.J. and Dick H.W. (2009). *The city in Southeast Asia: patterns, processes, and policy*. Singapore: NUS Press.

Roberts A. (2008). Privatizing social reproduction: the primitive accumulation of water in an era of neoliberalism. *Antipode*, 40, 535–560.

Robinson J.L. (2013). *Contested water: the struggle against water privatization in the United States and Canada*. Cambridge, MA: MIT Press.

Scruggs L. (1998). Political and economic inequality and the environment. *Ecological Economics*, 26, 259–275.

Setiawati I. and Muhammadi F.Z. (2013). Suez to offer city assistance to manage water. *Jakarta Post*, 6 August.

Sheehan J. (2005). The commodification of the Asian commons: water as a property right. *Asia Pacific Journal of Environmental Law*, 9, 87–104.

Skitka L.J. (2009). Exploring the 'lost and found' of justice theory and research. *Social Justice Research*, 22, 98–116.

Smith N. (2008). *Uneven development: nature, capital, and the production of space* (third edition). Athens, GA, and London: University of Georgia Press.

Soja E.W. (2010). *Seeking spatial justice*. Minneapolis: University of Minnesota Press.

Swyngedouw E. (2005). Dispossessing H2O: the contested terrain of water privatization. *Capitalism Nature Socialism*, 16(1), 81–98.

Swyngedouw E. (2004). *Social power and the urbanization of water: flows of power*. Oxford: Oxford University Press.

Syme G.J. and Nancarrow B. (2001). Social justice and environmental management: an introduction. *Social Justice Research*, 14(4), 343–347.

Texier P. (2008). Floods in Jakarta: when the extreme reveals daily structural constraints and mismanagement. *Disaster Prevention and Management*, 1(3), 358–372.

TNI – Transnational Institute (2015). Jakarta Court cancels world's biggest water privatisation after 18 year failure. Retrieved 11 May 2016 from https://www.tni.org/en/pressrelease/jakarta-court-cancels-worlds-biggest-water-privatisation-after-18-year-failure

Vidal J. (2015). Water privatisation: a worldwide failure? *Guardian*, 30 January. Retrieved 19 May 2016 from http://www.theguardian.com/globaldevelopment/2015/jan/30/waterprivatisationworldwidefailurelagosworldbank

Widiantono D.J. and Soepriadi I. (2009). Menakar kinerja kota-kota di Indonesia. *Bulletin Elektronik Departemen Pekerjaan Umum*, January–February.

World Bank (2015). Water and sewerage sector snapshots – private participation in infrastructure (PPI). Retrieved 19 May 2016 from http://ppi.worldbank.org/snapshots/sector/Waterandsewerage

World Bank (1995). Enhancing the quality of life in urban Indonesia: the legacy of Kampung Improvement Program. *Indonesia Impact Evaluation Report*. Washington, DC: World Bank.

World Health Organization (WHO) (2015). Meeting target 10: How much will it cost? *Asia Water Watch 2015*.

Young I.M. (1990). *Justice and the politics of difference*. Princeton, NJ: Princeton University Press.

Zwarteveen M.Z. and Boelens R. (2014). Defining, researching and struggling for water justice: some conceptual building blocks for research and action. *Water International*, 39(2), 143–158.

8 Ecological resilience and New York City's water supply system

The role of adaptive governance in combating vulnerabilities

Sarah E. Blake[1]

Introduction

Resource overconsumption is one of the most pressing issues facing societies today (Foster, Clark and York 2010; Rosa, Diekmann, Dietz and Jaeger 2010). Although societies depend on nature for survival and growth, we have long been consuming at an unsustainable rate (Foster 1999; Schnaiberg 1980). Unprecedented global growth has pushed us to a precipice, where we are beginning to see the disastrous effects of overconsumption in the forms of climate change and scarcity. Water scarcity, in particular, has become a global problem. As a necessary resource, clean drinking water is often thought of as a right. However, in our current capitalist system, access to clean drinking water is limited or diminishing in developed and developing regions throughout the globe (Barlow and Clark 2005).

The adaptive governance approach to managing sustainable social-ecological systems can be used to help combat overconsumption and scarcity. Adaptive governance "... is increasingly called upon by scholars and practitioners to coordinate resource management regimes in the face of the complexity and uncertainty associated with rapid environmental change" (Chaffin, Gosnell and Cosens 2014, 1). According to Dietz and colleagues (2003), adaptive governance should bring together stakeholders with different interests to create reflexive strategies to manage our common natural resources (Chaffin et al. 2014). To better understand these strategies in action, scholars have examined adaptive governance for numerous issues, including natural hazards, fisheries, and water management (Clark and Semmahasak 2013; Cosens and Williams 2012; Djalante, Holley and Thomalla 2011; Scholz and Stiftel 2005). Recent work has illuminated the importance of knowledge and timing in strategy implementation, and the differences between governance and co-management (Chaffin et al. 2014; Folke, Hahn, Olsson and Norberg 2005). However, the literature has two gaps: (1) it under-analyzes the role that power plays in the implementation of adaptive governance strategies; and (2) it has not examined the role of adaptive strategies to preserve unfiltered drinking water supplies.

This chapter addresses these gaps through a historical analysis of New York City's (NYC) water supply system, which provides a strong case for sustainable water management because: it is the largest municipal water supply system in the

U.S., it is located in a water-rich climate, and for the past 18 years it has been managed through an adaptive governance strategy that has been hailed as one of the most successful examples of adaptive management (Pfeffer and Wagenet 1999). Moreover, NYC's water supply is drawn from unfiltered water supplies, which are the result of a protected and sustainable environment, and which provide possible blueprints for successful adaptive governance strategies.

The case of the creation, extension, and preservation of NYC's water supply is used to answer three questions:

1. What are the roles of political and economic power in creating a sustainable and resilient water supply system?
2. What specific historical and political conditions mobilized stakeholders to begin the process of adaptive governance negotiations?
3. How are adaptive governance strategies linking powerful and vulnerable localities used to sustainably manage resources?

In what follows I discuss adaptive governance and its role in mitigating vulnerabilities and building resilience, focusing on the gaps within the literature that this project works to address. I then present NYC's water supply system, highlighting the vulnerabilities within the West of the Hudson watershed region and the city's political and economic power. Finally, the Memorandum of Agreement between the city and the watershed is presented as a model of adaptive governance, whose implementation was rooted in the city's economic power. The chapter provides an outline of adaptive governance implementation that integrates power, community movements, and bridging organizations as key components to negotiations. As well, it stresses the ability of a powerful locality, such as NYC, to use its political and economic power to help support and implement these programs, and demonstrates that adaptive governance strategies linking powerful and vulnerable locations can create a more resilient social-ecological system. Beyond understanding the NYC case, this analysis can serve as a guide for implementing sustainable land and resource management in other urban areas.

Vulnerability, resilience, and adaptive governance

Adaptive governance refers to a flexible and inclusive approach to sustainably managing common resources. Dietz et al. (2003) coined the term in their discussion of problems with common resource governance. Remarking on the fact that socio-ecological systems are dynamic and that environmental governance is impacted by many institutional and structural pressures, they emphasized that successful commons governance requires a capacity to adapt. In their original iteration Dietz, Ostrom and Stern (2003) suggested that a successful adaptive governance system should be able to accomplish five goals: (1) provide scientific and local knowledge; (2) address conflicts; (3) enforce rules; (4) create infrastructure; and (5) anticipate change. In this formulation adaptive governance captures the many institutional and structural pressures that impact environmental governance and can thus be seen as a possible solution to managing changing socio-ecological systems (Dietz et al. 2003; Folke et al. 2005; Folke 2006; Walker, Holling, Carpenter and Kinzig 2004). Moreover, much of the adaptive governance literature sees this approach as a precursor to sustainable development. Specifically, if we manage socio-ecological systems in a way that links scientific and local knowledge with the structure and legitimacy associated with governance, such systems can become more sustainable (Chaffin et al. 2014; Clark and Clarke 2011).

The adaptive governance literature views governance in terms of resilience: How can we manage our social-ecological systems in a way that allows for them to be resilient? According to Gunderson and Holling, ecosystem resilience can be understood as ". . . the magnitude of disturbance that can be absorbed before the system changes its structure by changing the variables and processes that control behavior" (2002, 28). Given that socio-ecological systems are perpetually changing, attempting to understand systems in terms of stability is unhelpful (Folke et al. 2005). Instead, researchers must try to understand how disturbances happen, how they can impact the system, and how they can present opportunities for adaptive management. Because a resilient system is able to bounce back from disturbances, the governance of the system must be flexible if it is to be effective (Gunderson 1999). From this perspective, ". . . the role of governance in socio-ecological systems is not inhibiting change, but managing the system to cope with, adapt to, and allow for further change" (Chaffin et al. 2014, 5). Adaptive governance achieves these goals.

However, not all systems that incorporate adaptive governance are resilient (Chaffin et al. 2014). The difference between a vulnerable system and a resilient system is that while the resilient system "bounces back" from disturbances, the vulnerable one is impacted by disturbances (Kasperson, Kasperson and Turner 2010). As clarified by Kasperson et al., vulnerability explains ". . . the degree to which a system or unit (such as a human group or place) is likely to experience harm due to exposure to perturbations or stresses" (2010, 236). Adaptive governance is one way to strengthen vulnerable socio-ecological systems, which may eventually become resilient systems.

While the adaptive governance literature provides a strong blueprint for sustainably managing communal resources, this chapter highlights two gaps, one empirical and one theoretical. First, the literature has yet to focus on unfiltered surface drinking water supplies. This is an important empirical lacunae because freshwater resources are indispensable to our survival and we are increasingly faced with issues of water scarcity, pollution, and privatization, which threaten our ability to provide clean drinking water to the global population (Barlow and Clark 2005). We must begin to understand how to sustainably manage this vital resource. Understanding surface drinking water management from an adaptive governance perspective can help to do this. As well, this analysis sheds light on sustainable land use and land management. Creating a sustainable water supply is inherently linked to creating a sustainable surrounding environment because water quality is largely determined by the run-off from the surrounding land (US EPA 2000). Therefore, any adaptive governance strategies that focus on unfiltered surface drinking water will also focus on protecting the surrounding environment.

The second lacunae is the literature's underdevelopment of power, particularly economic power. Mann emphasizes that "societies are constituted of multiple overlapping and intersecting socio-spatial networks of power" (1986, 1). Moreover, he discusses four overlapping sources of social power: political, economic, ideological, and military. The adaptive governance literature has touched upon political power in discussions of top–down versus bottom–up approaches and through various stakeholder involvement (Chaffin et al. 2014). However, both economic and ideological power are ignored. More attention needs to be given to the way these power dynamics influence a socio-ecological system's ability to implement adaptive governance strategies. While both of these issues are important, this chapter focuses on economic power (see Blake 2015 for a discussion of the role of ideological power in creating sustainable environments). Economic power is particularly important because it can be related to political power, as we will see in the case of NYC's water supply. While political power can assist in legitimating adaptive governance plans, little can happen without economic power to support this implementation. This relationship often shapes developed urban areas. Elucidating how adaptive governance is shaped by economic and political power can help to answer the sustainability scholars' call to understand how developed cities can foster global sustainability (Martine, McGranahan G., Montgomery M. and Fernández-Castilla 2008; Sanchez-Rodriguez 2008).

NYC's economic and political power

The NYC metropolitan area is the largest in the U.S. It boasts the country's biggest and most complex water supply system, including the most extensive catchment area in the country, with a watershed area that covers over 2,000 square miles (Gandy 2002). Miles of tunnels transport water from three upstate reservoir systems and provide over 9 million people with 1.3 billion gallons of drinking water per day (Delaney 1983; Gandy 2002). The system's direct beneficiaries are urban New Yorkers, but the water comes from rivers and streams in upstate New York (Blaine, Sweeny and Arscott 2006; Delaney 1983; Gandy 2002). To protect the city's drinking water, watersheds with strict environmental regulations have been created (Blaine et al. 2006; Finnegan 1997; Pfeffer and Wagenet 1999).

NYC's watershed areas are divided by the Hudson River. The Croton River System, which was constructed in the mid-1800s and was the city's original water supply system, lies east of the Hudson River. This watershed covers approximately 300 square miles of Westchester County, New York, and touches upon Fairfield County, Connecticut (Finnegan 1997; National Research Council 2000). The remaining 1,600 square miles of watershed lands lie on the western side of the Hudson River, in the counties of Greene, Sullivan, Ulster, Delaware, and Schoharie in New York state. This West of Hudson watershed provides 90% of NYC's drinking water (National Research Council 2000), and all lands in this watershed are preserved through adaptive governance strategies between the city and these watershed communities.

To understand how power has shaped NYC's water supply system and its watershed land preservation, it is useful to examine the power distribution within

New York state. The city's economic and political power is rooted in the trade growth that emerged after the American Revolution, when the city's international and domestic trade made it the nation's economic capital throughout the nineteenth century (Burrows and Wallace 1999). This economic dominance was due to the city holding the only ingress and egress to international, and until the early 1800s domestic, trade in the state. This put NYC in a powerful political position as the state's economy was essentially dependent upon the city's growth.

This economically dependent relationship was crucial to creating the city's water supply, as it needed access to rural areas outside the city to secure a "pure and wholesome supply" of water for its ever growing population (Burrows and Wallace 1999; King 1843). This chapter shows that the city's economic power resulted in New York state guaranteeing it political power over the rural hinterlands. To better understand the power dynamic between the city, the state, and the rural hinterland from which the city ultimately took its water, it is helpful to draw on Mann's discussion of "organizational outflanking" (Mann 1986).

Mann (1986) uses organizational outflanking to explain why the dominated tend to comply rather than revolt against the dominant. Mann explains that organizational outflanking is a result of institutionalized control, where "the few at the top can keep the masses at the bottom compliant [through] . . . the laws and the norms of the social group in which both operate" (1986, 7). The dominated are "outflanked" through institutionalized norms and are unable to revolt because these norms provide no opening for mobilization. Therefore, organizational outflanking is rooted in institutionalized laws and legislation. It is then strengthened through normalized interactions between those with power and those without. These normalized interactions reinforce the institutionalized stratification between the powerful and the dominated.

NYC's hinterlands demonstrate a case where organizational outflanking is at work as the state legislature institutionalized laws giving the city legal authority over these areas. Through these laws the city was able to select water sources, as well as the surrounding land, for acquisition through eminent domain (Laws of NY State 1833–1907). The hinterlands, on the other hand, are isolated rural areas and are relatively powerless. Moreover, the city's power of eminent domain meant rural residents had no means of resisting the city's land grabs. The city's institutionalized control over the hinterlands gave it a legitimate, systemic power that is rooted in the city's political and economic relationship with New York state. Moreover, the state's legitimation of the city's power ultimately allowed the city to mobilize its interests against those of its hinterlands (Logan and Molotch 2007; Mann 1986).

Extraterritorial control and environmental protection

The city's extraterritorial power enhanced, in two ways, the socio-ecological system's resilience. First, creating and maintaining a "pure and wholesome" water supply was integral to perpetuating NYC's capitalist growth, thereby enhancing its economic resilience (King 1843; Koeppel 2000). Second, beyond allowing the city to take land and water to create reservoirs, the extraterritorial power also allowed it to take land surrounding these planned reservoirs and to hold that land as protected space. This acquisition limited economic activities such as logging, and effectively mitigated the negative feedback loops within this socio-ecological system (Gunderson and Holling 2002). We will see that while the city's actions economically weakened an already vulnerable locality, it made the West of Hudson watershed more ecologically resilient.

In 1898, prior to the city's reach into the West of Hudson, the municipalities of Manhattan, Brooklyn, Queens, Staten Island, and the Bronx consolidated, securing the city's hold over the two biggest national ports and cementing the city's economic superiority (Burrows and Wallace 1999). However, this economic superiority would have been short lived if the city could not address the pending water crisis (Burrows and Wallace 1999). Access to West of Hudson water sources, granted in 1905, allowed for a 900% increase in the city's drinking water supply from 1900 to 1964 (nyc.dep.gov). This allowed the city to continue its growth, in terms of population and capital.

While the 1905 law allowed for continued growth in NYC, it led to growth restrictions on the towns in the West of Hudson watershed region. The land acquired during construction wiped out entire towns, which completely undermined the region's economy, leaving an already struggling rural region even more economically vulnerable (Burnett 2002; Steuding 1989; *Walton Reporter* 1958). An unidentified writer for the 1925 *Albany Evening News* described the Esopus Valley during the construction of the Schoharie Reservoir and Shandaken Tunnel:

> The dramatic story of a river turned back from its course and tunneled beneath a mountain and of a prosperous village buried 150 feet beneath an artificial lake unfolds toward its pathetic end here today. Last groups of Gilboa's 200 citizens are watching their hometown fall slowly in ruin, so that New York City's water supply can have a new reservoir. Before the town was to be flooded, it was supposed to be burned to the ground. There were a few movie companies competing for rights to film the final fire, before they were able to, however, the villagers torched the town to save what was left of their village's dignity.
>
> (Stratigos 1998, 73)

In 1954 the *Walton Reporter* described the Delaware River basin before the city built the Cannonsville and Pepaction Reservoirs and the Delaware Tunnel:

> Not long ago the little locomotive went down the valley twice daily, its whistle echoing back and forth across the hills as it can in no other place except the Catskills. Mail, passengers and freight were its burden, and great hopes were held for its future as a rail link to Scranton [Pennsylvania]. But somehow it was always plagued by financial troubles, and its doom was finally sealed when New York City picked the East Branch valley for a water site (page unknown).

The creation of the reservoirs not only destroyed numerous hamlets and villages in this region, it also rerouted roads and railroads, leaving the remaining towns more isolated than before. Taken together, this created an economically vulnerable region.

While the city's extraterritorial control had negative economic consequences for the watershed region, it enabled two important environment-preserving developments. First, the city was able to acquire large amounts of land – specifically in the West of Hudson region – as buffer zones around the reservoirs to protect them from potential run-off. Second, the city maintained control over all acquired land and instated NYC Department of Environmental Protection police throughout the region, to patrol all city-owned land and to enforce city-imposed environmental regulations. This control, combined with federal drinking water regulations passed in the 1970s and 1980s, preserved vast areas of land that might have been developed had the city not acquired the watershed region.

This discussion provides important context for understanding the adaptive governance entered into by the city and the West of Hudson watershed in subsequent years. It is clear that the state-granted power gave the city unprecedented control of the region. However, as we will see in the next section, the city's water supply expansion had consequences that prompted the watershed towns to organize a bottom–up response to further invasion, paving the way for adaptive governance.

Late-twentieth-century regulations

In 1974 the U.S. Congress passed the Safe Drinking Water Act, which "aim[ed] to ensure that public water supplies meet national standards that protect consumers from harmful contaminants in drinking water" (US EPA 1999, 4). By creating federal mandates the Safe Drinking Water Act made huge strides for water safety in the U.S. However, the 1974 standards, based on the 1962 Public Health Service guidelines, did not necessarily improve water quality as most states were already adhering to these standards. In NYC's case, the 1974 act had little effect on water quality as the city was already following the 1962 standards. However, the 1986 amendment to the Safe Drinking Water Act (SDWA) had important impacts on the city, its water supply, and its watershed areas.

The SDWA's Surface Water Treatment Rule section required filtration for all surface water supplies. However, supplies with "pristine and protected sources" could apply for and be granted a filtration waiver (US EPA 1999, 8). All systems that wish to qualify for filtration avoidance must be able to prove they can meet the above criteria, through a draft of regulations set to be enforced in the system's watershed. If the EPA determines the proposal feasible, they then issue a Filtration Avoidance Decision. The SDWA's 1986 amendment would become a turning point for NYC and its watersheds.

Capitalism and NYC's sustainable water supply system

As much of the environmental sociology literature tells us, capitalism is inherently unsustainable (Foster 1999; O'Connor 1987; Schnaiberg 1980). This chapter does not dispute that. However, in NYC's case it was the city's capitalist nature that led officials toward environmental sustainability. Capitalism's goal is to increase profits and minimize costs, and NYC's decision to file for EPA filtration avoidance was rooted in this ideology.

The estimated construction cost for filtering the city's water supply was between $6 billion and $8 billion, plus an estimated $5 million per year in operating costs. While filtration would have provided city residents with a cleaner water supply, it would also have strained city and state budgets. Moreover, money brought into the city would have been invested in filtration plants, instead of re-invested in the capitalist infrastructure, thereby undermining the city and state's economic power. It is with this financial burden in mind that the city began to look toward a more sustainable alternative, with the NYC mayor and the Department of Environmental Protection (DEP) commissioner ultimately choosing to apply to the EPA for filtration avoidance.

The EPA published filtration avoidance requirements in 1989, and the city immediately began working on a discussion draft of regulations, which they completed and sent to all involved parties, including watershed municipalities in 1990. Land acquisition was a major component of the initial draft, as the EPA recognized that

> land acquisition is one of the most effective, and therefore, important mechanisms to permanently protect the city's Catskill/Delaware watershed. The overarching goal [. . .] is to ensure that undeveloped, environmentally-sensitive watershed lands remain protected and that the watershed continues to be a source of high-quality drinking water.
>
> (2000, 48)

As NYC still held the power granted, under the 1905 state law, to acquire any land necessary to create and maintain the water supply, this was the focus of the original draft (EPA 2000).

Vulnerabilities and resistance

NYC's plan to acquire more land would have further weakened an economically vulnerable and isolated region – the West of Hudson watershed. It is with this case that we see hints of "injustices-in-waiting" (Caniglia, Frank, Delano and Kerner 2014). The communities in this region are rural, with little industry, and have average county incomes that fall below the New York state average (Headwaters Institute 2014). The proposed regulations would have eliminated any existing industry, making it extremely difficult to attract new industries and putting a very real strain on the town economies. NYC's previous land acquisitions compelled residents to fear the proposed regulations would bring a new bout of land seizures, resulting in the depopulation of the entire West of Hudson watershed region.

In sharp contrast to the city's previous interactions with the community, the watershed residents came together to fight the city's proposed regulations. In 1991 they created the Coalition of Watershed Towns, which sued the city after it submitted the draft regulations to the EPA. The lawsuit filed by the Coalition signifies the mobilization of local stakeholders in response to "a perception of crisis [regarding] . . . an undesirable state of environmental governance" (Chaffin et al. 2014, 56).

The lawsuit was significant because it severely impacted the city's ability to obtain filtration avoidance, and lay the groundwork for a shift in governance (Chaffin et al. 2014; Cosens 2013). When the lawsuit was officially filed (1993) the city had already filed a long-term plan with the EPA "that committed it to a seven-year program for acquisition of an additional 70,000 acres and up to $220 million in funding" (EPA 2000, 52). The EPA approved this plan on condition that "the City [. . .] assess the land acquisition program and [. . .] revise its long-term land acquisition plan [and] commit $201 million to acquiring or otherwise restricting use on a minimum of 80,000 acres in the Catskill/Delaware watershed" (EPA 2000, 52). When the EPA reassessed the application in 1994, no progress had been made on either of these requirements, due to the Coalition's litigation. It is here that the city began moving toward adaptive governance, as it saw no other economically viable option than negotiating with the West of Hudson Coalition.

Up until this point NYC's water supply system – encompassing both the city and its hinterlands – had been a relatively resilient socio-ecological system. Over the previous 180 years the city entered its hinterlands on four different occasions to satisfy its urban water needs, and each of these seizures can be seen as a disturbance to the system. However, the system was able to recover from each disturbance. From a social perspective, the hinterlands' waters allowed the city to grow economically and demographically, which enabled it to continue as the state's financial center. From an ecological perspective, we see a somewhat resilient system because it continues to meet the city's water needs without suffering from scarcity-related environmental problems. Water is abundant in New York state and the city's water needs did not leave upstate communities waterless or upstate rivers dry. However, the EPA's determination makes clear that the system was not pristine. So, although scarcity was not an issue, pollution, phosphorus increases due to runoff, and changes in water flows were major problems (epa.gov).

As previously discussed, NYC's initial response to these ecological problems was to acquire additional land through eminent domain. While this would have greatly benefited the system's ecology, it would have harmed the West of Hudson communities (epa.gov).

It is only after community stakeholders mobilized through the lawsuit that governance shifted from top–down to bottom–up. This corresponds closely with the adaptive governance literature. As Chaffin and colleagues (2014) discuss, most of the literature agrees that adaptive governance tends to emerge from leadership among local-level stakeholders. Often, as Walker et al. (2004) describes, there is a "window of opportunity" that leads local stakeholders to join together. In the current case it was the 1986 Safe Drinking Water Act amendment and the city's subsequent decision to apply for non-filtration that created a window of opportunity and motivated local leaders to advocate for their communities.

Building an agreement

Although the Coalition's lawsuit did not immediately steer the two groups toward adaptive governance, they eventually reached this stage through the help of a "bridging organization" (Folke et al. 2005). According to Folke and colleagues (2005), a bridging organization is one that assists in collaboration and conflict resolution, and in this case it was the state of New York that took on the role of a bridging organization.

Prior to the state's involvement, negotiations between the city and the Coalition were at a standstill, and the city was at risk of failing to meet the EPA's filtration avoidance decision (FAD) requirements.

> [By early 1995] It became clear that the land acquisition milestones [along with many of the other requirements] of EPA's second conditional FAD would not be met and that the city was in serious jeopardy of losing its filtration avoidance status for its Catskill/Delaware system.
>
> (EPA 2000, 52)

At that point the Governor's office stepped in and provided facilitators to help with the negotiation process, and an agreement slowly materialized, one that adhered to the EPA regulations set forth in the 1993 Filtration Avoidance Decision and still allowed for development within the West of Hudson watershed.

On January 21, 1997, NYC, New York state, the US EPA, the Coalition of Watershed Towns, the Catskill Watershed Corporation, Putnam County, Westchester County, municipalities within the EOH and WOH, and the environmental groups signed a Memorandum of Agreement (MOA). The MOA allows the city to meet the requirements set forth by the EPA's 1993 Filtration Avoidance Determination, but does so in ways that hold the city responsible for protecting their water supply and allows the West of Hudson communities to thrive.

The MOA provides a concrete example of adaptive governance strategies at work. According to the literature, adaptive governance should: (1) provide information (science and local knowledge); (2) deal with conflict; (3) induce rule compliance; (4) provide infrastructure; and (5) be prepared for change (Chaffin et al. 2014). The MOA works to accomplish each of these five points. Guided by the EPA and environmental scientists from Cornell University, the MOA implemented environmental and community programs based on scientific knowledge and has provided local education on the water supply's importance. It has implemented programs and put guidelines in place to both negotiate conflicts between the city and the watershed communities, as well as induce rule compliance. It has also provided infrastructure to the communities, the water supply system, and to programs implemented through the agreement. As well, it was developed to handle change, as it is evaluated and modified every five years.

The MOA satisfies each task required by the 1993 EPA Filtration Avoidance Decision, and in ways that hold the city responsible for protecting the water supply while allowing the watershed communities to thrive. The agreement allows for the much needed land acquisition, but in a way that is less authoritarian, stipulating that land acquisition in the West of Hudson and East of Hudson watersheds must be done through "willing buyer/willing seller" negotiations, meaning that NYC cannot acquire land within its watershed through eminent domain. It also enacts the Watershed Protection and Partnership Programs, which enable for education initiatives throughout the watershed areas, grants and funding for septic system upgrades, stormwater retrofits, forestry management programs, development funds, and tax consulting funds. Additionally, the MOA created two not-for-profit programs (the Catskills Watershed Corporation and the Watershed Protection and Partnership Council (MOA 1997)) to oversee the implementation of the new programs and to ensure that all parties involved carry out their designated roles to the best of their ability.

The MOA also demonstrates how adaptive governance strategies can link vulnerable and resilient localities in the common goal of creating a resilient social-ecological system. Previously, NYC had used its political and economic power to create an ecologically resilient water supply, but this resilience did not apply to the entire social-ecological system as the water system's creation left the West of Hudson region economically vulnerable. The MOA's completion helped transform this region and the entire NYC water supply socio-ecological system into a more resilient system because it addressed economic concerns and environmental concerns in the entire watershed.

The partnership programs set forth in the MOA mirror much of what Folke et al. (2005) see as making adaptive governance a successful strategy. These programs are based on scientific and local knowledge, but at the same time rely on both the political and economic support of NYC's Department of Environmental Protection and New York state's Department of Environmental Conservation. As Folke and colleagues explain, ". . . legislation and governmental policies support self-organization while framing creativity for adaptive co-management efforts" (2005, 441) help to make adaptive governance programs successful. While governmental policies can lend legitimacy to adaptive governance strategies, success is also based on creative solutions among a variety of stakeholders, not only those with political power.

Analyzing NYC's water supply system helps us see economic power's importance in creating adaptive governance programs. The programs implemented through the MOA are completely dependent upon the city's economic power. Without NYC's funding, the West of Hudson region would be in the same – if not worse – economic situation as prior to the MOA's implementation. It is only through the city's investment in MOA programs that the watershed region has been able to bolster its economy in an ecologically sustainable way, which underscores that both economic and political power are necessary in implementing adaptive governance strategies.

Conclusions: adaptive governance, water, and climate

This chapter's goal was threefold: (1) demonstrate the role of economic power in implementing adaptive governance strategies; (2) highlight key historical political conditions that allowed for stakeholder mobilization; and (3) demonstrate the ability of adaptive governance strategies to link resilient and vulnerable localities to sustainably manage our natural resources. NYC's water supply represents a case that successfully implemented adaptive governance strategies, using both political and economic power, to sustainably manage an unfiltered water supply system.

This analysis builds on the previous literature in two ways. First, it elucidates the profound role that economic power plays in the implementation of adaptive governance. NYC's economic power allowed for its reach into its hinterlands to acquire a water supply and enforce environmental regulations, but later this power was used to fund a successful adaptive governance model between the city and the hinterlands. Second, it articulates the way adaptive governance strategies can be used to sustainably manage unfiltered drinking water supplies. Adaptive governance strategies allowed two groups with conflicting agendas – economic growth versus environmental preservation – to join together and work toward the common goal of developing a sustainable social-ecological system within the city's watershed. Years later, this adaptive governance approach has been hailed as one of the most successful adaptive governance models to date (Pfeffer and Wagenet 1999).

These findings further our understanding of both adaptive governance implementation and their role in sustainable resource management. Regarding implementation, this analysis expands our understanding of adaptive governance negotiations. While stakeholders need a window of opportunity to broach the subject of adaptive governance, they also require a political climate conducive to negotiating with resistant stakeholders. Legislative action, such as the Surface Water Treatment Rule amendment, can lend political support to adaptive governance strategies. Without the appropriate political climate, powerful economic actors may be hesitant or – in the case of NYC – unwilling to engage in collaborative governance strategies that can consume large amounts of time and resources, and which may ultimately reduce their power. However, the appropriate political context strongly compels such actors to invest in such strategies. In turn, political and economic investments in adaptive governance programs allow for the sustainable management of resources, particularly fresh water sources and their surrounding environment.

A limitation with this case is NYC's water-rich location. The city has been able to create a resilient socio-ecological system around their water supply primarily because they are in a location where water is an abundant resource, and the issue of scarcity is not a major concern. This limits our understanding of an urban area's ability to foster similar adaptive governance strategies in arid climates. Therefore, further research is needed to determine the effectiveness of similar adaptive governance strategies for water management in arid or drought-ridden climates. As NYC is one of only five unfiltered surface water supplies in the United States – including San Francisco, a city in a state experiencing a five-year drought – a comparison of governance strategies across each of these five cases would provide a more in-depth understanding of power's role in adaptive governance strategies, and the ability of adaptive governance strategies to be used to preserve the watersheds of unfiltered surface water supplies.

Note

1 Washington State University, Department of Sociology, seblake@wsu.edu

References

Barlow M. and Clark T. (2005). *Blue gold*. New York: The New Press.

Blaine J.G., Sweeny B.W. and Arscott D.B. (2006). Enhanced source-water monitoring for New York City: historical framework, political context, and project design. *Journal of the North American Benthological Society*, 25, 851–866.

Blake S.E. (2015). *New York City's water supply: a case for a sustainable growth machine*. Unpublished doctoral dissertation. Pullman, WA: Washington State University.

Burnett N. (1997). The inside story of the watershed agreement: an oral history of the NYC watershed negotiations 1990–1997, set 1. Catskills Watershed Corporation. Retrieved April 1, 2014, from http://www.cwconline.org/behind_the_scenes.html

Burnett N. (2002). The inside story of the watershed agreement: an oral history of the NYC watershed negotiations 1990–1997, set 2. Catskills Watershed Corporation. Retrieved April 1, 2014, from http://www.cwconline.org/behind_the_scenes.html

Burrows E.G. and Wallace M. (1999). *Gotham: a history of New York City to 1898*. New York: Oxford University Press.

Caniglia B.S., Frank B., Delano D. and Kerner B. (2014). Enhancing environmental justice research and praxis: the inclusion of human security, resilience and vulnerabilities literature. *International Journal of Innovation and Sustainable Development*, 8, 409–426.

Chaffin B C., Gosnell H. and Cosens B.A. (2014). A decade of adaptive governance scholarship: synthesis and future directions. *Ecology and Society*, 19, 56–70.

Clark J.R.A. and Clarke R. (2011). Local sustainability initiatives in English national parks: what role for adaptive governance? *Land Use Policy*, 28, 314–324.

Clark J. and Semmahasak C. (2013). Evaluating adaptive governance approaches to sustainable water management in North-West Thailand. *Environmental Management*, 51, 882–896.

Clegg S. (1989). *Frameworks of power*. London: Sage Publications.

Dahl R.A. (1961). *Who governs? Democracy and power in an American city*. New Haven, CT: Yale University Press.

Delaney P. (Ed.) (1983). *Sandhogs: a history of the tunnel workers of New York*. New York: Compressed Air and Free Air, Shaft, Tunnel, Foundation, Casisson, Subway, Cofferdam, Sewer Construction Workers of New York and New Jersey and Vicinity.

Cosens B. (2013). Legitimacy, adaptation, and resilience in ecosystem management. *Ecology and Society*, 18, 1.

Cosens B. and Williams M.K. (2012). Resilience and water governance: adaptive governance in the Columbia River Basin. *Ecology and Society*, 17, 3–17.

Dietz T., Ostrom E. and Stern P.C. (2003). The struggle to govern the commons. *Science*, 302, 1907–1910.

Djalante R., Holley C., and Thomalla F. (2011). Adaptive governance and managing resilience to natural hazards. *International Journal of Disaster Risk Science*, 2, 1–14.

Espeland W.N. (1998). *The struggle for water: politics, rationality, and identity in the American Southwest*. Chicago: University of Chicago Press.

Finnegan M.C. (1997). New York City's watershed agreement: a lesson in sharing responsibility. *Pace Environmental Law Review*, 14, 577–644.

Folke C. (2006). Resilience: the emergence of a perspective for social-ecological systems analyses. *Global Environmental Change*, 16, 253–267.

Folke C., Hahn T., Olsson P. and Norberg J. (2005). Adaptive governance of socio-ecological systems. *Annual Review of Environmental Resources*, 30, 441–473.

Foster J.B. (1999). Marx's theory of metabolic rift: classical foundations for environmental sociology. *American Journal of Sociology*, 105, 366–405.

Foster J.B., Clark B. and York R. (2010). *The ecological rift: capitalism's war on the earth*. New York: Monthly Review Press.

Gandy M. (2002). *Concrete and clay: reworking nature in New York City*. Cambridge, MA: MIT Press.

Gunderson L. (1999). Resilience, flexibility, and adaptive management: antidotes for spurious certitude? *Conservation Ecology*, 3, 7.

Gunderson L.H. and Holling C.S. (2002). *Panarchy: understanding transformations in human and natural systems*. Washington D.C.: Island Press.

Headwaters Institute. (2014). Selected geographies: Delaware County NY, benchmark geographies: United States economic profile system-human dimensions toolkit, EPS-HDT. Retrieved 1 June 2015 from http://headwaterseconomics.org/wphw/wp-content/uploads/print-ready-measures-pdfs/36025_Delaware-County_NY_Measures.pdf

Jorgenson A.K. and Clark B. (2011). Societies consuming nature: a panel study of the ecological footprints of nations, 1960–2003. *Social Science Research*, 40, 226–244.

Kasperson J.X., Kasperson R.E. and Turner II B.L. (2010). Vulnerability of coupled human ecological systems to global environmental change. In E.A. Rosa, A. Diekmann, T. Dietz and C.C. Jaeger (Eds.) *Human footprints on the global environment: threats to sustainability*. Cambridge, MA: MIT Press.

King C. (1843). *A memoir of the construction, cost, and capacity of the Croton Aqueduct, compiled from official documents: together with an account of the civic celebration of the fourteenth October, 1842, on the occasion of the completion of the great work: Preceded by a preliminary essay on ancient and modern aqueducts*. New York: Charles King.

Koeppel G.T. (2000). *Water for Gotham: a history*. Princeton, NJ: Princeton University Press.

Logan J. and Molotch H. (2007). *Urban fortunes: the political economy of place*. Berkeley, CA: University of California Press.

Mann M. (1986). *The sources of social power*. Cambridge: Cambridge University Press.

Martine G., McGranahan G., Montgomery M. and Fernández-Castilla R. (2008). *The new global frontier: urbanization, poverty and environment in the 21st century*. London: Earthscan.

Montgomery M.R. (2008). The demography of the urban transition: what we know and don't know. In G. Martine, G. McGranahan, M. Montgomery and R. Fernandez-Castilla (Eds.) *The new global frontier: urbanization, poverty and environment in the 21st century*. London: Earthscan.

National Research Council (2000). *Watershed management for potable water supply: assessing the New York City strategy*. Washington D.C.: National Academy Press.

New York City Department of Environmental Protection (2015). History of New York Water supply system. Retrieved 4 June 2015 from http://www.nyc.gov/html/dep/html/drinking_water/history.shtml

New York State (1836). *Census of the State of New York, for 1835 Albany Croswell*. Van Benthuysen and Burt New York State Library.

New York State (1857). *Census of the State of New York, for 1855 Albany Charles*. Van Benthuysen New York State Library.

New York State Legislature (1834). *Laws of New York: Fifty-seventh session New York State*. New York State Library.

New York State Legislature (1836). *Laws of New York: Fifty-ninth session New York State*. New York State Library.

New York State Legislature (1837). *Laws of New York: Sixtieth session New York State*. New York State Library.
New York State Legislature (1838). *Laws of New York: Sixty-first session New York State*. New York State Library.
New York State Legislature (1839). *Laws of New York: Sixty-second session New York State*. New York State Library.
New York State Legislature (1840). *Laws of New York: Sixty-third session New York State*. New York State Library.
New York State Legislature (1842). *Laws of New York: Sixty-fifth session New York State*. New York State Library.
New York State Legislature (1843). *Laws of New York: Sixty-sixth session New York State*. New York State Library.
New York State Legislature (1845). *Laws of New York*. New York State Library.
New York State Legislature (1849). *Laws of New York: Seventy-second session New York State*. New York State Library.
New York State Legislature (1853). *Laws of New York: Seventy-sixth session New York State*. New York State Library.
New York State Legislature (1883). *Laws of New York: One hundred and sixth session New York State*. New York State Library.
New York State Legislature (1893). *Laws of New York*. New York State Library.
New York State Legislature (1905). *Laws of New York: One hundred and twenty-eighth session*. New York State Library.
New York State Legislature (1907). *Laws of New York: One hundred and thirtieth session*. New York State Library.
O'Connor J. (1987). Capitalism, nature and socialism: a theoretical introduction. *Capital Nature Socialism*, 1(Fall).
Parsons T. (1960). *The structure and process of modern societies*. Glencoe, IL: The Free Press.
Pfeffer M.J. and Wagenet L.P. (1999). Planning for environmental responsibility and equity: a critical appraisal of the rural/urban relations in the New York City watershed. In O.J. Furuseth and M.B. Lapping (Eds.) *Contested countryside: the rural urban fringe in North America* (pp. 179–206). Brookfield, VT: Ashgate.
Reisner M. (1987). *Cadillac desert: the American west and its disappearing water*. New York: Penguin.
Riverkeeper (2009). Riverkeeper timeline. Retrieved 1 June 2015 from http://www.riverkeeper.org/about-us/our-story/riverkeeper-timeline/
Sanchez-Rodriguez R. (2008). Urban sustainability and global environmental change: reflections for an urban agenda. In G. Martine, G. McGranahan, M. Montgomery and R. Fernandez-Castilla (Eds.) *The new global frontier: urbanization, poverty and environment in the 21st century*. London: Earthscan.
Rosa E.A., Diekmann A., Dietz T. and Jaeger C.C. (2010). *Human footprints on the global environment: threats to sustainability*. Cambridge, MA: MIT Press.
Schnaiberg A. (1980). *The environment: from surplus to scarcity*. New York: Oxford University Press.
Scholz J.T. and Stiftel B. (2005). *Adaptive governance and water conflict: new institutions for collaborative planning*. New York: Routledge.
Shonnard F. and Spooner W.W. (1900). *History of Westchester County New York: from its earliest settlement to the year 1900*. New York: The New York History Company.
Steuding B. (1989). *The last of the handmade dams: the story of the Ashokan Reservoir*. Fleischmann, NY: NY Purple Mountain Press.

Stratigos L.T. (1998). *Sesquicentennial: Gilboa, New York 1848–1998*. Gilboa, NY: Gilboa Historical Society.
US EPA (1999). 25 years of the Safe Drinking Water Act: history and trends. Retrieved 1 June 2015 from https://www.hsdl.org/?view&did=449348
US EPA (2000). Assessing New York City's watershed protection program: the 1997 filtration avoidance determination mid-course review for the Catskill/Delaware water supply watershed. Retrieved 1 June 2015 from http://www.epa.gov/region02/water/nycshed/fadmidrev.pdf
Walker B., Holling C.S., Carpenter S.R. and Kinzig A. (2004). Resilience, adaptability and transformability in socio-ecological systems. *Ecology and Society*, 9, 5.
Walton Reporter (1958). July 18.

Part III
Governance and policy

9 Rethinking the politics of water

Risk, resilience, and the rights of future generations

Joanna L. Robinson[1]

Introduction: commodity or commons?

Water is essential to life. It is deeply imbued with cultural and spiritual understandings. Water nourishes, cleanses, grows our food, and is fundamental to human health and survival. At the same time, the ability of global fresh water systems to adequately supply water services and sanitation to the world's population is under threat and millions of people around the world lack access to clean, safe drinking water (Bakker 2010). Pollution, climate change, and deforestation threaten the world's fresh water supply while global consumption of water is rising at a rate faster than population growth (Barlow and Clarke 2001). In the context of increased climate change, poverty, and urban migration, water – urban drinking water in particular – has emerged as a key issue globally. Debates about the management and conservation of water resources focus on scarcity and stewardship, ownership and control, and environmental and social justice (Bakker 2010; Conca 2006; Robinson 2013).

The key challenge for governments and policymakers is ensuring the protection and fair distribution of water in the face of the myriad threats to fresh water systems. Critical to this process is the recognition of inequities in access to clean drinking water and sanitation, a growing problem in global cities. A lack of infrastructure to supply water and sanitation services to urban poor populations, along with rising costs and the heightened risk of water-borne diseases, creates a context of vulnerability and growing social and environmental injustice.

Despite the push for increased public participation and equity into global water governance models (Bakker 2010; Ingram and Blatter 2001), many communities around the world facing water scarcity are subjected to contentious policy prescriptions, particularly with the rise of private sector involvement in water treatment and delivery (Bakker 2010; Robinson 2013). In many global cities, governance failure means poor and marginalized populations have unequal access to clean drinking water. Increased private sector investment in water treatment and delivery systems risks exacerbating this vulnerability, creating a context of "injustice in waiting" because of the failure to recognize these existing inequities and build system resilience (Caniglia, Frank, Delano and Kerner 2014).

Over the course of the last thirty years, international environmental agreements have emphasized the concept of sustainable development – incorporating environmental considerations into economic and social policy – as a means of resolving the conflict between economic growth and ecological degradation (Baker 2016). This concept has also been applied to water governance models, beginning with the 1992 "Dublin Statement on Water and Sustainable Development," adopted by the United Nations, which calls for reform of global water governance to increase efficiency and ensure sustainability and equity (Robinson 2013). The Dublin Statement promoted the notion of "water as economic good" for the first time in international policy, leading to intense debates about the role of the private sector in water governance (Rogers, de Silva and Bhatia 2002). Many water governance scholars have criticized the model of sustainable development in water governance and argue that it fails to account for ecological and social justice and promotes the commodification of global water resources (Bakker 2010; Ingram and Blatter 2001; Robinson 2013). These scholars point to the importance of incorporating notions of resilience, risk, and human security into water governance models in order to ensure both water conservation and equity (Bakker 2010; Ingram and Blatter 2001; Robinson 2013).

This chapter presents two policy models for addressing water scarcity and unequal access in global cities. The first proscribes a utilitarian economic framework to water conservation, placing an economic value on water. This model dominates public policy decision-making, especially in relation to urban water services. The second considers access to fresh water a human right and calls for the fair allocation of water resources. I argue that water policies based on market-based models are limited in ensuring both water conservation and the fair distribution of water to existing and future generations because they fail to account for inequities in the system, and assume that it is a substitutable commodity. As a result, vulnerabilities remain embedded in urban areas and marginalized populations susceptible to future ecological or economic shocks (Caniglia et al. 2014). To prevent or mitigate theses "injustices in waiting," water governance policies must provide frameworks for building social and ecological resilience that recognize the determinants of environmental harm before injustices occur (Caniglia et al. 2014; Klinenberg 2003). I contend that water governance policies based on ecological and distributive justice are more effective for ensuring the fair distribution of water for current and future generations and for building resilience precisely because they recognize existing inequities.

The global water crisis

The capacity to meet the needs of the current global population and future generations is at risk; close to 1 billion people lack access to fresh water, while over 2.5 billion lack sanitation services, and water-borne diseases kill over 2 million people every year, mostly children (Gleick and Ajami 2014). Municipal water systems are straining to provide safe drinking water, upgrade failing infrastructure, and ensure fair distribution in an era of declining public investment (Bakker 2010; Jehl 2004; Robinson 2013). Many water scholars argue that the crisis is largely rooted in governance failure and contend that new models of management must be adopted to deal with the ecological, economic, and social challenges of water treatment and delivery (Bakker 2010; Morgan 2011; Mullin 2011).

In the era of neo-liberal reforms, the global water crisis is largely being addressed through the privatization of water services (Bakker 2010; Morgan 2011; Roberts 2008). The decrease in public investment in infrastructure combined with new international trade regulations, the rise of multinational water firms and the push for private sector involvement by global financial institutions such as the World Bank and the IMF have impelled governments to turn to the private sector to help deliver water services (Morgan 2011; Robinson 2013). Proponents of market-based models argue that pricing water will increase private sector investment in infrastructure, reallocate water resources properly and ensure conservation (Bakker 2010; Low and Gleeson 1998). Water is thus considered an economic good to be regulated in the marketplace, where corporations compete for access to global fresh water resources.

The marketization of water and increased private sector involvement in water governance and management has resulted in a conflict over who controls water (Bakker 2010; Robinson 2013). Anti-water-privatization movements have emerged internationally to protest what they see as the commodification of water, with many successful outcomes, from Cochabamba, Bolivia, to Vancouver, Canada. These movements consider water a human right and a part of the global commons. As the water crisis worsens, understanding which water governance policies are best suited for creating system resilience to ensure conservation, equality of access, and intergenerational justice is imperative.

The social dimension of environmental resources

In the last half century, environmental concerns have moved to the forefront of the public agenda. While there are limitations in terms of concrete policy outcomes, what has occurred over time is a shift in the way nature is understood. The traditional division between society and the environment, made prominent in sociology as a result of its earlier anthropocentric nature, has largely waned as questions about human/nature interactions are increasingly incorporated into sociological debates about the ecological crisis (Pellow and Brem 2013). Environmental sociologists point to the development of new environmental norms (including, for example, policies that assess potential environmental harm from natural resource extraction) that are changing social practices and the relationship between humans and nature (Brulle 2000; Pellow and Brem 2013). While the critical importance of the environment as an object of inquiry is central to theories of environmental sociology, key debates remain over the scope of human-induced environmental harm and the range of solutions to the ecological crisis.

The major division in the field lies in the consideration of the role of technological innovation and private investment. Some scholars, most notably Schnaiberg and Gould (2000), argue that the root causes of environmental degradation are found in the dominant economic system. Market-based, capitalist economies are an enormous threat to the environment because of their need for continuous economic expansion and consumption. Schnaiberg and Gould (2000) refer to this problem as the "treadmill of production" and maintain that as long as unrestrained growth and development continue, the conflict between society and the environment will remain unresolved (Schnaiberg and Gould 2000; Schnaiberg, Pellow and Weinberg 2002). For many scholars, the capitalist mode of production is the root of the problem rather than the solution to ecological concerns (Dauvergne 2010; Schnaiberg and Gould 2000; Rubin 2012).

Other environmental scholars point to the innovative and creative nature of the capitalist system as spurring the kinds of developments necessary for environmental protection. The theory of ecological modernization, similar to the notion of "sustainable development," focuses on technological innovation and looks favorably on market-based solutions to the ecological crisis (Mol and Sonnenfeld 2000). Unlike theories that consider industrial and technological development as a threat to environmental well-being, ecological modernization points to the expansion of the modernization process and new ecologically focused innovations as driving the necessary institutional changes for mitigating environmental problems (Pellow and Brem 2013). Proponents of the ecological modernization model argue that increased technological innovation in the area of environmental governance and resource management will ensure that ecological issues become a central focus of political institutions and thus lead to policies that will reduce pollution, promote conservation, and increase energy efficiency, making environmental sustainability both economically and politically viable (Fisher and Freudenburg 2001; Spaargaren 1997).

The division between market-based models and those that problematize the capitalist economy results in a theoretical impasse: the enduring conflict between nature and society versus an overly optimistic claim that innovation will save us from ecological collapse (Beck 2008; Giddens 1998). The challenge remains how to move beyond this deadlock to develop a theory of ecological conservation that will be politically and economically feasible while also capable of generating solutions to global environmental challenges, including the world's water crisis.

In the context of water governance, I argue that it is important to interrogate the ecological modernization thesis because current public policy debates favour market-based proscriptions that claim economic growth and technological development will lead to improved environmental outcomes. From this perspective, the centrality of the economy, as a means to conserve and distribute resources fairly, is rarely questioned, nor is the assumption that economic growth is compatible with ecological integrity. It is important therefore to examine the capacity of market-based models to not only address conservation but also the fair distribution of resources. The call for more empirical studies of ecological modernization policies is prevalent in the sociological literature (Buttel 2000; Fisher and Freudenburg 2001). Fisher and Freudenburg (2001, 704) argue that scholarly research in this area should "work toward greater rigor in identifying conditions under which 'ecological modernization' outcomes are more or less likely."

It is essential to examine the applicability of ecological modernization for resources that are not readily treated as discrete variables, including air, water, and biodiversity. Most empirical applications of ecological modernization theory tend to focus on cases that can be easily made to fit the theory (Fisher and Freudenburg 2001), such as waste management (Gille 2000), renewable energy (Mol and Sonnenfeld 2000), and pulp and paper industries (Sonnenfeld 2000). The problem with focusing on particular industries or industrial processes is that it depends on two underlying assumptions: (1) that environmental issues can be examined as distinct cases; and (2) that they can be treated as commodities (Fisher and Freudenburg 2001). Yet as Polanyi (1944) reminds us, the environment is a "fictitious commodity" because it is not produced as an item to be sold in the marketplace. More specifically, Bakker (2004) refers to water as being an "uncooperative commodity" in relation to privatization because of its unbounded nature and the social and environmental complexities of water delivery. For these reasons, it is critical to test the viability of ecological modernization and other market-based theories for resources that cannot easily be considered in isolation of interdependent ecological systems – and are thus more easily described as "fictitious commodities."

Water is a unique case to examine sociologically in light of theories of modernization for several reasons. First, problems of extreme scarcity and unequal access to water and water services are widespread globally (Bakker 2010). A failure to recognize these injustices creates a context of vulnerability to future environmental and economic shocks for poor and marginalized populations. Second, water as a resource is not easily treated as a distinct, commodifiable resource. Third, water is an important case because the dominant policy prescriptions tend to promote market-based solutions to the water crisis, including privatization and water metering. Finally, as water is critical for human survival, it is essential to find viable and just solutions to global water crises, including building ecological and social resilience.

The liberal roots of market-based environmentalism

Modern resource and land-use management policies reflect the idea that liberty and moral rightness are founded on the pursuit of individuality and the right to own property as outlined in Locke's *Two Treatises of Government* (1967). By linking liberty and property, Locke argued that private property rights are an essential means of securing individual rights, and thus the protection of property is a critical function of government (Young 1996). This liberal notion of property rights and the moral obligation to transform nature continues to influence present-day environmental and land-use policies that consider resources as commodities to be regulated in the marketplace. The history of modern industrial development with its emphasis on property rights has trumped the individual rights of those who bear the negative consequences of such development in terms of unequal resource distribution and environmental degradation.

The prevailing model of public policy decision-making in contemporary society emphasizes property rights and is often market-oriented, where environmental protection is considered a function of the economy. Ecological modernization and other market-based models of conservation begin with the assumption that economic efficiency is the best way to deal with ecological degradation, through resource allocation and pricing, and this often includes valuing the ecosystem services traditionally left out of pricing natural resources (Costanza et al. 1997). Proponents of this perspective argue that because scarcity is on the rise, treating environmental resources as economic goods is necessary to ensure reallocation and efficiency through proper pricing and accountability (Bakker 2010).

Under this model, decisions about government regulation are made in terms of a cost–benefit analysis, whereby efficiency is achieved when the economic benefits outweigh the costs (Schnaiberg and Gould 2000). Assigning property rights to natural resources "will ensure efficient allocation of environmental values and thus prevent both the exhaustion of resources and the ruin of ecological systems" (Low and Gleeson 1998, 161–162). This model is based on a utilitarian argument, which assumes economic growth and continued expansion of the market will maximize the welfare of human beings (Wood 2000), although other scholars point out that utilitarianism may not always work to everyone's advantage, even if it does increase overall community happiness (Bell 2012).

Under this conception of resource use – similar to the ecological modernization paradigm – protecting the environment and conserving resources for future generations is best assured when they occur simultaneously with economic expansion and technological innovation (Pellow and Brem 2013). Although ecological modernization theorists recognize that many environmental problems resulted from industrialization and modernity, they argue that the solution is not to dismantle these institutions, but rather to further the modernization process as a means of reversing the ecological crisis (Mol and Sonnenfeld 2000; Spaargaren and Mol 1992). Further innovation, investment, and modernization will ensure that environmental problems are of central concern, with the development of new technologies that reduce pollution and increase energy efficiency (Spaargaren 2000).

Economic models are frequently proposed as a way of dealing with water scarcity and uneven access. Proponents of water privatization argue that regulating water through the marketplace will increase conservation and innovation and allow more equal distribution. They contend that treating water as a scarce economic resource and applying full-cost pricing will lead to more efficient use and conservation because higher prices for water will encourage people to use less (Bakker 2010; Rogers, de Silva and Bhatia 2002). Increased scarcity, it is argued, will drive technological innovation to increase efficiency and conservation through advancements in the infrastructure of water treatment and delivery systems (Conca 2006). Market-based theories also assume that water privatization will lead to more equitable distribution of and access to water, as the absence of clear property rights, it is argued, misallocates water resources (Low and Gleeson 1998).

Limitations to market-based conservation and ecological modernization

Many scholars are critical of the sustainable development/ecological modernization model of governing resources, as well as its capacity to address the pressing challenges of the ecological crisis, including inequities and ecological collapse. Ulrich Beck (2006) argues that the institutions and systems that emerged from modernization have resulted in a world of risks and threats ranging from environmental to economic, political, and social, and that looking to these same institutions for solutions is unrealistic as they are the cause of the crisis in the first place.

Part of the problem is that theories of ecological modernization are most often applied to resources that are, at least in theory, substitutable. This approach assumes that all resources can be substituted by another good or service in the case of depletion (Bakker 2007a; Shiva 2002; Wood 2000). Yet, when applied to resources that are not substitutable and necessary for human survival, the limitations to this model are striking. First, by favoring marketization, the model places an economic value on resources, treating them as distinct and measurable commodities. Yet water is not a substitutable resource. As Shiva (2002, 15) argues, "over-exploitation of water and disruption of the water cycle create absolute scarcity that markets cannot substitute with other commodities [. . .] when water disappears, there is no alternative. There is simply no substitute." Water is a clear example of Polanyi's fictitious commodity problem. Just as assumptions about labor as a commodity to be regulated by the market fail to take into account the social nature of humans and their differing motivations (Block 2003), assumptions about water as a commodity fail to take into account the ecological nature of water, including its unbounded properties and the fact that it has no substitute (Bakker 2010). This model also fails to account for existing social and ecological injustices, leaving poor and marginalized populations vulnerable to environmental harm (Caniglia et al. 2014). An economic-centered model of environmental policy disconnects humans from nature, which becomes simply another factor of production, obscuring the reality that human beings are intricately bound to, dependent on, and beholden to the natural world for survival.

Second, treating resources as individual goods that can be bought and sold in the marketplace does not account for how resources function within ecological systems (Wood 2000). Treating water as a commodity is problematic because it is unbounded and cannot be divided into separate parts to be allocated for ownership (Shiva 2002). Pricing water ignores the fluidity of environments as well as the full range of its uses, including cultural and spiritual beliefs, ecological integrity, and the necessity of water for human survival (Espeland 1998; Robinson 2013; Shiva 2002). Water and water services are part of larger systems that produce resources, maintain biodiversity and other life support systems and cycles, thus cannot be treated as discrete, substitutable goods (Low and Gleeson 1998; Shiva 2002; Wood 2000).

Watersheds work as natural purifiers of water; they help protect human health and the integrity of ecosystems (Shiva 2002). To protect watersheds and ensure clean drinking water, it is important to recognize that they are part of a system and that the integrity of water needs to be maintained from the beginning to end of the source (Dombeck 2003). The services provided by watersheds are for the most part external to the marketplace and while market-based approaches tend to assign a value to ecosystem services, they are "too often ignored or undervalued, leading to the error of constructing projects whose social costs far outweigh their benefits" (Costanza et al. 1997, 259). Ecological modernization solutions that treat water as a commodity are unable to capture this holistic view of the hydrological cycle and the social, cultural, and ecological services it provides (Ingram and Blatter 2001; Shiva 2002). When governance models do not recognize how watersheds are linked to other biological and natural systems – including forests and airsheds – as well as the necessity of building the resilience of these systems, they risk increasing social and ecological harm.

A fourth problem with market-based modernization models is that they assume that unrestricted freedom to contract is fair and that each individual consents to exchange good and services in the marketplace (Wood 2000). This assumption does not take into account structural inequalities that prevent all individuals from participating equally in society (Sen 1992). Full cost pricing of water in the marketplace threatens the ability of those who do not have the means to pay for water and, as a result, cannot ensure its fair distribution (Bakker 2010). Water pricing is thus insufficient in correcting the imbalance between private property and the rights of individuals to access resources because it does not address the tension that exists between the *rights* to resources and *access* to resources, what economist Amartya Sen labels the distinction between freedom and the means of freedom (Sen 1992). While proponents of water privatization often support the concept of the human right to water (Bakker 2007b; Goldman 2007), because they do not prioritize equity in terms of access, the emphasis remains on cost recovery.

Water privatization often exacerbates existing injustices and reduces community resilience in the face of environmental and social harm. This is not to argue that public systems are problem-free (governance failure and corruption are often at the root of the push for private investment) or that there have been no benefits from private sector water delivery in improving access and quality (Bakker 2010). Yet, there are several prominent cases where the privatization of municipal water services[2] has resulted in negative consequences for disadvantaged populations (Bakker 2010; Robinson 2013). In Cochabamba, Bolivia, the price of water increased to levels far beyond what poor families could afford after privatization by the national government. After the water system was privatized, rates rose as much as 300% above the previous cost, leaving many poor people cut off, while others were forced to pay over 25% of their salaries for water (Olivera and Lewis 2004). In Buenos Aires, Argentina, the price of water rose by more than 27% after the water system was privatized, while in Orange Farm, South Africa, hundreds of poor families lost access to clean water when water metering was installed. As a consequence, rates of cholera increased dramatically as residents were forced to drink unsanitized water (Barlow 2003).

Fifth, because ecological and social justice are inconsistent with private sector requirements to increase profits, policies based on models of economic efficiency or ecological modernization are insufficient for ensuring either long-term sustainability or equality of access. Commodification of nature means the push for profit will increase the demands on ecosystems, rather than increase efficiency and regulate scarcity, as any private company that owns and delivers water services will seek first to maximize their gain (Clarke 2003; Schnaiberg and Gould 2000). York, Rosa and Dietz (2003) argue that GDP is, in fact, a predictor of a nation's ecological footprint; as a country's economy expands and grows, so does its ecological impact.

Overcoming this problem is challenging as well-being and ecological improvements within countries are linked to increases in overall wealth or economic growth. Many environmental scholars are questioning the link between economic expansion and well-being, including Marxist-based treadmill of production critiques that underscore the inherent conflict between the capitalist economy and the environment (Jennings 2010; Pellow and Brem 2013). Others point to the need to consider economic activity as "consuming" or using up resources when assessing the production economy to allow for an assessment of what is consumed, the environmental risks that flow from this consumption, and the assigning of responsibility for environmental degradation (Princen 2002).

At the same time, these debates limit the discussion to the economy and the environment and often exclude the social dimension – the assumption being that we must give up social well-being (in that it is tied to increases in wealth) to make environmental gains. There is growing evidence that well-being, including mental and physical health and happiness, is not dependent on the increase in overall wealth of a society, but rather on the reduction of inequities within wealthy countries (Wilkinson and Pickett 2010). Research that decouples well-being from economic growth and points to the importance of reducing inequality moves the debate beyond the enduring conflict between the economy and the environment and demonstrates that environmental protection need not come at the expense of social well-being.

Finally, market-based conservation is problematic because it creates injustices in waiting for future generations by failing to recognize their right to have fair access to water resources. Private property rights and the right to exchange goods in the marketplace are only applicable to existing populations; the needs and rights of future generations are not considered in weighing the costs and benefits of current resource use (Wood 2000). Policies based on short-term economic gain leave no room for the moral obligation to consider future generations and, as a result, they will potentially inherit a world with limited resources and serious damage to life-sustaining systems. Even when sustainability is the goal, the rights of future generations are rarely considered (Wood 2000). The question then becomes how to ensure conservation of resources and equal distribution without relying on market-based mechanisms. What are alternative pathways to environmental conservation that mitigate the problems inherent in economic efficiency models?

One of the barriers to solving the ecological crisis are the stratified power structures that prevent equal access to capital and resources across populations and countries (Pellow and Brem 2013). Despite the ability of social movements to influence environmental policy, the general rule is that those with political and economic power – the treadmill elites – are the ones who make decisions about capital, labor, and resources (Gould, Schnaiberg and Weinberg 1996; Gould, Pellow and Schnaiberg 2004; Schnaiberg et al. 2002). The treadmill model suggests a fundamental restructuring of the political and economic institutions that currently dominate the global capitalist system, with increased democratic control over production to account for environmental problems. The challenge is ensuring decisions about resources and economic production are made in a more democratic, egalitarian way. I argue that models of distributive justice are useful in this regard as they provide the potential for a more equitable distribution of resources.

Alternatives to market-based modernization: theories of justice

Theories of distributive justice offer an alternative to the dominant model of utilitarian economic efficiency. John Rawls (1971; 1993) developed his theory of justice as an attempt to find alternatives to utilitarianism and deal with the shortcomings of economic liberalism by advocating an egalitarian model of society. His theory of justice emphasizes the equal distribution of resources and fair equality of opportunity across societies (over the economic and property rights of individuals), whereby economic opportunities are "to the greatest benefit of the least advantaged" (Rawls 1971, 302–303). Central to Rawls' conception of justice is the idea that resources, including the primary goods of freedom, opportunity, wealth, and self-respect, "are to be distributed equally unless an unequal distribution of any or all of these goods is to the advantage of the least favoured" (Rawls 1971, 303). His theory of justice is based on a non-utilitarian model of decision-making that incorporates the concept of social cooperation and mutual advantage rather than preference maximization or majority rule.

The value of Rawls' theory of distributive justice lies in its ability to recognize the social and environmental costs of economic policies and technological innovation. Rather than advocating market-based policies as a way of regulating scarcity and distributing resources, the theory of distributive justice advocates intervening in the economy, to mitigate the social and environmental costs of economic transactions that place people at a disadvantage relative to others (Bryner 2002). Utilitarian models of economic efficiency, in not allowing for equal competition in the marketplace, treat some individuals as a means to others' ends, making them beholden to others in market-based transactions (Wood 2000). Theories of justice correct this imbalance by arguing that citizens should be treated as equals and resources distributed fairly across societies.

Applying theories of justice to environmental conservation

Rawls' theory assumes that societies exist in a state of "moderate scarcity," and offers distributive justice as a way of overcoming the conflicts that might potentially arise from this type of condition (Rawls 1971, 127). Although Rawls does not specifically discuss how his theory is useful for ensuring environmental conservation, other scholars have pointed to its value as a framework for developing just and equitable environmental policies. For example, Wood (2000) argues that Rawls' theory of justice is useful in dealing with conflict over land use and development, and in managing the problem of biodiversity loss. He suggests that current forms of liberal democracy, in particular constitutional democracy, are inadequate for ensuring biodiversity protection because they cater to the short-term preferences of individuals and do not take into account the needs of future generations. By applying Rawls' theory of justice, he maintains that future generations will be seen as "the least favoured" and therefore become the beneficiary of policy decisions regarding the distribution of resources. As a result biodiversity will be protected for their future needs (Wood 2000).

With critical environmental resources in decline, we are clearly facing a condition of "moderate scarcity" and thus theories of justice are useful in dealing with conflicts arising from this social and environmental condition. First, the application of Rawls theory to conservation allows for public policy decisions to be made from the standpoint of justice and rights, rather than using goal-oriented arguments that are inherently utilitarian (Wood 2000). In this sense, environmental resources such as water can be treated as more than mere commodities to be bought and sold in the marketplace. Instead decisions about resources, including allocation and conservation, can be made based on the concepts of justice and fairness that recognize the complex properties and fluidity of natural resources as being part of the global commons (Wood 2000).

Second, the Rawlsian principle that the greatest benefit should go to the least advantaged supports the equal distribution and fair allocation of world's resources, including water, to those who are less well off. While economic efficiency assumes that the allocation of resources is fair, and ignores economic and social disadvantage, such as the ability to pay, theories of justice are able to deal with these problems of inequality through the premise that governments should treat their citizens with respect and ensure equal distribution of resources across populations.

Third, because Rawls' theory of justice allows for a shared morality that calls for the more fortunate to benefit from social and economic arrangements only if the less fortunate benefit more, the fate of future generations is considered. If we assume future generations are less fortunate because they are unable to participate in decision-making processes about resources on which they will depend for survival, conserving resources now is a form of intergenerational justice because it allows us to benefit now only if future generations benefit more (Wood 2000). Because future generations are disadvantaged, in that they do not have the equal opportunity to benefit from existing ecological resources, Rawls' theory of justice stipulates that they have equal access as those with advantage – in this case, current generations (Postma 2006; Wood 2000). As such, the only way to ensure that future generations have equal access to natural resources, including fresh water supplies, is to act now to protect and conserve resources for future use.

Finally, theories of justice support the notion of new forms of citizen-based environmental decision-making, what Shiva (2002) calls "ecological democracy," or the merging of ecological thinking with social justice. By rejecting a utilitarian model of decision-making that is both instrumental and based on majority rule, these theories embrace a model of political decision-making that is rights-based, allowing for the incorporation of marginalized views or values into policymaking. Environmental rights and the right to access environmental resources therefore trump other utilitarian or majority-rule policies – generally reflective of "top–down" politics – that characterize current decision-making processes.

Many solutions to the global environmental problems are being forged and implemented on the ground in local communities around the world, challenging both neo-liberalism and traditional models of top–down governance and decision-making (Robinson 2013). Peter Evans (2008) points to the myriad social movements that have emerged in response to neo-liberal globalization, including anti-water-privatization movements. He argues that locally based movements represent the "counter-hegemonic globalization" that is needed to oppose the destructive social, economic, and environmental policies of neo-liberal globalization and to ensure social and ecological justice. The challenge is how to recognize and include solutions proposed by community-based, local, and indigenous groups in working towards sustainability (Page 2014). For example, many of the proposed alternatives to the economic model of water conservation and delivery are community-based and informed by consensus decision-making. They include models of community ownership and watershed management that work within the natural ecological limits of specific locations (Schreier 2003). Theories of justice that call for more representative democracy are one way of ensuring increased democracy and justice by incorporating marginalized voices from local communities into the decision-making arena. One promising avenue is the growing importance of participatory democracy and the push for inclusion of marginalized voices in decisions about water governance and natural resource protection.

Expanding theories of justice: participatory democracy and politics from below

In trying to reform democratic institutions so that they embrace a full range of opinions and values, one challenge is to ensure non-elite actors and movements have their voices heard. This challenge is especially important when considering how environmental resources, including water, are distributed, because disadvantaged and marginalized populations are often the most threatened by ecological destruction and resource (mis)allocation (this includes future generations). Rawls' theory of justice, despite offering a useful model of distributive justice, is limited in its capacity to deal with marginalized people and issues. For example Sen (1992; 1999) questions the effectiveness of Rawls fair distribution thesis, arguing that it only takes into account the equal distribution of goods and does not address the way in which individuals can effectively use those goods to achieve their means. In the case of water, this has been particularly problematic. Governments and policymakers around the world have embraced the concept of water as a human right and yet this has rarely materialized into equity in terms of access to water services (Mirosa and Harris 2011).

The focus on the political arena as a site of decision-making power is equally problematic for dealing with individuals and issues that have traditionally been excluded from political power. Some feminist scholars have criticized liberal theories of justice for focusing exclusively on external social structures and institutions rather than the inequalities inherent in social relations and the gendered division of labor (Okin 1991). Iris Marion Young (2006) echoes this static vision of justice and points to the agency of citizens to take responsibility for ensuring justice is achieved. Further, Rawls' theory of justice, rooted in the Kantian notion of individual autonomy, places the individual at the center. This poses a challenge when attempting to apply Rawls' conception of distributive justice to environmental conservation (Wood 2000). The emphasis on individual rights that lies at the heart of modern Western society has often been blamed for the rise of environmental and social problems. Economic liberalism has led to a consumer society that puts increasing demands on the ever-fragile ecosystems on which we depend for survival (Beck 2006). If individualism is the problem, how is the tension between the individual bias in liberal democracy and the social problems that have emerged from this type of social organization to be resolved? We need to rethink the individual-based model of liberal democracy and citizenship to recognize the social and environmental contexts in which individuals are embedded, much like the concept of viewing resources as both part of and inseparable from ecosystems.

A useful model for this new conception of democratic decision-making is Habermas's theory of communicative action (1984), which defines the criteria for the inclusion of non-political elites into decision-making processes and does not privilege the political sphere over public and ecological domains. Habermas (1984; 1995; 1996) contends that we need to broaden the scope of the Rawlsian definition of justice to incorporate the public realm as a critical arena for democratic decision-making, arguing for a form of participatory democracy that will have emancipatory power for both societies and nature. According to Habermas (1974), if we continue to privilege the political sphere over the public sphere, social and political institutions and, by extension, public policy decisions will continue to be controlled by a technocratic elite. Hence civil society will remain alienated from political power.

Habermas (1984) calls for a social theory that recognizes the critical importance of both the everyday or public sphere (the lifeworld) and the structures that shape and are shaped by it (the system), including the processes of material production that bridge the social world with the natural world.[3] This is the kind of participatory democracy that many scholars argue will provide the basis for the development of a new form of environmental democracy that will allow for the principles of distributive justice to be incorporated into policy decisions about environmental resources (Klein 2014; Shiva 2002; Stevenson and Dryzek 2014).

Beck's (1996, 39) theory of reflexive modernization argues that power from below – or sub-politics – lessens the power of elites in the decision-making arena and paves the way for a "negotiation state." In his theory of the "world risk society," Beck (2006) goes further to contend that the ecological risks and harm caused by modernization have a potentially positive outcome – the enlightenment function – which allows us to move toward new ways of looking at environmental and social problems and developing institutional arrangements to deal with these challenges (Beck 2006). According to Beck (2006), there is the potential for empowerment through risk as public debates about environmental problems create a form of "involuntary democratization" or context of action to mitigate risk.

It is important to ensure this "involuntary democratization" allows for a plurality of voices and avoids "elite capture," where marginalized voices are excluded from the decision-making realm (Saito-Jensen, Iben and Thorsten 2014). Mansbridge (1992) argues for the institutionalization of deliberative processes of decision-making that bring together elites with rank-and-file members of interest groups to create a political process that reflects the interests of the broader public rather than a narrow group of self-interested groups. Additionally, Piven (2008) looks to the social interdependence that brings together non-elite actors to create new forms of power, using the tools of globalization – international networks and technological advances, such as the internet – to counter the power of multinational corporations. She argues that the complex global problems the world faces – from climate change and inequality to war and terrorism – need communal solutions, to work together across geographical, economic, and cultural boundaries.

It is clear that alternative water governance models based on equity and resilience are the exception rather than the rule. Part of the problem is the enormous imbalance of power that exists between policymakers and governments, corporations, international financial institutions, including the World Bank, and various international trade agreements and individual citizens and communities. According to Morgan (2011), the emergence of a new global water policy field has de-centered the state and made water a focus of economic restructuring, shifting power over water governance to global water firms and financing institutions. These institutions promote private sector participation in water treatment and delivery by lobbying and pressuring municipal governments to outsource public water services (Bakker 2010; Morgan 2011) and have become significantly more powerful in shaping water policies than other actors, including governments, unions, and civil society (Swyngedouw 2005). To adopt water governance models that are based on principles of equity and enhance resilience, it is necessary to address these power imbalances.

While power imbalances are difficult to overcome, there are myriad global examples that reflect the power of "politics from below" and the countermovement against global corporate control of resources (Bakker 2010; Robinson 2013). In relation to water equity, from Cochabama, Bolivia, to Stockton, California, grassroots movements have formed in opposition to water privatization, and there is a growing global water movement advocating for including the fundamental right to water in the United Nations Declaration of Human Rights (Mirosa and Harris 2011). Community knowledge and collective action are playing a central role in the way water is regulated, distributed, and socially constructed. New forms of deliberative democracy and collective negotiation are gaining ground and proving to be valuable forms of decision-making when it comes to the way we view and regulate natural, economic, and social resources (Bakker 2010; Bruns and Meinzen-Dick 2000; Robinson 2013; Schreier 2003; Weinberg, Pellow and Schnaiberg 2000).

A recent case from British Columbia, Canada, highlights the potential success of collective negotiation and participatory planning. In January 2016, after a 20-year struggle between environmentalists, government, the forestry industry, and First Nations, a historic agreement to protect the Great Bear Rainforest – the largest coastal temperate rainforest in the world – was reached (Hunter 2016). The agreement was the result of a participatory framework that allowed for equal representation of these stakeholders and the recognition of aboriginal rights to share decision-making power over natural resources (Page 2014).

This example demonstrates that strengthening the capacity of institutions at the community level as well as recognizing the rights of marginalized groups has the potential to enhance community resilience and environmental stewardship.[4] While it is difficult to imagine a world where power shifts from the hands of the elites into the hands of the global citizenry, the recent expansion of transnational movements, coupled with the global financial crisis, provide an opportunity for reimagining how power is organized and a new way of dealing with the social, economic, and environmental problems we face.

Conclusion

Increased globalization and the ensuing pressures on the environment and fresh water supplies mean the "water as a commodity" versus "water as a human right" conflict will be at the forefront of the social agenda for years to come. Understanding the processes of decision-making that shape conservation policies is critical for reducing conflict, ensuring the ecological protection and equitable access to life-sustaining resources.

Beyond fair access, fresh water systems must be conserved for future generations. This chapter presents two models for making policy decisions around water distribution. The first emphasizes the economic value of water as a commodity, while the second model stresses the importance of allocating resources equitably across current and future generations. As I demonstrate, market-based ecological modernization models are inadequate in dealing with the conservation and fair distribution of water to current and future generations because they treat water as mere commodity rather than as an integral component of global ecosystems, they ignore inequalities between individuals in their ability to access and compete for water resources, and do not allow for a moral obligation to conserve water.

172 *Joanna L. Robinson*

Theories of distributive justice provide a useful framework for dealing with the problem of water scarcity and unfair allocation, because they begin with the premise that resources should be allocated fairly to current and future generations. I argue that in order to ensure that power structures are not dominated by elites, Rawls' theory should be broadened to include a conception of decision-making that is based on participatory or deliberative democracy. I contend that Habermas's theory of communicative action provides a starting point for the development of ecological democracy and constitutional justice that can guarantee environmental rights and the rights of future generations to access resources. As the dominant economic paradigm continues to threaten the survival of the planet's life-support systems, it is crucial that we adopt new ways of thinking about how to conserve resources. Ecological democracy provides the means to achieve that end.

Notes

1 Glendon College, York University, Department of Sociology, jrobinson@glendon.yorku.ca
2 For the purposes of this chapter, water "privatization" refers to the contracting of public services to the private sector by governments. Privatization of municipal water services is commonly referred to as a form of "public–private partnership" (P3s), which is typically a complex agreement between governments and private sector firms for the building or upgrading of capital-intensive infrastructure and delivery of services (for more information on the history of P3s see Pierre 1998, and the application of P3s to water see Bakker 2004; 2010).
3 Some scholars question the application of Habermas's social theory to ecological conservation because of his privileging of human emancipation over the natural world and his position that we can only understand nature as a way to advance human societies. Eckersley (1990) argues that Habermas's anthropocentric stance makes it impossible to envision a cooperative relationship between society and nature. On the other hand, Brulle (2002) argues that we can, in fact, look to Habermas's critical theory as providing the means to developing a new environmental ethic because it provides the social conditions (i.e., participatory democracy) that will pave the way for the construction and enactment of a binding environmental ethic.
4 Local involvement has allowed for the inclusion of less powerful stakeholders into decisions about water management. Research on community-based water management in Nepal demonstrates that involving local communities in planning and management of water systems increases efficiency and sustainability of the water systems (WaterAid Nepal 2008). Yet, local involvement does not always lead to increased capacity or power of the local community to shape policy. In their research on transboundary water governance in Canada and the United States, Norman and Bakker (2009) demonstrate that an increase in local stakeholder involvement did not translate into more power over decision-making for local stakeholders. In this case, a lack of institutional capacity at the local level, coupled with asymmetrical power between different scales of governance meant that federal governments continued to have a monopoly over decision-making about transboundary water management even after local stakeholders were given a voice. To reduce conflict between levels of government, water scholars thus emphasize the importance of integrated water management policies that recognize the interconnectedness of scales of governance and range of water uses, and promote collaboration of stakeholders across these scales (Blatter and Ingram 2000; Bouwer 2002; Norman and Bakker 2009).

References

Baker S. (2016). *Sustainable development*. London: Routledge.

Bakker K. (2004). *An uncooperative commodity: privatizing water in England and Wales* Oxford: Oxford University Press.

Bakker K. (2007a). Neoliberalizing nature? Market environmentalism in water supply in England and Wales. *Annals of the Association of American Geographers*, 95(3), 542–565.

Bakker K. (2007b). The 'commons' versus the 'commodity': alter-globalization, anti-privatization and the human right to water in the global south. *Antipode*, 39(3), 430–455.

Bakker K. (2010). *Privatizing water: governance failure and the world's urban water crisis*. Ithaca, NY: Cornell University Press.

Barlow M. (2003). The world's water: a human right or a corporate good? In B. McDonald and D. Jehl (Eds.) *Whose water is it? The unquenchable thirst of a water-hungry world*. Washington: National Geographic Society.

Barlow M. and Clarke T. (2001). *Blue gold: the battle against corporate theft of the world's water*. Toronto: Stoddard Publishing.

Beck U. (1996). Risk society and the provident state. In S. Lash, B. Szerszynski and B. Wynne (Eds.) *Risk, environment and modernity: towards a new ecology* (pp. 27–43). London: Sage.

Beck U. (2006). Living in the world risk society. *Economy and Society*, 35(3), 329–345.

Beck U. (2008). *World at risk*. London: Polity Press.

Bell M.M. (2012). *An invitation to environmental sociology* (4th ed.). Los Angeles: Sage Publications.

Blatter J. and Ingram H. (2000). States markets and beyond: governance of transboundary water issues. *Natural Resources Journal*, 40, 439–473.

Block F. (2003). Karl Polanyi and the writing of "The great transformation". *Theory and Society*, 00, 1–32.

Bouwer H. (2002). Integrated water management for the 21st century: problems and solutions. *Journal of Irrigation and Drainage Engineering*, 128(4), 193–202.

Brulle R.J. (2000). *Agency, democracy and nature: the U.S. environmental movement from a critical theory perspective*. Cambridge, MA: MIT Press.

Brulle R.J. (2002). Habermas and green political thought: two roads converging. *Environmental Politics*, 11(4), 1–20.

Bruns B.R. and Meinzen-Dick R.S. (2000). *Negotiating water rights*. London: Intermediate Technology Publications.

Bryner G.C. (2002). Assessing claims of environmental justice: conceptual frameworks. In K.M. Mutz, G.C. Bryner and D.S. Kenney (Eds.) *Justice and natural resources: concepts, strategies, and applications*. Washington: Island Press.

Buttel F.H. (1986). Sociology and the environment. *International Social Science Journal*, 109, 337–356.

Buttel F.H. (2000). Ecological modernization as social theory. *GeoForum*, 31, 57–65.

Buttel F.H. (2000). World society, the nation state and environmental protection: comment on Frank, Hironaka and Schofer. *American Sociological Review*, 65, 117–121.

Caniglia B.S., Frank B., Delano D. and Kerner B. (2014). Enhancing environmental justice research and praxis: the inclusion of human security, resilience and vulnerabilities literature. *International Journal of Innovation and Sustainable Development*, 8(4), 409–426.

Catley-Carlson M. (2003). Working for water. In B. McDonald and D. Jehl (Eds.) *Whose water is it? The unquenchable thirst of a water-hungry world*. Washington: National Geographic Society.

Clarke T. (2003). Water privateers. *Alternatives Journal*, 29(2), 10–15.
Conca K. (2006). *Governing water: contentious transnational politics and global institution building*. Cambridge, MA: MIT Press.
Costanza R., d'Arge R., de Groot R., Farberk S., Grasso M., Hannon B. et al. (1997). The value of the world's ecosystem services and natural capital. *Nature*, 387, 253–260.
Dauvergne P. (2010). *The shadows of consumption: consequences for the global environment*. Cambridge, MA: MIT Press.
Dombeck M. (2003). From the forest to the faucet. In B. McDonald and D. Jehl (Eds.) *Whose water is it? The unquenchable thirst of a water-hungry world*. Washington: National Geographic Society.
Eckersley R. (1990). Habermas and green political theory: two roads diverging. *Theory and Society*, 19(6), 739–776.
Espeland W.N. (1998). *The struggle for water: politics, rationality and identity in the American Southwest*. Chicago: University of Chicago Press.
Evans P. (2008). Is an alternative globalization possible? *Politics and Society*, 36(2), 271–305.
Fisher D. and Freudenburg W. (2001). Ecological modernization and its critics: assessing the past and looking toward the future. *Society and Natural Resources*, 14, 701–709.
Giddens A. (1998). *The third way*. Cambridge: Polity Press.
Gille Z. (2000). Legacy of waste or wasted legacy? The end of industrial ecology in post-socialist Hungary. *Environmental Politics*, 9(1), 203–231.
Gleick P.H. and Ajami N. (2014). *The world's water volume 8: The biennial report on freshwater resources*. Washington: Island Press.
Goldman M. (2007). How 'water for all!' policy became hegemonic: the power of the World Bank and its transnational policy networks. *Geoforum*, 38(5), 786–800.
Gould K.A., Schnaiberg A. and Weinberg A.S. (1996). *Local environmental struggles: citizen activism in the treadmill of production*. Cambridge: Cambridge University Press.
Gould K.A., Pellow D. and Schnaiberg A. (2004). Interrogating the treadmill of production: everything you wanted to know about the treadmill but were afraid to ask. *Organization and Environment*, 17(3), 296–316.
Habermas J. (1974). *Toward a rational society: student protest, science and politics*. Boston: Beacon Press.
Habermas J. (1984). *The theory of communicative action, volume one: reason and the rationalization of society*. Boston: Beacon Press.
Habermas J. (1995). Reconciliation through the public use of reason. In J. Habermas (Ed.) *The inclusion of the other*. Cambridge, MA: MIT Press.
Habermas J. (1996). *Between facts and norms: contributions to a discourse theory of law and democracy*. Cambridge, MA: MIT Press.
Hunter J. (2016). Final agreement reached to protect B.C.'s Great Bear Rainforest. Retrieved 25 April 2016 from http://www.theglobeandmail.com/news/british-columbia/final-agreement-reached-to-protect-bcs-great-bear-rainforest/article28475362/
Ingram H. and Blatter J. (2001). *Reflections on water: new approaches to transboundary conflicts and cooperation*. Cambridge, MA: MIT Press.
Jehl D. (2004). Introduction. In B. McDonald and D. Jehl (Eds.) *Whose water is it? The unquenchable thirst of a water-hungry world*. Washington: National Geographic.
Jennings B. (2010). Toward an ecological political economy: Accommodating nature in a new discourse of public philosophy and policy analysis. *Critical Policy Studies*, 4(1), 77–85.
Klein N. (2014). *This changes everything: capitalism vs. the climate*. Toronto: Knopf.

Klinenberg E. (2003). *Heat wave: a social autopsy of disaster in Chicago*. Chicago: University of Chicago Press.
Locke J. (1967). *Two treatises of government*. Retrieved 29 April 2016 from http://socserv2.socsci.mcmaster.ca/econ/ugcm/3ll3/locke/government.pdf
Low N. and Gleeson B. (1998). *Justice, society and nature: an exploration of political ecology*. London: Routledge.
Mansbridge J. (1992). A deliberative perspective on neocorporatism. *Politics and Society*, 20(4), 493–505.
Meinzen-Dick R.S. and Ringler C. (2008). Water reallocation: drivers, challenges, threats, and solutions for the poor. *Journal of Human Development*, 9(1), 47–64.
Mirosa O. and Harris L. (2011). Human right to water: contemporary challenges and contours of a global debate. *Antipode*, 44(3), 932–949.
Mol A.P.J and Sonnenfeld A. (Eds.) (2000). *Ecological modernisation around the world: perspectives and critical debates*. London: Routledge.
Mol A.P.J. and Spaargaren G. (2000). Ecological modernisation theory in debate: a review. In A.P.J. Mol and D.A. Sonnenfeld (Eds.) *Ecological modernisation around the world: perspectives and critical debates*. London: Routledge.
Morgan B. (2011). *Water on tap rights and regulation in the transnational governance of urban water services*. Cambridge: Cambridge University Press.
Mullin M. (2011). *Governing the tap: special district governance and the new local politics of water*. Cambridge, MA: MIT Press.
Norman E.S. and Bakker K. (2009). Transgressing scales: transboundary water governance across the Canada–U.S. border. *Annals of the Association of American Geographers*, 99 (1), 99–117.
Okin S.M. (1991). *Justice, gender and the family*. New York: Basic Books.
Olivera O. and Lewis T. (2004). *Cochabamba! Water rebellion in Bolivia*. New York: South End Press.
Page J. (2014). *Tracking the great bear: how environmentalists recreated British Columbia's coastal rainforest*. Vancouver: UBC Press.
Pellow D.N. and Brem H.N. (2013). An environmental sociology for the twenty-first century. *Annual Review of Sociology*, 39, 229–250.
Pierre J. (Ed.) (1998). *Partnerships in urban governance: European and American experience*. New York: Palgrave Macmillan Ltd.
Piven F.F. (2008). Can power from below change the world? 2007 presidential address. *American Sociological Review*, 73, 1–14.
Polanyi K. (1944). *The great transformation*. Boston: Beacon Press.
Postma D.W. (2006). *Why care for nature? In search of an ethical framework for environmental responsibility and education*. New York: Springer.
Princen T. (2002). The consumption angle. In T. Princen, M. Maniates and K. Conca (Eds.) *Confronting consumption*. Cambridge, MA: MIT Press.
Rawls J. (1971). *A theory of justice*. Boston: Harvard University Press.
Rawls J. (1993). *Political liberalism*. New York: Columbia University Press.
Roberts A. (2008). Privatizing social reproduction: the primitive accumulation of water in an era of neoliberalism. *Antipode*, 40(4), 535–560.
Robinson J. (2013). *Contested water: the struggle against water privatization in the United States and Canada*. Cambridge, MA: MIT Press.
Rogers P., de Silva R. and Bhatia R. (2002). Water is an economic good: how to use prices to promote equity, efficiency, and sustainability. *Water Policy*, 4(1), 1–17.
Rubin J. (2012). *The end of growth*. Toronto: Random House Canada.

Saito-Jensen M., Iben N. and Thorsten T. (2014). Beyond elite capture: community-based natural resource management and power in Mohammed Nager village, Andhra Pradesh, India. *Environmental Conservation, 37(3)*, 327–335.

Schnaiberg A. and Gould K.A. (2000). *Environment and society: the enduring conflict.* New York: Cambridge University Press.

Schnaiberg A., Pellow D.N. and Weinberg A.S. (2002). The treadmill of production and the environmental state. In A.P.J. Mol and F.H. Buttel (Eds.) *The environmental state under pressure.* Amsterdam: Elsevier Science.

Schreier H. (2003). Mountain wise and water smart. In B. McDonald and D. Jehl (Eds.) *Whose water is it? The unquenchable thirst of a water-hungry world.* Washington: National Geographic Society.

Sen A. (1982). *Choice, welfare and measurement.* Cambridge: Cambridge University Press.

Sen A. (1992). *Inequality reexamined.* Oxford: Clarendon.

Sen A. (1999). *Development as freedom.* New York: Anchor Books.

Shiva V. (2002). *Water wars: privatization, pollution and profit.* New York: Southend Press.

Sonnenfeld D.A. (2000). Contradictions of ecological modernisation: pulp and paper manufacturing in South-east Asia. *Environmental Politics, 9(1)*, 235–256.

Spaargaren G. (1997). *The ecological modernization of production and consumption: essays in environmental sociology.* Wageningen, Netherlands: Wageningen University.

Spaargaren G. (2000). Ecological modernisation theory and the changing discourse on environment and modernity. In G. Spaargaren, A.P.J. Mol and F. Buttel (Eds.) *Environment and global modernity.* London: Sage.

Spaargaren G. and Mol A.P.J. (1992). Sociology, environment, and modernity: ecological modernization as a theory of social change. *Society and Natural Resources, 5*, 323–344.

Stevenson H. and Dryzek J.S. (2014). *Democratizing global climate governance.* Cambridge: Cambridge University Press.

Swyngedouw E. (2005). Dispossessing H_2O: the contested terrain of water privatization. *Capitalism, Nature, Socialism, 16(1)*, 81–98.

Terhorst P. (2008). 'Reclaiming public water': changing sector policy through globalization from below. *Progress in Development Studies, 8(1)*, 103–114.

WaterAid Nepal (2008). Nepal's experiences in community-based water resources management. *WaterAid Nepal Field Work Paper.*

Weinberg A.S., Pellow D.N. and Schnaiberg A. (2000). *Urban recycling and the search for sustainable community development.* Princeton, NJ: Princeton University Press

Wilkinson R. and Pickett K. (2010). *The spirit level: why greater equality makes societies stronger.* New York: Bloomsbury Press.

Wood P. (2000). *Biodiversity and democracy: rethinking society and nature.* Vancouver: UBC Press.

York R., Rosa E. and Dietz T. (2003). Footprints on the earth: the environmental consequences of modernity. *American Sociological Review, 68*, 279–300.

Young I.M. (2006). *Responsibility for justice.* New York: Oxford University Press.

Young J.P. (1996). *Reconsidering American liberalism: the troubled odyssey of the liberal idea.* Boulder, CO: Westwood Press.

10 The pitfalls and promises of climate action plans
Transformative adaptation as resilience strategy in US cities

Chandra Russo[1] and Andrew Pattison[2]

Introduction

In the face of established scientific consensus that climate change is already under way (IPCC 2014), the United States has proven largely ineffectual in passing meaningful legislation to curb its own greenhouse gas emissions or to prepare its citizenry for a warming climate. This seems a cruel if perhaps carefully designed irony as the US, along with China, leads the globe as the largest contributor to carbon emissions. In the absence of action at the federal level, local governments in cities, counties, and states have taken the most consequential steps to curb climate change emissions through the advent of climate action planning (Bulkeley 2013; Ramaswami et al. 2012).

A climate action plan (CAP) describes the set of policies or programs a subnational entity hopes to implement in order to reduce greenhouse gas emissions.[3] The proliferation of CAPs across US cities is an important advance for impacting upon climate change. For the purposes of this discussion, which focuses on urban resilience, we highlight two shortcomings in CAPs. First, most CAPs to date focus on climate change *mitigation* – decreasing greenhouse gas emissions – yet do little in the way of *adaptation* – implementing socially and culturally appropriate measures to better prepare for the impacts of climate change. Second, and likely more endemic to urban policymaking as a whole, CAPs have been weak in addressing social equity concerns. When CAPs neglect adaptation and/or give insufficient regard to the environmental ravages of social inequity, the shortterm health and long-term security of marginalized communities and entire cities are threatened.

This chapter proceeds with cautious optimism about the role that local climate change planning *can* play. Local government processes are often more responsive to community demands and more directly connected to the lived experiences of urban communities than state and federal policy-making (Bulkeley and Betsill 2003; Giddens 2011). This potential is key to why we think city CAPs deserve heightened focus from environmental justice scholars and activists committed to securing climate change resiliency in the short-term as part of a long-term sustainability program. In order to achieve this potential, however, we argue for the importance of transformative adaptation measures as a foremost means of making US cities more resilient and ultimately more sustainable. Transformative adaptation is here defined as merging climate change preparedness measures with a serious reworking of the traditional urban planning framework so that the interests of communities are valued over those of wealthy developers (Pelling 2010; Revi et al. 2014).

In what follows, we begin by discussing key concepts, such as vulnerability, resilience, and sustainability. In moving toward greater urban resilience and ultimately sustainability, we make a case for the importance of doing transformative adaptation (Pelling 2010; Revi et al. 2014). We then look to municipal climate action plans, where there are scarce instances of adaptation and a general neglect of issues of social equity. Finally, we elaborate a framework for transformative adaptation at the city level through examples drawn from five US-based CAPs: Boston 2014, NYC 2015, Portland 2015, Seattle 2013, and Washington DC 2010. Revi and colleagues (2014) suggest that cities have not been studied through the lens of transformative adaptation and that "it is too early to be able to claim that transformative adaptation is strongly evident at the city level" (27). Agreeing with this assessment, we consider what transformative adaptation might look like in the climate action planning of US cities.

What we identify here as a coupled weakness – insufficient attention to adaptation and to social equity concerns – is not merely a pitfall but an area of burgeoning potential. Adaptation strategies are still in their infancy, even if they are a necessary part of how cities will need to prepare for and protect themselves from climate change impacts that are already under way. For this reason, there is great promise for incorporating social equity objectives into adaptation planning. We argue that a transformative adaptation agenda is our best bet in securing more resilient and sustainable cities

Transformative adaptation

The impacts of a changing climate are already beginning to challenge urban infrastructures and population well-being and will continue to do so (IPCC 2014). More frequent and enduring temperature extremes will increase the need for energy-intensive cooling and heating processes (Panteli and Mancarella 2015). Precipitation decreases will lead to water scarcity while population demand remains constant or grows (Bulkeley 2013). Sea-level rise will threaten low-lying coastal cities. Stronger and more frequent storm surges will pose new risks to urban infrastructure. Vector-borne diseases will increase in frequency and regional sprawl (IPCC 2014). All of these impacts have the potential to lead to increased physiological stresses and mass community displacements (Hunt and Watkiss 2011). In essence, climate change introduces and will continue to generate a set of vulnerabilities that our civilization has not previously witnessed.

The Intergovernmental Panel on Climate Change defines vulnerability as "the propensity or predisposition to be adversely effected [. . .] including sensitivity or susceptibility to harm and lack of capacity to adapt" (IPCC 2014, 128). Yet vulnerability is not merely a question of exposure to the physical impacts of climate change, but is produced through social, political, and economic dynamics. Environmental justice scholars have long demonstrated that communities plagued by injustice, poverty, and a lack of sociopolitical access are more vulnerable to environmental destruction and less resilient in the face of environmental change. Low-income communities of color are disproportionately exposed to environmental harms (Bullard 2000), less able to respond and recover from environmental ills ranging from what Robert Nixon (2006) calls the "slow violence" of environmental injustice to the more acute disasters catalyzed by climate change. In the face of more frequent and intense urban heatwaves, the poor cannot afford air conditioning and are the most likely to face severe consequences when the electric grid fails (Panteli and Mancarella 2015). When decaying urban infrastructure and climate crises lead to flooding and other weather-related emergencies, communities that rely on public transportation lack the escape mechanisms that wealthier urban residents with private vehicles may possess (Elliot and Pais 2006; Angotti 2013). These groups are also the least able to return to their homes after the forced evacuations spurred by climate-related catastrophe (Fussell, Sastry and Vanlandingham 2010). Because certain communities have been structurally abandoned by the social and political system, they have been rendered less resilient and less able to adjust, adapt, and respond to the impacts of climate change.

Caniglia and colleagues (2014) suggest that an attention to making societies more resilient to environmental changes places a keener focus on timescale than many previous environmental analyses and planning efforts. Though vulnerabilities to climate change are socially produced and unevenly distributed, the topography of urban vulnerabilities is often hard to map until *after* a climate change impact is experienced. In this way, the impacts of climate change have a way of exposing "injustices in waiting." The physical realities of environmental risk dovetail with long-standing forms of inequality to reveal the full extent of social injustices. The now canonical instance of this is Hurricane Katrina, which revealed at multiple levels how extreme weather events are unevenly experienced by coastal residents in both the short and long term, from immediate disaster relief to efforts at relocation and then return. An emphasis on resilience as the effort to make cities less vulnerable and more holistically prepared to endure the impacts of climate change demonstrates the importance of "recognizing such vulnerabilities before environmental harms can take place, and [building] resilience by lessening known vulnerabilities"(Caniglia, Frank, Delano and Kerner 2014, 417). Resilient cities are proactive rather than reactive; they have foresight in lieu of mere hindsight.

A second point in regards to resilience and timescale is here in order. There has been some suggestion that "resilience" is the new "sustainability" (Davidson 2010, cited in Caniglia et al. 2014). Just as sustainability was once a buzzword for environmental activists and scholars, resilience is today's environmental vogue. It is featured centrally in cutting-edge environmental literatures and holds mass appeal to urban policy experts, from city planners to disaster managers. This is not to say that either sustainability or resilience are empty concepts. They each have great utility, and we wish to hold on to both in our analysis. Rather than suggest the two are interchangeable, however, they can be distinguished in terms of timescale. If the IPCC (2014) defines sustainability as "a dynamic process that guarantees the persistence of natural and human systems in an equitable manner" (127), we would further specify this to add "over the long term." In other words, while resilience might be regarded as a proactively generated, short-term ability to encounter and recover from disturbance, sustainability is the more enduring socio-ecological capacity to support livelihood.

The role of timescale in climate change response is also helpful for pivoting to a core concept in this chapter, that of transformative adaptation. In order to understand what climate change *adaptation* seeks to accomplish, it is helpful to juxtapose *adaptation* to the much more commonly implemented *mitigation*. Climate change *mitigation* strategies seek to curb the devastating impacts of human behavior on the environment (Bulkeley 2013). Colloquially, these are efforts to lower the "carbon footprint." Mitigation is rooted in the acknowledgement that we can and need to find ways to reduce the level of carbon emissions released into the atmosphere. This is certainly future-oriented thinking. However, climate change *adaptation* is a bit different. Adaptation measures are rooted not solely in hedging against further environmental destruction but in the acknowledgement that some form of climate change is inevitable and already under way (Bulkeley 2013). The human-generated GHG emissions of the past century will have real environmental impacts to which cities need to adapt. In terms of timescale, both *mitigation* and *adaptation* are future-oriented, though *adaptation* might be understood as having a different orientation to the past and present. *Adaptation* must respond to climate impacts already under way due to past and present socio-ecological processes. Table 10.1 lists some examples of policies that address mitigation versus adaptation and inequality concerns.

While climate policy experts agree that adaptation and mitigation are complementary strategies for addressing climate change, to date, the vast majority of municipal climate change policies have focused on mitigation. Adaptation strategies, in contrast, are implemented much more rarely and are only in their earliest phase of development (Zimmerman and Faris 2011). The hindrances to creating and implementing adaptation measures are twofold: techno-scientific and sociopolitical. In terms of the techno-science, there is still a great deal of uncertainty about what risks are going to be experienced, where, how, and when. Indeed, experts argue that adaptation done without a complex assessment of various timescales as well as the shifting risks that climate change introduces can actually render populations more vulnerable to impacts (Dilling, Daly, Travis, Wilhelmi and Klein 2015). In the case of mitigation, it is much easier to measure levels of GHG emissions and atmospheric conditions, assessing relative efficacy and progress toward stated reductions targets. Adaptation is "messier"; it depends upon various institutions and actors whose successes may only be measured in the aftermath of socio-ecological catastrophe (Berrang-Ford, Ford and Paterson 2011). In conjunction with this, then, is the sociopolitical conundrum of dedicating what are already perceived to be scarce time, money, and energy toward

Table 10.1 Examples of policies that address mitigation vs. adaptation and inequality concerns

	Examples of traditional mitigation policy	Examples of adaptation policy (and inequality concerns)
Energy sector	Promotion of renewable energy generation (as a percentage of total fuel profile) to replace traditional carbon-intensive fossil fuels	Smart meters and smart-grid technologies Decentralization of electricity generation
Transportation sector	Switching to alternative fuels vehicles (e.g., electronic) and/or more fuel-efficient vehicles Upgrade and promote existing public transit	Low-carbon urban development requiring less individual transit (e.g., mixed-use and transit-oriented development) Improve the walkability and multi-modal transit options in communities (e.g., improve sidewalks and neighborhood connectivity to amenities)
Built environment	Energy-efficiency improvements to municipal buildings Mandatory renewable generation on-site for new buildings (e.g., solar hot water or photovoltaic panels)	Addressing and coping for risk associated with sea-level rise (where applicable) Stormwater management planning to address increased frequency and intensity of storms and flooding in vulnerable areas (e.g., improving infrastructure) Assess risk and prepare for increasing frequency and more prolonged heatwaves in vulnerable areas (e.g., cooling centers and "heatlines" to call for help or heat warnings)
Waste	Methane recovery from landfills	Promotion of community gardens and composting programs in underserved "food desert" neighborhoods

Source: IPCC (2007)

threats that are hard to measure and upon which little consensus rests (Pelling 2010; Laukkonen et al. 2009).

As a basic overview, Revi et al. (2014, 15) suggest that adaptation can be assessed based on four guidelines:

1   the proportion of residents served with risk-reducing infrastructure and services;
2   the proportion living in housing built to appropriate health and safety standards;
3   local government capacity; and
4   the levels of risk from climate change's direct and indirect impacts.

Like most policy goals, there are numerous ways in which adaptation has been practicably addressed as well as conceptually elaborated. Instructive to our assessment is the idea that adaptation exists along a spectrum that might be understood as conservative at one end, maintaining social systems and structures as they are, and transformational at the other, re-imagining the social and ecological interplay of the urban landscape (Pelling 2011). We believe that in order to make a real contribution to cities' short-term resilience and longer-term sustainability transformative adaptation is necessary. This kind of adaptation "brings an ethical and practical requirement to consider social justice as well as risk management concerns [. . .] to consider the root and proximate causes of risk that lie within and are reproduced by dominant development practices and pathways" (Revi et al. 2014, 25). As adaptation measures might be the most available and effective means for making climate change planning more just and equitable – and thus our cities more resilient – this socio-politically transformative model of adaptation has great promise. We now turn to a more specific discussion of climate action plans, the subnational urban planning tools where the vast majority of climate change policy in the US is being developed.

The coupled weakness of CAPs

In 2005 Seattle Mayor Greg Nickels launched the US Mayors Climate Protection Agreement to advance the goals of the Kyoto Protocol, an international agreement to address climate change that the US refused to join. The mayors' agreement, which over 1,000 mayors from 50 states have signed, encouraged US cities, counties, and states to adopt CAP, and to date, hundreds of cities have done so (EPA 2015; USCMCPA 2015). CAPs generally seek to alter the most energy-intensive elements of urban infrastructure in order to reduce a city's carbon emissions and energy dependency. Examples include increasing renewable energy generation, such as wind power and solar; making built structures more energy-efficient; and reducing transportation-related emissions.[4] While the past decade has seen CAPs become more explicit in terms of stated goals, policy details, and assessment measures (Krause 2011; Rabe 2004; Ramseur 2007), there is still significant divergence in how specific such plans are. Many CAPs are still structured as "big picture" documents that do not delineate a clear action plan or state how new initiatives will be funded (Galucci 2013). Nevertheless, the proliferation of CAPs across US cities is an important advance for impacting upon climate change.

For the purposes of this discussion, with its focus on boosting urban resilience, we highlight two shortcomings of CAPs: adaptation measures have not been planned or implemented and issues of social equity have been widely neglected. In the last section, we outlined why climate change adaptation is rarely done, for reasons both techno-scientific and sociopolitical. The second way in which CAPs fall short in building toward urban resilience is in the neglect of equity issues. Environmental policymaking has often erased the needs of disenfranchised communities, displacing increased financial and environmental burdens on the poor (Douglas et al. 2012; Finn and McCormick 2011). In previous work, we suggest that the most common mitigation measures undertaken by CAPs do not merely neglect issues of equity, but may actually exacerbate injustice and social vulnerability (Russo and Pattison forthcoming). Mitigation efforts are forged in a dominant urban development framework, which privileges the interests of those with investment capital over redistributive policies. In contrast to CAPs' more established mitigation measures, adaptation strategies are in a much earlier stage of development. This means it is both necessary to make adaptation a priority in preparing cities to be more resilient and sustainable, and that there is opportunity to push for transformative adaptation, climate change preparedness that addresses the deeply stratified allocation of resources and power in US cities.

A framework for transformative adaptation in CAPs

Transformative adaptation can work at many different scales, from project-specific sites to the level of the nation-state, though there are suggestions that smaller-scale initiatives may be the easiest and most effective way to do transformative adaptation (Bulkeley 2013). We aim to articulate how transformative adaptation might look through city-level climate action plans. In order for such plans to move cities toward transformative adaptation, we suggest that four key principles must be in place:

1 establish equitable adaptation;
2 pursue equitable transportation-oriented development;
3 include robust social policies;
4 ensure procedural equity.

In what follows, we elaborate on these principles with examples from five US city CAPs: Boston 2014, NYC 2015, Portland 2015, Seattle 2013, and Washington DC 2010. Our data are constrained to CAPs as public documents along with other secondary journalistic and scholarly sources. We do not incorporate surveys or interviews with community members and so cannot comment in detail on the involved social and political dynamics that have informed the CAPs we review. Nor can we speak to the lived experiences of inclusion or exclusion faced by vulnerable communities in these cities.

Establishing equitable adaptation

In order for a CAP to pursue a transformative adaptation agenda, this influential document needs to name and explain that adaptation is centrally about equity. The city must clarify what priority it places on adaptation, often also termed "preparedness," and how this is linked to ameliorating enduring structures of urban stratification. Incidentally, most CAPs that expressly pursue equitable adaptation explain this objective as key to attaining greater urban resilience.

Washington DC's 2010 CAP offers a good example of this, asserting early in the document that equitable adaptation is a foremost means for making the most vulnerable more resilient, and that this concern for equity is key to understanding the purpose of adaptation. The document begins:

Climate change adaptation activities focus on the ways in which vulnerable populations, including those living in urban environments and particularly lower-income residents, can prepare for and cope with the threats posed by climate change (Climate of Opportunity: a Climate Action Plan for the District of Columbia 2010, 5).

Seattle's 2013 CAP offers a similar declaration that adaptation must be attuned to equity concerns:

> Our most vulnerable populations, including lower income, recent immigrant, and older residents, are at greater risk from the impacts of climate change and they often have the fewest resources to respond to changing conditions. Fostering the resilience in these more vulnerable residents and supporting their recovery after extreme events is critical.
> (Seattle Climate Action Plan 2013, 54)

While the DC plan offers a conceptual framework for equitable adaptation, Seattle's plan goes a bit further in offering a rubric of how adaptation will ensure greater equity. First, the city will prioritize those practices that ensure vulnerable groups are more able to respond to the impacts of climate change. Second, the "input and perspectives from members of vulnerable groups" will centrally inform climate change preparedness measures, a call for procedural equity to which we return (Seattle Climate Action Plan 2013, 54).

Boston's 2014 Climate Action Plan notes that in pursuing adaptation, the city is "inspired by the environmental justice movement" (Greenovate Boston 2014, 16). Boston elaborates on how an environmental justice lens informs adaptation, noting, "minority and low-income communities must not be disproportionately impacted by climate hazards" and that the "benefits from climate mitigation and preparedness efforts should be shared equally among all groups of people" (Greenovate Boston 2014, 6). Boston foresees that sea-level rise and heatwaves will pose some of the more significant threats to "the wellness and resilience of vulnerable populations" (Greenovate Boston 2014, 16), and so the 2014 CAP will prioritize addressing such impacts through collaboration across various named city departments.

The adaptation or "preparedness" portion of Portland's 2015 CAP also makes social equity central. The document notes, "in Portland, communities of color and low-income populations experience disparities that result in disproportionate vulnerabilities to the impacts of climate change" (Climate Action Plan, City of Portland 2015, 25). The disparities listed include health risks, lack of quality affordable housing, limited access to transportation and open spaces, and higher mortality. Portland's CAP also notes that "other legacies of inequitable public policies" (Climate Action Plan, City of Portland 2015, 25) create increased vulnerability for certain urban communities. This is a rather transformative acknowledgement that urban development processes have long contributed to greater social inequality and that adaptation measures must actively seek to undo such unjust arrangements of power and resources.

This portion of the plan explains that the pursuit of "climate resilience" must "ensure that the benefits of taking actions to prepare for climate change are shared by the whole community and across multiple generations" (Climate Action Plan, City of Portland 2015, 25).

Establishing that equitable adaptation is a priority can take many forms, and in most CAPs it is offered as more of a vision statement than a set of plans and initiatives of its own. Rather, it can serve as an important framing device in which to situate the rest of the plan. We now turn to more practice-oriented initiatives that a transformative adaptation agenda should include.

Equitable transportation-oriented development

Broadly defined, transportation-oriented development (TOD) seeks to create denser, mixed-use urban spaces that are easily walkable, bikeable, and navigable by public transportation as a means of reducing carbon emissions and energy dependence (Belzer and Poticha 2009). TOD also aims to put people near transit, and housing near jobs (Belzer and Poticha 2009). TOD is arguably the single most socially impactful aspect of CAPs in that it fundamentally reorganizes the urban environment, which is why we focus on it specifically. Scholars as well as community leaders argue that *equitable* TOD might be the climate policy that most benefits low-income and other underserved communities (Belzer and Poticha 2009). Since TOD is about access to not just transportation but also housing, services, and goods, it portends the greatest benefits for those urban residents who spend a disproportionate amount of their income on housing and transportation costs as compared with other communities (Belzer and Poticha 2009). Because TOD ensures appropriate urban density is well served by diverse transportation modes, such development is also key to climate change adaptation. Through TOD, urban communities are better served by emergency responders and have easier access to evacuation measures in the case of disaster (McGregor, Roberts and Cousins 2012). In some cities that are already immensely well serviced by public transport, such as NYC, TOD is going to look different than in smaller cities and towns. However, the basic principles remain. Transportation should be safe, reliable, and accessible to all communities so that residents can meet their daily needs and obligations in an equitable and energy-efficient manner.

Unfortunately, the vast majority of TOD has neglected or displaced, rather than better served, low-income communities, making it a highly unjust climate policy (Wood and Brooks 2009). In some cities, TOD has been viewed as somewhat experimental, working against decades-long historical trajectories. Much US urban infrastructure has been developed to support the automobile industry as well as the placement of white, nuclear families in suburban outskirts, away from city centers (Lipsitz 1998). Municipalities have funded this kind of development through incentives to private investors through tax credits, which means the wealthy design TOD to best suit their interests. Lower-income residents are often structurally prevented from helping to plan these new communities and thus benefit little from them (Belzer and Poticha 2009). Those with disposable income are granted superior shopping opportunities while communities of color, the working classes, new immigrants, and other groups are priced out and forced elsewhere.

Many CAPs are seeking to do TOD equitably. Portland's 2015 CAP offers one of the more explicit and robust discussions of TOD, including what the stakes are for social equity and how the city plans to address these issues. The CAP explains that since lower-income households drive less and spend a greater percentage of their income on transport, transit investments should be targeted to serve these communities first and foremost (Climate Action Plan, City of Portland 2015, 47). Thus, while the city seeks to increase the percentage of its residents using low-carbon transit options from 22% to more than 60% by 2030, it understands that a key focus on equity in this regard is necessary. The plan explains that TOD, if necessary for achieving the city's mitigation and adaptation priorities, will also "attract new residents, which can increase gentrification and displacement (voluntary and involuntary) pressures on existing residents and neighborhood small businesses" (Climate Action Plan, City of Portland 2015, 47). Portland has thus set up a series of processes for "understanding and minimizing the effects of gentrification, assessing the risk of gentrification for different neighborhoods, and identifying and implementing best practices" (Climate Action Plan, City of Portland 2015, 48), through various tools and resources developed by the Equity Working Group.[5]

The Portland plan is specifically interested in doing TOD in the eastern section of the city, where a quarter of the city's residents live. East Portland is inhabited by nearly 40% of people of color, is much more racially diverse than the rest of the city, and has a higher concentration of people living in poverty. East Portland, the CAP explains, has been underserved by city planning procedures, especially when it comes to low-carbon transportation options, such as buses, cycling lanes, and even sidewalks for pedestrians (Climate Action Plan, City of Portland 2015).

The Portland CAP offers a series of initiatives to be achieved by 2020. Primary among these is to ensure that affordable housing has "safe, direct bicycle and pedestrian access to transit" (Climate Action Plan, City of Portland 2015, 81). The city plans to identify where more affordable housing needs to be created, with a particular focus on bettering transport options in these communities. There are also calls to repeal state zoning legislation that would prohibit such equity-focused development objectives (Climate Action Plan, City of Portland 2015). Finally, the plan calls for improving design and development standards for the multifamily buildings in which so many East Portland families live, as well as improving landscaping and open space to promote community walkability.

TOD is potentially the most socially significant climate mitigation and adaptation strategy and should be included in any effort at transformative adaptation. However, transformative adaptation also requires cities to go beyond traditional climate policy to combat the various urban planning legacies that have led huge swathes of the American population to be vulnerable to climate change in the first place. We now turn to these.

Robust social policies

Since underserved and underrepresented urban communities are more vulnerable to climate change impacts and hence less resilient, a transformative adaptation will include policies that may not appear to be climate related on their face. Examples include plans and benchmarks to address issues as broadly considered as affordable housing and job security. In this way, CAPs can address more than emissions targets and infrastructure adjustments to confront the underlying dynamics of social stratification. Such policies work proactively to remedy so-called "injustices in waiting."

While some CAPs proffer limited poverty reduction goals, few cities have made robust social policies part of their climate action plans or integrated such considerations into how they think about adaptation. The recently released OneNYC 2015 is distinctive in this regard. As a climate action plan, OneNYC is likely the most ambitious poverty reduction program being undertaken nationally through efforts that range from education to job growth, affordable housing to health care. Nobel-winning economist Joseph Stiglitz called the plan "unprecedented" in its targets for reducing urban poverty (Flegenheimer 2015). Obviously, New York City is unique as the most populous US city with unmatched urban resources. Nevertheless, while NYC is an outlier among US cities, our national and global population is increasingly living in large urban areas, so focusing on this city may be more instructive in thinking about transformative adaptation than it first appears.

NYC has one of the greatest wealth gaps among American municipalities (Roberts 2014). These serious issues of inequality threaten the city's resilience. As the OneNYC document explains, income inequality continues to rise, with nearly half of city residents living at or near the poverty line. Almost one and a half million residents face serious food insecurity, and more than half of those renting in the city spend more than 30% of their income on housing. This is combined with continuing epidemics of homelessness and environmentally produced disease, from asthma to diabetes, which plague low-income neighborhoods (OneNYC 2015, 25). The OneNYC plan positions itself within this context of serious urban equity issues coupled with the political and economic resources of a global city poised to aggressively address climate change.

OneNYC lays out a series of social policies as part of its vision for addressing climate change. These include increasing workforce participation through industry-focused training. The aim is to train 30,000 workers each year, so that by 2020 a greater proportion of NYC's public school graduates will receive college degrees (OneNYC 2015). The plan also calls for raising the minimum wage to $13 by 2016, a legislative mandate that would have to be implemented at the state rather than city level (Flegenheimer 2015). In terms of affordable housing, by 2024, OneNYC will finance the construction of 80,000 new affordable housing units and invest in preserving 120,000 existing affordable housing units (OneNYC 2015). OneNYC also proposes a variety of infrastructure development plans to ensure underserved communities have access to safe, reliable, and efficient transport as well as broadband internet by 2025. Both of these aims are crucial for day-to-day well-being, affordability, and social mobility, as well as disaster preparedness and resilience in the case of extreme weather events, from heatwaves to hurricanes.

One of the more surprising aspects of OneNYC, however, might be the priority it places on cultural institutions as a means of making the city more resilient and sustainable. New York City is world renowned for its museums and theaters, galleries and artists, which this CAP acknowledges to be crucial to social well-being in various ways. OneNYC explains that "culture" grows economic opportunities, providing New Yorkers with thousands of needed jobs and attracting tourists. Investment in cultural institutions is central to quality of life considerations, what OneNYC describes as "critical to ensuring the well-being of residents, improving social connections, lowering stress, improving school effectiveness, raising community awareness, and enhancing civic engagement" (OneNYC 2015, 78). Yet outside of Manhattan, and in low-income areas across the city's boroughs, scant resources have supported cultural initiatives and programming (OneNYC 2015, 78). The plan suggests this to be a formative barrier to urban resilience and long-term sustainability and sets itself the goal of an "increase in cultural and civic events in community districts with the highest rates of poverty and lowest rates of public cultural and civic programming" (OneNYC 2015, 78).

A plan like OneNYC does not come out of nowhere. It is not the creative product of city officials who merely wish to do better by the disenfranchised and structurally excluded. While Mayor Bloomberg's 2007 PlaNYC was in many ways ahead of its time in proposing adaptation measures, it fell short on social equity issues in very public ways. For instance, the city was sued for violating the Americans with Disabilities Act, when during Tropical Storm Irene in 2011, mandatory evacuations were ordered without considering the mobility needs of people with disabilities (Peterson 2015). PlaNYC was also criticized for evading the city's established mechanisms for producing and approving plans, relying on disorganized ways of soliciting community response through emails with no transparency for how feedback was to be incorporated in the plan (Angotti 2012; Paul 2007). Many suggested that calls for public participation in PlaNYC were an afterthought, a public relations strategy to hide the corporate interests driving the plan. As Yosef Jabareen (2014) assesses in his close reading of the document, "PlaNYC encourages community involvement in significant planning issues *in the future* and reflects little interest in community involvement during the preparation of the plan itself" (5908). As a final principle, we suggest that the pursuit of procedural equity is a foremost means for creating a transformative adaptation agenda, keeping such a framework in place and on track.

Procedural equity

Environmental justice scholar Robert Bullard (2000) argues for the importance of procedural equity in planning for sustainability. Procedural equity is defined here as the assurance that all community members are subject to the same rules, regulations, and avenues of access to the political process (Bullard 2000). Procedural equity prevents undemocratic decision-making and other practices that exclude already marginalized and vulnerable communities from participatory activities. These might include holding public hearings that are hard for people to attend, whether because of timing or location, or creating materials that are inaccessible, due to language barriers, lack of cultural competency, or other obstacles to literacy (Bullard 2000). Ensuring the involvement of all members of the community has long been regarded as foundational to doing successful climate change planning. Public support and involvement is key to shifting social attitudes and practices so as to adequately address environmental impacts. Building on Mark Roseland's work, it is evident that transformative adaptation will not be a top–down endeavor, as "real visions for change rarely come from government or from the market place but from civil society" (2005, 27, cited in Paul 2007). However, if broad-based participation is understood as the goal of climate change planning, specific attention needs to be paid to ensuring that historically underrepresented communities are brought into the planning process in meaningful ways.

All of the CAPs examined for this chapter are the products of struggles not just for better climate change policies but for greater equity and broader community participation. Sara Bernard (2015) explains how Portland's 2015 CAP came to centrally address issues of environmental justice. While Portland was the first US city to develop a plan to lower its carbon emissions as early as 1993, when such policies were hardly discussed at any level of government, it was not until 2009 that the city actively pursued community feedback. When consulted, residents made clear that they wanted Portland to "*increase the emphasis on equity*" (Bernard 2015). As the "whitest city in America," according to the 2010 census, Portland's demographic is rapidly changing, and many community organizations have worked tirelessly to ensure that low-income communities of color are as prepared for climate change impacts as everyone else. Ensuring that all communities get to participate in city planning for climate change preparedness is essential.

In addition to equity considerations woven throughout the 2015 Portland CAP, this plan actually names "procedural equity" as a central goal. The CAP explains that, "government programs and policies have historically been designed for a dominant culture, which can inhibit successful participation by other cultural communities" (Portland CAP 2015, 149). For this reason, Portland proposes four ways that programs and policies can be socio-culturally competent:

1. use people-friendly and culturally responsive strategies such as translated materials, childcare and food;
2. partner with and support cultural liaisons;
3. coordinate administrative processes to simplify community interaction;
4. adapt program delivery to meet a community where it is.

(Portland CAP 2015, 149)

Seattle's climate planning also advocates for environmental justice activism. Seattle's 2013 CAP includes promising commitments to equity and adaptation.

Nevertheless, on August 22, 2015, Seattle Mayor Ed Murray's office launched the Equity and Environment Initiative (EEI), bringing the city together with community groups and private funders "to deepen Seattle's commitment to race and social justice in environmental work" (Office of Mayor Murray 2013). The EEI, which is initiated and run out of the same division that has designed the city's CAPs, focuses on procedural equity, ensuring that the residents most vulnerable to climate change are considered centrally in climate action planning. The EEI seems to further Seattle's work towards transformative adaptation by pursuing what the Mayor's office explicitly names an "environmental justice" framework (Office of Mayor Murray 2013).

OneNYC is the clear response to the weaknesses around equity contained in the previous PlaNYC. The new plan includes a section on "how New Yorkers shaped OneNYC" (OneNYC 2015, 18). More than 8,000 residents were surveyed online and by telephone. Over 1,000 New Yorkers attended 40 community meetings held in every borough. Nearly 200 civic organizations, 50 elected officials, leaders from other state cities and counties, and 125 representatives from the city's 70 agencies all played a role in developing the new plan. Education and housing were the most important issues to the New Yorkers surveyed. Residents also emphasized the importance of having transit access between home and work (OneNYC 2015). These social considerations then became central to the plan (OneNYC 2015). The fact that the city explains in detail the ways in which feedback was solicited and implemented in the new plan means that procedural equity and participatory development are important priorities in these most recent climate action planning efforts.

Implementing transformative adaptation?

City-level planning is rife with challenges, foremost among these being issues of equity (Harvey 1973; Molotch 1976). Publicly established frameworks can hardly be assessed as effective without the more rigorous examination of implementation practices that so much important scholarship today examines (Jabareen 2014; Roseland 2005). While we have selected those CAPs that appear to be the most explicitly focused on equity in their adaptation aims, there is significant variation in how these documents assert they will pursue their objectives. Many of the most promising features of these plans, including those to which we draw attention, remain overly vague. We acknowledge that this leaves such frameworks open to significant diversion in implementation. Nevertheless, by looking to existing CAPs and accompanying documents, we believe it is possible to point to ways that US cities can take steps toward climate change adaptation with a primary focus on social equity issues. In so doing, we point to how cities might pursue a transformative adaptation agenda necessary for both short-term resilience and long-term sustainability.

With climate change impacts already under way and the social inequities that have long plagued US cities still firmly in place, environmental justice scholars have good reason to support a transformative adaptation agenda. Similarly, with the absence of climate action at the federal level, municipal climate action planning across the US appears to be the most substantial governing effort to acknowledge scientific predictions and protect diverse communities as well as future generations. At the same time, climate action plans have a long way to go in becoming the kinds of specific and aggressive policy-driving frameworks current climate change predictions require. Two of the foremost weaknesses in current plans include a lagging attention to adaptation measures and a continuing neglect of social equity issues, a coupled weakness that means CAPS currently do little to address "injustices in waiting."

Without suggesting that such a coupled weakness can become an automatic potential, we believe that environmental justice advocates and scholars have space as well as leverage to push for a transformative adaptation agenda in US municipal CAPs. By articulating four components of what a transformative adaptation should include, we hope to contribute to conversations about the necessity of doing adaptation equitably in order to heighten urban resilience and push toward the long-term sustainability of US cities.

Notes

1 Associate Professor of Sociology, Colgate University, Department of Sociology and Anthropology, crusso@colgate.edu
2 Gretchen Hoadley Burke '81 Endowed Chair for Regional Studies, Visiting Professor of Environmental Studies, Colgate University, apattison@colgate.edu
3 We use the nomenclature of climate action plan/CAP to delineate any city-level comprehensive plan that seeks to address climate change through planned actions, and hence do not constrain our examples to city documents that are explicitly labeled "Climate Action Plan."
4 Though CAPs do incorporate plans for more conservative water usage and system-wide waste reduction, such concerns have been lesser priorities until recently (Bulkeley 2013, 127).
5 Source www.portlandoregon.gov/bps/67908

References

Angotti T. (2013). New York after Sandy. *Progressive Planning*, 194, 2–11.
Belzer D. and Poticha S. (2009). Understanding transit-oriented development: lessons learned 1999–2009. In *Fostering equitable and sustainable transit-oriented development*. Center for Transit-Oriented Development.
Bernard S. (2015). Can the whitest city in America deliver green living for all? *grist*. Retrieved 31 October 2015 from http://grist.org/cities/can-the-whitest-city-in-america-deliver-green-living-for-all/
Berrang-Ford L., Ford J.D. and Paterson J. (2011). Are we adapting to climate change? *Global Environmental Change*, 21, 25–33.
Bulkeley H. (Ed.) (2013). *Cities and climate change*. New York: Routledge.
Bulkeley H. and Betsill M. (Eds.) (2003). *Cities for climate change: urban sustainability and global environmental governance*. London: Routledge.
Bullard R. (2000). Environmental justice in the 21st century. *People of Color Environmental Groups Directory*, 1–21.

Caniglia B.S., Frank B., Delano D. and Kerner B. (2014). Enhancing environmental justice research and praxis: the inclusion of human security, resilience and vulnerabilities literature. *International Journal of Innovation and Sustainable Development*, 8, 409–426.

Climate Action Plan, City of Portland, Oregon, Mulnomah County (2015). Retrieved 31 October 2015 from https://www.portlandoregon.gov/bps/article/531984

Climate of Opportunity: a Climate Action Plan for the District of Columbia (2010). Retrieved 31 October 2015 from http://doee.dc.gov/sites/default/files/dc/sites/ddoe/publication/attachments/ClimateOfOpportunity_web.pdf

Davidson D.J. (2010). The applicability of the concept of resilience to social systems: some sources of optimism and nagging doubts. *Society and Natural Resources*, 23(12), 1135–1149.

Dilling L., Daly M.E., Travis W.R., Wilhelmi O.V. and Klein R.A. (2015). The dynamics of vulnerability. Why adapting to climate variability will not always prepare us for climate change: dynamics of vulnerability. *Wiley Interdisciplinary Reviews: Climate Change*, 6, 413–425.

Douglas E.M., Kirshen P., Paolisso M., Watson C., Wiggin J., Enrici A. and Ruth M. (2012). Coastal flooding, climate change, and environmental justice: identifying obstacles and incentives for adaptation in two metropolitan Boston Massachusetts communities. *Mitigation and Adaptation Strategies for Global Change*, 17, 537–562.

Elliot J.R. and Pais J. (2006). Race, class and Hurricane Katrina: social difference in human responses to disaster. *Social Science Research*, 35(2), 295–321.

Environmental Protection Agency (2015). State climate and energy program: state examples climate change action plans. Retrieved 31 October 2015 from http://www3.epa.gov/statelocalclimate/index.html

Finn D. and McCormick L. (2011). Urban climate change plans: how holistic? *Local Environment*, 6(4), 397–416.

Flegenheimer M. (2015). New York City's environment program will focus on income inequality. *New York Times*. Retrieved 31 October 2015 from http://www.nytimes.com/2015/04/22/nyregion/new-york-citys-environment-program-to-focus-on-income-inequality.html

Fussell E., Sastry N. and Vanlandingham M. (2010). Race, socioeconomic status, and return migration to New Orleans after Hurricane Katrina. *Population and Environment*, 31(1), 20–42.

Galucci M. (2013). 6 of the world's most extensive climate adaptation plans. *Inside Climate News*. Retrieved 31 October 2015 from http://insideclimatenews.org/news/20130620/6-worlds-most-extensive-climate-adaptation-plans

Giddens A. (Ed.) (2011). *The politics of climate change* (2nd ed.). Cambridge: Polity.

Greenovate Boston: 2014 Climate Action Plan Update (2014). Retrieved 31 October 2015 from http://www.cityofboston.gov/eeos/pdfs/Greenovate%20Boston%202014%20CAP%20Update_Full.pdf

Harvey D. (Ed.) (1973). *Social justice and the city*. Athens, GA: University of Georgia Press

Hunt A. and Watkiss P. (2011). Climate change impacts and adaptation in cities: a review of the literature. *Climatic Change*, 104, 13–49.

Intergovernmental Panel on Climate Change (2007). *Climate change 2007: working group II: impacts, adaptation and vulnerability*. Retrieved 18 August 2016 from https://www.ipcc.ch/pdf/assessment-report/ar4/wg2/ar4_wg2_full_report.pdf

Intergovernmental Panel on Climate Change (2014). *Climate change 2014: synthesis report*. Stockholm: IPCC.

Jabareen Y. (2014). An assessment framework for cities coping with climate change: the case of New York City and its PlaNYC 2030. *Sustainability, 6*, 5898–5919.

Krause R. (2011). Policy innovation, intergovernmental relations, and the adoption of climate protection initiatives by U.S cities. *Journal of Urban Affairs, 33(1)*, 45–60.

Laukkonen J., Blanco P.K., Lenhart J., Keiner M., Cavric B. and Kinuthia-Njenga C. (2009). Combining climate change adaptation and mitigation measures at the local level. *Habitat International, 33*, 287–292.

Lipsitz G. ed. (1998). *Possessive investment in whiteness.* Philadelphia, PA: Temple University Press.

Mayor Murray launches first-of-its-kind Equity & Environment Initiative. April 22, 2015. Mayor Murray. Retrieved 31 October 2015 from http://murray.seattle.gov/mayor-murray-launches-first-of-its-kind-equity-environment-initiative/

McGregor A., Roberts C. and Cousins F. (Eds.) (2012). *Two degrees: the built environment and our changing climate.* New York: Routledge.

Molotch H. (1976). The city as a growth machine: toward a political economy of place. *American Journal of Sociology, 82(2)*, 309–332.

Nixon R. (2006). Slow violence, gender and the environmentalism of the poor. *Journal of Commonwealth and Postcolonial Studies, 13.2–14.1*, 14–37.

OneNYC (2015). New York the plan for a strong and just city. Retrieved 31 October 2015 from http://www.nyc.gov/html/onenyc/downloads/pdf/publications/OneNYC.pdf

Panteli M. and Mancarella P. (2015). Influence of extreme weather and climate change on the resilience of power systems: impacts and possible mitigation strategies. *Electric Power Systems Research, 127*, 259–270.

Paul B. (2007). PlaNYC: a model of public participation or corporate marketing. Retrieved 31 October 2015 from http://www.hunter.cuny.edu/ccpd/repository/files/planyc-a-model-of-public-participation-or.pdf

Pelling M. (2010). *Adaptation to climate change: from resilience to transformation.* London: Routledge.

Peterson M. (2015). Cities urged not to ignore marginalized communities in climate change plans. *ThinkProgress.* Retrieved 31 October 2015 from http://thinkprogress.org/climate/2015/05/20/3660371/national-climate-adaptation-forum-equity/

Rabe B. (Ed.) (2004). *Statehouse and greenhouse: the emerging politics of American climate change policy.* Washington DC: Brookings Institutional Press.

Ramaswami A., Bernard M., Chavez A., Hillman T., Whitiker M., Thomas G. and Marshall M. (2012). Quantifying carbon mitigation wedges in U.S. cities: near-term strategies analysis and critical review. *Environmental Science and Technology, 46(7)*, 3629–3642.

Ramseur J. (2007). *Climate change: action by states to address greenhouse gas emissions.* Washington DC. Congressional Research Service.

Revi A., Satterthwaite D., Aragón-Durand F., Corfee-Morlot J., Kiunsi R.B., Pelling M. et al. (2014). Towards transformative adaptation in cities: the IPCC's fifth assessment. *Environment and Urbanization, 26*, 11–28.

Roberts, S. (2014). Gap between Manhattan's rich and poor is greatest in U.S., census finds. *New York Times,* September 17. Retrieved 18 August 2016 from http://www.nytimes.com/2014/09/18/nyregion/gap-between-manhattans-rich-and-poor-is-greatest-in-us-census-finds.html

Roseland M. (Ed.) (2005). *Toward sustainable communities.* Gabriola Island, British Columbia: New Society Publishers.

Russo C. and Pattison A. (forthcoming) Climate action planning: an intersectional approach to the urban equity dilemma. In P. Godfrey and D. Torres (Eds.) *Systemic crises of global climate change: intersections of race, class and gender*. New York: Routledge.

Seattle Climate Action Plan (2013). Retrieved 31 October 2015 from http://www.seattle.gov/Documents/Departments/OSE/2013_CAP_20130612.pdf

US Conference of Mayors Climate Protection Agreement (USCMCPA) (2015). Retrieved 31 October 2015 from http://www.usmayors.org/climateprotection/agreement.htm

Wood D. and Brooks A. (2009). Overview of briefing papers. Retrieved 31 October 2015 from http://www.hud.gov/offices/cpd/about/conplan/pdf/Fostering_Equitable_and_Sustainable_TOD.pdf

Zimmerman R. and Faris C. (2011). Climate change mitigation and adaptation in North American cities. *Current Opinion in Environmental Sustainability*, 3, 181–187.

11 Resisting environmental injustice through socio-spatial tactics
Experiences of community reconstruction in Boston, Havana, and Barcelona

Isabelle Anguelovski[1]

Introduction

While early environmental justice (EJ) activism seemed often associated with fights against the disproportionate impacts of toxic contamination on minority or low-income residents, the more recent EJ agenda combines environmental sustainability and equitable community development. It includes demands for well-connected, affordable, and clean transit systems (Lucas 2004); healthy, fresh, local, and affordable food; community food security (Alkon and Agyeman 2011; Gottlieb 2009; Gottlieb and Joshi 2010; Hess 2009); as well as jobs, training, and other opportunities in the green economy (Fitzgerald 2010). In their struggles, urban activists pay much attention to comprehensive community reconstruction and neighborhood livability initiatives, since much environmental degradation, long-term abandonment, and trauma takes place at the local scale (Anguelovski 2014).

These struggles are intrinsically linked to issues of spatial justice – that is, the equitable allocation of socially valued resources, such as jobs, political power, social services, environmental goods in space, and the equal opportunities to utilize these resources over time (Marcuse 2009; Soja 2009). A promising way to remediate urban spatial injustices is to analyze the social processes that can address neighborhood environmental degradation and new injustices-in-waiting, and achieve environmental equality for vulnerable residents. Yet, to date, we lack an understanding of the socio-spatial strategies and tactics that urban environmental justice activists have developed to address environmental toxics, rebuild distressed urban neighborhoods, and achieve spatial justice.

This chapter attempts to address this gap by examining the socio-spatial strategies developed by activists in three minority and low-income urban neighborhoods that are centrally located: Casc Antic (Barcelona), Dudley (Boston), and Cayo Hueso (Havana). Each neighborhood has been very active and visible over the past two decades as residents and their supporters organized toward improved environmental quality. These are neighborhoods who successfully asserted their claims to planners and policymakers, leading to improved environmental and health conditions through a variety of projects: parks and playgrounds, sports courts and centers, urban farms, farmers' markets and healthy food providers, and waste management.

Analyzing these cases is particularly valuable for uncovering how activists manage to advance their claims for equitable and green neighborhoods, adapt them through time and space, and resist emerging pressures that might undermine their achievements. Additionally, because they are located in different political systems, a comparative analysis enables us to see whether activist strategies are affected by such political differences. This comparative approach is motivated by a commitment to providing a strong theoretical understanding of urban neighborhoods with comparable spatialities, connections, and processes (McFarlane 2010; Robinson 2011) – uneven development, socio-racial marginalization, abandonment, and revival – despite the fact that they are also located in different political systems.

Here, I argue that these neighborhoods have developed similar socio-spatial strategies and tactics, despite the fact social movement scholarship suggests tactical repertoires will vary among different political systems and contexts (Tilly 1978, 2001). The similar strategies and tactics included broad and "unexpected" coalitions of activists, bricolage techniques, a strategic use of the political environment, and leveraging access to technical experts and funders, who in turn became activists and advocates on behalf of residents. In the next section I present existing scholarship on strategies and tactics adopted by activists in historically deprived neighborhoods, which provides a general framework for understanding the development and rationale of local citizen mobilization. I then proceed to analyze the activists' strategies and tactics in Boston, Barcelona, and Havana, before discussing the relevance of my findings for urban environmental justice scholarship.

Environmental justice and the selection of strategies and tactics

Historically, minority and low-income urban neighborhoods have suffered more environmental harm from waste sites, disposal facilities, transfer storage, incinerators, refineries, and other contaminating industries – what is traditionally known as locally unwanted land uses (LULUs) (Downey and Hawkins 2008; Lerner 2005; Mohai, Pellow and Roberts 2009; Sze 2007). At the same time, such neighborhoods have been particularly affected by contentious or failed urban regeneration, or revitalization programs (Crisp 2013; Lawless 2011; Matthews 2012). More than others, residents of historically marginalized neighborhoods are threatened by labels such as "ghettos," by urban renewal policies and ensuing gentrification processes (Fullilove 2004; Otero 2010; Pattillo 2007; Smith 1982). Consequently, they often organize to contest territorial stigmas associated with degradation and neglect and, in turn, create meaningful and autonomous images of place and community (Garbin and Millington 2012; Millington 2015; Wacquant 2007).

In resisting disruption and threats to their communities and rejecting market-based neighborhood revaluations, activists develop numerous coping mechanisms against oppressive and exploitative transformations. Through different "democratic attitudes" and strategic choices, they attempt to create a different type of citizenship, alter power relations, strengthen citizen control over decision-making and planning processes, and promote the radical democratization and transformation of cities (Purcell 2008, 2009). They are often democratic movements that reject dominant neoliberal assumptions about urban development and pursue goals of more humane, equitable, and socially cooperative futures in cities (Purcell 2008).

In social movement theory, strategies and tactics are understood as the range of direct action and institutional means that groups and movements develop to advance concrete objectives. Historically, strategies and tactics have been shown to have greater influence over their target if they choose culturally-accepted strategies (Tilly 1978) while being innovative (Tarrow 2011). Movements able to alternate between more confrontational tactics and direct negotiations with state actors tend to have a greater chance to achieve their goals (Pellow 2001; Polletta 2005; Porta and Rucht 2002; Tilly 1978). Yet, as their members draw upon a variety of strategies and tactics, they do not all have access to the same resources. Lower financial resources, education level, status, and time constitute barriers to participation and mobilization among seemingly powerless groups (Fagotto and Fung 2006; Schneider 2007). However, if they are able to show resourcefulness and strategic capacity – that is, the access to salient information, heuristic facility, presence of privileged outsiders (including skilled and charismatic supporters), and motivation – groups can compensate for their lack of material resources (Ganz 2000; Tarrow 2011).

One widely used social movement strategy is to build coalitions. Groups who can demonstrate broad support increase their chances of exercising power (Gamson 1990; Tilly 1978). Additionally, constructing wider coalitions between groups and beyond classes seems to help activists successfully pressure state actors and corporations (Di Chiro 2008; Gould, Lewis and Roberts 2004; McGurty 2000; Polletta 2005; Staggenborg 1998; Tarrow 2011). In the US, for example, broad urban coalitions such as the "Right to the City Alliance"[2] have brought together activists from different social movement traditions, including labor and environmental justice activists (Connolly and Steil 2009; Marcuse 2009). Previous studies have shown that coalitions are more likely to emerge when resources are abundant (Staggenborg 1986; Zald and McCarthy 1987), the identity of movement members is quite unified, and their collective identity is strong. Coalitions also emerge when their members perceive exceptional threats might prevent them from attaining their objectives individually and when external circumstances might threaten the goals of social movement organizations (McCammon and Campbell 2002; Van Dyke 2003), including a change of political regime.

Regarding tactics, coalitions have used three different types. Direct and confrontational tactics – lawsuits against companies, direct denunciations and shaming, or pressure for greater government oversight – allow marginalized communities to address environmental inequities and contamination (Bandy and Smith 2005; Pellow 2001, 2007). In other cases residents use more collaborative approaches by successfully pressuring contaminating companies to participate in multi-party dialogue processes and negotiations (Susskind and Macey 2004). In still other cases activists combine professional techniques, scientific studies on contamination impacts, and the experiences from affected residents to "co-produce knowledge," which, in turn, improves the likelihood that public agencies or corporations will respond to residents' demands (Corburn 2005).

In distressed urban neighborhoods, collective action is considered more effective when accompanied by community organizing and empowerment, and when supported by dedicated individuals and cadres – including those working in community development corporations (CDCs) – who provide technical assistance, political savviness, grant resources, motivation, and create policy networks beyond the neighborhood (Scally 2012; Von Hoffman 2003; Williams 1985). However, local activists must often compromise with external organizations over the definition and scope of objectives and the radicalism of their approach (Davis 1991). For instance, foundations have been shown to steer social movements away from radicalism, and toward moderate objectives that better fit their own goals (Bartley 2007).

This variety of strategies and tactics raises the question of what determines the adoption of repertoires of action. At the national level, institutional policy environments tend to shape the types of engagement that activists can adopt with decision-makers (Kitschelt 1986). When structures for political input and citizen participation are more open, activists engaged in protests are more likely to achieve their goals and influence policy. As argued by traditional social movement scholars, political systems tend to influence the initiation, forms, and outcomes of collective action (Tilly 2001). For instance, democratic regimes are more likely to accept confrontation and other direct tactics. As well, collective action – and more direct and violent collective action – arises in contexts where political repression is less likely (Tilly 1978). Movements often organize collective action on the basis of whether factors align positively for them, including whether political opportunities are expanding (McAdam 1982; Tilly 1978).

In sum, coalitions, outside supporters, shared values and interests, and a favorable political system are particularly helpful to the mobilization of historically marginalized groups. To date, however, most social movement studies examine single-issue coalitions, coalitions organized around protests, and the conditions for their emergence. The development of long-term strategies and tactics used by urban neighborhood activists mobilizing in a context of neighborhood abandonment and later environmental revival has been understudied. This chapter attempts to fill this gap by examining the development of socio-spatial tactics for urban environmental justice in three cases.

From neighborhood abandonment to socio-environmental transformations in Boston, Barcelona, and Havana

For this chapter I purposely selected neighborhoods – Dudley (Boston), Casc Antic (Barcelona), and Cayo Hueso (Havana) – representing different political systems to analyze how these conditions affect (or not) the strategies and tactics of historically distressed residents and their supporters. I examined how activists within degraded neighborhoods in dissimilar political settings mobilize against similar environmental and health challenges, and how they receive support for their community projects and leverage power, and at times alliances, in their relations with decision-makers. Here, I classify political systems according to the level of political rights and citizens' participation, protection of civil liberties, and presence of guaranteed democratic elections (Tilly 2006). Following this logic, Boston illustrates a case of well-established democracy with historic roots of civic engagement and high protection of liberties and regular elections at multiple levels. Barcelona represents a young democracy re-established in 1977 with growing and intense level of citizens' participation and civil liberties. Havana is an example of an autocratic and centralized government with weak opportunities for citizens' engagement in decision-making, low respect of civil liberties, and closed elections at the national level.

This study is based on semi-structured interviews with 45 participants in Barcelona, 49 participants in Havana, and 50 participants in Boston identified through snowball sampling techniques. Among others, I conducted interviews with community-based organizations, NGOs, and local residents mobilizing for improving local environmental conditions. My goal was to understand the relations they developed with planners and officials, the tactics they used to achieve their projects, and the coalitions they have built. Interview questions also examined the broader context of urbanization and how historical conditions of degradation and exclusion have influenced neighborhood organization. Additionally, I conducted interviews with officials and professionals from governmental organizations, whose work and opinions influenced community organization. Here, I sought to understand the broader political environment in which activists organized their actions, and which official plans and participation forums they responded to. Lastly, I interviewed institutional funders, whose financial and organizational support to Dudley, Casc Antic, and Cayo Hueso appeared to have been decisive. During my fieldwork I also attended meetings and events as a participant observer, to better understand the development of activists' work. All this data was analyzed using grounded theory and process tracing techniques to reconstruct the process of strategic and tactical selection and the intervening factors that motivated activist choices. In the next subsection, I briefly present neighborhood changes in each city (see also Table 11.1) and then analyze strategies and tactics.

Boston

Dudley is a Boston neighborhood in the district of Roxbury with a large number of low-income African-American, Cape Verdean, and Latino residents. In the 1980s more than half of land parcels in Dudley were vacant, due to years of dumping, arson, and abandonment by affluent property owners and by the city (Layzer 2006). However, since the end of the 1980s, residents and local organizations have organized against illegal dumping and abandonment through the "Don't Dump on Us"[3] campaign, which led to a shared vision of a sustainable and safe "urban village," and through several community planning exercises and redevelopment tools. The neighborhood also took over 1,300 parcels of abandoned land after the City of Boston granted the Dudley Street Neighborhood Initiative (a new community organization made of active residents fighting environmental dumping and disinvestment) the power of eminent domain (Layzer 2006).

Table 11.1 A summary of neighborhood changes in Dudley, Casc Antic, and Cayo Hueso

Dudley	Casc Antic	Cayo Hueso
• Majority of low-income African-American, Cape Verdean, and Latino residents • 1,300 vacant lots by the mid-1980s, the majority of them contaminated and abandoned by the City of Boston and affluent property owners • Illegal trash transfer stations • Lack of parks and recreational facilities • Food desert, 50% of children below poverty line • Since 1984, community-led land clean-up, management and (re)development of parcels into urban farms, gardens, community gyms, and healthy food businesses	• 31% of residents as foreigners, and majority of them in poverty • Legacy of Franco: crumbling housing, poor waste management, and abandoned and unsafe public spaces • 1980s: unequal developments with the PERIS urban plans with acute social and environmental impacts • Urban conflicts since the end of the 1990s (i.e., Forat de la Vergonya), occupation and auto-reconstruction of abandoned park • 2000s: community-based environmental revitalization projects and advocacy for improvement in socio-environmental conditions directed at the City of Barcelona	• Dense and predominantly Afro-Cuban neighborhood in Centro Habana • By 1989: degradation of buildings and sanitation and further decay during the Special Period crisis • More than 50% of residents without daily access to potable water • Few green areas and safe public spaces • 1990s–2000s: workshops for the Comprehensive Transformation of the Neighborhood (TTIBs) promoted by the GDIC planning agency as autonomous community-based revitalization projects • 1990s–2000s: independent resident projects around public space and recreational and sports facilities

Since 2011 new community development models have taken root in Dudley, combining job creation and training, community wealth creation, and environmental justice. New partnerships between nonprofits, small businesses, and residents are facilitating integrated food networks by bringing together growers (i.e., City Growers, The Food Project), processors (i.e., the food incubator Commonwealth Kitchen), retail and restaurants (i.e., Dorchester Food-Coop, Haley House, Dudley Dough, food trucks and local corner stores such as Davis Market), waste management, and community land trusts (i.e., Dudley Land Trust). Through a partnership called the Dudley Real Food Hub (DRFH), community members work together to address complex development issues and increase affordable fresh produce, provide healthier restaurants, offer healthier school food, reuse vacant lots for growing food, develop community-owned food businesses and jobs, and help create new ventures around food waste collection, management, and recycling. They are working for a more resilient form of economic development in view of environmental gentrification threats – economic development that can also benefit long-term residents and avoid creating new environmental injustices-in-waiting.

Barcelona

In Barcelona, 31% of Casc Antic residents are foreigners (including many North African, Latino, Pakistani, and Chinese immigrants), and a large number of residents remain poor (Anguelovski 2014). The early years of the post-Franco era were characterized by crumbling housing, poor waste management, and abandoned public spaces. To address the neighborhood's decay, the democratic Municipality of Barcelona, in the 1980s and 1990s, revitalized degraded areas, promoted tourism, and improved much of the local infrastructure (Monnet 2002). However, since the mid-1990s, conflicts in the Casc Antic – especially around a four-block area destroyed and left vacant space called the Forat de la Vergonya – have emerged between authorities and residents who are protesting against city-sponsored real estate speculation and expropriations, gentrification, and continuing neighborhood degradation in some areas. Over time, the Forat has become an example of community-managed parks and gardens, and has been later rebuilt by the City of Barcelona as a permanent green space.

In parallel, other environmental and health initiatives have taken root through community organizations successfully advocating for improved street infrastructure, green space, housing, and waste management investment. Community organizations, such as Mescladis,[4] are also working on immigrants' integration through training in food preparation and processing. They are creating new economic opportunities for residents so that they can be more resilient in view of new gentrification and displacement pressures.

Havana

Located in the borough of Centro Habana, Cayo Hueso has historically been an Afro-Cuban neighborhood. The neighborhood's density is extremely high, with 40,000 residents living in highly degraded buildings covering 0.83 km2 (Spiegel et al. 2001). In the 1990s the so-called "Special Period" of economic crisis and restructuration prompted residents to participate in revitalization projects through the Talleres Integrales de Transformación del Barrio (TTIB) (Anguelovski 2014). Those "talleres" were workshops for neighborhood transformation, sponsored by the Group for the Comprehensive Development of the Capital (GDIC) (a decentralized planning agency), which offered new opportunities for participatory urban development by promoting neighborhood reappraisals (Hearn 2008) and the improvement of environmental and health conditions in Cayo Hueso.

Additionally, independent leaders were able to jumpstart other initiatives around park green space development, street beautification, and urban agriculture. Here, local activists attempted to create greater individual and community resilience in view of the multiple environmental, social, and economic challenges brought by the Special Period crisis. In the next section, I examine the strategies and tactics developed in each neighborhood (see Table 11.2 for a summary).

Table 11.2 Strategic and tactical development in Dudley, Casc Antic, and Cayo Hueso

	Dudley (Boston)	Casc Antic (Barcelona)	Cayo Hueso (Havana)
Coalition development	– Broad and unexpected coalitions for environmental projects, including several university departments, cafés, youth networks	– Broad and unexpected coalitions for environmental projects, including squatters, historic preservation groups, artists, publishing companies	– Broad and unexpected coalitions for environmental projects, including Afro Cuban artists, international NGOs, athletes from Latin America, and US universities
Bricolage techniques	– Bricolage techniques for quick project initiation to respond to chaos and deep environmental damage – Use of volunteers, especially youth and children – Creative forms of protest and resistance (i.e., human chains on streets, occupation of parks)	– Bricolage techniques for quick project initiation and response to government neglect in the neighborhood – Use of volunteers, especially children, youth, and older residents – Radical forms of protest and resistance (squatting, chaining oneself on building)	– Bricolage techniques for quick project initiation ("resolver") and respond to the crisis and lack of governmental resources – Use of volunteers, especially youth, artists, and children – More subdued occupation of space
Ingenious use of the political environment	– Occupation of empty political space in neighborhood – Relationship-building with municipal offices (BRA and DND) and politicians at the city level	– Occupation of empty political space in neighborhood – Engagement with administrative staff (Cap de Territori) and officials (Regidor) at the local district level	– Occupation of empty political space in neighborhood – Clever use of new national policies (i.e., Urban Agriculture, laws on NGO funding) and structures (Brigades, CDRs) and connections with national decision-makers
Secured access to technical experts and funders	– Legal and technical assistance from environmental NGOs, public health design schools, and community development organizations, who in turn helped access funders – Engagement with foundations who advocated on behalf of community members to local government	– Legal and technical assistance from lawyers and social architects – Filing of official claims by experts – Little engagement with the municipality, except for more technical organizations (GENAB environmental NGO and sports groups such as AECCA)	– Legal and technical assistance from health research centers, centers for community initiatives, international NGOs – Engagement with locally based international NGOs who negotiated with government on behalf of activists or helped access other funders

The development of socio-spatial strategies and tactics for environmental justice

Large and flexible community coalitions

In seeking to achieve their environmental goals, the main umbrella strategy used by Barcelona, Boston, and Havana activists was to form broad – and often unexpected – coalitions. In Barcelona, long-time residents formed coalitions in the early 2000s with the Casc Antic Neighbors' Associations, historic preservation groups, squatters, urban gardeners, students, lawyers, architects, publishing companies, professors, mayors of foreign cities, and movie directors. Such broad coalitions came to number over 5,000 people, who turned out in force during protests and demonstrations. Their members worked on defending the Forat de la Vergonya empty lots, cleaning them up, regenerating them, and constructing permanent environmental amenities on them, as well as side projects such as a local recycling center, street greening, and the upgrading of local playgrounds and plazas. More recently, new organizations (i.e., Mescladis) and residents joined efforts to further develop the new community garden and promote culturally valued and healthy food in the neighborhood.

Similarly, in Boston in the late 1980s and early 1990s, residents fighting illegal dumping and working on Dudley's environmental revitalization connected with a variety of groups and organizations: community organizations (i.e., Dudley Street Neighborhood Initiative (DSNI), Alianza Hispana), community development corporations (i.e., Dorchester Bay, Nuestra Comunidad), NGOs (i.e., Alternatives for Community, the Environment, Boston Urban Gardeners), religious leaders, and universities, among others. Those organizations worked on pressing issues: mounting protests; filing lawsuits against illegal trash transfer stations; declaring sites as toxic waste sites and advocating for their remediation and cleanup by the MA Department of Environmental Protection; cleaning up lots and converting them into community gardens, playgrounds, or parks; building green affordable housing units, and advocating for local transit justice. Side coalitions were also built around healthy eating and fresh food, which included organizations such as: the Food Project, the Dudley Street Neighborhood Initiative, Alternatives for Community and the Environment, the Boston Natural Areas Network, the Haley House, Project Right, Children's Hospital, schools, the Boston Collaborative for Food and Fitness, Commonwealth Kitchen, City Growers, and local corner stores. A smaller coalition also exists around open space revitalization and park stewardship.

As for Cayo Hueso, in the early 1990s community leaders managed to recruit the help of local teachers, doctors, musicians, and athletes to clean up and transform degraded spaces. International coalitions and collaborations have been a strong part of the community projects' successes. For example, staff members from the GDIC planning agency initiated partnerships with university planning departments in Latin American, European, and US universities. In the United States, the MIT Department of Urban Studies and Planning worked closely with the GDIC and later with Joel Díaz to establish multidisciplinary workshops that, over time, became the TTIBs. Additionally, international NGOs, such as Oxfam and Save the Children, teamed up with the GDIC and local NGOs to secure access to land and new funding sources.

The coalitions in the three neighborhoods have been broad, flexible, diverse, and united through time by core interests and values, which has helped residents respond to environmental needs in a more creative and resilient way. In Boston, for example, university schools and departments (i.e., schools of public health, planning departments) have supported community organizers in their environmental assessment needs and in the environmental design of community gardens, while local artists assisted them by drawing murals with neighborhood children around the gardens. In all three cities, these coalitions have remained flexible, with ties and contacts being generally loose, but tightening during crucial moments of neighborhood organization, such as protests or advocacy work. In Barcelona, for example, cleaning up empty lots in the Forat de la Vergonya was a crystallizing task for all activists as the neighborhood struggle around the Forat symbolized the coalition's commitment to community land control and land redevelopment. Over time, coalition members also remained united around common values of solidarity, altruism, and the vision around community control.

Coalition diversity and flexibility also offered activists the benefit of having different activist traditions come together to achieve shared goals. In Barcelona, combining the organizing capacity of younger social sectors (who held strong ideological positions and favored more direct tactics) with the rallying work of long-term residents has contributed to success in neighborhood struggles and to more resilience vis-à-vis new types of degradation or redevelopment pressures. Similarly, in Dudley neighborhood leaders' spontaneity and community-organizing capacity were complemented by the professionalism and experience of organizations such as DSNI, ACE, Project Right, and La Alianza Hispana. In Cayo Hueso, NGOs such as Ayuda Popular Noruega (PNA) and Oxfam America elicited the support of respected intellectual Cuban institutions, such as the journal *Temas*, with whom they shared interests in public debate and autonomous participation, in order to ensure the legitimacy of and support for their projects.

The development of broad coalitions in Boston, Barcelona, and Havana can be explained by the importance of implementing concrete change, building new relationships to consolidate projects, further anchoring them in the community, and building resilient networks for long-term environmental transformation. With these coalitions in place, community groups then developed a variety of tactics to enhance their neighborhoods' environmental quality. In the next few subsections I examine these tactics in greater detail, with a particular focus on those using socio-spatial capital.

Spatial capital refers to levels of urban vitality, which includes interactions and activities occurring within neighborhoods, as well as network-building (Chion 2008, 2009). It is developed through informal relations built during encounters in neighborhood streets or local public life (Chion 2009). As I analyze in the next sections, diverse activist coalitions in Dudley, Casc Antic, and Cayo Hueso used the neighborhood spatial capital to advance their environmental goals through bricolage tactics, a strategic use of the surrounding political environment, and the leverage of technical and funder activism.

Bricolage tactics

Bricolage refers to actions and thoughts based on objects that pre-exist in someone's environment (Lévi-Strauss 1962), and these are the techniques that street activists used when they began organizing their neighborhoods. People creatively pieced or assembled disconnected material and non-material resources, and often behaved in inventive ways to solve immediate challenges. For example, in Barcelona, during the spontaneous reconstruction of the Forat empty spaces, some neighbors brought plants, others constructed benches and playgrounds, a mayor from Sicily, whom residents knew, shipped trees to the neighborhood, older residents created community gardens, and young squatters worked on the maintenance of the space. All of this was accomplished without any major investments and in a spontaneous way. Activists pieced resources and materials together through bricolage techniques to achieve what some called "quick wins," that is, a concrete visual neighborhood environmental transformation. During interviews they justified this bricolage approach by the need to promptly address the environmental neglect and to clean up construction debris left throughout the neighborhood. Continuing with this tradition, today, during celebratory events around the community garden, garden leaders call upon neighbors to organize pot-luck meals using plants or vegetables from the garden and other ingredients offered by residents.

During the early years of Dudley's neighborhood activism, residents assembled objects or materials together to achieve the rapid construction of parks, playgrounds, and community gardens – in a context of environmental damage, empty lots, and abandonment. They felt the need to achieve quick esthetical changes in the neighborhood, in order to enlist new residents in their projects and to visually demonstrate to outsiders that their neighborhood was changing. Dudley Square's dense network of community organizations has helped community leaders successfully develop their bricolage projects. For instance, the founder of the Haley Bakery was able to build her bakery, obtain fresh produce, and recruit participants in her workshop, thanks to her relationships with and knowledge of five different community organizations around the bakery.

In Havana several projects (i.e., the Quiero a mi Barrio gym, the Callejón de Hamel, and the Beisbolito Park) originated in the creativity of their leaders piecing materials together, finding neighbors to help clean degraded space, and international individual donors offering to send equipment. For example, in the Callejón de Hamel, Salvador (a local artist) stitched together various materials to create the green and art-based street. He secretly gathered ink from printers that companies were throwing into dumpsters, convinced a neighbor to keep paint for him in a house barrel, managed to obtain pieces of electric wire to paint at night with a light that he built, used old bathtubs to create benches, and neighbors brought trees and plants from their small rural lots to plant throughout the Callejón. Cubans call this "resolver" – to seek informal help from collaborators to solve issues quickly (often in an unofficial or illegal way). This became a pressing tactic in the context of an international crisis and a historical neglect of urban neighborhoods in Havana.

The use of bricolage techniques was often illustrated through the recruitment of different types of volunteers to execute specific tasks linked to the development of their activities. Recruiting volunteers has been a spontaneous and compensatory tactic to address the lack of budget to hire professional planners, designers, and environmental staff. Some organizations or groups, such as the Food Project or the Youth Environmental Networks in Boston, the community garden in the Casc Antic, and the environmental brigades in Cayo Hueso, were essentially built around youth who helped run activities. These initiatives rallied new supporters and participants, including children, because of what leaders saw as their fresh and spontaneous way of integrating themselves in projects and activities.

Additionally, community leaders and workers used bricolage techniques to recruit participants for demonstrations, sit-ins, picketing, and protests. This practice took place through door-to-door recruiting, word of mouth, or taking advantage of social and cultural events to identify new participants. In the Casc Antic, between 2002 and 2006, such recruitment led residents, squatters, students, and artists to organize sit-ins or stand-up demonstrations in the Forat, asking for, among other things, ending police violence against the neighborhood and putting a park in the Forat de la Vergonya. In another case, dozens of community activists chained themselves to the City of Barcelona's main building. In Dudley, in the early years of neighborhood reconstruction, out of desperation and in an attempt to send a message, residents organized massive protests and human chains of residents at street corners to expel dumping offenders. In Cayo Hueso, community leaders, such as the founder of the Casa del Niño y de la Niña, illegally occupied spaces they planned to clean up and rebuild. Yet, their protests had to be more subtle than those carried out by activists in Boston and Barcelona because these leaders knew that open protests were not allowed in Cuba.

The strategic use of the external political environment

The diverse coalitions of Dudley, Casc Antic, and Cayo Hueso activists also made the best use of political opportunities around them. Political opportunity structures refer to the context and resources that encourage or discourage collective action (Della Porta and Tarrow 2005; Tarrow 1994), and indicate a social movement's capacity to respond strategically to a favorable political environment (Gamson 1990).

First, activists used windows of political opportunities to initiate their projects. More specifically, during the early years of neighborhood activism, the state's presence in each neighborhood was so insignificant that residents decided to fill this vacuum through autonomous cleanup and rebuilding initiatives. In the Casc Antic, squatters saw a political opening in 2001 that compelled them to occupy empty buildings around the Forat, as well as start cleaning up and greening the space. In Dudley, the absence of law and order in the neighborhood in the late 1980s prompted residents to autonomously move forward with the removal of waste and with space cleanup.

In Cayo Hueso, the top–down and centralized policymaking context led community leaders to take advantage of not only the local political context, as in Dudley and Casc Antic, but also of favorable national political circumstances and policies. At the end of the 1980s, when the GDIC decentralized planning agency gained the Cuban government's support to start autonomous community-based planning and regeneration, they created the first TTIB neighborhood transformation workshop in Cayo Hueso and initiated participatory urban planning. Such state concessions to decentralized agencies also reflected the incapacity of the Cuban government to respond to community needs and invest in urban neighborhoods. Additionally, Cuban nonprofit organizations were granted the right in 1993 to receive international funding, which encouraged TTIB workshop leaders to create partnerships with international NGOs based close to Cayo Hueso.

Furthermore, activists in all three neighborhoods managed to navigate their way through municipal offices and local political structures to obtain targeted support or authorizations for their projects. In Boston, community leaders and community organizations (i.e., Project Hope, the Food Project, or the Nonquit Street Association) used their contacts in the Department of Neighborhood Development (DND) to negotiate access to land for new gardens and playgrounds. Similarly, Barcelona community organizations who worked on sports programs, such as AECCA or Fundació Adsis, often called specific municipal staff, such as the Cap de Territori (a neighborhood-based municipal worker), to successfully negotiate access to schools and sports grounds for their activities. Cayo Hueso is the neighborhood where community leaders had to most directly engage with and negotiate with existing political institutions and structures, because of the known importance of winning their managers' official or tacit approval, who in many cases were still very skeptical towards community-based and decentralized initiatives. For example, TTIB members made sure to regularly attend neighborhood meetings from the Committees for the Defense of the Revolution (CDR), to demonstrate an active presence in Cuban political organizations and build allies in those organizations.

Third, activists who consider themselves less radical and more conciliatory in their demands developed tactical and instrumental relations with elected officials, to gain broader receptiveness to their work and seal some deals – including gaining long-time access to land or space for the projects. For example, in the Casc Antic the GENAB (Ecological Group for the Old Quarter of Barcelona) environmental NGO maintained good communication flows with high-level elected officials and was able to successfully negotiate the opening of the recycling center, the Punt Verd. Other residents relied on public officials to gain support for transforming the Forat into a green zone. In many cases, they had met those officials in previous protests and social struggles, and identified them as new potential allies. This was the case with Itziar Gonzalez, the former Casc

Antic City Manager who had met squatters in other Barcelona protests; he had offered them technical advice and had acted as a mediator in several urban conflicts. In Cuba, in the early 1990s, TTIB workshop leaders decided to gain access to high-level politicians in the national and local government, to make them realize that supporting community projects could be a way to avoid having large numbers emigrate from Cuba. The GDIC staff, in particular, informed Cuban officials how they could harness political benefits from supporting community projects, arguing that the neighborhood was needed [to prevent protests and/or exile] ("Se hacia falta el barrio").

At times, however, cultivating ties with public officials has resulted in Dudley and Casc Antic activists realizing that they needed to ensure that their choices still ultimately represented community voices. Risks of co-optation by municipal officials explain why tensions were at times acute within activist groups, especially when tactical choices needed to be made while maintaining legitimacy. For instance, Barcelona squatters and community organizations disagreed at times over the engagement with municipal officials. Squatters distrusted the municipality's community engagement practices and wanted to solve problems autonomously, while community organization members showed more pragmatic engagement practices. In contrast, political support from public officials is so important in Cuba that all activists agreed early on that building relationships with public leaders was important.

In sum, activists in all three neighborhoods made strategic use of their external political structure, institutions, and historical context, which enabled them to gain political legitimacy, harness official support for their community initiatives, and access funding or land to further develop their projects.

Leveraging access to technical expertise and funders

Upon initial successes in environmental protests, space occupation, and/or project start-up, activist coalitions in all three neighborhoods managed to access technical and knowledge-based experts, who became activists themselves. Accessing technical expertise was a tactic coalitions used to gain credibility and moral authority for their projects, as well as access more stable or more established funding sources for community reconstruction work. These experts often had close socio-spatial ties to the neighborhoods and, over time, both technical experts and funders often became neighborhood activists, supporting the residents' demands and fights. In turn, this support has helped neighborhoods be more resilient to new outside threats of unequal development.

In Dudley a variety of community organizations and city-wide groups provided technical environmental expertise to help residents assess and denounce environmental contamination or industry malpractices, and to clean up hazardous sites. In the early 1990s, the NGOs DSNI and ACE, which were well integrated in Dudley, helped residents lobby the Massachusetts Department of Environmental Protection to declare parts of Dudley as hazardous sites, thereby helping them obtain restoration funds. While nonprofit organizations might not have the funding capacity or authority to restore sites, they have the technical capacity and moral authority to prove that agencies are engaging in discriminatory environmental practices. Local nonprofits (e.g., the Food Project) also provided technical support to local gardeners by testing the soil, providing compost, and building raised beds. Some other organizations facilitated and organized design workshops with residents to create a unified community vision around new projects. In some cases, technical experts came from outside Dudley, through residents or workers in Dudley who already knew them. For example, Wellesley College faculty members built close historic ties in the neighborhood through friends and colleagues who had been active in Dudley since the 1970s. In the early 1990s public health studies conducted by researchers at Wellesley College and the Harvard School of Public Health helped ACE and the Food Project monitor local air and soil quality. The results of such studies, combined with advocacy, influenced public decision-making and resulted in the closure of toxic facilities and the restoration of waste sites.

Similarly, in the Casc Antic, NGOs offered technical or legal support to residents, though their focus was on fighting housing expropriation or denouncing illegal municipal projects. During the 2001–06 period, the historic preservation group Veins en Defensa de la Barcelona Vella, whose founder was himself a neighborhood resident, gave legal assistance to resident victims of tenant harassment and building degradation. The NGO founder also filed an official denunciation, in Brussels, against the Municipality of Barcelona for misusing European Union public funds. In another case the Barcelona-wide organization Architects without Borders, whose members were themselves neighborhood squatters or friends of squatters, supported activists at protests and facilitated discussion around redesigning the Forat into a permanent green zone.

In Cayo Hueso a series of individuals and organizations offered technical help to the TTIB workshop members and to individual neighborhood leaders, in order to assess the public health benefits of neighborhood environmental projects or to plan community design workshops. In 1998–99, the Cayo Hueso TTIB collaborated with the Hygiene, Epidemiology, and Microbiology National Institute (INHEM) and with Canadian universities on the "Ecosystem Health" project, to evaluate the health and environmental aspects of the TTIB work and document its benefits to Havana officials.

Activists have also used technical expertise to find and access national and international partners. For example, nonprofit organizations such as the Information and Referral Center for Community Initiatives (CIERIC) prepared training workshops on topics to help local leaders develop grant proposals. Similar to Dudley and Casc Antic, organizations such as the Martin Luther King Center engaged residents in community planning and participatory budgeting to help them take greater ownership of renovation projects in residential buildings. In sum, through technical and legal expert support, community leaders and workers have managed to strengthen community action and the legitimacy of community projects.

Upon initial legal victories or site remediation, community groups used their success to harness greater financial support for future projects. In Dudley, the construction of the Jardín de la Amistad garden allowed the Alianza Hispana community organization to demonstrate concrete and esthetically-transforming achievements to members of the Riley and the Ford Foundations, who subsequently invested hundreds of thousands of dollars in the neighborhood. In Cayo Hueso, in the late 2000s, community leaders took local Save the Children staff on several tours of their projects to demonstrate the socio-environmental changes they were able to bring, especially for school-age children, and obtain financial support from the international NGO. Similarly, in Barcelona, residents in the Casc Antic built strong ties with leaders of the Fundació Comtal, Fundació Adsis, and Fundació Ciutadania Multicultural, who then started assuming the responsibility of addressing the social needs of vulnerable youth and migrants in the neighborhood.

Lastly, over time some technical and funder experts became activists themselves by reaching out to municipal or national government entities to obtain long-term political or financial support for community projects (in Dudley and Cayo Hueso) or by denouncing local governmental practices in the press (in the Casc Antic). In Havana, the NGO Save the Children negotiated access to schools with the Ministry of Education by highlighting to some of its staff how it had managed to build a partnership with the Casa del Niño y de la Niña and how it is actively working in the neighborhood. In Boston, the Croc Foundation advocated extensively for Dudley's latest community center – the Croc Center – and for securing land for it. Its main staff member in Boston met several times with former Mayor Menino to ensure that the center would be built on a site easily accessible and visible to residents. In other words, at times the foundations, international cooperation agencies, and technical NGOs became the voice and advocates of the neighborhood they were inserted in. Over time their engagement in the neighborhood meant they were willing to play a broader advocacy role on behalf of vulnerable groups who generally did not have a meaningful say in decision-making. Accessing new sources of financial support might eventually allow residents to avoid new injustices-in-waiting when their neighborhood becomes attractive to outsiders – and potential gentrifiers.

Discussion and conclusions

This chapter has examined the development of long-term strategies and tactics used by urban neighborhood activists, who are mobilizing against spatial injustice and neighborhood abandonment and striving toward environmental justice and livability. My comparative approach has revealed that, despite existing scholarship on institutional contexts and political systems (Kitschelt 1986; Tilly 1978, 2006), activists tend to converge toward similar strategic and tactical choices, including developing coalitions, resorting to bricolage techniques, strategically using the political environment, and leveraging access to technical experts and funders. These similarities suggest that the experiences of historically marginalized residents living in urban distressed neighborhoods with poor environmental quality, territorial stigmatization, and abandonment from public authorities and investors are closely associated with certain strategies and tactical choices.

National policies or constraints (such as living in an autocratic regime) did not matter much to local activism development because local authorities were not as present in the different neighborhoods, thereby giving residents and their supporters much leeway to develop their strategies. National authorities were also interested in physical and environmental improvements to the neighborhood and accommodated innovative arrangements. These similarities in the development of socio-spatial strategies also reveal how neighborhoods play a triple role for activists – as a motivator for action, a goal (i.e., place-(re)making), and a strategy – linked to experiences of grief and hope. Such an analysis is particularly relevant for understanding how EJ activists achieve their goals for more equitable and green neighborhoods, adapt them through time and space, and resist new emerging pressures that might undermine their activism. These experiences provide valuable lessons for social and environmental justice activists, community leaders, nonprofits, foundations, and local governments committed to building green and equitable neighborhoods.

It is, however, important to note that tactical nuances exist between Havana, Barcelona, and Boston. For example, there are differences in the transparency of resource seeking and sharing (from less in Havana, to medium in Boston, to high and visible in Barcelona) and in the length and intensity of contestation (less in Havana). In an autocratic country like Cuba, radical protests are not possible. However, a more clever type of contestation, such as children – as core members of the Cuban revolution – writing open complaint letters supported by a respected community leader (the founder of the Casa del Niño y de la Niña) with strong ties to political officials was a politically acceptable tactic. Additionally, activists in the three neighborhoods had different fundraising approaches: Cayo Hueso residents had to seek international funding because of the Cuban government's inability to invest massive resources in neighborhood revitalization, while Barcelona residents obtained funds through public resources, after years of civic demands. In Boston activists sought a combination of private and public investment for neighborhood greening and revitalization. In other words, rather than core differences among neighborhood tactics, it seems more relevant to speak of idiosyncratic adaptation of tactics and implementation of community activism. In all cases, municipal authorities were at times willing to accommodate innovative arrangements because they sometimes benefited from them, and community initiatives filled a void that public authorities were not willing or did not have the capacity to fill.

In Barcelona, Boston, and Havana, environmental justice activists built on spatial capital ties and took advantage of neighborhood socio-spatial dynamics and resources – being either volunteers, protesters, political allies, experts, or funders. Results reveal three complementary levels and types of activism: street activism, technical expert activism, and funder activism. Street activism consisted in volunteers and protestors stitching together material and nonmaterial resources to jumpstart projects and to organize protests and demonstrations. Additionally, street activists had connections with experts, such as lawyers, architects, planners, and environmental health specialists, who backed up their claims and provided technical, legal, and scientific skills they were able to use against illegal actions perpetrated in their neighborhood. By proving their commitment to the neighborhood and the tightness of networks, street and expert activists eventually attracted a diversity of funding sources who, in turn, acted as catalysts for projects benefiting residents.

Yet, today, environmental justice activism is at a crossroads: as many of the revitalized neighborhoods benefit from parks, playgrounds, or urban farms, investors are starting to value them again, putting neighborhood residents at risk of environmental gentrification (Checker 2011). This might well be the ultimate conundrum for environmental justice activism. Environmental justice scholars thus need to examine more closely how community strategies and tactics evolve in view of these new threats and how local coalitions manage to remain resilient in the face of new displacement and exclusionary pressures – that is, of new injustices-in-waiting. New research needs to look at the conditions under which EJ activists address the apolitical and technocratic discourse of sustainability or green city planning, and reassert the social and political dimensions of sustainability and their right to the city. EJ scholars and practitioners also need to rethink how to achieve urban sustainability in ways that address environmental gentrification, encroachment, affordability issues, and greening as possibly the new "urban frontier."

Notes

1 Institute for Environmental Science and Technology (ICTA), Universitat Autònoma de Barcelona (UAB) – Spain, Isabelle.Anguelovski@uab.cat
2 For more information, see http://www.righttothecity.org/our-history.html
3 For more information, see http://www.dsni.org/dsni-historic-timeline/
4 For more information, see http://www.mescladis.org/es/

References

Alkon A.H. and Agyeman J. (2011). *Cultivating food justice: race, class, and sustainability*. Cambridge, MA: MIT Press.
Anguelovski I. (2014). *Neighborhood as refuge: environmental justice, community reconstruction, and place-remaking in the city*. Cambridge, MA: MIT Press.
Bandy J. and Smith J. (2005). *Coalitions across borders: transnational protest and the neoliberal order*. Oxford: Rowman & Littlefield.
Bartley T. (2007). The construction of an organizational field and the rise of forest certification. *Social Problems*, 54, 229–255.
Checker M. (2011). Wiped out by the "greenwave": environmental gentrification and the paradoxical politics of urban sustainability. *City & Society*, 23, 210–229.
Chion M. (2008). Production of street life in San Francisco. *Justice et Injustice Spatiales* Nanterre.

Chion M. (2009). Producing urban vitality: the case of dance in San Francisco. *Urban Geography*, 30, 416–439.
Connolly J. and Steil J. (2009). Can the just city be built from below: brownfields, planning, and power in the South Bronx. In P. Marcuse (Ed.) *Searching for the just city: debates in urban theory and practice*. New York: Routledge.
Corburn J. (2005). *Street science: community knowledge and environmental health justice*. Cambridge, MA: MIT Press.
Crisp R. (2013). "Communities with oomph"? Exploring the potential for stronger social ties to revitalise disadvantaged neighbourhoods. *Environment and Planning C: Government and Policy*, 31, 324–339.
Davis J. (1991). *Contested ground: collective action and the urban neighborhood*. Ithaca, NY: Cornell University Press.
Della Porta D. and Tarrow S. (2005). *Transnational protest and global activism*. Lanham, MD: Rowman & Littlefield.
Di Chiro G. (2008). Living environmentalisms: coalition politics, social reproduction, and environmental justice. *Environmental Politics*, 17, 276–298.
Downey L. and Hawkins B. (2008). Race, income, and environmental inequality in the United States. *Sociological Perspectives*, 51, 759–781.
Fagotto E. and Fung A. (2006). Empowered participation in urban governance: the Minneapolis neighborhood revitalization program. *International Journal of Urban and Regional Research*, 30, 638–655.
Fitzgerald J. (2010). *Emerald cities: urban sustainability and economic development*. New York: Oxford University Press.
Flora C. and Flora J. (2006). Creating social capital. In W. Vitek and W. Jackson (Eds.) *Rooted in the land: essays on community and lace*. New Haven, CT: Yale University Press.
Fullilove M. (2004). *Root shock: how tearing up city neighborhoods hurts America, and what we can do about it*. New York: One World/Ballantine Books.
Gamson W. (1990). *The strategy of social protest*. Belmont, CA: Wadsworth Publishing.
Ganz M. (2000). Resources and resourcefulness: strategic capacity in the unionization of California agriculture, 1959–1966. *American Journal of Sociology*, 105, 1003–1062.
Garbin D. and Millington G. (2012). Territorial stigma and the politics of resistance in a Parisian banlieue: la courneuve and beyond. *Urban Studies*, 49, 2067–2083.
Gottlieb R. (2009). Where we live, work, play and eat: expanding the environmental justice agenda. *Environmental Justice*, 2, 7–8.
Gottlieb R. and Joshi A. (2010). *Food Justice*. Cambridge, MA: MIT Press.
Gould K., Lewis T. and Roberts T. (2004). Blue-green coalitions: constraints and possibilities in the post 9-11 political environment. *Journal of World-System Research*, 10, 90–116.
Hearn A. (2008). *Cuba: religion, social capital, and development*. Durham, NC: Duke University Press.
Hess D.J. (2009). *Localist movements in a global economy: sustainability, justice, and urban development in the United States*. Cambridge, MA: MIT Press.
Kitschelt H.P. (1986). Political opportunity structures and political protest: anti-nuclear movements in four democracies. *British Journal of Political Science*, 16, 57–85.
Lawless P. (2011). Understanding the scale and nature of outcome change in area-regeneration programmes: evidence from the New Deal for Communities programme in England. *Environment and Planning C: Government and Policy*, 29.
Layzer J. (2006). *The environmental case: translating values into policy*. Washington: CQ Press.

Lerner S. (2005). *Sacrifice zones: the front lines of toxic chemical exposure in the United States*. Cambridge, MA: MIT Press.
Lévi-Strauss C. (1962). *La pensée sauvage*. Paris: Plon.
Lucas, K., (2004). *Running On Empty: Transport, Social Exclusion and Environmental Justice*. Bristol: The Policy Press.
Manzo L.C. and Perkins D. (2006). Finding common ground: the importance of place attachment to community participation and planning. *Journal of Planning Literature*, 20, 335.
Marcuse P. (2009). *Searching for the just city: debates in urban theory and practice*. New York: Routledge.
Matthews P. (2012). From area-based initiatives to strategic partnerships: have we lost the meaning of regeneration? *Environment and Planning C*, 30, 147.
McAdam D. (1982). *Political process and the development of black insurgency, 1930–1970*. Chicago: University of Chicago Press.
McCammon H. and Campbell K. (2002). Allies on the road to victory: coalition formation between the suffragists and the Woman's Christian Temperance Union. *Mobilization*, 7, 231–251.
McFarlane C. (2010). The comparative city: knowledge, learning, urbanism. *International Journal of Urban and Regional Research*, 34, 725–742.
McGurty E. (2000). Warren County, NC, and the emergence of the environmental justice movement: unlikely coalitions and shared meanings in local collective action. *Society and Natural Resources*, 13, 373–387.
Millington N. (2015). From urban scar to "park in the sky": terrain vague, urban design, and the remaking of New York City's High Line Park. *Environment and Planning A*, 0308518X15599294.
Mohai P., Pellow D. and Roberts J.T. (2009). Environmental justice. *Annual Review of Environment and Resources*, 34, 405–430.
Monnet N. (2002). *La formación del espacio público: Una mirada etnológica sobre el casc antic de Barcelona*. Los Libros de la Catarata.
Otero L. (2010). *La calle: spatial conflicts and urban renewal in a southwest city*. Tuscon: University of Arizona Press.
Pattillo M. (2007). *Black on the block: the politics of race and class in the city*. Chicago: University of Chicago Press
Pellow D. (2001). Environmental justice and the political process: movements, corporations, and the state. *Sociological Quarterly*, 42, 47–67.
Pellow D. (2007). *Resisting global toxics: transnational movements for environmental justice* Cambridge, MA: MIT Press.
Polletta F. (2005). How participatory democracy became white: culture and organizational choice. *Mobilization*, 10, 271–288.
Porta D.D. and Rucht D. (2002). The dynamics of environmental campaigns. *Mobilization*, 7, 1–14.
Purcell M. (2008). *Recapturing democracy: neoliberalization and the struggle for alternative urban futures*. New York: Routledge.
Purcell M. (2009). Resisting neoliberalization: communicative planning or counter-hegemonic movements? *Planning Theory*, 8, 140–165.
Robinson J. (2011). Cities in a world of cities: the comparative gesture. *International Journal of Urban and Regional Research*, 35, 1–23.
Rootes C. and Leonard L. (2009). Environmental movements and campaigns against waste infrastructure in the United States. *Environmental Politics*, 18, 835–850.

Saegert S., Thompson J.P. and Warren M. (2001). *Social capital and poor communities.* New York: Russell Sage Foundation.
Scally C.P. (2012). Community development corporations, policy networks, and the rescaling of community development advocacy. *Environment and Planning* C, 30, 712.
Schneider S. (2007). *Refocusing crime prevention: collective action and the quest for community.* Toronto: University of Toronto Press.
Smith N. (1982). Gentrification and uneven development. *Economic Geography*, 58, 139–155.
Soja, E. (2009). The city and spatial justice. *Spatial Justice*, 1, 31–38.
Spiegel J., Bonet M., Yassi A., Molina E., Concepcion M. and Mast P. (2001). Developing ecosystem health indicators in Centro Habana: a community based approach. *Ecosystem Health*, 7, 15–26.
Staggenborg S. (1986). Coalition work in the pro-choice movement: organizational and environmental opportunities and obstacles. *Social Problems*, 33, 374–390.
Staggenborg S. (1998). The consequences of professionalization and formalization in the pro-choice movement. *American Sociological Review*, 53, 585–606.
Susskind L. and Macey G. (2004). *Using dispute resolution techniques to address environmental justice concerns: case studies.* Harvard Program on Negotiation and US EPA.
Sze J. (2007). *Noxious New York: the racial politics of urban health and environmental justice, Environmental justice in America: A new paradigm.* Cambridge, MA: MIT Press.
Tarrow S. (1994). *Power in movement: social movements, collective action, and politics.* Cambridge: Cambridge University Press.
Tarrow S. (2011). *Power in movement: social movements and contentious politics.* Cambridge: Cambridge University Press.
Tilly C. (1978). *From mobilization to revolution.* Reading, MA: Addison-Wesley Pub. Co.
Tilly C. (2001). *Coercion, capital, and European states, AD 990–1992.* Oxford: Blackwell.
Tilly C. (2006). *Regimes and repertoires.* Chicago: University of Chicago Press.
Van dyke N. (2003). Crossing movement boundaries: factors that facilitate coalition protest by American college students, 1930–1990. *Social Problems*, 50, 226–250.
Von hoffman A. (2003). *House by house, block by block: the rebirth of America's urban neighborhoods.* New York: Oxford University Press.
Wacquant L. (2007). Territorial stigmatization in the age of advanced marginality. *Thesis Eleven*, 91, 66–77.
Warren M. (2001). *Dry bones rattling: community building to revitalize American democracy.* Princeton, NJ: Princeton University Press.
Williams M.R. (1985). *Neighborhood organizations – seeds of a new urban life.* Westport, CT: Greenwood Press.
Zald M. and McCarthy J. (1987). *Social movements in an organizational society.* New Brunswick, NJ: Transaction Publishers.

12 Environmental justice initiatives for community resilience
Ecovillages, just transitions, and human rights cities

Jacqueline Patterson[1] and Jackie Smith[2]

Introduction

Global financial, ecological, and geopolitical crises are exacerbating the threats to the livelihoods of the most vulnerable groups, and now they are increasingly impacting more privileged groups that had previously been shielded from such threats. These developments heighten popular awareness of the global capitalist system's inherent contradictions, opening possibilities for exploration of alternatives that are better suited to meet human needs and protect the environment. For instance, following the 2005 Hurricane Katrina, activists in the U.S. gulf region began coming together with others around the country to resist displacement and to demand a "right to the city" (Gotham and Greenberg 2014, 133), and following the 2008 global financial collapse, the World Social Forum was organized around the theme "The Crisis of Civilization." This meeting helped bring more widespread attention to ideas that have long been central in indigenous cultures and that are integral to the environmental justice framework—the notions of *buen vivir*, or living well and in harmony with the earth, as an alternative organizing principle for society, and the related idea of rights for Mother Earth (Smith 2014).

The environmental justice framework that guides this volume views climate change and other environmental degradation as a result of systematic inequalities and exclusions that have made communities of color, low-income people, and indigenous communities the disproportionate bearers of the costs of fossil-fuel-intensive development (Pellow 2000). Accordingly, efforts to mitigate environmental devastation and transform destructive practices require changes to the day-to-day operations that reproduce the global capitalist order. As our analysis shows, in response to climate change, activists in places around the world have been working to disrupt the inter-related processes of global capitalism—including globalization (or delocalization), proletarianization, depeasantization, commodification, and industrialization—that threaten human survival. Each of these processes reinforces hierarchies and divisions among people and between humans and the earth. Each externalizes the social and environmental costs of capitalist production, displacing such costs away from those who benefit from capitalist production to the environment, communities of color, workers, and the larger society. Through various strategies, the environmental justice movement helps disrupt capitalism's competitive logic and the externalization of costs to people and the environment. The movement does so by promoting cooperative practices that reduce the distances between sites of production and consumption, redefining development and core social values, and valorizing the work and identities that have been devalued by prevailing logics. In doing so, movement activists help advance community resilience by nurturing social cohesion and harmonious relations with the earth. We argue that by examining responses of communities most impacted by capitalism's devastation, we can gain knowledge about advancing social transformation that produces community resilience.

The environmental justice movement

The environmental justice movement has emerged over recent decades in response to the inability of the capitalist system to provide for the needs and security of the people and communities on whose work it depends. It is a form of resistance to the systemic tendency to impose environmental hazards disproportionately on low income and communities of color and indigenous peoples. The movement has emerged from several strands of organizing in different parts of the world, but in the United States it grew out of an explicit critique of the mainstream environmental movement, which had "blatantly omitted" the environmental claims being made by communities of color and indigenous groups (Taylor 2010, 6).

In October 1991, the Southwest Network for Environmental and Economic Justice convened the First National People of Color Environmental Leadership Summit in Washington, DC.[3] The meeting brought together more than 650 grassroots and national leaders from all 50 states, Washington DC, Puerto Rico, Mexico, and Marshall Islands, and it generated a set of Environmental Justice Principles[4] that continue to define and guide the environmental justice movement today. Representatives from the summit subsequently shared these principles when they attended the 1992 Earth Summit, where activists from around the world had gathered to discuss environmental organizing strategies (Chavis Jr. 1993). Many of the networks formed at the Earth Summit persisted and grew over time, and these networks and their activities helped create spaces for transnational dialogue and exchange, though not without much difficulty and unevenness (Brooks 2005; Conway 2012; Moghadam 2012).

Over time, and through years of collective struggle and occasional movement convergences, the environmental justice framework has expanded both in the U.S. environmental movement and globally (Bullard 1993; Faber 2005; Rothman and Oliver 1999). The movement has helped to center discussions of race and colonialism and to bring attention to the experiences of indigenous peoples and communities of color, which are made invisible in mainstream public discourse. The movement has drawn attention to the "frontline communities" that are most impacted by climate change and by the industrialization that fuels it, and members of those communities have played vital leadership roles. At the same time, the movement has helped develop or drawn attention to alternative models that can help advance human and environmental well-being. Such alternatives are often based in indigenous cultures or in the traditional knowledge and experiences of frontline and other oppressed communities. The success of the environmental justice movement in transforming U.S. and global activist discourse is evident in the responses to recent social and ecological crises, including responses to Hurricane Katrina and superstorm Sandy in the United States. Recognizing patterns of post-crisis redevelopment that have displaced low-income groups and people of color from urban neighborhoods, heightened their exposures to risks, and undermined their capacities for resilience, new coalitions are forming around a broader, systemic critique of globalized capitalism (Gotham and Greenberg 2014). Globally, we have seen a dramatic shift in global climate activism by 2007, where a more confrontational, system-challenging climate justice movement became prominent (Bond 2012; Hadden 2015; Reitan and Gibson 2012).[5]

The coalescence of the climate justice movement in global spaces such as UN meetings and the World Social Forums, and its basis in the frontline communities most impacted by climate change and environmental injustice, helped radicalize global environmental debates and bring together activists from a diverse array of struggles around a common focus that has become increasingly clear in the demand for system change. In spaces such as the World Social Forums, climate justice activists from around the world have met and developed their analyses and strategies as well as their relationships with other movements. These movements have also worked to engage with governmental actors who shared at least some of their political aims, and these relationships have helped bring some environmental justice ideas and projects onto government agendas.[6]

In 2010, activists came together in the World Peoples Conference on Climate Change (WPCCC) and the Rights of Mother Earth, an international conference organized by the Bolivian state in response to the failed intergovernmental climate negotiations. The WPCCC developed a People's Agreement[7] that reinforces and helps spread many of the ideas, projects, and analyses that had been developed by the climate justice movement—ideas such as ecological debt, food sovereignty, rights for Mother Earth, and the need to build a powerful social movement to confront capitalism as the driver of climate change. Subsequent to the WPCCC, activists and sympathetic government leaders have continued to develop their strategic thinking and to challenge elites' inaction in the face of climate change.[8] The broader field of climate justice activism, moreover, continues to build on many years of grassroots organizing and trans-local relationship-building that has helped broadcast and clarify a global climate justice perspective constituted of a global protagonist, or agent for climate justice (Evans 2002; Wiesner 2014). This movement has also been generating ideas and implementing projects aimed at addressing community needs and building resilience. We discuss a few examples of such projects below, including ecovillages, human rights cities, and just transition projects.

Community resilience initiatives

Resilience refers to the ability of communities to survive, rebuild, and thrive following devastation. Environmental justice advocates have been working to identify strategies for building such resilience, which center around countering or disrupting the competitive and extractive logics of capitalism that are reinforced through processes of globalization, proletarianization, depeasantization, commodification, and industrialization, among others. For it is these processes that reproduce what Gotham and Greenberg (2014, 136) call the "uneven landscapes of risk and resiliency." Each of the projects we explore helps reduce communities' reliance on industrial capitalism for their survival, promotes greater cooperation among people as well as harmonious relations between humans and the earth, and reprioritizes human rights over the needs of capital.

In their analysis of the coupled human and natural systems (CHANS) literature, Caniglia and her collaborators (2014) identify some of the lessons about how societal resilience can be strengthened. These include:

- learning to accept change and actively building an understanding of and response to inevitable change;
- utilizing planning, innovation, and collective action to [ensure that basic needs are met];[9]
- developing and engaging diverse resources;
- becoming active agents in bringing about resilience.

To this list, and based on our observations of movement practices, we would add:

- cultivating an *environmental justice constituency* that supports ecologically grounded rights-based projects.

Our discussion below points to the ways that three overlapping contemporary social movement initiatives—ecovillages, just transition, and human rights cities—serve to build community resilience in the face of the kinds of threats cities are facing and will continue to face as climate change continues. We situate community activism in the larger context of a global climate justice movement that has generated critical ideas and trans-local networks that shape local actors' understandings and choices and disseminate alternative ideas and models to a global audience. We draw from these cases some lessons of how urban planners and municipal officials can better support community resilience.

Here we define "projects" as sets of practices that are embedded in logics and political imaginaries that enable them to be adaptive and responsive to a variety of local conditions. Such projects are both locally emergent and linked to global social movements. They are often iterative, evolving over time through dialogic processes that are integral to movements, and they are typically informed by both local experiences and global analyses that are reflected in various movement settings.

In varying ways and to different degrees, each of the projects we examine here demonstrates an acceptance that climate change is happening, and indeed it is a major driver of the project. All of these projects also engage in explicit work to articulate innovative models and to plan collective action aimed to advance goals of community resilience. Many of the leading proponents of these initiatives are motivated by the concern for community survival. Moreover, their systemic analysis compels them to help others who have not yet experienced the same degree of threat prepare for what activists know will eventually impact other communities.[10] Significantly, all these projects involve "movement building" efforts to develop multisectoral alliances and to maximize the resources available for advancing the project. To support their visions, these projects engage people in outreach and public education work to transform passive consumer-citizens or victims into critical agents of social change. This includes working to create a supportive political environment by actively cultivating a constituency that understands and supports environmental justice and community resilience. This work helps "challenge what critical global scholars call 'neoliberal governmentality,' that is, a policy of creating responsible, private economic subjects whose actions further corporate globalization" (Desai 2009, 94–95). The innovative models described in this chapter offer an alternative lens to the concept of *injustice-in-waiting* proposed by the editors. The full extent of inequalities burdening vulnerable populations is not made visible just by crises, disasters, or extreme events. Rather, these groups have long experienced injustices, and the deepening ecological and social crises are serving to exacerbate these injustices even further. What is "in waiting," then, is even graver injustices and more widespread experiences of environmental risks and costs in the population if alternative models that strengthen *a priori* community resilience are not pursued.

Ecovillages

Cooperative, eco-friendly, sharing economy traditions and practices that are rooted in communities date back to the beginning of time. In Jamaica and other countries in the Caribbean, people have a practice called "throwing a partner," which is an informal revolving loan fund/group savings plan mechanism that is usually handled by a matron of the community. While community-owned solar has just taken off in the past couple of years, we see historical parallels to such local, renewable energy projects in cases like the Muheza Hospital in Tanzania, which began pioneering a microgrid for the rural community there more than thirty years ago. Recycling traditions from melting and repurposing scrap metal to passing on hand-me-down clothing, previously the norm, have been eroded by the glut of production and consumerism in today's society, although we now see a resurgence of this in communities around the world.

Ecovillage projects essentially revitalize and modernize these traditional practices and link them with other innovations in intentional community models that prioritize social, economic, and ecological sustainability. Ecovillage participants seek to develop and institutionalize alternatives to ecologically destructive systems for the provision of transportation, food, energy, water, and waste management. Inherent in this model is the belief that the breakdown of traditional forms of community, wasteful consumerist lifestyles, the destruction of natural habitat, urban sprawl, factory farming, and over-reliance on fossil fuels trends must be changed to avert ecological disaster and create richer and more fulfilling ways of life. Ecovillages offer small-scale communities with minimal ecological impact or regenerative impacts as an alternative. Many advocates also seek independence from existing infrastructures, although others pursue more integration with existing infrastructure.

Ecovillages, whether urban or rural, tend to integrate community and ecological values within a principle-based approach to sustainability (Van Schyndel 2008). Johnathon Dawson, former president of the Global Ecovillage Network, describes five ecovillage principles in his 2006 book *Ecovillages: New frontiers for sustainability*:

1 Grassroots initiatives, not government-sponsored projects;
2 Residents value and practice community living;
3 Residents are not overly dependent on government, corporate or other centralized sources for water, food, shelter, power, and other basic necessities. Rather, they attempt to provide these resources themselves;
4 Residents have a strong sense of shared values, often characterized in spiritual terms;
5 Ecovillages often serve as research and demonstration sites, offering educational experiences for others.

Explicit in the idea of ecovillages is that they can be replicated and scaled up. Indeed, as many participants quickly learned, achieving their goals requires changes in the larger set of relationships within a (bio)region. Thus, the vision of the ecodistrict model is that of just, resilient, and sustainable cities, from the neighborhood up. The concept of ecodistricts is based on "urban regeneration and community development rooted in a relentless commitment to authentic collaboration and social, economic and ecological innovation that reimagines the future of cities" (EcoDistricts 2016) and advocates for the following values:

- Neighborhoods and districts are the building blocks of sustainable cities;
- Everybody—regardless of class, race, age, religion, gender identity, or sexual orientation—deserves to live in healthy, safe, connected, and vibrant neighborhoods;
- Economic opportunity, community well-being, and ecological health are fundamental ingredients for sustainable neighborhoods and cities;
- Neighborhood sustainability requires a new model for action—rooted in collaboration and greater inclusion—to co-create innovative district-scale projects;

- Rigorous, consistent, and transparent reporting in the areas of governance, environmental, and social performance is fundamental to effectively promote and manage long-term sustainability;
- Social equity, inclusion, and democracy are essential to sustainable neighborhood development.

Ecovillages and districts thus offer models that foster sustainability for the planet and address the societal fragmentation that has resulted in compromised health, increased crime, and a breakdown in access to basic needs such as breathable air, drinkable water, affordable, nutritious food, affordable electricity, and uncontaminated land. Also incorporating elements for strengthening local economies and advancing democracy, these local models provide microcosms for the change we must see in the world to realize a society that upholds human and civil rights.

> If you live in the urban development space, you've likely heard this fact: the zip code a child is born into determines his or her quality of life more than any other factor. If that phrase isn't alarming to you, it should be. Why? Because the way we build our cities has historically been inequitable. Urban development conversations often include the same faces at the decision table, and these faces haven't adequately represented the diverse needs of the neighborhood they represent. The result has often been gentrification, displacement and the concentration of low-income, minority communities with poor access to transportation, walkable neighborhoods, local employment opportunities, safe public spaces and social services. Fortunately, the concept of equitable development is gaining significant traction, and both the public and private sectors are acknowledging that equity-focused urban development is now imperative. EcoDistricts has been working with communities and projects across North America to learn what it will take to build just cities for all.
>
> (Schaefer-Borrego 2016)

Two U.S.-based examples of communities adopting a hybrid of the ecovillage model are Gulfport, Mississippi, and Longview, Texas. These communities have undergone a process of reimagining community design and have begun to implement a suite of activities designed to have more sustainable systems that strengthen the local economy, erode the dependence on corporate entities for providing basic goods and services, while delivering the needs of community members.

Community supported agriculture (CSA) in Longview, as part of their, "Safe Inviting Green Neighborhoods (SIGNS)" initiative, is implemented through a network of community gardens on the lands of houses of worship to advance food security, particularly in the context of the shifting agricultural yields resulting from climate change. The project grows fruits and vegetables and members of the community harvest what they need and the CSA managers take the excess and provide it to a local mission to share with their patrons. Similarly, in Gulfport community members have been granted a plot of land by the local government, upon which they grow fresh fruits and vegetables which are shared with those in need.

Located in ground zero of the U.S. hurricane zone, the Gulfport ecodistrict project has recognized that uplifting human and civil rights in the context of disaster is critical to building climate resilience at the community level. Therefore, they have prioritized convening clergy, municipal leaders, other community members, and so on, to engage with emergency management officials so that the community members and leaders understand the system and practices and so that emergency management officials better appreciate the kinds of reforms necessary to meet the needs of marginalized populations within the communities. Such work helps reduce the inequities that intensify the vulnerabilities of low-income and people of color.[11]

In Longview, there was a recognition of differential participation in recycling. So the project engaged in a campaign to increase engagement in recycling by increasing awareness of the damage to the environment that landfills cause. Through community cooperation in a public education and mobilization campaign, the Longview project has been able to increase participation in the recycling program.

Though each community is in the relative infancy of their ecodistrict/ecovillage work, each draws from the models generated by ecodistricts and ecovillages elsewhere. In each place there are plans to expand to include green schools, community owned solar, storm water management, and other initiatives to their suite of projects aimed at strengthening local economies while uplifting human and civil rights. Residents in Gulfport and Longview have identified as the key to building community resilience their collective capacity to resist corporate control of the commons and to implement alternative systems and practices that are cooperative and regenerative.

The principles and practices articulated in the model of ecovillages are also evident in the other projects we examine below on emerging communities seeking to address inequities and vulnerabilities in an era of ecological and social crisis. There is a great deal of overlap in these models, yet each reflects different starting points and community conversations. However, we expect that activists engaged in each of these projects overlap in use of human rights language, environmental justice and sustainability, and notions of collective action and well-being, generating a greater convergence in how these models are articulated by an increasingly interconnected and informed global movement.

Just transition

> Eliminating a socio-economic system requires a profound mass movement that changes socio-political systems and alters human behavior, particularly the behaviors that guide our collective choices about who decides what we produce and consume, why we produce and consume it, and why what we produce and consume is distributed in the unequal and inequitable manner that it is. In effect, we need a mass movement for a Just Transition and we have to build it! (Source http://ggjalliance.org/just-transition-assemblies)

In June 2013, the Climate Justice Alliance (CJA), a collaborative of more than 35 grassroots organizations in low-income and communities of color around the United States, launched the Our Power Campaign: Communities United for a Just Transition. The goal of the Our Power Campaign is to "bring together frontline communities to 'build the bigger we' for a just transition toward local, living economies."[12] The idea of just transition refers to the notion that the costs of shifting to a low-carbon society as well as of the experiences of climate change must be shared in a just and equitable way, recognizing that vulnerable groups are already bearing disproportionate costs. CJA works to strengthen relationships between these frontline communities facing a variety of environmental threats and other sectors of progressive organizing, including environmentalists, labor unions, food sovereignty organizations, among others. Such alliances help raise consciousness about the real costs of fossil-fuel-intensive capitalist production on communities. At the same time, the alliance works to ensure that people most impacted by economic and environmental crises lead efforts to resist and transform their conditions. The CJA organized assemblies at the U.S. Social Forum in Detroit (2010) and sent delegations to international climate conferences, including those in the context of the United Nations and the World People's Conference on Climate Change and the Rights of Mother Earth, held in Bolivia in April 2010. The Our Power Campaign grew from the discussions and analyses that emerged from these varied gatherings of activists and their engagements with other movements.

Reflecting the commitment to movement-building that is central in the resilience projects we examine, a key element of the Our Power Campaign strategy is to hold a series of "Just Transition Assemblies" around the country to provide spaces for people to come together to discuss what a just transition should look like. Such assemblies allow community residents to learn about the issues and to see what models are already available, what challenges there are to realizing necessary changes, and to develop their shared thinking about how groups and communities can work to advance the goal of a just transition. In the words of campaign organizers:

> The process in which we challenge capitalism and create our own solutions and alternatives is through Just Transition. Just Transition is not the final state we want to end up in, rather it is the process for us to begin to envision and practice an anti-capitalist way of living. A Just Transition includes a framework for governance, for how we relate to the Earth, how we produce and consume, for reparations within the US and in the Global South, for how work is defined and valued, and for how people relate to each other. It is a step towards a complete re-imagination of our world, grounded in practice and solutions offered up by communities that have been the most exploited and neglected by capitalism. At the end of the day, we are not talking about a gentler capitalism, we are talking about transforming the way we relate to the world and each other.
> (Source http://ggjalliance.org/just-transition-assemblies)

Thus far, two such assemblies have taken place, one in Jackson, Mississippi, and the other in Bellingham, Washington. Three others are planned for the spring and summer of 2016, following the CJA's mobilization around the December 2015 climate negotiations (COP) in Paris. The aim of these assemblies is to help transfer information between global and national organizing sites and local communities and to enable conversations to develop across time and place as participants in these assemblies gain deeper understandings of the issues and of the possibilities for collective action.

Assemblies such as these are essential tools for building community resilience, since they mobilize and engage residents in conversations about how to respond to the dramatic threats posed by climate change. In effect they enact each of the elements for strengthening community resilience identified above: they explicitly acknowledge climate change and the need to transition; they create spaces for participants to be creative in planning alternatives and developing strategies to realize these; they offer opportunities to mobilize diverse allies and resources; they invite leadership and help cultivate the skills needed for participants to become active agents for just transition; and they provide opportunities for expanding the constituencies for environmental justice through both outreach/mobilizing work and through the implementation of concrete projects.

The essential demands and visions that have emerged from CJA's Just Transition campaign include (Our Power Campaign 2015):

- ending our carbon-intensive society;
- promoting real economic and political democracy—ensure that communities most affected by extractive industry and pollution shape discussions about how to respond to climate change;
- creating a system where workers have an equitable stake in the ownership of essential resources and in decisions about the production and distribution of goods and services;
- ensuring environmentally sustainable economic opportunities for all;
- creating a system that operates in harmony with the earth and promotes ecological restoration.

Conversations at the assembly in Jackson were organized into thematic groups that focused on workers, youth, women, and gender justice as well as energy democracy. Participants were asked to discuss what they saw as the challenges in each of those areas, the actual or potential actions that could help realize a just transition, and how they would organize collective actions to achieve these goals. An important backdrop for the assembly was the setting in Jackson, Mississippi, where the assembly's host organization, Cooperation Jackson,[13] has been implementing an ambitious and inspiring agenda for addressing racism, social exclusion, and environmental degradation. It has done so by providing various kinds of support for local cooperatives, advancing a sustainable communities initiative that includes a community land trust and numerous cooperative projects, and by making Jackson a Human

Rights City.[14] Cooperation Jackson leaders have helped craft Jackson's Just Transition Plan, which includes work to promote clean energy; move towards zero waste; advance regional food systems; promote efficient, affordable, and durable housing; and provide for ecosystem restoration and stewardship (Acuno 2015, 22–23).

Like the ecodistricts example above, advocates of a just transition are rejecting the mainstream media and political discourses that suggest that climate change can be addressed without a radical transformation of our economic and social systems. The idea of just transition disrupts the system's emphasis on delocalization, economic competitiveness, and growth, emphasizing instead community needs and abilities and the development of social or cooperative economies. A just transition discourse also centers on human rights and makes visible those actors whose experiences and even whose very existence is obscured if not erased when it comes to planning and policy. It promotes practices that reduce the distance between production and consumption, which necessarily limits environmental and social externalities. Through movement-building, project implementation, and communication and public education work, just transition advocates are helping advance a counter-narrative to global capitalism that fosters community resilience.

Human Rights City initiatives

Given the centrality of human rights to the community resilience initiatives we have discussed thus far, we draw attention to another social movement initiative that complements and reinforces—and that encompasses—projects such as ecovillages/districts and just transition, the human rights cities initiative. Human rights cities are "cities that explicitly refer to international human rights norms in their activities, statements or policy" (van den Berg and Oomen 2014, 13). Such cities have been on the rise in recent years due partly to pressures caused by economic globalization such as migration and urbanization, financial crisis, and the devolution of state authority. Cities are where human rights are experienced, and local authorities typically have greatest influence over their protection. Yet, international human rights treaties are negotiated among national governments, and national authorities are legally responsible for implementing them. Human rights advocates have thus been working to hold municipal officials accountable for enforcing international law. As communities face intensified pressures from the forces of globalization, these movements are gaining momentum (van Lindert and Lettinga 2014).

While human rights cities can take many different forms, the model Human Rights Cities initiative was launched by the Peoples Decade for Human Rights Education[15] (PDHRE) in the wake of the 1993 World Conference on Human Rights in Vienna. The initiative aims to mobilize people in communities to "pursue a community-wide dialogue and to launch actions to improve the life and security of women, men and children based on human rights norms and standards" (Marks, Modrowski and Lichem 2008, 45). The process of becoming a Human Rights City can vary, and some communities start with a city council resolution designating the city a Human Rights City. In other contexts, such as Jackson, Mississippi, organizers work to develop broad community alliances to support human rights principles before seeking a formal Human Rights City designation. The key element is residents' intention of using human rights as a framework for community governance and the active engagement of popular groups in support of this aim (Acuno 2015).

Rosario, Argentina, became the first Human Rights City in 1997, motivated by residents' desires to prevent another military dictatorship and to reduce overall violence and social exclusion (Oomen and Baumgärtel 2012). Since then, activists around the world have been developing this model for transforming policymaking and raising public consciousness. The idea of Human Rights Cities has been spread especially by PDHRE through a variety of mechanisms, including the World Social Forums, where tens of thousands of social justice organizers have gathered on an annual or bi-annual basis since 2001. Currently there are more than two dozen Human Rights Cities around the world, with growing numbers in the United States.[16]

Recognizing that prevailing social policies have done little to effectively address social problems such as poverty and social exclusion, Human Rights Cities advocates help mobilize civil society actors in support of a policy agenda that prioritizes social justice and community needs over values such as economic growth and "development," which define conventional policy agendas. While conventional approaches allow business and other elites to define priorities and policies, the Human Rights City initiative:

> Encourages local communities to take charge of their own future by understanding their needs and the causes of the various forms of deprivation [. . .] and acting on that understanding. Where a vibrant civil society and responsive local government exist, human rights communities complement and reinforce their efforts to tackle poverty and social ills. The added value of the Human Rights Cities Program in such a context is to channel those efforts around national and international commitment to human rights. Where local government is ineffective, corrupt, or non-existent and few opportunities are available to mobilize beyond the family and clan, a Human Rights Cities initiative is a vehicle for raising awareness and transforming that awareness into action for social change.
> (Marks et al. 2008, 18)

Beyond providing a model for local organizing, the Human Rights City initiative is also valuable for its ability to connect local communities with a global human rights movement. It thus offers a rich body of international human rights law that validates and reinforces local claims. The value of such international connection cannot be underestimated for its role in motivating and supporting community engagement, providing resources as well as models for local action, and gaining attention from policymakers and other elites in the community.

PDHRE's examination of the impacts of Human Rights City organizing in cities around the world led to the conclusion that:

> Those who have participated in the creation of Human Rights Cities have acquired a skill set and confidence for questioning those power relations that make deprivation of human rights possible. They use the legal and administrative systems to their advantage and address problems of urban poverty as participants in change rather than victims of fatality or recipients of charity. They develop the ability to analyze problems in terms of deep causes rather than merely treating symptoms. The idea that social and economic injustice is "the way the world is" yields to awareness that people can change their condition by civic engagement for societal development based on human rights.
> (Marks et al. 2008, 146–147)

With this very invitation to residents to envision what it would mean to have a city that prioritized and actively worked to promote human rights, Human Rights City initiatives are disrupting dominant narratives and invoking creative social and political leadership from people and communities, just as the invitations to envision "Just Transitions" has done. Explicit attention to the human rights framework can help broaden the possible base of support while also helping both participants and a larger public better appreciate the intersections of human rights and environmental degradation.

When residents are asked to consider how to advance the ideal of a Human Rights City, concerns for ending environmental racism and ensuring the needs of vulnerable communities and future generations in the face of climate change come readily to the fore. In addition, such conversations tend to emphasize the need for building strong movements that bridge divisions across race, sector, location, and other divides.[17] And within this framework, proposals such as the Universal Declaration of the Rights of Mother Earth,[18] an initiative that emerges from the global climate justice movement and that has been supported in documents such as the People's Agreement of the World Peoples Conference on Climate Change and the Rights of Mother Earth,[19] provide natural focal points around which to mobilize communities.

Akin to ecovillages and just transition, human rights movements are helping to delegitimize prevailing models of governance and authority which have consistently failed to provide for people's basic needs, while offering promising alternatives. By appealing to international human rights laws and principles, activists are holding public officials to account for both the gaps between the ideological justifications and the actual operation of the prevailing system. They also illuminate the institutional gaps that deny local authorities the capacity to carry out their responsibilities under international law. By creating spaces where residents can reflect on the social and ecological costs of capitalist development, define and advocate for community needs and values, and where they can consider preferable alternatives to the status quo and build diverse alliances, leadership skills, and a broad constituency for environmental justice, Human Rights Cities serve as a model for enhancing community resilience.

Lessons for urban planners and policymakers

Prevailing neoliberal, capitalist ideology and policies undermine community resilience. People from historically oppressed groups see and experience the contradictions most intensely, and thus they are most aware of the need for fundamental, systematic change that emphasizes human needs and survival over economic growth. Our discussion illustrates how environmental justice initiatives, led by low-income, people of color, and indigenous communities, are articulating alternative ideologies and values that disrupt the dominant logics of capitalism and help reorient governance in ways that enhance community resilience. Such projects counter capitalism's competitive and exploitative hierarchies with practices that preserve communities and that privilege human rights, dignity, and ecosystem sustainability over material wealth. In doing so they foster values of social cohesion and harmonious relationships with nature, both of which are essential to community resilience.

Drawing from the examples above, we identify some key lessons that can guide urban planners and policymakers in efforts to build resilient communities. It bears repeating that planners need to begin from the recognition that the existing capitalist system is not a resilient one, and that community survival demands that we find alternatives to this system. All work must begin from this recognition and identify paths from a failing system toward more just and ecologically sound alternatives.

> **Broaden participation in public policymaking.** In each of these initiatives activists are working to create more inclusive policy spaces where the most vulnerable groups are engaged in decision-making. Metzger (2015) found that including historically underrepresented groups and academics alongside policymakers and business leaders led to openings "on both a political and epistemological level" (346). In particular, the inclusion of academics in policy debates led to more evidence-based policymaking, which can be helpful in countering the systematic exclusion of particular groups.
>
> **Engage human rights discourses and institutions.** Our examples also point to the utility of the human rights framework as a tool for advancing environmental health and community resilience. "This is because there is already wide recognition that many human rights are dependent on our relationship with a clean, healthy, and sustainable planet. Moreover, some regional charters do in fact recognize a clean and healthy environment as a basic human right (e.g., the African Charter on Human and People's Rights and the American Convention on Human Rights)" (Shilomboleni 2015, 323).
>
> **Utilize transnational networks and resources.** Policymakers and planners can find important resources and policy innovations in transnational social movements and in the policies of other national and local governments. Each of our examples above emerge from globally connected movements, and each benefits from the cross-cultural sharing of experiences and analyses. Bolivia's sponsorship of the World People's Conference on Climate Change and the Rights of Mother Earth provides an important example of how national governments,

working together with social movements, can provide leadership to advance community resilience. The ideas shared in forums like this one also tend to find their way—often as a result of social movement mobilization—into national and local policies. Thus, planners should look outside a single country's borders to search out examples of community resilience.

Remove policy barriers to resilience. Implementation of projects that enhance community resilience often require changes in national and local regulations and policies. Such policies were designed to advance capitalist processes such as industrialization and globalization/delocalization that contribute to climate change. For instance, laws that impinge on the creation of cooperatives, and regulations regarding the production and distribution of food and energy, are often designed to favor large-scale producers in a capitalist economic order. This has obstructed the development of alternative models, and urgent attention is needed to remove policy barriers to resilience and to enhance financial mechanisms and legal-support systems for resilience projects.

Create spaces for developing community cohesion and other values that foster resilience. Another important element of each of the cases we examined is the creation of spaces where diverse community residents can come together across racial, class, neighborhood, sectoral, and other divides to discuss policies and develop connections with each other and with allies outside the community. Such spaces are essential for raising public consciousness about the nature of environmental threats and interdependencies as well as about the viable alternatives to prevailing development practices. Community members need spaces to meet one another and to develop shared understandings of community values. They need to be able to develop trust and build commitment to working together for the large-scale social transformation needed for community resilience. Capitalism's logics create hierarchies and segregate communities, and thus intentional efforts must be made to create these kinds of spaces. Public planners can work to ensure that local regulations don't inhibit such activities, and in fact it seems appropriate to utilize public resources to help incubate and develop social cohesion.

In sum, frontline communities and groups most harmed by fossil-fuel-intensive capitalist development have played a critical role in building a global environmental justice movement that has helped generate and disseminate valuable ideas and models for building community resilience. At the core of these projects are processes that directly counter key logics and practices of capitalism and that serve to revitalize community relationships (including relationships between people and ecosystems), re-localize production, reduce fossil-fuel-dependence, and restore/reclaim traditional values and practices. Building urban resilience will require new models of governance that incorporate marginalized and excluded groups not only to prevent more extreme environmental injustice but also to help mobilize the knowledge and skills needed to help us all survive and thrive in a warming world.

Notes

1 Climate Program-National Association for the Advancement of Colored People (jpatterson@naacpnet.org).
2 Department of Sociology, University of Pittsburgh (jgsmith@pitt.edu)
3 The Southwest Network for Environmental and Economic Justice includes activist leaders from the U.S. southwest, including Native American leaders. Also present were health advocates and researchers whose discussions at the 1985 Urban Environmental Health Conference and at the 1990 Race and the Incidence of Environmental Hazards Conference helped bring together evidence and clarify understandings of environmental racism (Taylor 1993).
4 See http://www.ejnet.org/ej/principles.html
5 The 2007 meeting of the UN Framework Convention on Climate Change in Bali marked a critical split in the activist community, and "Climate Justice Now!" was formed as an alternative to the Climate Action Network, which had been the major platform for civil society groups at previous UN meetings and embraced a more reformist approach. Climate Justice Now! embraced an anti-capitalist critique and refused to engage in negotiations on what it deemed the "false solutions" to climate change being offered in official UN meetings. The network was shaped in part by an influx of activists from the global justice movement, which had been building during the 1990s and early 2000s (Bond 2012; Hadden 2015; Reitan and Gibson 2012).
6 For instance, a number of state constitutions recognize the rights of nature, and the concept of "food sovereignty" has been accepted in some official documents, including those of the Organization of American States.
7 The People's Agreement of the World Peoples Conference on Climate Change and the Rights of Mother Earth can be found at: https://pwccc.wordpress.com/support/
8 In 2015, the Bolivian government under President Evo Morales held a follow-up to the WPCCC in Tiquipaya, Bolivia, called the "World Peoples Conference on Climate Change and the Defense of Life" (http://www.radiomundoreal.fm/get.php?file=IMG/pdf/statement-world-people-tiquipaya-ii_12.10.pdf&type=application/pdf).
9 Original wording was "to maintain a system's functioning." We interpret "system" here as the system of social reproduction rather than the dominant socio-economic order.
10 For instance, Gotham and Greenberg (2014) demonstrate how activists in New York City reached out to their counterparts in New Orleans after Hurricane Katrina to warn them about how to avoid being marginalized by powerful advocates of market-oriented redevelopment following the crisis, as they had been following the 9/11 attacks in 2001. Gotham and Greenberg argue that capitalist globalization has made *all* cities more crisis-prone, and they show how cities' "uneven landscapes of risk and resiliency" are reinforced when disasters create opportunities for powerful actors to use their political influence to shift more risks and costs onto less powerful groups.
11 See http://ecoadapt.org/webinars/feb-webinar-2015
12 See http://ggjalliance.org/ourpowercampaign
13 See http://www.cooperationjackson.org/
14 For details on cooperatives see: http://www.cooperationjackson.org/; on the sustainable communities initiative see: http://www.cooperationjackson.org/sustainable-communities-initiative/; on the Human Rights City initiative see: http://www.cooperationjackson.org/announcementsblog/2015/1/10/the-human-rights-city-campaign. For a more in-depth look at the strategic thinking that guides Cooperation Jackson's work, see this interview with organizer Kali Acuno: http://grist.org/people/a-green-utopia-deep-in-mississippi-this-guy-has-a-game-plan/ (interview by Sara Bernard for Grist.org, December 9, 2014). For an in-depth exploration of the broader Jackson initiative, see Acuno (2015).
15 Source http://www.pdhre.org/

16 Washington D.C. became the first U.S. Human Rights City in 2008, followed by cities including Eugene, Oregon; Chapel Hill, North Carolina; Boston; Seattle; Pittsburgh; and most recently Jackson, Mississippi.
17 For instance, see the report from Pittsburgh Human Rights City Alliance on its 2014 event marking International Mother Earth Day (http://pgh-humanrightscity.wikispaces.com/file/view/Report%20on%20Mother%20Earth%20Day%202014.pdf/507287904/Report%20on%20Mother%20Earth%20Day%202014.pdf).
18 See http://therightsofnature.org/universal-declaration/
19 See https://pwccc.wordpress.com/support/

References

Acuno K. (2015). Casting shadows: Chokwe lumumba and the struggle for racial justice and economic democracy in Jackson, Mississippi. Retrieved 4 April 2014 from http://www.rosalux-nyc.org/casting-shadows/

Bond P. (Ed.) (2012). *Politics of climate justice: paralysis above, movement below*. Scottsville, South Africa: University of Kwazulu-Natal Press.

Brooks E. (2005). Transnational campaigns against child labor: the garment industry in Bangladesh. In J. Bandy and J. Smith (Eds.) *Coalitions across borders: transnational protest and the neoliberal order* (pp. 121–140). Lanham, MD: Rowman & Littlefield, Boulder.

Bullard R.D. (1993). Anatomy of environmental racism and the environmental justice movement. In R.D. Bullard (Ed.) *Confronting environmental racism: voices from the grassroots* (pp. 15–40). Boston: South End Press.

Caniglia B.S., Frank B., Delano D. and Kerner B. (2014). Enhancing environmental justice research and praxis: the inclusion of human security, resilience and vulnerabilities literature. *International Journal of Innovation and Sustainable Development*, 8(4), 409–426.

Chavis Jr. B. (1993). Foreword. In R.D. Bullard (Ed.) *Confronting environmental racism: voices from the grassroots* (pp. 3–5). Boston: South End Press.

Conway J.M. (Ed.) (2012). *Edges of global justice*. New York: Routledge.

Dawson J. (2006). *Ecovillages: new frontier for sustainability*. Shumaker Briefings. Cambridge: Green Books.

Desai M. (Ed.) (2009). *Gender and the politics of possibilities: rethinking globablization*. Lanham, MD: Rowman & Littlefield Publishers.

EcoDistricts (2016). Vision, mission, and values. Retrieved 3 March 2016 from http://ecodistricts.org/about/vision-mission-values/

Evans P. (2002). Introduction: looking for agents of urban livability in a globalized political economy. In P. Evans (Ed.) *Livable cities? Urban struggles for livelihood and sustainability* (pp. 1–30). Berkeley: University of California Press.

Faber D. (2005). Building a transnational environmental justice movement: obstacles and opportunities in the age of globalization. In J. Bandy and J. Smith (Eds.) *Coalitions across borders: transnational protest and the neoliberal order* (pp. 43–68). Lanham, MD: Rowman & Littlefield, Boulder.

Gotham K.F. and Greenberg M. (Eds.) (2014). *Crisis cities: disaster and redevelopment in New York and New Orleans*. New York: Oxford University Press.

Hadden J. (Ed.) (2015). *Networks in contention: global civil society and the divisive politics of climate change*. New York: Cambridge University Press.

Marks S.P., Modrowski K.A. and Lichem W. (2008). *Human rights cities: civic engagement for societal development*. New York: People's Movement for Human Rights Learning & UN Habitat. Retrieved 4 April 2016 from http://www.pdhre.org/Human_Rights_Cities_Book.pdf

Metzger M. (2015). Thinking forward in global food governance—synthesis paper. *Global Food Governance in an Era of Crisis-Special Issue: Mapping the Global Food Landscape*, 2(2), 345–349.
Moghadam V. (Ed.) (2012). *Globalization and social movements: Islamism, feminism and the global justice movement* (2nd ed.). Lanham, MD: Rowman & Littlefield, Boulder.
Oomen B. and Baumgärtel M. (2012). Human rights cities. In A. Mihr and M. Gibney (Eds.) *The SAGE handbook of human rights* (pp. 709–729). Thousand Oaks, CA: Sage.
Our Power Campaign (2015). Report on the summer of Our Power Southern People's Movement Assembly on Just Transition for Climate Justice, Economic Democracy, and a Regenerative Economy. Retrieved 4 April 2016 from http://ggjalliance.org/sites/default/files/PMA-Just-Transition—Web-Final.pdf.
Pellow D.N. (2000). Environmental inequality formation toward a theory of environmental injustice. *American Behavioral Scientist*, 43(4), 581–601.
Pittsburgh Human Rights City Alliance (2014). Pittsburgh's human rights city alliance hosts event to recognize Mother Earth Day. Retrieved 4 April 2016 from http://pgh-humanrightscity.wikispaces.com/file/view/Report%20on%20Mother%20Earth%20Day%202014.pdf/507287904/Report%20on%20Mother%20Earth%20Day%202014.pdf
Reitan R. and Gibson S. (2012). Climate change or social change? Environmental and leftist praxis and participatory action research. *Globalizations*, 9(3), 395–410.
Rothman F.D. and Oliver P.E. (1999). From local to global: the anti-dam movement in Southern Brazil 1979–1992. *Mobilization: An International Journal*, 4(1), 41–57.
Schaefer-Borrego A. (2016). EcoDistricts. Retrieved 4 April 2016 from http://ecodistricts.org/what-will-it-take-to-build-just-cities-for-all/
Shilomboleni, H. (2015). Sustainable food systems and global environmental change—Synthesis paper. *Global Food Governance in an Era of Crisis-Special Issue: Mapping the Global Food Landscape*, 2(2), 321–325.
Smith J. (2014). Counter-hegemonic networks and the transformation of global climate politics: rethinking movement-state relations. *Global Discourse: An Interdisciplinary Journal of Current Affairs and Applied Contemporary Thought*, 4(1), 1–19.
Taylor D. (1993). Environmentalism and the politics of inclusion. In R.D. Bullard (Ed.) *Confronting environmental racism: voices from the grassroots* (pp. 53–61). Boston: South End Press.
Taylor D.E. (2010). Introduction. In D.E. Taylor (Ed.) *Environment and social justice: an international perspective* (pp. 1–27). Bradford, UK: Emerald Group Publishing Ltd.
van den Berg E. and Oomen B. (2014). Towards a decentralization of human rights: the rise of human rights cities. In T. van Lindert and D. Lettinga (Eds). *The future of human rights in an urban world: exploring opportunities, threats and challenges*. Retrieved 4 April 2016 from http://www.amnesty.nl/sites/default/files/public/the_future_of_human_rights_in_an_urban_world_0.pdf
van Lindert T. and Lettinga D. (Eds.) (2014). *The future of human rights in an urban world: exploring opportunities, threats and challenges*. Netherlands: Amnesty International. Retrieved 19 August 2016 from http://www.amnesty.nl/sites/default/files/public/the_future_of_human_rights_in_an_urban_world_0.pdf
Van Schyndel K.D. (2008). Redefining community in the ecovillage. *Human Ecology Review*, 15, 12–24.
Wiesner C. (2014). Global climate politics: paralysis above and movement below. Retrieved 4 April 2016 from http://youtu.be/xDa51ZLzFpM

13 Conclusion

Beatrice Frank,[1] Beth Schaefer Caniglia[2] and Manuel Vallée[3]

The chapters in this volume have examined the intersections between environmental justice and resilience in urban environments. Part I examines the theoretical challenges that have, to date, kept resilience studies from actively addressing the inequalities that perpetuate vulnerabilities in socio-ecological systems. The case studies in Part II serve to highlight various types of legacies that produce inequalities, including land tenure, racism, histories of disenfranchisement, and the concentration of power among local authorities and corporations. Finally, Part III – on governance and policy – explores various alternative practices that have emerged in the planning, development and policy arenas that can both help place justice at the forefront of proactive risk and climate change planning, and push toward a *just resilience*, one that allows us to foresee, prevent or alleviate injustices-in-waiting.

Theoretical insights

Resilience theory is based upon systems theory. Our authors carefully examined the underpinning assumptions of systems theory – especially those stemming from structural-functionalism – and found features of the theory that fail to address injustice. Specifically, resilience theory focuses on how specific characteristics of a system either resist or recover from an external shock to the system. The primary goal of the research program that surrounds this question is to identify key functions of the current system and predict how well those will withstand external shocks or recover from them. All three of our primary theoretical contributors identified this approach as failing to ask a fundamental question: when we define whether or not a system is resilient, we almost always fail to ask, resilient for whom? This shortcoming is a built-in weakness of the theory itself and the authors in the theoretical framework section address this gap through different approaches that intersect, complete and enrich each other.

Pellow starts in Chapter 2 by offering a comprehensive approach that merges critical race theory, feminist theory, ethnic studies and political ecology, among others, proposing a new field of study called critical environmental justice studies. He elaborates four primary pillars of this approach:

Pillar 1: Pay greater attention to how multiple social categories of difference are entangled in the production of environmental injustice, from race, gender, sexuality, ability and class to species.

Pillar 2: Embrace multiscalar methodological and theoretical approaches to studying environmental justice (EJ) issues, in order to better comprehend the complex spatial and temporal causes, consequences and possible resolutions of EJ struggles.

Pillar 3: Develop a deeper grasp of the entrenched and embedded character of social inequality – including speciesism – in society, and therefore a reckoning with the need for transformative approaches to realize environmental justice.

Pillar 4: Pay greater attention to and articulate the ways humans and more-than-human actors are indispensable to the present, and for building sustainable, just and resilient urban spaces.

In Chapter 3, Mayer bridges the psychology of resilience with community resilience studies to propose a meso-level approach to resilience that emphasizes adaptive capacity over preserving the status quo. Mayer states: "community resilience can be defined as the enduring capacity of geographically, politically, or affinity-bound communities to define and account for their vulnerabilities to disaster and develop capabilities to prevent, withstand, or mitigate for a traumatic event" (p. 41). Mayer adds to the definition a focus on resilience as a process, and an emphasis on networked capacities. He highlights that empirical evidence suggests "fairly robust inverse relationships between social vulnerability and community resilience" (p. 42). He argues that the community resilience approach offers the best option for creating resilience in ways that concentrate resources and skills and foster social change and long-term adaptive capacity – because of the fact social capital and community collaboration are at the center of such an approach.

Caniglia and Frank suggest a similarly explicit approach to resilience planning in Chapter 4. After building a broad understanding of resilience theory – by synthesizing findings from the vulnerabilities, human security, coupled human and natural systems, and environmental justice literatures in a previous contribution – the authors suggest studies of disaster preparedness should begin by critically assessing existing equality, rather than assuming that the current institutions need to be maintained. This analysis should address questions that highlight leverage points for strengthening the resilience of the most vulnerable populations. Their recommendations boil down to three best practices that are gaining traction in the planning, sustainability and resilience fields:

1 Actively build ties of trust with all communities, especially those on the front lines of short- and long-term disasters.
2 Plan ahead. Climatological surveys and downscaled climate models point to increases in particular risks in the face of climate change. Advanced

planning allows us to strengthen adaptive capacity of communities, thus lessening vulnerabilities and sensitivity toward uncertainty and change.
3   Invest in fostering the adaptive capacity and social capital of the most vulnerable populations. Providing infrastructure that encourages social activities in vulnerable neighborhoods frequently pays off when disasters strike. When social ties and capital exist, they can be activated for the common good. We can call this step-wise social capital formation – a strategy for adaptive capacity that pays dividends at multiple levels.

Caniglia and Frank point out that structural-functionalism begins by presuming that the key features and patterns characterizing systems are functional and adapted for the surrounding environment. While this weakness led sociologists to ultimately abandon structural-functionalist explanations by the mid-1960s, the revival of structural-functionalism via resilience theory requires a new evaluation of its opportunities and limits. Mayer poses a similar critique: "a more conflict-oriented approach that views resilience as a process as opposed to an outcome would emphasize adaptation toward a desired outcome instead of the maintenance of the existing status quo" (p. 41). Pellow's critique goes much deeper. He begins by arguing that existing social institutions, such as governments and markets, were never meant to provide equal access or outcomes for everyone. In fact, those institutions were designed to advance and protect the privilege of whites and, in particular, white men. An explicitly *unjust resilience* has accumulated through a legacy of explicit oppression and biased legal mechanisms that favor the existing rich over the poor and minorities. *Just resilience*, in contrast, would be characterized by social and environmental justice and might be based upon the definition of "just sustainability" (Pellow, p. 26): "the need to ensure a better quality of life for all, now and into the future, in a just and equitable manner, while living within the limits of supporting ecosystems."

The three theoretical chapters take an interdisciplinary approach that is grounded in more critical perspectives vis-à-vis resilience theory and its forerunner, systems theory, both of which stem from the biophysical sciences. When we apply theories from outside of our home disciplines, it is necessary to take a close look at the underpinning assumptions. Otherwise, we blindly build those assumptions into our models. In the case of resilience theory, the costs are considerable, as it leaves behind the most vulnerable groups. More theoretical work is therefore needed to use and embrace concepts, theories, frameworks and applied approaches developed in other disciplines. Until such a shift is fostered, it will remain challenging to establish new paths and processes that help enhance local and global *just resilience and sustainability*. We therefore invite scholars, practitioners and experts to build upon the environmental justice and resilience theoretical frameworks offered in this book, utilizing this momentum to further challenge the status quo and institutional powers that limit our ability to develop *just* socio-ecological systems for all.

Lessons from the case studies

Part II is filled with case studies that illuminate social forces that undermine the potential for resilience. Specifically, these studies highlight the role of historical, political, economic and power forces in creating contemporary vulnerabilities and perpetuating injustices-in-waiting. In Chapter 5, Mix, Raridon and Croff, for example, trace contemporary food inequalities to the legacy of Tulsa's 1921 race riots. Those riots devastated infrastructure within the North Tulsa black community, which perpetuated inequalities and created a food desert – also defined in this chapter as food injustices-in-waiting. Without addressing deep-rooted injustices, such as historical inequalities, populations remain vulnerable and the ability to foster community sustainability and resilience becomes elusive. The laissez-faire approach embedded in societies' governance structures and the failure to acknowledge how current contexts are shaped by historical injustices, as elucidated in Chapter 4, perpetuates environmental injustices and a blindness toward the inequalities that surround us. In turn, injustices-in-waiting become more and more ingrained, to the point that vulnerable populations are the ones who suffer the highest economic and human losses during crises and disasters.

In Chapter 6, Manuel Vallée shows how the New Zealand lumber industry led the country's Ministry of Agriculture and Forestry to pursue a mass urban pesticide campaign to eradicate a non-native moth, thereby subjecting trusting citizens to repeated chemical exposures that predisposed them to illness – which the chapter defined as chemical injustices-in-waiting – and undermined local ecosystem resilience. Potential community opposition was defused by government naturework – ideological work that encouraged citizens to view the moths as a biosecurity threat to be eradicated and pesticides as a necessary evil for participating in a "modern" society – that nurtured an acquiescence to toxicity. This work underscores that governments can play a crucial ideological role in the growing toxification of space, which disproportionately impacts the poor and people of color. It also exposes that governments have a tendency to prioritize corporate profits over human well-being. As Pellow highlights in Chapter 2, existing social institutions are often poor mechanisms for increasing ecological resilience and environmental justice, for humans and other species alike, as they are often designed to exploit the many for the benefit of increasingly fewer elites. Vallée ends his chapter by calling for a human rights approach to pesticides, and toxicants more generally, which would prioritize human health and well-being over industry profits, and would reduce chemical injustices-in-waiting and enhance human and ecosystem resilience.

The need for and challenges involved with public–private partnerships are highlighted by Padawangi and Vallée in Chapter 7, which analyzes efforts to provide Jakarta's urban poor with access to fresh water. In this case, a public–private partnership was created to increase fresh water connections for those lacking access in Jakarta, Indonesia. While the partnership's first stage failed to significantly improve the urban poor's water access, the partnership's second stage was designed in accordance with the World Bank's output-based aid funding mechanism, which directs water utility partners to build water hook-up infrastructure for the poor. This program succeeded in increasing the number of urban poor households connected to the freshwater network, thereby seemingly alleviating water justice issues and improving community resiliency. However, the progress was, in fact, quite limited, as a focus on increased connections did little to address the quality of service experienced by the poor, or Jakarta's underlying social justice issues, which feed into the water justice issues. If anything, the program's limited success helped legitimize a market-based approach that reduces water to an economic good, obscures water's non-market values – including socio-ecological values, political values, as well as individual and collective values – and maintains deep-seated social justice issues that perpetuate injustices-in-waiting and keeps poor communities vulnerable.

Power dynamics are also a key component of Chapter 8, in which Sarah Black traces the availability of clean drinking water for New York City (NYC) to the state's legacy of granting preferential treatment to the megacity's economic power. While previous case studies demonstrated that deep-rooted inequalities are fostered through institutional and governance systems, New York City's water supply system represents a case where a more just resilience was pursued. However, this outcome did not come without a fight, as New York City used both political and economic power to expropriate its hinterlands' water supplies, until a new law required NYC to negotiate a mutually beneficial relationship with her surrounding communities. The new law provided an opportunity for NYC's hinterlands to mobilize a set of demands that built social capital and financial opportunity for themselves, in exchange for protecting and sharing the pristine water supply sought by the city. This case study supports the idea that a more *just resilience* can be fostered when political and economic power is mobilized to link powerful and vulnerable locations in creating a more resilient social-ecological system. As advocated by Mayer, resilience that emphasizes adaptive capacity, instead of preserving the status quo, can lead to social change and long-term sustainability, especially when social capital and community collaboration are key elements of such an approach.

The first three case studies discuss perpetuated injustices that reduced socio-ecological resilience. However, Blake's case study of New York City provides a different story, as it offers an example of a community moving toward more resilient systems. Specifically, it illustrates how political and economic power were used to link powerful and vulnerable locations in creating a more just social-ecological system. Yet, even in this positive story, power is in the hands of government, with vulnerable communities playing a minor role in promoting resilience in ways that foster social change and long-term adaptive capacity. This is not the case in Part III, where governments and environmental justice movements develop alternative and often complementary solutions in building resilient and sustainable socio-ecological systems.

Policy, governance and planning solutions

Alternative policies, governance structures and planning solutions are explored in Part III to challenge the current status quo of institutions and power, and thus propel a shift toward the development of *just* socio-ecological systems for all. Many argue that public–private partnerships and other market-based frameworks for natural resource management are incompatible with achieving justice, equality and resilience for the poor. This is the firm stance that Joanna Robinson adheres to in Chapter 9. To build her case, she engages two mainstream environmental sociology theories: ecological modernization and the treadmill of production. Focusing on water, Robinson lays out the dire need to ensure adequate water supplies for poor and vulnerable groups, as well as future generations. While ecological modernization posits that efficiencies arise from centralization, privatization and other market-based mechanisms, Robinson argues that water violates a central assumption of ecological modernization approaches: substitutability. Water is not, in fact, substitutable. Given that water is essential for life in all its forms, Robinson argues that ecological and distributive justice policies are needed to ensure water for the most vulnerable and for future generations. Instead of ecological modernization's utilitarian approach, Robinson advocates drawing from Rawls' theory of justice, which stipulates that the disadvantaged should always be prioritized for the greatest benefits. In other words, perhaps a rights-based approach to resource allocation is a better way to ensure that the poor are taken care of in the face of environmental and climate change pressures.

In Chapter 10, Chandra Russo and Andrew Pattison highlight similar values and approaches in the process of creating city climate action plans. These plans are generally produced by government, industry and citizen partnerships to design adaptation and mitigation plans that are responsive to local needs. Faced with federal government recalcitrance to respond to impending climate change, the term climate action plan "describes the set of policies or programs a subnational entity hopes to implement in order to reduce greenhouse gas emissions" (p. 177). However, rather than accept the need to preserve the existing relationships and patterns within a community, *some* climate action plans take the planning process as an opportunity to place equity and justice at the forefront. In this way, Russo and Pattison argue that climate action plans can be a source for *transformative adaptation* and increased resilience for the most vulnerable groups. To begin with, they argue that "resilient cities are proactive rather than reactive." Additionally, transformative adaptation is "climate change preparedness that addresses the deeply stratified allocation of resources and power in US cities" (p. 183). Certain adaptations – such as affordable housing, access to transportation and open spaces – may not appear to be directly related to climate adaptation. However, by addressing existing vulnerabilities, they prevent injustices-in-waiting and build resilience to future ecological change.

Local community activism and empowerment can also lead to equity and justice being placed at the forefront of resilience-building. Disadvantaged populations can become promoters of environmental sustainability and equitable community development, in order to improve environmental quality, resilience and justice in their own neighborhoods. In Chapter 11, Isabelle Anguelovski looks at three minority and low-income urban neighborhoods in different geographical locations that undertake similar socio-spatial strategies and tactics to resist emerging pressures, such as space toxification and degradation, territorial stigmatization, abandonment from public authorities and investors, and possible future gentrification. While these three neighborhoods have different governance and power structures, they use broad and "unexpected" coalitions of activists, bricolage techniques, a strategic use of the political environment, and technical experts and funders to foster urban socio-ecological justice. It is possible to build green and equitable cities when government entities ensure rights-based resource allocations, and place equity and justice at the forefront of planning. However, this case demonstrates it is equally important that local coalitions have social capital to remain resilient in the face of displacement and exclusionary pressures. This study reiterates Mayer's position that community resilience approaches offer the best option for creating resilience in ways that concentrate resources and skills, and foster social change and long-term adaptive capacity. As demonstrated by Anguelovski, social capital and community collaboration are powerful elements in building resilient neighborhoods, mobilizing against spatial injustice and striving toward just and sustainable socio-ecological systems.

In Chapter 12, Jacqueline Patterson and Jackie Smith highlight other programs that have emerged from grassroots and the environmental justice movement. Ecovillages exemplify community resilience programs based in neighborhoods or districts that prioritize building local social and economic capital. They are driven by innovation from the grassroots, rather than fueled by government entities. The basic values characterizing ecovillages include: inclusion, democracy, transparency, community health and well-being, and equity. A second set of programs, just transition programs, are specifically designed to recognize vulnerabilities that emerge with economic and ecological change. The new energy economy, for example, requires decline in some sectors and creates opportunity in others. Just transition programs target those whose jobs are vulnerable to elimination and provides them with social networks and training. Finally, Patterson and Smith describe the ways human rights cities place equitable and democratic progress at the center of their planning processes. By infusing their policies and planning documents with the principles found in the United Nations Declaration on Human Rights, human rights cities adopt the values of the Declaration in all of their interactions. This new language also brings new constituents to the table, helping to ensure citizen engagement and building collective capital.

Part III illustrates strongly that human security insights provide important frameworks for understanding the contexts of vulnerabilities in cities. Specifically, governance, economics, food security, and community social capital can enable or constrain resilience. They also show that using alternative models and proposing new pathways can lead to vulnerable populations' engaging in decision-making, and building social capital, which in turn allows socio-ecological systems to become more resilient and sustainable for all. Such approaches can prevent that creation and embedding of injustices-in-waiting as vulnerabilities are considered in advance rather than addressed once they become exposed through disasters. Only by embracing and further pushing policies, governance models and planning solutions that include socio-ecological justice in our theories, practices, and governance and policies will cities become bastions of resource efficiency and sustainability for everybody.

A pathway for the future

Although this volume represents only a first attempt at synthesizing the fields of resilience and environmental justice in urban contexts, there are clear patterns that emerge for future research. The urgency of impending climate change, along with the extent of existing climate injustices, necessitates a meeting of the minds across these disciplines. From the above we distill a series of best practices for better pursuing environmental justice and resilience for all.

Justice and equity should always come first in the resilience planning process. Legacies of racial, gender, ethnic, age, class and other cross-cutting forms of disadvantage mediate resilience. Local authorities will fail to address the matrices of vulnerabilities affecting the poor if they begin with the assumption that current institutions are designed to serve everyone equally. Instead, the best programs designed for decreasing vulnerabilities among the poor begin by acknowledging and assessing the legacies of exclusion that produced those inequalities to begin with. Human rights cities, ecodistricts, grassroots activism and justice-centered climate action plans are just a few best practice examples provided by our authors.

Community engagement practices must be undertaken at every stage of project planning and implementation. These chapters confirm the empirical evidence of decades of natural resource management research and show that: (1) projects conceived without community input often fail at the community level; and (2) community engagement at each stage of project planning, design and implementation increases project acceptance, builds local social capital and increases long-term resilience.

The environmental justice movement is an excellent source of transformative approaches to resilience in the face of climate change. Movement members are knowledgeable of local community concerns and preferences, but they are often also knowledgeable of the resilience models and best practices being advocated at the global level. Several of our authors highlight the role the environmental justice movement played in the case studies reviewed in this volume. Therefore, when communities begin resilience planning, it makes sense to start by checking with the community organizations most likely to be involved in the environmental justice movement for insights and collaborations.

Lessons for those in the academic fields engaged in resilience studies are twofold. First, the assumptions underpinning systems theory need to be balanced by a healthy dose of critical theory. Our scholars put forth a clean consensus that systems theory's desire to preserve the central features and relationships among institutions in the social system will preserve existing inequalities, rather than seek to alleviate those vulnerabilities before the effects of environmental and climate change advance more severely. Second, continued efforts at inter- and trans-disciplinarity – specifically those that bring in expertise in the areas of stratification and inequalities – are needed. The contributions in this volume from sociology, political ecology, Rawls' political justice theory, along with feminism, critical race theory and ethnic studies have revealed severe oversights and blind spots that have endured for too long in resilience studies.

Finally, rather than setting our resilience goal to avoid a state change in the face of climate change and other disasters, our goal should be to seek a state change *before* such disasters strike, a state change that lessens the vulnerabilities of the poor and people of color, who often stand on the front lines when disasters strike. Only proactive acknowledgement and planning, coupled with community engagement, can ensure we target the matrices of inequalities that have produced the existing system, and perpetuate both environmental injustices and injustices-in-waiting.

Notes

1 Regional Parks, Capital Regional District of Victoria, bfrank@crd.bc.ca
2 Director of the Sustainable Economic & Enterprise Development (SEED), Institute and Faculty Research Director in the College of Business and Economics at Regis University, beth.caniglia@oksatate.edu
3 Sociology Department, University of Auckland, m.vallee@auckland.ac.nz

Index

ability 21, 29, 235
Abramson, D.M. 47
acquiescence to toxicity 100, 109–110, 111, 237
activism 30, 195–212, 216, 239–240, 241; bricolage techniques 202, 205–206; climate action plans 189–190; Climate Justice Now! 231n5; coalition development 202, 203–205; Coalition of Watershed Towns 145–146; community resilience 219; food justice 82, 91; global climate 218; strategic use of the political environment 202, 206–208; technical experts and funders 202, 208–210; water 131; *see also* protests; social movements
adaptation 8–9; climate change 177–182, 183–191, 239; resilience 38, 41–42, 45–46, 51, 52, 60; resources for 7; urban 51
adaptive capacity 10, 52, 238; community resilience 41–42, 240; incremental changes 46, 50; planning 235–236; psycho-social resilience 44
adaptive governance 138, 139–141, 144, 146, 147–149
Adger, W.N. 40, 48
Adorno, T.W. 69
advocacy 210
African-Americans 23–24, 67–68, 79–80; Dudley 200; food insecurity 82, 85; Hurricane Katrina 6, 91; poverty 83; Tulsa 89–90; *see also* people of color; race
age: critical environmental justice 29; ecodistricts 221; inequality 67; legacies of disadvantage 241; United States 67; *see also* children; elderly people; youth
agency 41, 43, 45, 50, 52, 59

agriculture: community supported 222; organic 103; policies 24–25; vulnerability to climate change 1
Agyeman, J. 26
Anderson, S.A. 82, 86
Anderton, Jim 105, 107
Anguelovski, Isabelle 195–215, 240
Argentina 164, 227
Asian Development Bank 118, 119, 128, 133
asthma 23, 103, 104
Auckland 9, 98, 99, 100–112
Australia 100–101, 105–106, 109

Bakker, K. 120, 161, 172n4
Barcelona 195, 198–212
Basel Convention 49
Beck, Ulrich 163, 170
Benford, Robert 25
Berkes, F. 41
Bernard, Sara 189
biodiversity: ecological modernization 161; impact of pesticides on 97, 102–103; manufacturers of disease 112; Painted Apple Moth framed as threat to 107–108; Rawls' theory of justice 167; urban expansion 4; water 163
biosecurity threat, Painted Apple Moth framed as a 104–109, 110, 111–112
Blake, Sarah E. 138–153, 238
Bolivia 164, 171, 231n8
Boston 178, 184, 195, 198–212, 232n16
Brazil 3
bricolage techniques 196, 202, 205–206, 240
bridging organizations 147
Brisman, A. 31
British Columbia 98, 171
Brulle, Robert J. 17, 172n3

Buenos Aires 164
built environment 181, 182, 186
Bullard, Robert 26, 188–189

California 98, 171
Canada 98, 171, 172n4
Caniglia, Beth Schaefer 1–14, 19, 57–75, 179, 219, 234–242
capacity-building 10, 171
Capek, Stella 100
capital, spatial 204–205
capitalism 69–70, 98, 99, 159–160, 165; costs of 228; counter-narratives to 226; critique of 218; environmental justice and 216–217, 219; globalization 231n10; just transition 224; neoliberal ideology 229; New York City's water supply 142, 144–145; policy barriers to resilience 230
CAPs *see* climate action plans
carbon emissions 23, 177, 180, 182, 189
Carpenter, S.R. 40
Carson, Rachel 97
Casc Antic 195, 198–212
Cayo Hueso 195, 198–212
CBOs *see* community-based organizations
CDCs *see* community development corporations
Chaffin, B, C. 138, 140, 146
change: adaptability to 38; adaptive governance 139, 147; *see also* social change
CHANS *see* coupled human and natural systems
Chapel Hill, North Carolina 232n16
Charmaz, K. 85
chemical terrorism 110
children: critical environmental justice 22; food insecurity 83; pesticide-induced health risks 98, 103, 104; poverty 67; psycho-social resilience 39; urban activism 206, 211; vulnerability 1, 61; water-borne diseases 158; *see also* youth
China 3, 177
Ciplet, D. 2–3, 68–69
cities 1–2; climate change adaptation 178, 183–191; definition of 1; ecodistricts 221–222; human rights 219, 226–228, 240, 241; inequality 57; pesticides 98; resilience and 51; urban activism 196–197, 198–212, 240; urban socio-ecological systems 4–6, 7, 9, 10; water injustices 123, 157

citizen complicity 100
citizenship 18
CJA *see* Climate Justice Alliance
class: community cohesion 230; critical environmental justice 19, 21, 29, 235; ecodistricts 221; environmental justice 49; environmental protection policies 24; inequalities 17, 18, 67; legacies of disadvantage 241; networked capacities 42; pesticide-induced health risks 98; Tulsa 80
cleanup initatives 206–207
climate action plans (CAPs) 177–178, 182–191, 239, 241
climate change 2–4, 17, 23, 66, 177–194, 239, 241–242; certainty of 1; community resilience initiatives 219–220; critical environmental justice 28–29; human rights cities 228; inequalities 216; just transition 224–226; need for communal solutions 170; pesticides 98, 110; planning 235–236; resource overconsumption 138; transformative adaptation 177–178, 180–182, 183–191; water 157
climate injustice 2–4, 68–69, 218
Climate Justice Alliance (CJA) 224–225
Climate Justice Now! 231n5
Coalition of Watershed Towns 145–146, 147
coalitions 196, 197, 198, 202, 203–205, 208, 212, 240
Cochabamba 164, 171
collective action 198, 219, 223, 225
commodification of water 123, 132, 158, 163, 165, 171
communicative action 169, 172
community-based organizations (CBOs) 130
community-based revitalization 200, 201, 207
community cohesion 230; *see also* social cohesion
community development corporations (CDCs) 198, 203
community gardens 87, 92, 181, 201, 203, 205, 222
community involvement 168, 172n4, 188, 189, 241
community ownership 168
community resilience 38–39, 41–43, 46, 51–52, 240; capacity-building 171; definition of 41–42, 235; food justice

81, 82–83; human rights cities 228; initiatives 219–220, 229; just transition 225, 226; lessons for urban planners and policymakers 229–230; Resilience Activation Framework 47–48; social cohesion 217; urban activism 201; water privatization 164
community supported agriculture (CSA) 222
conflict: adaptive governance 139, 147, 149; bridging organizations 147; Casc Antic 200, 201; Rawls' theory of justice 167; social resilience 58
conservation: ecological modernization 160; fresh water systems 171; Rawls' theory of justice 167–168, 169
conservation of resources model 47
consumption 4, 165, 217; just transition 226; overconsumption 138
Cooperation Jackson 225 226
coping skills 39, 40
Cosens, B.A. 138
cost-benefit analysis 162
Costanza, R. 164
Cote, M. 43, 45, 46
coupled human and natural systems (CHANS) 7, 59, 219, 235
critical animal studies 20, 22, 29, 30
critical environmental justice 8, 17, 19–32, 51, 52, 234–235
critical race theory 22, 26–27, 29, 30, 69, 242
critical theory 66–71, 241
Croff, Julie M. 79–96, 237
CSA *see* community supported agriculture
cultural institutions 188
culture 48

Davis, K. 65–66
Dawson, Johnathon 221
decision making 168, 169; participatory democracy 170, 172; politics from below 170–171; procedural justice 121
Deepwater Horizon oil spill (DWHOS) 46–47, 49–50
deforestation 51, 157
deindustrialization 81
Delano, D. 19, 179
democracy 167, 199; deliberative 171, 172; ecological 168, 172; ecovillages 222, 240; just transition 225; participatory 168, 169–170, 172
Derraik, J. 105–106

Desai, M. 220
Diamond community 23–24
Dietz, T. 138, 139, 165
disability studies 22
disabled people: critical environmental justice 22; PlaNYC 188; vulnerability to climate change 1
disasters 4, 5, 10, 57, 68, 231n10; climate change 179, 188; food insecurity 92, 93; inequality 17, 66; laissez-faire approaches to recovery 63; networked capacities 42; preparedness 51, 60–61, 70, 71–72, 235; social resources 48; transport-oriented development 185; vulnerability to 68, 242; *see also* flooding; Hurricane Katrina
discrimination: food insecurity 81, 85, 88, 89–91, 93; Hurricane Katrina 91; water access 132–133
disease 3, 69, 71, 157, 158, 178
distributive justice 9, 121, 158, 166 169, 170, 172, 239
Downey, Liam 68, 81
droughts 5, 61, 68, 69, 92
Dublin Statement on Water and Sustainable Development 158
DuBois, W.E.B. 27
Dudley 195, 198–212
Durkheim, Emile 62

Earth Summit (1992) 217
earthquakes 5, 92
Eckersley, R. 172n3
eco-feminism 22
ecodistricts 221–223, 241
ecological biodiversity *see* biodiversity
ecological democracy 168
ecological justice 31–32, 158, 165, 239
ecological modernization 160–161, 162, 163–165, 171, 239
ecological resilience 40, 57, 58, 112
economic crisis 64–65, 123, 216
economic development 6, 18, 200
economic growth: adaptive governance 149; ecological modernization 160; privileging of 99; sustainable development 157–158; utilitarianism 162
economic power 141–142, 148–149, 238
economics 4, 240; economic security 7; Painted Apple Moth framed as economic threat 108–109
ecosystem services 4, 102, 162

ecosystems: just resilience 236; lack of education about 111; resilience 6–7, 140; vulnerability to climate change 1; water 163–164
ecovillages 219, 220–223, 240
education 111, 220, 223, 226
elderly people: critical environmental justice 22; pesticide-induced health risks 98; policies 72; vulnerability to climate change 1, 2, 69, 71; vulnerability to shocks 61, 64
elites 68, 166, 169–170, 172, 227, 237
eminent domain 142, 146, 148, 199
employment 4, 25, 195
energy: climate change policies 181; Jackson's Just Transition Plan 226; just transition 240; renewable 181, 182; vulnerability to climate change 1
engineering resilience 58
environmental bads 5–6, 7–8, 9, 99
environmental degradation 57, 161, 195, 196, 216; capitalism 159–160; Cooperation Jackson 225; ecological modernization 162; environmental justice movement 49; responsibility for 165; *see also* pollution
environmental gentrification 200, 212
environmental justice 5, 10, 29–32, 217–218, 241; activism 195, 211, 212; biodiversity protection policies 112; climate action plans 184, 189–190, 191; community resilience initiatives 219–220, 229, 230; critical 8, 17, 19–32, 51, 52, 234–235; disruption of capitalism 216–217; ecovillages 223; government decision-making processes 112; human rights cities 228; injustices-in-waiting 7–8; overview of the field 17–19; redefinition of concept 31; regime shifts 59; resilience 49–51, 52, 57–58; socio-ecological systems 66–67; socio-spatial strategies and tactics 203–210; transformative adaptation 190, 191; vulnerability 179; water 157; *see also* justice
Environmental Justice Principles 217
environmental protection 24, 142–143, 165
Environmental Protection Agency (EPA) 144, 145, 146, 147
environmental revitalization 200, 201, 203, 211
environmental sociology 159

environmental violence 99
EPA *see* Environmental Protection Agency
equilibrium 40, 45, 58, 62
equitable community development 195
equity 43, 241; climate action plans 90, 177, 178, 182, 183–185, 189–190, 191, 239; ecovillages 222, 240; procedural 183, 184, 188–190; transport-oriented development 185–186; *see also* inequality; justice
ethnic studies 26–27, 29, 30, 242
ethnicity: community resilience 48; environmental justice 49; inequality 67; legacies of disadvantage 241; *see also* race
Eugene, Oregon 232n16
Evans, B. 26
Evans, Peter 168
expendability 26–27, 29, 31
extraterritorial control 142–144

feminism 69, 169, 242; critical race 22, 29, 30; critiques of structural-functionalism 63; ecological 20, 29
filtration 144, 145, 147
First National People of Color Environmental Leadership Summit (1991) 217
First Nations 171
Fisher, D. 160
flooding 5, 49, 71, 92, 179; climate change 66, 69, 181; legacy of colonialism 68; New Orleans 6
Folke, C. 147, 148
food: food deserts 81–82, 83, 84, 181, 200, 237; food justice 9, 80–93, 237; food networks 200; food security 7, 10, 60, 195, 240; food sovereignty 231n6; Jackson's Just Transition Plan 226; New York City 187; regulation 230; urban activism 203
forests 1, 164, 171; *see also* plantation forestry industry
fossil fuels 3, 23, 26, 69, 220, 224, 230
Foster, John Bellamy 97, 99, 110
Fox, Michael 22
Frampton, Ruth 107
Francis, Pope 28
Frank, Beatrice 1–14, 19, 57–75, 179, 234–242
Frankfurt School 69
freedom 164

Freudenburg, W. 22, 160
Frickel, S. 22
Fry, R. 64
functionalism 28, 41, 43, 44, 45; structural-functionalism 61–66, 234, 236
funders 196, 202, 207, 208–210, 211–212, 240
future generations 165, 167–168, 171, 172

gender 18–19; community resilience 48; critical environmental justice 19, 20, 21, 29, 235; ecodistricts 221; inequality 67; legacies of disadvantage 241; networked capacities 42; *see also* women
gender studies 22
genetically modified organisms (GMOs) 103
gentrification 4, 186, 196, 200, 201, 210, 212, 222
Giddens, A. 40
Gleeson, B. 162
globalization 4, 168, 171, 219, 226, 230, 231n10
GMOs *see* genetically modified organisms
Gonzalez, Itziar 207–208
Gosnell, H. 138
Gotham, K.F. 219, 231n10
Gould, K.A. 159–160
governance 7, 9, 10, 240, 241; adaptive 138, 139–141, 144, 146, 147–149; ecodistricts 222; new models of 230; resilience 42, 45, 59; water 157–159, 160, 164, 170, 172n4; *see also* policies; regulation
Gramling, R. 22
green neighborhoods 196, 211
Greenberg, M. 219, 231n10
greenhouse gas emissions 177, 180, 239
Gulfport 222–223
Gunderson, L.H. 41, 45, 140

Habermas, Jürgen 69, 169–170, 172
Harlan, S.L. 3
Harrison, J. 99
Harvey, David 99, 112
Hatt, K. 45
Havana 195, 198–212
hazards 5, 43, 49, 81
health: access to healthcare 7, 60; disparities 184; food-related knowledge 86–88; insecurity 2; Jakarta's water supply 129; Painted Apple Moth framed as threat to 105–107; pesticide-induced health risks 97, 98, 102, 103–104, 110, 111; upstream public health approach 112; urban activism 209; vulnerability to climate change 1; water-borne diseases 157, 158
heat waves 66, 68, 71, 181, 184, 188
hegemony 19, 25, 26, 100
herbicides 24
Hispanics 67; *see also* Latinos
Hobbs, Marian 105, 106
Hobfoll, S.E. 47
Holling, C.S. 6, 39, 40, 41, 45, 47, 140
Horkheimer, M. 69
Hornborg, A. 45, 46
housing: access to 4; Casc Antic 200; climate change adaptation 181, 187, 239; disparities 184; Jackson's Just Transition Plan 226; Jakarta 124; racial segregation 91; transport-oriented development 185; urban activism 203, 209; vulnerability to climate change 3
Howard, J. 97, 99–100
Hudson River 141, 143
human rights approaches 229; ecovillages 222, 223; human rights cities 219, 226–228, 240, 241; just transition 226; pesticides 110–111, 112, 237; water 158, 159, 164, 169
human security 7, 59–60, 158, 240
Hurricane Katrina 5–6, 7, 26, 38, 52, 179, 216, 218, 231n10
hurricanes 5, 49, 66, 188

ideology 67, 70, 141
IFC *see* International Finance Corporation
immigrants: Casc Antic 201; critical environmental justice 22; environmental justice studies 17; transport-oriented development 186
India 3
indigenous peoples: critical environmental justice 22; environmental justice movement 17, 18, 217, 218, 229; rights 171; vulnerability to climate change 1, 28, 216; vulnerability to shocks 64
indispensability 26–29, 31, 235
individual resilience 39–40, 44, 47–48, 201; *see also* psycho-social resilience
inequality 2, 7, 46, 220, 241–242; cities 51; climate action plans 184; climate injustice 3; community resilience 38–39, 46; critical environmental

justice 19–20, 21, 22, 24–26, 28–30, 235; critical theory 69, 71; debates on 65–66; environmental justice 17–18, 49, 50, 52; food justice 80–81, 82, 83, 85; Hurricane Katrina 6; legacies of disadvantage 241; need for communal solutions 170; networked capacities 42; New York City 187; Rawls' theory of justice 167; reforms 72; social injustices 5; social resilience 57–58; structural 43, 81, 164; Tulsa 80, 237; United States 64, 67–68; utilitarianism 99; water access 118–119, 120–121, 123–124, 131–133, 157–158, 161, 171; *see also* equity; injustice
infrastructure 51, 179, 236; adaptive governance 139, 147; Casc Antic 201; climate change adaptation 181; ecovillages 221; Jakarta 124, 127; social policies 187–188; transportation 185; water 157
injustice 5, 10, 230, 242; climate 2–4, 68–69, 218, 241; climate change mitigation 182–183; critical environmental justice 21, 31; human rights cities 228; King on 28; "slow violence" of 179; spatial 121, 123–124, 131, 132–133, 195, 240; water 119, 121, 122–133, 163; *see also* inequality
injustices-in-waiting 5–6, 7–8, 9, 220, 240–241, 242; climate change 179, 191, 239; critical environmental justice 26; critical theory 71; economic development 200; food justice 81, 83, 85, 91–93, 237; market-based approaches 165; New York City's water supply 145; pesticides 98, 107, 109, 110, 237; resilience thinking 38; social policies 187; toxification 97; urban activism 195, 210, 212; water 123, 129–130, 131, 132, 157, 158, 238; *see also* inequality
institutions 171, 236, 237; critical theory 67, 69, 70, 71; cultural 188; international 68, 170; resilience 48, 59–60; structural-functionalism 63–64, 66; systems theory 241–242
interactive justice 121
interdisciplinarity 17, 18, 236, 242
Intergovernmental Panel on Climate Change (IPCC) 3, 49, 178, 180
International Finance Corporation (IFC) 118, 119–120

intersectionality 18, 22
Ioris, A.A.R. 120
IPCC *see* Intergovernmental Panel on Climate Change
Island Resource Allocation Hypothesis 107–108, 109

Jabareen, Yosef 188
Jackson, Mississippi 225–226, 227, 232n16
Jakarta 9, 118, 119, 120–121, 123–133, 237–238
Jamaica 220
just resilience 8, 25–26, 32, 50, 52, 71, 236, 238
just transition 219, 223–226, 240
justice 19, 25, 241; climate action plans 239; distributive 9, 121, 158, 166–169, 170, 172, 239; ecological 31–32, 158, 165, 239; food 9, 80–93, 237; global climate 228; interactive 121; procedural 121, 183, 184, 188–190; spatial 195; *see also* environmental justice; equity; injustice; social justice

Kasperson, R.E. 140
Kerner, B. 19, 179
Khan, M.R. 2–3, 68–69
King, Martin Luther Jr. 28
Kinzig, A. 40
knowledge: adaptive governance 139, 140, 147; co-production of 197–198; food-related 86–88
Krippner, S. 61

laissez-faire approaches 63, 64, 65, 72, 237
land acquisition 142–143, 145, 146, 147–148
land use 140, 161, 167
Landy, Benjamin 64
Lansley, Stewart 65
Laszlo, A. 61
Latinos 80, 83, 200; *see also* Hispanics
lawsuits 145–146, 202, 203
liberalism 169
Lichem, W. 226
Light Brown Apple Moth 98
local citizen mobilization 196, 198; *see also* activism
local government 177, 181, 211
locally unwanted land uses (LULUs) 196
Locke, John 161
Longview 222–223

Low, N. 162
LULUs *see* locally unwanted land uses

Mann, M. 141, 142
Mansbridge, J. 170
manufacturers of disease 112
marginalization 2, 8, 22, 59, 93, 132–133, 196
market-based approaches 120, 159, 160, 161–162, 239; limitations to 158, 163–166, 171; neighborhood revaluations 196; output-based aid 119, 122–123, 132; water injustices 121, 238; *see also* privatization
markets 63, 64, 65
Marks, S.P. 226, 227
Márquez, John 26–27
Marx, Karl 69
Marxist approaches 165
Masten, A.S. 39
materiality 121, 132
Mayer, Brian 37–56, 235, 236, 238
McKinlay, John 112
Meehan, K. 121
megacities 1–2
Memorandum of Agreement (MOA) 147–148
metering, water 127, 161, 164–165
Metro Manila 133
Metzger, M. 229
Mills, Charles 27
mitigation 177, 180–181, 182–183
Mix, Tamara L. 79–96, 237
MOA *see* Memorandum of Agreement
mobile grocers 83, 85, 91, 92–93
modernization: ecological 160–161, 162, 163–165, 171, 239; reflexive 170
Modrowski, K.A. 226
Moore, W. 65–66
Morgan, B. 170
Murray, Ed 190

Native Americans 23
natural disasters *see* disasters
nature 99, 100, 159, 161, 229
naturework 100, 104, 110, 237
neoliberalism 44, 46, 50, 159, 168, 197, 220, 229
Nepal 172n4
networked capacities 42, 235
New Orleans 5–6, 7, 38, 52, 91, 92, 231n10
New York City (NYC): activism 231n10; air pollution 23; climate action plan 178, 185, 187–188, 190; water system 9, 138–139, 141–149, 238
New Zealand 98–99, 100–112, 237
NGOs *see* non-governmental organizations
Nibert, David 22
Nightingale, A.J. 43, 45, 46
Nixon, Robert 179
non-governmental organizations (NGOs): climate change 3; Jakarta's water supply 121, 130; urban activism 202, 203–204, 207, 208–210
Norco 23–24
Norman, E.S. 172n4
Norris, F.H. 38, 42, 47
Nyseth Brehm, H. 81

OBA *see* output-based aid programs
Oklahoma 83
OneNYC 187–188, 190
Ontario 98
Oomen, B. 226
oppression 22, 67, 69–70
Orange Farm 164–165
organic agriculture 103
"organizational outflanking" 142
Ostrom, E. 139
Our Power Campaign 224, 225
output-based aid (OBA) programs 119, 120–123, 125–131, 238
overconsumption 138

Padawangi, Rita 118–137, 237–238
Painted Apple Moth 98–99, 100–112
panarchy 41
Parks, B. 68
Parsons, T. 45, 63
participatory democracy 168, 169–170, 172
Patterson, Jacqueline 216–233, 240
Pattison, Andrew 177–194, 239
PCPs *see* pentachlorophenol
PDHRE *see* Peoples Decade for Human Rights Education
Peck, J. 44
Pelling, M. 51
Pellow, David N. 8, 17–36, 50, 81, 99, 234–235, 236, 237
pentachlorophenol (PCPs) 106
people of color 9, 57, 99, 179; critical environmental justice 22; disasters 63, 242; economic vulnerability 61, 65; environmental justice movement

Index 249

17, 18, 217, 229; expendability 27, 29; policies 72; Portland 186, 189; transport-oriented development 186; vulnerability to climate change 1, 2–3, 28, 69, 71, 216; vulnerability to shocks 64; *see also* African-Americans; race

Peoples Decade for Human Rights Education (PDHRE) 226–228

personal security 7

pesticides 9, 24, 97–117, 237

Pfefferbaum, B. 38

Pfefferbaum, R.L. 38

Philippines 133

Pittsburgh 232n16

Piven, F.F. 170

planning 235–236; *see also* urban planning

plantation forestry industry 108–109, 110, 112, 237

PlaNYC 188

Polanyi, K. 161, 163

policies 9, 72, 99, 239; adaptive governance 148; barriers to resilience 230; biodiversity protection 112; climate action plans 182–191, 239, 241; climate change adaptation 180–182; climate change mitigation 180, 181; critical environmental justice 24–25; human rights cities 227; international climate 3; market-based 161–162, 163; pesticides 111; public participation in policymaking 229; social 183, 187–188; strategic use of the political environment 240; urban activism 211; urban renewal 196; water 157, 158, 161; *see also* governance; regulation

political ecology 42, 43, 242

politics: activism 196, 198, 199, 211; adaptive governance 141, 149; from below 170–171; Habermas' theory 169–170; New York City's water supply 139, 141–142, 148–149, 238; strategic use of the political environment 196, 202, 206–208

pollution 5, 17, 57, 99; cross-border 20, 23; ecological modernization 160; just transition 225; pesticides 97; water 24–25, 140, 146, 157

poor people 9, 57, 99; disasters 242; environmental justice studies 17; policies 72; vulnerability to climate change 1, 2–3, 28, 69, 71, 216; vulnerability to shocks 64; water access 118–119, 120–125, 127–128, 130, 132–133, 238; water privatization 164–165; *see also* poverty

Portland 178, 184–185, 186, 189

poverty 2, 66; Casc Antic 200; climate action plans 187; Dudley 200; food insecurity 86; human rights cities 227, 228; Jakarta 127; psycho-social resilience 44; racial inequality 67–68, 83; Tulsa 89, 91, 92; vulnerability 179; water 157; *see also* poor people

power 8, 10, 50; adaptive governance 138, 141, 149; critical environmental justice 19, 24, 26; critiques of resilience 45, 46; New York City's water supply 139, 141–143, 144, 148–149, 238; state 19, 21, 24, 30; stratified structures of 166; urban activism 196; water governance 170

precautionary principle 110–111

preparedness 51, 59, 60–61, 70, 71–72, 235; climate change 184, 188, 239; just resilience 8; networked capacities 42

prevention 9

principle of reverse onus 110–111

privatization 118, 119–122, 140, 159, 161; definition of 172n2; harms from 164–165; Jakarta 124–125, 130, 131–132, 133; proponents of 162, 164

procedural justice 121, 183, 184, 188–190

property rights 161–162, 165, 166

protests: anti-water-privatization 159, 168; pesticide use in Auckland 100; urban activism 202, 203, 206, 209, 211, 212; *see also* activism

psycho-social resilience 39–40, 44, 47–48, 51–52; *see also* indigenous peoples

public engagement 111

public transport 88, 179, 185–186

queer theory 22, 69

race: community cohesion 230; community resilience 48; critical environmental justice 19, 21, 29, 235; critical race theory 22, 26–27, 29, 30, 69, 242; ecodistricts 221; environmental justice 49, 217; exposure to risk 5; food insecurity 82, 83, 85, 88, 89–91, 93; human rights cities 228; inequalities 17, 18; legacies of disadvantage 241; networked capacities 42; racial expendability 26–27, 29; racial indispensability 27, 28, 29; Tulsa 79, 83,

85, 93, 237; *see also* African-Americans; ethnicity; people of color
racism: Cooperation Jackson 225; critical environmental justice 22, 24, 30; environmental 18, 23, 24, 27, 28, 30, 228; food justice 80; inequality 67; institutional 80, 81, 90; King on 28; racial indispensability 27
RAF *see* Resilience Activation Framework
Raridon, Andrew 79–96, 237
Rawls, John 166, 167–169, 172, 239, 242
recession 64–65
recovery resources 7, 42, 61, 68, 70, 71–72
recycling 200, 220, 223
reflexive modernization 170
regulation: adaptive governance 148, 149; Jakarta's water supply 128, 130; New York City's water supply 141, 144; "organizational outflanking" 142; pesticides 111; policy barriers to resilience 230; *see also* governance; policies
Reid, J. 44
renewable energy 181, 182
repertoires of action 198
reservoirs 143–144
resilience 6–8, 9–10, 37–52, 57–72, 234–236, 241–242; adaptive governance 140, 148; basic understanding of 58–59; cities 51; climate change 177–178, 179, 182–183, 185, 188, 191, 239; concept of 179–180; critiques of 43–46; Deepwater Horizon oil spill 46–47; definitions of 38; ecological 57, 58, 112; engineering 58; environmental justice 49–50, 52, 57–58; food justice 93; general model of social 59–61; impact of pesticides 97–98; initiatives 219–220; just 8, 25–26, 32, 50, 52, 71, 236, 238; manufacturers of disease 112; New York City's water supply 142–143, 146, 148, 149; policy barriers to 230; psycho-social 39–40, 44, 47–48, 51–52; Resilience Activation Framework 47–48, 50, 51–52; social support 2; socio-ecological 37–38, 40–41, 44, 45–46, 49–52, 60; systems theory 61–66; water governance 158, 170; water privatization 164; *see also* community resilience
Resilience Activation Framework (RAF) 47–48, 50, 51–52
Resilience Alliance 41

resistance theory 58
resource overconsumption 138
resources: adaptive governance 138, 139, 140, 149; ecovillages 221; non-substitutability 163; Rawls' theory of justice 166, 167–168; recovery 7, 42, 61, 68, 70, 71–72; Resilience Activation Framework 47, 48; rights and access to 164; societal resilience 219
reverse onus, principle of 110–111
Revi, A. 178, 181, 182
Right to the City Alliance 197
rights 164, 169; aboriginal 171; ecological democracy 168, 172; "right to the city" 216; to water 171, 239; *see also* human rights approaches
riots 79–80, 237
risk: buffers 8; climate change 181; exposure to 5; risk society 170
Roberts, J.T. 2–3, 49, 68–69
Robinson, Joanna L. 120, 157–176, 239
Rosa, E. 165
Rosario 227
Roseland, Mark 189
Ross, H. 41
rules 139, 147
Russo, Chandra 177–194, 239

Safe Drinking Water Act (SDWA) 144, 146
safety 7
Salt, D. 58
sanitation 157, 200
scale 20, 21, 22–24, 30, 46, 235
Schaefer-Borrego, A. 222
Schlosberg, D. 19
Schnaiberg, A. 159–160
SDWA *see* Safe Drinking Water Act
sea-level rises 49, 178, 181, 184
Seattle 178, 182, 184, 189–190, 232n16
segregation 2, 24, 67, 81; disaster recovery 92; New Orleans 91; Tulsa 79, 80, 89, 91, 92
self-esteem 39, 40
Sen, Amartya 164, 169
Sewell, W.H. 40, 50
sexuality 18–19; critical environmental justice 19, 20, 21, 22, 29, 235; ecodistricts 221
Shell 23–24
Shilomboleni, H. 229
Shiva, V. 163, 168
Smith, Jackie 216–233, 240

Index

social capital 2, 83, 235, 240; access to 61; community engagement 241; ecovillages 240; low levels of 92; New Orleans 6; New York City's water supply 238; social resilience 59, 60; step-wise social capital formation 236; urban activism 240

social change 20–21, 220, 238; community resilience 240; critical environmental justice 25, 30; critical theory 67; human rights cities 227

social cohesion 59, 217, 229, 230

social justice 43, 51, 165, 236; climate change adaptation 182; ecological democracy 168; human rights cities 227; water 119, 121, 122, 132–133, 157, 238

social movements 166, 168, 196–198, 219; critical environmental justice 24, 30; human rights cities 219, 226–228; just transition 219, 223–226; transnational networks 229–230; *see also* activism; protests

social networks 8–9, 92

social policies 183, 187–188

social resilience 7, 41, 57–58, 59–61

social sciences 37, 41, 45, 61–62, 65; constructivist 43; critical theory 66; Frankfurt School 69; vulnerability and resilience 42; water privatization 120

social support 2, 48

social systems 7, 45, 51, 59, 66, 70; *see also* socio-ecological systems

social well-being 165

socio-cultural systems 62, 63

socio-ecological systems 4–6, 7, 9, 10, 239; adaptive governance 139–140, 141, 148, 149; climate justice 3; inequality 66–67; just 236; New York City's water supply 142–143, 146, 148, 149; resilience 37–38, 40–41, 44, 45–46, 49–52, 60; systems theory 62; urban activism 240

socio-spatial capital 204–205

socio-spatial strategies 195, 196, 203–210, 211, 240

socionatures 22

South Africa 164–165

Southwest Network for Environmental and Economic Justice 217, 231n3

spatial capital 204–205

spatial injustices 121, 123–124, 131, 132–133, 195, 240

specieism 21, 22, 24, 235

stakeholders: adaptive governance 141, 149; New York City's water supply 145–146, 147; participatory planning 171; resilience 50; water governance 172n4

state 25, 31, 44; biosecurity frame 112; dominance 26; pesticides 99; power 19, 21, 24, 30; toxification of society 98

Stern, P.C. 139

Stevens, S.P. 38

stewardship 171, 226

Stiglitz, Joseph 187

stigma 89–90

storms 3, 68, 71, 178, 181

strategies, activist 195–198, 202, 203–210, 211, 212, 240

street activism 211–212

structural-functionalism 61–66, 234, 236

structures 62

subsidies 122–123, 128

Suckling, D. 107–108

supermarkets 82

sustainability 6, 10, 179–180; activism 212, 239–240; adaptive governance 141; concept of 38; definition of 180; ecological modernization 160; ecovillages 220, 222, 223; food justice 93; impact of pesticides 97–98; just 26; neighborhood 221–222

sustainable development 49, 81, 157–158; adaptive governance 140; critiques of 163; food insecurity 82; water 158

sustainable land use 140

sustainable water management 138–139, 140, 144–149

Sutton, Jim 105, 106, 107, 108

Swyngedouw, E. 121

symbolic interactionism 100

systems theory 44, 45, 61–66, 71, 234, 236, 241–242

tactics, activist 196, 197–198, 202, 203–210, 211, 212, 240

Tanzania 220

tariffs 120, 124–125, 130

Taylor, P. 64

technical experts 196, 202, 208–210, 211–212, 240

technology 159, 160, 162

temperature rises 1, 61, 69

temporality 23

Tickell, A. 44

timescales 179–180

Tizard, Judith 107, 108

TOD *see* transport-oriented development
Toffolon-Weiss, M.M. 49
tornados 5, 92
toxification of society 97–98, 99–100
toxins 5, 17, 49, 99; *see also* pesticides
trade 4
training 187, 200, 240
transformative adaptation 177–178, 180–182, 183–191, 239
transnational networks 229–230
transport-oriented development (TOD) 183, 185–186
transportation: climate action plans 182, 183, 185–186, 187–188; climate change policies 181, 239; disparities 184; equitable community development 195; food insecurity 88; lack of access to 3, 179; urban expansion 4; vulnerability to climate change 1
"treadmill of production" model 5, 160, 165, 166, 239
trust 235
Tulsa 9, 79–81, 83–93, 237
Tumin, Melvin 65–66

uncertainty 8, 38, 59, 180, 236
United Nations 119, 158, 218, 224
United Nations Declaration of Human Rights 171, 240
United States: climate action plans 178, 182–191, 239; Climate Justice Alliance 224–225; critical environmental justice 23–24; economic crisis 64; environmental justice movement 217–218; greenhouse gas emissions 177; inequality 65, 67–68; racism 28; Tulsa 9, 79–81, 83–93, 237; urban coalitions 197; water governance 172n4; *see also* New York City
Universal Declaration of the Rights of Mother Earth 228
urban planning 178, 186, 207
urban renewal policies 81, 196
urban socio-ecological systems 4–6, 7, 9, 10; *see also* socio-ecological systems
urban sprawl 4, 88
urbanization 4, 51, 57, 226
utilitarianism 99, 112, 158, 162, 166, 168

Vallée, Manuel 1–14, 97–117, 118–137, 234–242
values 100, 118, 217; community 230; ecovillages 221, 240; human rights cities 227, 228, 240; water 120, 238

Van den Berg, E. 226
violence, environmental 99, 179
volunteers 202, 206, 211
vulnerability 2, 43, 57, 61, 71–72, 240–241; adaptive governance 140; climate change 1, 68–69, 178–179, 182–183, 184; community resilience 42, 235; critical theory 71; definition of 178; disasters 68; food insecurity 82, 83; Hurricane Katrina 6; injustices and 7; lack of resilience 59; New York City's water supply 139, 145–146, 148, 149; Tulsa 80; water 157, 158, 161

wage-productivity gaps 65
Walker, B. 40, 58, 146
Warren, W.A. 40
Washington DC 178, 183–184, 232n16
waste: climate change policies 181; Jackson's Just Transition Plan 226; urban activism 199, 200, 201, 203
water 9, 118–137, 157–176, 237–238, 239; Cayo Hueso 200; contamination 51, 92; ecological modernization 161; global water crisis 158–159; injustices 119; materiality 121, 132; New York City 138–139, 141–149, 238; pesticide persistence 103; policies 158; politics from below 170–171; pollution 24–25, 97, 140, 146, 157; power imbalances 170; Rawls' theory of justice 167; scarcity 138, 140, 157, 161, 162, 163, 172, 178; urban expansion 4; vulnerability to climate change 1
water privatization 118, 119–122, 140, 159, 161, 162; definition of 172n2; grassroots opposition to 171; harms from 164–165; Jakarta 124–125, 130, 131–132, 133
Weber, Max 69
well-being 165, 221, 223, 237, 240
Welsh, M. 46
Westley, F. 45
White, R. 31
White-Spotted Tussock Moth 104, 106, 108
wildlife 102, 107–108
women: critical environmental justice 22; vulnerability to climate change 28, 71; vulnerability to shocks 64; *see also* gender

Wood, P. 167
Woodhouse, E. 97, 99–100
World Bank 118–119, 120, 122, 128, 130, 159, 170, 238
World People's Conference on Climate Change (WPCCC) and the Rights of Mother Earth 218, 224, 228, 229–230
World Social Forums 218, 227

Wright, M.O. 40
Wyche, K.F. 38

York, R. 165
Young, Iris Marion 169
youth: policies 72; urban activism 202, 206; vulnerability to climate change 71; vulnerability to shocks 64; *see also* children

Made in the USA
Lexington, KY
28 December 2018